# A Charmed Life

*by*

Nancy Manther

**All characters appearing in this work are fictitious. Any resemblance to real persons, living or dead, is purely coincidental.**



Published by eBookIt.com

ISBN-13: 978-1-4566-0866-8

For Adam, my very first charm ~

# Table of Contents

# Prologue

Strains of cello music played while the casket was being closed for what would be forever and always. The rich, low tones touched the hearts of Annie's children. She loved this music and while it was moving and sad, it was also beautiful. It was their mother. This hadn't been the only type of music she had loved – there were many -- just as there were many facets to the woman she had been. The emotions that the cello stirred made it the only choice for this moment. This was a moment they would remember forever.

The sun shone through the stained glass windows at a slant and made the funeral director's black suit a colorful mosaic. His work at the casket was reverent and private. His movements, thoughtful and deliberate. In fact, it seemed as if he was moving in slow motion. It was both touching and painful to witness. The ray of sunlight captured the scene like a spotlight. The irony of it was lost on no one. Annie always hated being the center of attention and now here she was, front and center, in a spotlight that was sent from heaven, just for her. It was finally her moment.

After the casket was closed he walked over to the front pew with something in his hands. Annie's children knew what he held there. They had been anticipating this moment. Annie had instructed that this exchange would occur at precisely this moment in the ceremony. It had been so important to her, so special. They both thought it seemed a bit melodramatic, but they knew better than to tamper with her wishes.

Into each of their outstretched hands he placed a treasure, so precious, so wonderful. Something such as this they'd never known --- they'd never held before. He transferred it to each of them as though it were Annie's body itself. It took their breath away, as well as that of those gathered there to say good-bye. This was because he'd just given them much more than their mother's body. He'd just given them her life.

The charms were still sort of shiny, but had been well worn and much loved. Scratched and smudged, Annie had worn the bracelets every day for years, both of them on her right wrist, one above the other. Her children held them gently, as if to protect them from anymore loss, anymore pain. Neither of them looked to see which one they held, and no one turned to look. Everyone seemed to recognize how private and intimate this moment was; that Annie had just given her children one last gift; the charms that were her life.

# **The Blue Star**

This was the charm that always made Annie's heart hurt. It represented Dillon, her first baby, who was stillborn. Every time she looked at the brilliant blue star, she remembered him, no matter how many years had passed. Of course, thinking of him was no amazing feat, because she had a hard time recalling even a day since he'd been born that she hadn't, even if only for a moment. Even if she barely caught it herself; if the thought was so fragile and fleeting that she nearly missed it, he was always there, close to her heart. What no one seemed to understand, was that Dillon's dying had changed her life forever. It had changed *her*.

It was the first time Annie could recall that her prayers weren't answered. To be honest, they were the first prayers that had ever really mattered. They might have been the only prayers. All of that fell by the wayside when Dillon was born; when he was born dead.

There had been a warning sign, but she hadn't realized it. At around thirty-two weeks she had developed a rash – a non-specific rash, the midwife had called it. No one seemed concerned. It was also June and one of the hottest anyone could remember. The mercury hit ninety degrees more than once that summer. It was probably just a heat rash – no big deal. Annie's maternal radar had been activated. She was worried.

A little over a week later, she felt the cramps. They were mild at first – she chalked them up to a normal discomfort of pregnancy. After all, she was in her last trimester. She was bound to be getting uncomfortable. They had been sporadic during the day; a little more bothersome by evening.

Eric had been at work, as usual. He worked a lot of late evenings then as a new accountant. He got home shortly after 11:00 p.m. that night and tumbled into bed next to her, exhausted. She'd been sleeping but was restless, because of the cramps and the heat. The small oscillating fan perched on the dresser blew a weak but steady breeze over the bed, but it wasn't enough. She stirred and looked over at Eric with heavy eyes.

"Hey you," she whispered, "long day?"

He slung his arm over her belly. "The longest." He was lying on his back, eyes closed, his other arm flung over his head. Within seconds he was sleeping.

*Great*, she thought, *he wakes me up and now that I'm awake, he's asleep.* She smiled at him tenderly in spite of her thoughts. He had been working harder than ever now that the baby was coming. He had become "Eric, The Provider" - hunting money to take care of his new little family. With a sigh of resignation, she realized she had to go to the bathroom. She wanted to ignore the urge, but knew that would be an exercise in futility. There was no denying it. She swung her leg over, to give her the leverage she needed to get out of the waterbed, and schlepped down the hall to the bathroom. When she sat down on the toilet she had no idea that her world would change only moments later. There, on the toilet paper, was a brown, slimy blob. It made her cringe to look at it. She knew what it was, what it meant. It was the mucus plug she'd read about in her pregnancy books, and it only meant one thing - that she would be in labor very soon.

It struck a chord deep inside her - this wasn't good. Annie made her way back to the bedroom, every step gentle and soft, so as not to disturb the baby any further.

"Eric," she said and nudged her snoring spouse. He was sound asleep now, and simply rolled over, away from her – away from the source of irritation. "Eric, wake up." This time she shook his shoulder more vigorously, her heart pounding as her terror increased. She felt like she was going to throw up.

"What!" He barked as he opened his eyes a little. "I just fell asleep."

"I think I lost my plug", she whispered, trying hard not to fall apart.

He looked at her blankly. "That's supposed to happen, isn't it?"

She sighed and took a deep breath. Hadn't he been listening in childbirth classes? This wasn't supposed to happen *now*, it was too soon. She was terrified. Annie looked at Eric and fear dug its gnarled fingers deep into her heart. He looked like he was shutting down, going into his denial mode. The way that Eric chose to handle her problems was to ignore them until she went away. She knew this problem was not going to go away. Some sixth sense had kicked into high gear. The nightmare had begun.

Annie sat down on the edge of the bed, her back to Eric. The cramps she had dismissed as "nothing" earlier, were starting to return. She grasped the wooden edge of the bed frame and held on tightly. If she let go, she was afraid she'd lose any self-control that was left. Eric raised himself up on his left elbow, pushing his hair out of his eyes with his right hand. He looked at his wife's back through bleary eyes, heavy with sleep. He reached over and placed his hand on her shoulder.

"What should we do?" he asked in a quiet voice.

"We need to call the doctor – the hospital, I mean. Labor and Delivery." Annie's eyes were filling with frightened tears that threatened to spill over any minute. "Where's the phone?" It was a rhetorical question – she knew where it was – but it seemed too daunting a task to reach over and get it off the nightstand.

They were told to come right away. The rest was a detailed blur. The feelings remained strong and sharp, but gradually it all melted together.

When they arrived at the hospital, a stocky nurse with short brown hair that had been permed one time too many, brought them to a room on the Labor and Delivery unit. It was too soon to be there, but Annie knew that it was for the best. Where else should you be when you're in labor? Labor. It was much too early. Surely, they'd be able to stop it. What if they couldn't? She didn't think she could handle having a preemie. The myriad of thoughts that always clogged her mind when she thought about "what if?" were running rampant. She was having trouble staying calm.

"Eric" she whispered as her eyes filled with tears, "I'm scared." He patted her leg, trying to reassure her.

"It'll be okay," he whispered. "Try not to worry."

*Not worry,* she thought, *why not tell me not to breathe?* How could she not worry? This was their baby – their child. Suddenly things were off course. She didn't know what to do. She didn't want to make Eric worry and certainly didn't want to be any trouble, but she was terrified. Her intuition, her sixth sense, and her gut were all screaming at her at the same time. Listening to them made her afraid and sad, so she did her best to ignore them and to put on a "happy" face. It was more of a mask than a face, and one that she'd be wearing for years.

An attractive young woman with long dark hair and big brown eyes strode into the room. She was wearing a white lab coat and carried a clipboard in her left arm. A blue stethoscope was draped around her neck. She approached Annie and Eric with confidence and certainty.

She stretched out her right arm for a handshake. "I'm Dr. Lewis, the resident on duty."

She was very businesslike and brusque, but she seemed to know what to do and for that Annie was grateful. The last thing they needed was to have some rookie who was as lost and afraid as they were. After examining Annie, the diagnosis was that she was in premature labor. At thirty-three weeks, it was too soon to have the baby, she explained, so they would give her a drug, Ritadrine, to stop the contractions and hopefully stop the labor. She would have to be on bed rest – possibly for the remainder of the pregnancy, or at least until the baby was big enough to be born.

Annie's blood became ice in her veins. While she appreciated the resident's confidence, every alarm in her body was going off. This was not good; the fairy tale was definitely over.

"We'll keep you on a monitor to keep an eye on the baby's heart rate and we'll get that IV with the Ritadrine started," Dr. Lewis continued, unaware of the terror spreading through Annie. "Any questions?" She finally looked up at them and was shocked to see tears running down Annie's face.

"Is our baby going to be okay?" The question came out as a whisper; that's all Annie could manage. If she forced out any more sound, she was afraid she'd lose control and start screaming at the tops of her lungs.

The young doctor hesitated before she spoke. She looked very thoughtful, as though she was formulating just the right answer in her head before she answered. She walked around to the foot of the bed. A safer place to share less than wonderful news.

"We're going to do everything we can to keep your baby where it belongs. The best place for it is inside of you. You are the best incubator. There's no reason to believe it won't be fine, as long as you do everything we tell you." She smiled weakly at them.

*Oh great*, Annie thought grimly, *it's all up to me. What if I do something wrong? What if I don't rest enough? What if I'm not good enough?*

"Do you know what could have caused the premature labor?" She asked the resident. "Did I do something wrong?"

"It's unlikely that you did anything to cause it, but let's rule out the obvious." She continued to ask Annie a list of questions about her behavior – did she smoke cigarettes or drink alcohol? How much caffeine did she consume? What about drugs, street or prescription? Was she eating properly? Did she get enough rest? What kind of exercise did she get?

The barrage of questions made her feel like a criminal on the witness stand. She had followed her midwife's orders to the letter and had read every book about pregnancy that she could get her hands on as well. She was a model expectant mother, and yet this snippy young doctor was implying otherwise. Of course, that would make her job easier; then they'd have a reason.

"She's been perfect," Eric interjected. Annie looked at him gratefully. Until this point he'd been uncharacteristically quiet. It felt good to have him defend her. "And she'll do everything you tell her to," he added. Again, it seemed that it was all up to her.

"Well, sir, it's not quite that easy," Dr. Lewis said. "It took both of you to get this baby started and it's going to take both of you to get it safely to its due date. Bed rest means bed rest. No chores, no walking around, no nothing. Annie, you can only get up to go to the bathroom. That's it." She converged on Eric again. "So, you will be doing the cooking and cleaning and everything, so that all your wife has to do is rest and grow this baby. Do you understand?" Her eyes could have bored holes into Eric's forehead.

"Yes, I understand. I'll wait on her hand and foot. I'll treat her like a queen," he squeezed her foot as he spoke, smiling at her. Annie smiled back weakly.

"But for now, we'll take care of you here," she continued. "Until the contractions have stopped with the IV and then stay controlled with oral medication, you'll be right here." She made this statement emphatically, as though they would find comfort in it. She even gave her head one short nod, as if to punctuate the order. "We'll move you to a room as soon as one is ready. Mr. Morgan, you'll need to go down to Admitting and take care of the paperwork." And with that, she was gone.

Annie and Eric looked at each other. Twenty-four hours ago things were fine. How could they have ever guessed that this waited for them?

"I'm sorry," she murmured. He didn't seem to know what to say, so he said nothing. She sank back into the pillow and turned her head toward the window. She had to be strong. She would not cry – but that's all she wanted to do.

"I better go downstairs and admit you," he said. "And have a smoke." He nervously felt his shirt pocket for the pack of Marlboro Lights, just to be sure it was still there. It had been a couple of hours since he'd had one.

"Okay." She knew that smoking was the first thing he'd do. Everything and everyone else secondary until that first hit of poison was inhaled. Only then did the rest of the world exist.

The minute he left the room, the tears came. She welcomed them as they ran down her cheeks. What was she going to do? How would they ever get through this? Bed rest meant she couldn't work anymore. What would they do for money? How was this going to work? Her brain was bombarded with questions, her heart was burdened with worries. Just then, the baby gave her a little kick, as if to say, "Remember me?" and she wept even more. She cradled her belly in her arms, loving her little one the best she could.

"I know you're worth it," she cooed, patting her tummy, wishing she could reach inside and hold him. "We'll have such good stories to tell you about all of this someday." She willed herself to be calm for the baby, knowing that any undue stress could be harmful. This led her to another train of thought – had this been caused by stress? She didn't think she'd been under much, but this was all new, and she was worried about so many things. The thought made her feel queasy. How could she have put her child in danger with her own petty worries? Hadn't Eric always told her to settle down, to stop worrying? Would he ever forgive her if something went wrong? Would it be her fault? Her thoughts were interrupted by a nurse who bustled into the room, pushing a wheelchair.

"How's it going?" she asked much too cheerfully. She was about Annie's age, but seemed much younger. "We get to move to a new room!" It sounded like she was announcing that Annie's just won the lottery.

"Lucky us," replied Annie, trying so hard to sound upbeat instead of sarcastic. She plastered a polite smile on her face. This young nurse had adopted the "we" lingo that health care professionals so frequently used when talking to patients. It made Annie feel like either a child or an old person, weak and vulnerable. She didn't like it one little bit.

The nurse's name was Melanie. She was very attractive, with curly blonde hair, that was pulled back into a loose ponytail. She wore just enough make-up to look pretty, not trashy. She was tiny – about 5'2" and couldn't have weighed more than 100 lbs. soaking wet. She had the type of figure that Annie had always coveted – narrow hips and thighs and a fairly large bosom. It was the type of figure that she always worried Eric coveted too. He'd dated a girl in high school who he had described as always needing a swimsuit top two sizes larger than the bottoms. Annie had always had the opposite problem and felt inadequate and dumpy every time she heard that story.

She felt especially like that now – like a beached whale – as the petite little nurse helped her slowly from the bed to the wheelchair. She wasn't an invalid, but Melanie handled her very gently, as though she might break. They had just gotten her settled into the wheelchair when Eric strode back into the room.

"Hey there," he said to them both, "Am I too late to help?" Then he extended an outstretched hand to Melanie, "I'm Eric Morgan, Annie's husband."

Melanie was busy collecting Annie's things from the windowsill and threw a glance in his direction instead of shaking his hand.

"Nice to meet you. We're moving your wife to a new room." She handed him Annie's purse and a plastic bag which held the clothes she had worn to the hospital. "Would you mind carrying these?" She was business-like and professional and Annie couldn't have loved her more at that moment. The last thing she needed was to watch Eric be his charming, flirtatious self.

"Sure," he said, as he took the items. A concerned look clouded his face. "But is she ready to be moved? Isn't it kind of soon?"

"No – don't worry." Melanie started pushing the wheelchair toward the door. "As long as a room is available, we need to move her. We need to free up the birthing room. She'll be fine." And with that, they started down the hall to the elevators.

The words "birthing room" stung Annie's heart. She knew it was too soon for the baby to be born, but she wanted it all to be over, with a happy ending. The unknown loomed in front of her and as hard as she tried, she couldn't see around it.

They kept her in the hospital four more days. It was nearly unbearable. She felt as though she didn't belong, but there was no way she wanted to go home. At least she felt safe there, the fetal heart monitor strapped around her belly like a big hug. She had become accustomed to the gentle, rhythmic beating of her baby's heart. She heard it first thing in the morning and it was her lullaby as she fell into a restless sleep each night. The thought of going home without being able to hear it every second terrified her. How would she know the baby was okay?

Another thought, one that kept nagging at her, terrified her as well. The baby hadn't been as active since she'd been in the hospital. She'd mentioned it to the doctors and nurses, but they didn't seem concerned. They reassured her that the heartbeat was strong and regular, that everything was fine. No amount of reassurance could comfort her. She just couldn't shake the fear that something was wrong.

There was a soft knock at the door. "Ready for dinner?" She turned her head to see Eric coming in with a bag from Burger King in one hand and a Dairy Queen bag in the other. Her appetite had all but left. It wasn't that the hospital food was that bad, she just wasn't hungry. Eric had cajoled her into agreeing to a fast food dinner. French fries could usually cheer her up.

"I got all of your favorites," he announced proudly as he wheeled the tray table over to her. He proceeded unpack the goodies in the bag. "I got you a Whopper, a large fry and an apple pie. Last but not least," he said with a flourish, "a Peanut Buster Parfait. A meal fit for a queen!" He beamed at her.

"Thanks," she said quietly, smiling at him. "It looks great. Did you get something for you?" It didn't look great to her at all; the smell made her feel a little nauseous, but it had been so nice of him to bring it. She had to at least try to eat.

"No, I'll get something later. I'm going to meet some of the guys from work at the Outpost." The Outpost was the favorite watering hole of Eric's office. He'd been stopping there more frequently these past few months. She chalked it up to her not being able to drink or stay up very late and her resemblance to a Beluga whale. "But you go ahead. Dig in!"

Her heart sank. It was one thing for him to go out when she'd been at home, happily and normally pregnant, but nothing was happy and normal anymore. That had ended the day she'd walked into the hospital.

"What time are you doing that?" She had to swallow hard to get rid of the tears that were building with incredible speed.

"Not for a while yet," he replied as he pushed the buttons on the bed railing to change the channel on the T.V. "What time is it anyway? The ball game should be on." He impatiently surfed through the few channels that were available until he found the baseball game.

Annie looked at her food. Now that Eric was going to be leaving, she had even less of an appetite. Her heart hurt at the thought of spending another night there alone, another night of trying to ignore her fears. In many ways she felt safe there, but also very much alone. She knew that part of the reason she felt that way was because she was keeping so many of her feelings from him. Annie didn't think he wanted to hear about it, so she kept quiet. Tears burned her eyes. She averted her gaze toward the window, away from Eric, so he wouldn't see. He'd always hated it when she cried about anything. It was a sure fire way to lose his attention. Her throat ached with trapped sobs and unspoken fears.

"You better start eating before it gets cold," his voice broke her concentration. "Aren't you hungry? You've got to eat, you know."

She blinked once and the tears spilled down her cheeks.

"What's the matter?" asked Eric. He sounded totally baffled as to why she would be crying. "Did you want a Big Mac instead?" He was trying to be funny.

"I'm sorry," she whimpered. If she said much more, all of the emotion would escape. "I can't help it."

He had one eye on the baseball game, flashing on the T.V. screen in the corner of the ceiling. "What's wrong? Didn't the doctors say everything's going to be okay?"

"They don't know," she said carefully, trying to maintain control. "They can't make any promises. I'm just so scared." Now she turned toward him, hoping for some comfort.

Eric was now completely engrossed in the baseball game. He seemed oblivious to her worries. She looked at him tenderly, but the tenderness was quickly replaced with frustration.

"Did you hear what I just said?" she asked. The irritation was heavy in her voice. He looked at her, confused.

"What?" Now he sounded irritated too.

"Never mind," she murmured, convinced he wouldn't understand. She really thought that keeping her true feelings from him would help, that somehow it would protect him and make things better. Thus the pattern was set. Set in stone.

The doctors sent her home when the contractions had stabilized enough for their criteria. The only way the contractions would be be stable enough for Annie, was for the doctors to give her a signed and sealed guarantee – which she knew they couldn't provide. So she went home, scared to death. The elevator ride was a nightmare. There she was, new moms all around her, bringing their babies home, and she had no idea what her future held. Would she be one of them someday? She could only hope and pray. She found it painful to even look at them, all sweet and rosy in their newborn glow. Would she ever know that joy? She desperately wanted to believe that she would, but a tiny place in her soul held the truth.

Eric had opened up the hide-a-bed sofa that was in the den for her to use for her bed rest. He thought it would be better than having her secluded upstairs in the bedroom away from everything. He'd put clean, crisp sheets and a light blanket on it, and had fluffed and arranged the pillows in a cozy heap. It looked so comfortable and inviting, she wanted to climb right in and hide for the next seven weeks straight.

"It looks great," she crooned, "It's so sweet of you to get it all ready like this."

Eric looked up from the stack of mail in his hand and smiled. "It's the least I could do."

"Well, I appreciate it," she said as she reached over to give him a hug. His attention was now riveted on the pile of bills and the smile that had just been there was replaced by a frown. Worry gnawed deeper in her gut once again when she saw his expression.

She knew he was worried about how they were going to pay the bills, with her suddenly not being able to work. They hadn't been able to save much money to live on during her maternity leave, but they'd managed to put some aside. This unexpected bump in the road would use that up and more. Tears burned her eyes again. Would this never end?

"I'm sorry." She felt like it was all her fault. His silence wasn't helping her feel any differently. He turned to look at her, his expression guarded.

"It'll be okay," he said as he squeezed her shoulder, "Don't I always take care of you? I'll figure something out."

She wanted his assurance to comfort her, but it didn't. All she could think about was the money she wouldn't be making for the next three months. If she went full term, she'd be on bed rest for seven weeks. She'd be lucky if she could take the minimum six weeks of maternity leave at that point. Annie knew she'd feel compelled to cut it short for the sake of their budget. All of these worries stacked themselves neatly upon her shoulders as well as her heart, and she felt as though she were made of lead.

Eric helped her get settled into her new accommodations. The hide-a-bed was positioned exactly in front of the T.V. and a stack of current women's magazines sat on the end table next to the bed. A tall glass of ice water sat nearby, tiny droplets of condensation running down its sides, forming a ring on the table below. The phone was placed within close reach. She climbed into her new nest.

"This is really comfy," she said to him as she sank back into the mound of pillows. "I hope I still think that a month from now."

"Why wouldn't you? I'd give anything to be able to lie around in bed and be waited on for weeks! You've got it made!"

Annie knew he was just trying to be jolly and keep her spirits up, but really - who was he kidding? Did he really think this was great? That she was lucky? She didn't want to think about it or talk about it now. She just wanted to fast forward to her due date and deliver their healthy little baby.

"Are you hungry?" Eric asked. "It's almost lunchtime."

"No, not really. Maybe later." She pulled the sheet up under her chin. "I think I'll sleep for a while." Now that she thought about it, she was exhausted – and besides that, she wanted to escape. Sleep worked well that way.

"Okay," he started, "Well, if you're going to sleep, I think I'll go in to the office for a while. There's a ton of work I need to get caught up on."

"That's fine." She snuggled down under the covers and looked up at him. He leaned down and kissed her forehead lightly before he turned to leave. "Why don't you give Sally a call and ask her to come and stay with you?"

"Did you forget? Frank and Sally are on a sabbatical in India for a month." The thought of the aunt and uncle who were her only family, being so far away, made her feel especially lonely. She needed them now, much like she did after each of her parents had died, so many years ago.

"Oh yeah, that's right. Well, you'll be fine. Who knows? By the time they get back, we'll probably have a baby!" And with that, he kissed the top of her head, and left for the office.

Annie wondered what happened to being treated like a queen and being waited on hand and foot. They had only been home a half hour and she was already on her own. Then she berated herself for being so self-absorbed. Of course he needed to go to work – they needed the money more than ever now. She closed her eyes before the tears could start because she knew that Eric needed to escape for a while too. The thought that her husband needed to get away from her and their baby, from the fear and uncertainty that engulfed her, made the pit of her stomach sting with despair.

A day and a half later, she had an appointment at the clinic to see how things were going. The baby had been less active, but she attributed that to the fact that she was less active as well. The appointment was with Dr. Hayes, a doctor she'd never heard of, but he was the only one with time available. The nurse midwives she'd been seeing at the clinic considered her too high risk; she needed a "real" doctor now.

He strode into the small exam room with the self-assurance of a movie star, a quarterback, a god. Later on Annie couldn't decide if these were qualities that she gave to him or if he was really like that. At any rate, he exuded confidence. The confidence faltered a bit when the Doptone couldn't find the baby's heartbeat.

"I've always hated these things," he said, his face reddening with every syllable. "I'll get the stethoscope." He untangled a goofy looking contraption with tubes and metal earpieces from a hook on the wall. It also had a strange metal headband on it, which Annie would've found amusing if it were another situation. It looked like something from Dr. Frankenstein's laboratory.

Dr. Hayes placed the bell of the instrument on her belly and listened carefully. You could've heard a pin drop, but all that they listened for was a heartbeat. It seemed that everyone was holding their breath. He frowned and repositioned the stethoscope, and waited intently for what seemed like forever. Beads of perspiration formed on his forehead as he bent over Annie. He moved it around, hoping to find the precious sound.

Annie looked up at the ceiling of the exam room, her heart beating wildly. She tried her best to calm it down, but it was no use. If only she could give some of her heartbeats to her baby, then everything would be okay. She said a brief prayer, asking God for the strength she was going to need soon.

The doctor straightened up while removing the stethoscope from his forehead which was dripping with nervous perspiration. His expression was grim. He looked as though he would rather be anywhere but where he was at that moment. He wiped the sweat from his brow with his forearm and placed the stethoscope on the counter top.

"Annie, Eric," he said in a quiet but strong voice, "I can't find a heartbeat. That doesn't mean it isn't there, but just that it's too faint for me to find with my ears alone. I want you guys to go down to the hospital for an ultrasound. Just so that we know what's going on."

It was only a fifteen minute drive to the hospital, but it was the longest and yet the shortest drive of Annie's life. As the skyline of downtown Minneapolis came into view, she knew that she'd think of this moment whenever she saw it, for the rest of her life. The sooner they got there, the sooner they'd know 'what's going on.' In her heart she knew what the doctor was trying not to say, but she couldn't let herself even think it, let alone utter the words to Eric. They rode in silence.

Silence and denial became the modus operandi for their lives. Any tendencies they had to ignore the obvious and live in oblivion became cemented in their repertoires during that ride to the hospital. They were changed forever.

Once at the hospital, they were ushered to the ultrasound room. There had been no reason to have an ultrasound before this, so it would be Annie's first. The room was dark, with an exam table in the middle. It was covered with white paper like all exam tables were, but there was also a large hospital pillow there for her head. They were greeted by a familiar face. Dr. Lewis, the young resident, was waiting for them.

"Hi Annie, Eric," she said gently, "I'm on call tonight so I'll be helping Dr. Hayes – he's on call too. Let's have you get up on the table here."

Annie carefully scooted up onto the exam table and lied down. The starched white pillow felt cool as she rested her head on it. Dr. Lewis wheeled a cart over next to her that had a large monitor on it, connected to a keyboard and some other equipment. The ultrasound technician squirted some gel on Annie's belly and proceeded to slide a thing that looked like a microphone around in circles.

"I'm looking for your baby's heartbeat right now," she said, her voice almost a whisper. Their eyes were all transfixed on the screen. Annie and Eric had no idea what they were looking for, but the tech and the doctor seemed to know what they were doing.

There was no movement on the screen. There were no sounds. There was no life, no heartbeat. The baby had died. *Their* baby had died. There were no words after that. Life as they knew it was over.

The Ritadrine was stopped and the pains of labor began in earnest. They were even more painful because their result was not a vibrant, screaming, healthy infant, but a quiet, still, lifeless one. The pain had no purpose but to cause more pain.

Family and friends gathered at the hospital. It was the last place Annie wanted them to be. The best place they could be was anywhere but near her, but Eric needed them close by, so she did her best to deal with it. They ogled at her self-control and pain tolerance while trying to decide what to order from the restaurant on the corner. Even given the state of shock she was in, their behavior struck

Annie as odd. She prayed for strength and grace. She also prayed for it to be over, while wanting it to last forever.

"Annie, it's time to push." The nurse had checked her seconds before and she was dilated to ten centimeters. Time to push. This was supposed to be a happy moment or at least a moment of relief. The only thing her mom had ever told her about childbirth, was that 'it feels so good when they finally say you can push.'

She bore down, just like the nurse had instructed. Because this was happening prematurely, they hadn't gotten to this stage in the childbirth classes yet. She had no idea what to do, but grasped her knees and pushed hard. Pain seared through her body. It felt as though a thousand bees were stinging her. This was almost worse than the contractions because it was so unexpected. Her mom had been mistaken; this didn't feel good at all.

"You're doing great, Annie," said Dr. Hayes, "just one more push -" Normally he would've finished with, "and we'll have a baby!" But he stopped short of that. Just one more push.

The baby came quickly. It was startling how easily he slipped out into the doctor's large, outstretched hands. The room was silent and still, just as the birth had been.

"He's beautiful," the nurse said as she placed him in Annie's arms. He was wrapped in a white blanket that had pink and blue stripes on it. His little face was so sweet and peaceful. He looked like he was sleeping.

"He looks perfect," whispered Eric, as he gently pushed the blanket away from the baby's chin. "He's so cute." His voice was quieter than usual, choked with emotion.

Annie looked down at her peaceful, perfect little boy. The nurse was right – he was beautiful. She tried to keep her emotions at bay, so she could take this moment to memorize everything about him. This would be her only chance and she instinctively knew that she had to make the most of it.

She traced his profile with the index finder of her left hand. He had an abundance of dark hair and his little brow was furrowed as though he was having a serious dream. He had a little rosebud mouth that was just like Eric's. Closing her eyes for just a moment, she tried to memorize how he felt in her arms. Once they took him away, her arms would be so empty.

"How much does he weigh?" she asked.

The nurse brushed away a tear as she answered: "4 lbs. 10 oz. And he's nineteen and a half inches long."

*A bag of sugar*, thought Annie, *he's almost as big as a bag of sugar*. Out loud she said, with pride in her voice, "He's not so little."

"No," Eric added, "he's a big boy. He would've been a bruiser if he was full term!"

Annie nodded and cradled her son's head in her hands and gently planted a kiss on his little forehead. She let her lips linger there, and inhaled deeply, as if to breathe in his very essence.

Just then the nurse who had been with them all night asked, "Annie, Eric, would you like me to baptize him?"

They looked at each other for a second and then both nodded their heads in agreement. Their Catholic upbringing kicked into full gear; baptism was important, although Annie knew that he was already in Heaven.

"What are you going to name him?" the nurse asked quietly.

"Dillon Paul," Annie replied softly.

Eric quickly cleared his throat. "Are you sure we should use our boy name? Maybe we should save it for our next baby." He said it carefully and quietly. They had a tough time finding and agreeing on the name. It seemed logical and reasonable to save it for another baby.

She looked at him like he'd lost his mind. "But Dillon is *his* name. We can't use it for another baby."

This wasn't the time to challenge her. When they had another boy, they'd find a different name. She knew that Eric hadn't been that crazy about the name Dillon anyway – especially the way Annie insisted they spell it.

"Okay, okay. We'll name him Dillon." He smiled at Annie and the nurse and then looked at his little boy. Dillon. He did look like a Dillon.

The nurse took the pink and blue striped bundle from Annie's arms. Her arms were trembling as she held this most precious little person. She'd never had to baptize a stillborn baby before. As reverently and calmly as she could, she made a sign of the cross on the infant's forehead and said, "Dillon Paul Morgan, I baptize you in the Name of the Father and of the Son and of the Holy Spirit. Amen." She patted his head affectionately as she said the final word and gently gave him back to Annie.

The moment was holy. It was the only word Annie could think of to describe it. She felt so close to God and Dillon at that moment, and wouldn't have traded it for anything. Anything, except a healthy baby, alive and crying in her arms. Feeling so close to God at that moment, she would've been crazy to lie about how she really felt.

Dr. Hayes knocked gently on the door and came in. "How are you two doing?" he asked quietly.

Annie looked at him, tears welling up in her eyes. What could she say? How *were* they doing? She didn't pretend to know.

"Are you ready to say good-bye?" he asked, his voice breaking. He had only met Annie and Eric that day, but seemed to feel such a bond, such responsibility for these young parents.

Annie looked down at Dillon tenderly. How could she ever let him go? He'd been her constant companion for the past eight months. He'd been her dream forever. She knew that it was time to say good-bye. Her tiny son was already starting to feel cold when she placed one last kiss on his cheek.

The nurse came and ever so quietly took him from her arms. It happened so gently that when she looked back on it later, it was difficult to pinpoint the exact moment of separation.

The room was dark and silent. There was such an emptiness now that Dillon was gone. Her arms ached as well as her heart – they were both so empty. Annie laid back in the hospital bed, exhausted. She fixed her gaze on the night sky because there was no where else to look. Eric was wrapping himself up in his feelings of loss and numbness. She respected his need to approach things in his own way, but it left her very much alone.

It was then that she saw it – a tiny star, glistening and shiny brightly, all alone in the darkness. She closed her eyes and looked again. It hadn't been there a minute before – was she hallucinating? No, there it was, twinkling and shining more than it had before.

Suddenly a feeling of warmth and peace enveloped her. She smiled because she knew that Dillon was in Heaven. He was telling her that by making his little star shine brighter than all the others. He would always be in her heart, swaddled in a blanket of the memories of this night and all the days preceding it. Every time she looked at the night sky and saw his star or any star, she'd know that she was not alone.

Much of what happened next was a blur. Because she was no longer pregnant, she could have a room on a regular floor rather than the maternity floor, in case it would be too difficult for her to be around babies. Even through her newborn grief, she knew enough to sense that they wanted to get rid of her, to remove the pain and stigma of a pregnancy gone wrong.

"I'd like to be where people know how to take care of me," she told Dr. Hayes. "This is my first baby..."

"Then that is what you will have," he declared. "And you'll have a private room. That's the least we can do."

This followed the discussion about how long she should stay home from work. The doctor was definitely her advocate. Eric suggested that since she didn't have a newborn to care for, perhaps she'd need less time to recuperate. Dr. Hayes dismissed his comment without missing a beat.

"Annie had a baby - she needs the customary six week maternity leave." He wrote his orders: a minimum of six weeks.

It was a relief to know that the time she'd need was validated, but she knew she'd go back to work sooner than that because they needed the money. While she was pregnant, she brought up the possibility of her working part-time after the baby came.

"There's no way we can afford that," Eric stated firmly. She took him at his word and didn't argue because she knew he was right. Now, even though there was no baby, she regretted her decision not to fight for time with him. Having just held him and smelled his tiny newborn head made her realize how precious that time would have been, and she felt awful for having been so willing to give it away.

Her arms literally ached for wanting to hold him, not only for a moment but for the rest of her life. She was shocked at the intensity of her feelings. Not only did her arms ache, but her heart hurt as well. It was unlike any pain she'd ever felt before, either physical or emotional. It was exquisitely perfect, a vast collection of contradictions. The baby that had brought her so much joy was now the cause of unimaginable pain. The emptiness inside of her where he had just spent his entire little life was such a vast chasm of grief and loss, she could not begin to comprehend it. Her wounds were fresh and raw and she had no idea how she was going to live until tomorrow or the next five minutes without him.

According to her wishes, she was moved to a room – private – on the maternity floor. Eric was given a cot to sleep on next to her bed, and there they spent the rest of the night. They didn't speak or touch. Each of them lay in their cocoons, alone and apart from each other.

Annie could never remember when she'd felt more alone. She gazed out the window at the now predawn sky. A chill ran from her forehead to her little toe, and she pulled the thin hospital blanket up under her chin to keep warm, to protect herself. The memory of Dillon's birth was still strong in her mind, and she closed her eyes and did her best to relive it. As painful as it was, she never wanted to forget a moment of it. She had to remember it. That was all she'd ever have of him.

Her thoughts were interrupted by the voice of a nurse and a hand on her shoulder.

"Annie. Hi. How are you doing?" She had a kind, soothing voice.

"Okay, I guess."

"Are you having much pain?" The question was perfectly normal and valid, but Annie wanted to scream, 'YES. You have no idea!' But, of course, she didn't. She simply said, "Not too much."

"Well, that's good," the nurse replied, "but I'm afraid I'll be causing you some - I have to knead your tummy."

Annie looked at her, perplexed. "You have to what?"

"I have to knead your uterus. It makes it shrink." She set to work, massaging and pushing on Annie's abdomen as if it were a blob of bread dough instead of the sacred vessel that had just held her baby. As the nurse pushed and prodded, she closed her eyes and tried to transport herself to another place, to another place in time. She wanted to be taken care of properly, but this was too invasive. Her first instinct was to clutch her belly, to protect the place that had been Dillon's home for the past thirty-four weeks. As the nurse did her job, she felt that her very soul was being touched. She felt pain on so many levels, it was difficult to tell where it started. There was supposed to be a squalling baby latching onto her breast to make this happen, not a nurse simulating the event. It broke her heart yet again.

"Normally nursing your baby takes care of this because it releases hormones that do the trick, but..." Suddenly she realized what she was saying and to whom she was saying it. Her demeanor changed abruptly. "So, that should be good for now. Be sure to press the call button if you need anything." With that, she turned on her heel and hurried from the room, her head down, going about one hundred miles an hour.

Annie winced at the cramps the nurse's massaging caused, as well as the knowledge that she had become a pariah through no fault of her own. While they meant well, none of the staff seemed to know what to do with her. They chose to work on the maternity floor because they loved the joy that every day brought with new moms and new life. She was the anvil on their stethoscopes that brought them back to earth, back to the reality that things didn't always go the way they were supposed to; there wasn't always a happy ending. It hurt to be the source of such abhorrence. Instinctively, she knew she better get used to it.

She breathed her way through the discomfort, using the technique the labor nurse had shown her. Dillon came before they had finished the childbirth classes, so she had no idea what to do. They had procrastinated about practicing all of those "dumb breathing exercises" as Eric had dubbed them. They seemed dumb to her too, until she was in the throes of labor and then she more than understood their value. The thought of all the other couples in their class having healthy babies was a slap in the face she hadn't expected, and she winced. The tears started again.

Eric stirred restlessly. He rolled over and squinted at the light sneaking in from around the edge of the door. The nurse had left it open a crack in her haste to leave.

"What's going on?" he asked in a half whisper. He put his forearm over his eyes to block out the light as well as the reality that came flooding back.

"Oh, nothing," she replied. "The nurse just came in for a minute." She decided to spare him the details. She wanted him to rest. "Go back to sleep, okay?"

"I don't think I can," he said, sitting up and stretching tiredly. Standing up, he came over to the bed. "How did you sleep?"

He leaned over and kissed her softly on the cheek and tasted the tear that was making its way to her chin. He put his arms around her and held her close. "Aw, Annie." It was all he said. It was all he had to say. The tears came more freely now, for both of them. They sat there for a few minutes, just holding each other. It was the closest they'd been in days and she needed the comfort. This was new terrain, a new journey for which she wasn't prepared.

Out in the hall were the sounds of the hospital waking up for the day. Tall metal carts with stacks of breakfast trays were rolled down the hall by food service workers. Plastic bassinets with newborn babies followed them, pushed by busy nurses. After all, the babies needed their breakfasts too and each room held a mom or two waiting to feed their new little bundles of hungry joy. Except Annie's room, of course. Her room was quiet and still. The days of eating for two were over.

"Knock, knock," a friendly voice said. It belonged to a young woman they'd never seen before. She had light brown hair that was pulled back in a ponytail. She was wearing black pants and a white blouse. Around her neck was a thin gold chain with a small gold cross dangling from it. "Hi, Annie, Eric, I'm Susan Phelps, one of the hospital chaplains. Dr. Hayes told me about your son. I'm so sorry." She stood near the end of the bed, not too close, but not too far away, either. "Can I get you two some breakfast?"

Annie shook her head. "None for me, but Eric would probably like some."

"You have to eat too," he chimed in. "You have to keep up your strength."

"I'm not very hungry, but you know what I would like," she said, her eyes lighting up a little. "Coffee – with caffeine!" She'd been so careful to avoid caffeine or anything harmful throughout the pregnancy. It was time for some "forbidden fruit." If she'd been offered a Bloody Mary she would've taken that as well – maybe even two of them.

The young chaplain smiled as she slipped out into the hallway to grab Eric a breakfast tray. She not only brought Annie a cup of coffee, but an entire pot.

"Here you go," she said as she poured the hot, steaming liquid into a Styrofoam cup, "coffee with caffeine!" She handed the cup to Annie carefully. "Be careful – it's really hot."

Annie wrapped her hands around the cup, grateful for the warmth, the aroma and the young woman's kindness. Eric brought his tray of food over to the chair by the window and sat down to eat. He lifted the round, plastic cover from the plate, to expose a plate of scrambled eggs, bacon, fresh fruit, and whole wheat toast. The chaplain continued to visit with them while Eric devoured his breakfast and Annie sipped and savored her coffee.

"It's normal to feel sad and hopeless," she started, "but time heals all things. Someday, years from now, you might be feeling sad and not know why. Then you'll remember that it's this day and what happened...."

She continued to talk, but Annie stopped listening. The chaplain was very nice and meant well, but didn't know what she was talking about. Be feeling sad and not know why? And then remember what happened?!

There was no doubt in Annie's mind that she would never forget the day Dillon was born. It would never creep up on her, no matter how many years had passed. Every day would bring thoughts of him, if only for a second. Of course there would be the "milestone" events – the birthdays each year, each Christmas, what would have been his first day of kindergarten, and his last day of high school, but she knew there would be more. Every time she'd see another child, she'd remember what she was missing. She'd think of him when the first snowflakes would drift gently down from the sky and collect in a pile in the yard or when after a sun shower a rainbow would stretch from here to forever. She would have run to get him from his crib or his toys to show him how wonderful it was. When a spider would magically appear from nowhere, lowering itself through the air on a silken thread, she would have shown him how to look for its beautiful, intricate web. "A tiny, little spider made that, Dillon, all by himself!" She could imagine him clapping his chubby little hands together and squealing with delight. The thought brought a small smile to her lips.

"Annie." Eric's voice brought her back to reality. Both he and the chaplain were looking at her expectantly and she wondered how long she'd been off in her own little world.

"I'm sorry," she stammered, "I'm just really tired. I didn't sleep much last night."

"That's to be expected, Annie," said the chaplain. "Grief can be exhausting."

*Really*, she wanted to say. She felt the urge to scream again, but only nodded her head in agreement. She hoped the visit was almost over and looked to Eric for help. Maybe he could read her eyes and do something to make it end. He was distracted by now as well, his hand on his shirt pocket, feeling for his smokes.

"Well, you two must be tired, so I'll be going now." With that, the young woman with the ponytail walked to the door. She turned toward them before she walked out into the hallway. "I really am so very sorry."

Annie looked after her, not sure what to think of this angel of mercy who brought them food and drink and the most misguided advice she could imagine. She meant well, she told herself. Little did she know that these words would become her new words to live by. They would bring her little comfort, but they'd help her hold onto her sanity, one well-meaning person at a time.

She pushed open the back door and stepped slowly into the kitchen. Everything was exactly as it had been when they left to go to the clinic the day before. The dishes she had eaten her lunch on had been washed and set in the dish drainer in the stainless steel sink.

"I didn't remember you doing the dishes yesterday," she said to Eric as he followed her in.

"Oh – Terri did them. You know my sister. She can't stand to see a dirty dish," he replied, shaking his head.

"When was she here?" It bothered Annie to know that Eric's sister had been there when she'd been in the hospital. Terri never thought that Annie's housekeeping skills were good enough; she always found fault with something and then took it upon herself to report it in detail to the rest of the family. Annie had no idea what shape the house had been in – she'd had other things on her mind.

"She offered to come over and straighten things up before you came home, so you wouldn't have to worry about it. I thought it was pretty nice of her."

"I guess so." She tried to choose her words carefully, not wanting to put Eric on the defensive about his sister. "I just don't remember how messy it was -"

He interrupted her. "It's fine – it wasn't that bad. She just wanted to help." The tension in his voice was so brittle she was afraid it would shatter and cover the floor with shards of what had been their life before all of this had happened. She feared that if that happened, they would never be able to piece it back together again. It struck her as ironic that her life had become a metaphor for Humpty Dumpty. Were they going to be broken forever?

"Okay – sorry. That was really kind of her. I just -"

"I know – you *just.*" He went back outside to have a cigarette, letting the screen door slam behind him.

Annie sighed and walked into the living room. Everything felt so empty – the house, the room, her arms. She sank down onto the couch and put her head in her hands. What was going to happen to them? How were they going to get through this? Her heart pounded in her chest as the questions raced through her head. She grabbed a pillow that was nearby and held it tightly, needing to hold onto something because it hurt too much not to.

Her thoughts drifted to Dillon. She wondered what it would have been like if everything had been all right and he had been born strong and healthy. What would be the first thing she'd do when they brought him home? She imagined bringing him into the nursery, gently laying him on the changing table and kissing his little toes when she unwrapped the receiving blanket. Eric would be there next to her, marveling at his newborn little boy, beaming with pride.

Cigarette smoke wafted in through the screen door from the backyard and brought her back to reality. Giving the pillow another squeeze, she stood up and walked to the spare bedroom. She'd been keeping the few baby things she had gotten in the closet since it had been too soon to prepare the nursery. She needed to go through them, to hold them and touch them. She needed a tactile connection to Dillon that only the little undershirts and sleepers could provide. He'd never worn them, but it seemed to be the only way she could feel close to him right now.

Her heart started beating wildly when she opened the closet door. Where were all the baby things? She was sure she had stacked them in a neat little pile on a box in the left hand corner. The box was there, but the baby clothes were gone. Annie felt her face flush as she searched every nook and cranny for the missing items. Maybe she had absent-mindedly put them in the back of the closet or on the right-hand side. Perhaps she'd stuck them up on the shelf and had forgotten about it. She dragged a step stool out from behind the garment bag of winter coats, and climbed up onto it to get a better view of the top shelf. Frantic now, she felt as though she was not just looking for little t-shirts, but for Dillon himself. For a split second she hoped that she'd actually find him, snuggled up in the corner, but then realized how crazy that was.

*Am I losing my mind?* She comforted herself with the thought that if she really were crazy, she wouldn't be able to even ask the question. But where were those damn baby clothes?

She smelled Eric approaching before she saw him – the cigarette smoke announced his arrival. Before he could say anything, she confronted him. "Where are the baby clothes? Where are Dillon's things?" Tears stung her eyes and she felt as though she was going to be sick.

Eric sighed heavily at the sight of her rummaging around in the closet and again shook his head, in what she interpreted as disgust.

"Would you please relax?" he said, the impatience in his voice nipping at her soul. "Terri thought it would upset you to have them here."

"So, where are they?" It was so hard to maintain civility and control.

He lowered his head a little and muttered, "I don't know. I just told her to take them away. I thought it would be too hard on you to see them."

Try as she might to hear the words he was saying, all that came across was that he meant well. Terri meant well. The chaplain meant well. Was the future going to be dominated by those who meant well but who were tearing out her heart in the process?

She wanted to shout at him. '*Last night I held our dead baby in my arms. What could be harder than that?*" She wanted to, but she didn't. He was hurting too. It wouldn't be fair to lash out and cause more pain. Instead she pictured herself as a huge, almost empty duffle bag into which she'd stuff the hurt, pain, and sadness. Putting her feelings there would be so much easier on everyone, at least for now.

They decided that a small graveside service would be best, since he had "never really lived" and "no one had ever known him". Annie didn't really have a say in the decision and years later could never remember how it had all transpired. Their priest had said that it was what was typically done in "situations like this" and they just obediently followed his directions. Money was also an issue. Funerals were expensive.

The morning after Dillon was born, while Annie had still been in the hospital, Eric and his mother had gone to the funeral home to make the arrangements. She wasn't even told about it until after everything was in order, another attempt to protect her from something that would be too hard on her. She felt cheated out of making those important final decisions about her baby, but dismissed it as being a good thing for Eric to be able to do for Dillon. He hadn't known him in the intimate way she did during the pregnancy, so maybe this would be a way he could feel some closeness.

The funeral was on Monday, two days after he had been born. Annie couldn't fit into any of her regular clothes yet and didn't feel up to shopping, so she had to wear one of her maternity dresses. She chose a navy blue sleeveless one, since it was a close to black as she could get. It was a warm day, a balmy eighty degrees.

Even though it wasn't supposed to be a "real" funeral, they had a little procession from their house to the cemetery. Eric had a large family, so there was more than just a handful of people. It was thoughtful of them to come, but Annie felt as though some of them were there out of curiosity more than concern. If nothing else, they just wanted to see how she and Eric would cope at their baby's funeral. She might have done the same thing, so she tried not to judge them. She ached with longing for Sally and Frank. Their absence magnified the emptiness within her.

The line of cars wound its way around the graceful curves of the cemetery. Just when Annie thought they'd be stopping, there was yet another curve to go around and follow. Finally Eric pulled over to the side of the road and stopped the car. He turned off the engine.

"Well," he said, looking straight ahead through the windshield, "here we are."

Annie looked out the window and saw the decorative sign that labeled this section of the cemetery: "Babyland." It gave her chills at first, but then she felt an odd sort of comfort and camaraderie. All the babies who had been put to rest here had parents who were feeling just like she and Eric were at that very moment. It helped her feel less alone and gave her the strength she needed to get out of the car.

"It looks nice," she said quietly. "It's very pretty." She gave Eric's hand a little squeeze and they turned to walk over to the grave. When she looked in that direction, she gasped sharply. There, sitting on a little platform, was a small, white container that looked a lot like a cooler. She looked at Eric, questions in her eyes. He nodded and said, "That's him."

She wasn't sure exactly how to react, there were so many emotions competing for her attention at once. Not only had she just arrived at her child's funeral, but she had to deal with the fact that he was sealed inside of a casket that looked just like the Rubbermaid cooler they had at home. They had just used it for a picnic they had been invited to earlier that summer. That day seemed like a million years ago – so much had happened since then. A group of friends, about five couples, had decided to get together for a picnic at Minnehaha Falls. It had been a glorious summer day, the kind that is perfect for relaxing on a blanket and watching the clouds change form. She didn't know if she'd ever want to use it again.

*Okay, Annie,* she told herself, *you can handle this. This is how baby caskets look. Accept it and move on.*

She glanced at Eric for guidance what to do next, but he was distracted, talking to some of their friends. Looking around, she made a conscious effort to notice who took the time out of their busy lives to be there. Standing in a small cluster near the road stood some of Eric's coworkers. She was a little surprised to see them here, since they had decided that only family and a handful of close friends should attend the service, but what could she do? Ask them to leave? She had never even met two of the women in the group. One of them was rather plain and dowdy, wearing a shapeless cotton dress that was made out of a small floral print. Her hair was light brown and pulled back into a thin ponytail. She had a kind, but plain face, her eyebrows knit into a furrow of sadness and concern. Her eyes remained focused on the ground. It seemed to Annie that she was afraid to look up, to see the reality of what was happening around her. Annie found herself empathizing with the strange woman, because she felt much the same way.

The other woman was a different story. She was not plain and dowdy, but just the opposite. She was stunning.

Tall and slender, she wore her sleeveless black sheath with graceful elegance. Her arms were tanned and toned as were her bare legs that seemed to go on forever. Blonde hair gently grazed her shoulders and glistened in the sun. She was not looking down, but rather was surveying the area with a boldness that seemed out of place. When their eyes met, the hairs on the back of Annie's neck stood up and she had a sick feeling in the pit of her stomach. She had seen the woman only a couple of weeks before, the day a limo had arrived at the house to take Eric to a work event at a water park in Wisconsin. It had caused a huge fight when he returned home, since he'd been out nearly all night. Shaken by this visceral reaction, Annie averted her gaze to Dillon's little casket. Oddly enough, that seemed to calm her down, comfort her and allow her the time she needed to gather her composure. Why had the blonde woman chosen to come? Annie's heart was beating wildly even thinking about it.

Her thoughts were interrupted by a gentle hand on her shoulder. It was the priest. He quietly said, " Should we get started?" Looking at him, she nodded.

She knew she had to go through this, just as she had gone through the labor and delivery. She remembered her Grandma's favorite saying: "What doesn't kill you, makes you stronger." *But I don't want to be stronger*, she thought. *I just want Dillon back.* Again she looked for Eric. She needed him near her now, next to her. She felt frail and fragile and ready to break into a thousand tiny pieces as she stood there. Alone.

The priest had made his way over to where the Rubbermaid casket sat on top of the green crushed velvet drape that covered a mound of dirt and busied himself looking over the passages from Scripture he had chosen to read that afternoon. Sunlight bounced off the white plastic finish of the casket as the branches of nearby trees were blown gently around by the balmy June breeze. It made Annie sad to think of Dillon being there all alone, and she walked over to be near him. She reached out her hand and patted the casket softly, as though it were his newborn baby cheek. *It's okay, sweetie,* she thought, *Mommy's here.*

Suddenly it seemed very quiet. A hush had descended upon the group gathered there. She glanced around and realized that everyone had taken her walk over to the casket as a signal that the service was about to start.

They had formed a small semicircle behind her and all stood there looking at her. Some were crying, others were dry-eyed but composed. There were a few whose eyes were focused on the grass or the trees or the pair of geese that basked in the sunshine at the base of a large, marble monument nearby -- anywhere but at Annie and the tiny white box. They could not bring themselves look at her or at the casket because it simply made them too uncomfortable. In her mind's eye she could see herself as they saw her and couldn't blame them -- it was a painful sight to behold.

Eric appeared at her side, seemingly from out of nowhere. His hand found hers and gave it a squeeze. The priest must have been waiting for this, because upon seeing Eric, he began the service. Annie's mind drifted during the priest's opening remarks about the uncertainty and unfairness of life and how someday we would see Dillon again. She let it drift on purpose, because to listen to his well meaning words would have surely made her run up there and strangle him. He meant well. He was just doing his job and he truly believed what he said. After all, he was a priest. How could he know? Had his baby ever died? The voice of one of her best friends reeled her back to reality. She was reading from The Little Prince by Saint-Exupery, just as Annie had requested.

*In one of the stars I shall be living. In one of them I shall be laughing. And so it will be as if all the stars were laughing, when you look at the sky at night...You - only you will have stars that can laugh!*

The words reminded her of the night Dillon was born and the star she had seen from the hospital window. She had read The Little Prince in high school and for some reason had remembered the part about the star at the last minute. She would never forget the courage and kindness it took for her friend to read it that day. It was the final reading of the service, the last words spoken.

No one knew what to say or do. Eric's parents invited everyone to their house for something to eat. It was the logical thing to do -- it seemed too early to go home, Eric had reasoned. One by one people said quick good-byes and walked to their cars parked one behind the other along the edge of Babyland. Bits and pieces of their words floated toward Annie through the humid air.

"See you at the house."

"Be there in a few minutes."

"You can follow us, if you want."

Annie was riveted to the spot where she stood next to Dillon's casket. It was as though her feet had grown roots that ran deep -- roots that would cradle her baby underground, keeping him safe and warm forever. How could she just leave him there, all alone? Again, as they had so many times in the days since he had come into the world, her arms ached and her heart hurt. She wrapped her arms around herself, as if to give herself some comfort.

"Come on, Annie," Eric said as he walked up behind her and put his hands on her shoulders. "It's time to go." He remained there, keeping his distance from the casket.

"It seems so cruel to just leave him here," she said, her voice nearly a whisper.

"Well, you can't stay here," the weariness in his voice was deafening.

"I know, but he's all alone."

Eric looked around as the last of the mourners got into their cars and prepared to leave.

"Annie, everyone's going to my parents' house now. We're supposed to be there. Come on -- let's go." He took a few steps away from her, as if that would make her leave.

When she failed to follow him, he stopped and sighed, his frustration breaking through the thin veneer of patience and control. "Annie, come on. People are going to think you're crazy if you stay here much longer."

She turned toward him in slow motion, her heart pounding. She squeezed her hands into fists, her arms stiff and close to her sides. She opened and closed her fists several times and took a couple of deep breaths before she spoke, "Let them think I'm crazy."

Even though her voice was barely audible, it was strong and clear. Eric squinted and tilted his head in her direction, straining to hear what she had said.

"What did you say?" he asked, almost afraid that he'd heard her correctly the first time.

"I said, let them think I'm crazy!" she repeated, saying each word more loudly than the last. By the time she finished the sentence, she was shouting. The priest, who was getting into his car at that moment turned and looked in their direction. He froze in place, balanced precariously between offering some assistance or driving away as quickly as possible. He offered up a fervent prayer, ducked into his Volkswagen Beetle and slowly inched his way away from the painful scene.

Eric stared at her, not knowing what to do or what to say. He looked over toward the cars by the curb and hoped the people inside of them hadn't heard his wife's outburst. Finally he just said, "Annie." He looked at her helplessly, hoping she'd snap out of this strange behavior. "You'll feel better if you get away from here."

"I'm tired of being told how I feel or how I should feel! My baby is in that casket -- my baby! He's so tiny and all alone. I can't leave him. I just can't."

She was sobbing now, struggling to breathe in between each word. Annie stood there alone, her arms folded across her chest. She winced when her arms brushed her engorged breasts that Eric had helped her wrap with an ACE bandage. Her milk had come in that morning, filling her up with sweet milk that no baby would drink.

One of the nurses had explained that when the milk came in, it would be very painful for a day or two until it dried up on its own. "With no baby nursing, the milk production will stop by itself," she had said in a very matter of fact way. "It can be rather uncomfortable, so sometimes it helps to bind them with an ACE bandage. Any questions?" She looked up from her list of topics to go over with new mothers, peering at Annie over the half-glasses that were perched on the end of her nose. She seemed perplexed to see Annie staring back at her with a horrified expression on her face. The nurse shook her head and smiled, "Oh honey -- don't worry about it -- you'll be just fine. It's just what happens if you decide not to breast feed, which by the way, is the best thing to do for your baby. So, let's see -- what's next here? Oh yes --" she looked up at Annie, "what type of formula will you be feeding your baby?"

"My baby died," Annie said softly. She gazed out the window at white fluffy clouds on a background of brilliant blue sky. She swore the clouds were taking the shape of a baby sleeping on its tummy. She blinked hard and looked again only to find it was gone.

"What was that, hon?" the nurse asked distractedly as she organized her paperwork.

Suddenly she stopped, her head snapping up to look at Annie. "Oh my God -- you had the stillborn, didn't you? Oh dear - I am so sorry! Oh, you poor thing - I am so sorry! I'll - I'll be right back." She scurried out of the room.

Annie just sat there, feeling guilty for ruining the woman's day. She caught a glimpse of her out at the nurse's station, talking excitedly, wringing her hands as she spoke to the other nurses. At one point they all turned and looked toward Annie's room and shook their heads sadly. She couldn't believe this was happening to her and yet somehow she could. Nothing would surprise her ever again. She and Eric just had the ultimate surprise -- nothing she could think of could top it.

Eric's somber voice brought her back to the moment. "He's my baby too, Annie. I know how you feel --"

Annie's words pounced on him. "You don't know how I feel! You don't know! Do you feel empty inside? Are you filling up with milk that has nowhere to go? Are you the one who failed?" She stood there, almost daring him to contradict her. Then she saw how dejected and confused he looked and sighed heavily. She walked over to him and put her arms around him. She laid her head on his chest. He in turn wrapped his arms around her gingerly, as though she might break so as not to cause her any more pain.

"Yes, Eric. He was your baby too."

They stood there together for a few more minutes, looking at the little white casket and then very slowly and gently, Eric guided Annie toward the car. There, on the other side of the street, she saw the blonde in the black dress, wave good-bye as she drove away.

# The Photograph

"Can I get you some, um, coffee or something?" Eric's younger brother Joe asked Annie awkwardly, interrupting her thoughts.

She was standing near the dining room table laden with "funeral food" -- lunch meats, buns, potato chips, macaroni salad, jello, bars and cookies -- when he approached her. She wasn't the least bit hungry, but she knew she'd be prodded to eat something. She looked up at Joe, surprised and relieved to have something to do, someone to talk to.

"Yes, I'd like that. Thank you." He handed her the cup of steaming coffee that he already had in his hand. "Thanks, Joe." She held it in both hands and blew on it a little to cool it off.

Joe nodded, embarrassed, but proud to have helped her in this small way.

Not knowing what to do or say next, he backed away from her and escaped to the other side of the room. She smiled, touched by his sweet, awkward gesture.

Annie surveyed the food again. She knew she needed to eat, but the knot in her stomach was taking up more than its fair share of the room. It was strange, because she hadn't noticed feeling that way until she saw the blonde woman at the cemetery. Grief had robbed her of an appetite during the past couple of days, but she hadn't felt the queasy tension that she did now. It gnawed at her relentlessly. She wondered if a Rice Krispie bar would make her feel better and was walking over to the table to get one, when she heard them.

"I just can't get over how much he looks like Jessica," Terri exclaimed to Eric's mother. "They have the same eyebrows, the same mouth. It's kind of eerie."

"They do look alike, but Jessie is changing so much every day. Two months ago when she was first born, though, they could have been twins." Both women stood next to each other, shaking their heads back and forth slowly. It seemed to Annie that they were looking at something on the table in front of them.

"I'm just glad I had Jessie first. Can you imagine how it would be if I'd had her after all this happened?"

"It sure would've been hard to enjoy it."

"Enjoy it? Yeah -- I really enjoyed that back labor," Terri said sarcastically. "And colic is such a treat." She took a bite of the sandwich she held in her free hand.

Annie stepped up next to the table to see what they were looking at and froze in her tracks. There on the white lace tablecloth were the Polaroid pictures the nurse had taken of Dillon right after he'd been born.

"Where did you get those?" Annie asked, shaken by the sight of her child, the child she had left behind at the cemetery less than an hour before.

Up snapped their heads as well as the pictures as Evelyn, Eric's mother grabbed them and pulled them close to her chest as if trying to hide a good poker hand.

"Now, Annie, you shouldn't be looking at these right now."

"And you should?" Annie shot back at her without thinking. "Where did you get them?" She demanded again. By now a hush settled over the room, everyone riveted to the scene.

"The nurse at the hospital gave them to Eric and I thought that I should hold onto them until you were ready to see them. They'll only upset you right now, dear," she said, reaching out to pat her hand. Annie pulled back, nearly spilling her coffee. "As you can see, I'm right."

"Please give them to me," Annie said as calmly as she could. She put down the Styrofoam cup and held out her hand toward her mother-in-law. She was raging inside, furious that so many decisions were being made about her behind her back, but she knew that if she unleashed her anger, that would confirm in everyone's minds that she was losing it. She wasn't losing it -- she was grieving.

"I only want what's best for you," said Evelyn, still holding the pictures tightly. The two women stood there in what appeared to be a stand off. Annie couldn't think of anything to say that wouldn't come out as a shriek, so she just stood there motionless, looking the older woman squarely in the eye. Evelyn was flustered but it was due more to anger than concern. No one told her what to do. "I'll just keep them until you're ready." She tucked them into her apron pocket, patting it in a quietly deliberate motion.

"When will that be, Evelyn?" Annie's voice was losing a little of its control. "How will you know when I'm ready?"

The room was completely quiet. The only sounds that could be heard were the birds chirping in the trees outside and Evelyn's increasingly heavier breathing as she tried to think of an answer. Suddenly the slam of the screen door shattered the silence. The piercing sound made everyone jump. It was Eric coming inside from having a cigarette. He strode into the room, his stress having just been lifted and blown away like the smoke he'd just exhaled out on the front porch. Oblivious to the heavy plaque of tension that coated every surface in the room, he promptly went to the table, grabbed a plate and started piling some potato salad onto it. It took him a few seconds to notice that all eyes were on Annie and his mother.

"What's going on?" he asked. "Did I miss something?" He put the serving spoon back into the tangerine-colored Tupperware bowl that held what had to be a vat of potato salad. It flipped over the edge and landed on the tablecloth with a muffled thud. There was an audible intake of air, as though the room itself had been holding its breath. Everyone knew how fussy Evelyn Morgan was about her tablecloths. Terri grabbed a napkin and swooped in to clean up the spill before anyone was able to exhale. "Nice going," she hissed at her brother as she gave him a dirty look.

"Like I said, what's going on? Annie?" The activity at the table and hearing Eric say her name broke Annie's concentration and made her look in his direction. There he stood, Chinet plate balanced on his left hand, looking at her expectantly. Why couldn't he just put down the plate and come to her side, to her rescue? Why did she have to feel so alone?

"I asked your mom to give me the pictures she has of Dillon." Annie did her best to state her case with as little emotion as possible. After the scene in the cemetery, she knew that he already thought she was going crazy. She didn't want to add any ammunition to his artillery by letting her feelings get in the way. "And she refused."

Eric sighed. He felt his mother's gaze upon him and exhaled again, a deep, defeated sigh.

"Mom, just give me the pictures, okay?" He held out his hand, waiting for her to comply. His mother hesitated for a second and then reached into her pocket to retrieve them. She looked at them one last time before handing them over to her son. Terri, who was standing behind her, peeked over Evelyn's shoulder as they were passed to Eric. "I still can't believe how much he looks like Jessica."

Without saying a word, Annie quietly walked to the front hall, took her purse off the hook on the wrought iron coat tree, and left.

"That was real nice of you to just leave me there like that," Eric stated as he walked into their living room later that evening. 'What were you thinking?"

He threw his keys down on the end table. They landed in a jumbled heap in front of her, startling her awake. She'd fallen asleep after having dissolved in an avalanche of tears on the couch when she'd gotten home several hours before. She was confused, not knowing how much time had passed.

"What time is it?" she asked, groggy and puffy-eyed. Trying to focus on the watch on her right wrist, she blinked and pushed her hair back. "Is it really 8:00 p.m.?" She'd left his parents' house five hours ago. Then she looked at Eric again. "Did you just get home?"

He sat down in the armchair across from her, shaking his head in disbelief.

"Yes, I just got home. Since you took the car, I needed to get a ride. I didn't think there was a rush. Besides, you seemed like you wanted to be alone." He looked at her with hard, cold eyes. When she tried to look more deeply into them, past the anger, he shifted his gaze to the other side of the room.

"I'm sorry -- but I had to get out of there. If I said anything I would have lost it. I just had to go."

"Why? What was the big deal?" Eric bounced his leg nervously, still not looking at her.

"The big deal was that your mom had pictures of Dillon that I didn't even know she had, and she wouldn't give them to me. Then Terri kept saying how much he looked like Jessica. It was just too much." She could feel her blood pressure rising as she spoke. Her heart pounded so hard she could feel it pulsating down to her feet. She curled her toes in an attempt to keep them from shaking.

"Well, he did look a lot like Jessie -- they would have been cousins, you know. They're only a couple of months apart. She didn't mean anything by it."

"It was still hard," she said, sniffling. She couldn't believe that he was being so casual about it -- wasn't it hard for him too? "Do you have the pictures?" She clutched the couch pillow tightly, squeezing the piping on its edge.

"Yes, but I don't think you should have them right now." He stood up, feeling his shirt pocket. She thought he was going to take the pictures out of it, but he removed his cigarettes instead. "They'll just upset you."

"No, they won't," she protested. "How could I be any more upset? Eric, please give them to me. Please."

The expression on his face was a mixture of pity, unease, and resignation. He started walking toward the door to go outside for a smoke and then retraced his steps back to her. He reached into his pocket and took out the two nearly square photographs. He dropped them on top of the pillow she was holding in her lap. "Just promise you won't go crazy on me." With that he left the room.

Annie grasped the two precious pieces of paper and plastic in her hands. She didn't look at them right away, but closed her eyes and tenderly felt the edges and the smooth, flat surfaces with her fingertips. Ever so slowly, holding her breath, she opened her eyes to look, only to realize that she had them upside down. Shaking her head and smiling a little in embarrassment, she turned them over. Her smile grew even bigger when she laid her eyes upon her little boy. He was even more perfect than she'd remembered -- he was beautiful -- and he didn't look anything like his cousin.

The top picture was a close up of Dillon. Eric had unwrapped the blanket he'd been bundled in, so that his entire body was visible. At the time she'd thought it a little strange and voyeuristic but now she was glad she could see so much of him. It was good to be able to see his little feet and hands, his tummy and his chest. She remembered holding his tiny feet, one at a time, in her left hand -- counting his toes. She'd lifted his fingers to count them as well and had given each of them a kiss in the process. The memory made her smile. How could this be bad for her? How could she not be ready?

The second picture made her heart take an unexpected leap and then break into a million pieces. It was a picture of her holding Dillon right after the nurse had given him to her. He was wrapped in the white receiving blanket with blue and pink stripes on each end. It was shocking to see herself holding her child. She looked like someone else -- someone too young to be going through something so tragic. The expression on her face was serious but serene. What had she been thinking at that moment? What had she been feeling? It struck her how incredibly sad the picture was, especially for someone from the outside looking in. It was heartbreaking. And it was her.

Tears streamed down her face and dripped from her chin onto the pillow. She moved the pictures so that they wouldn't get wet but didn't even try to wipe the tears away. In the last two minutes, these had become her most prized possessions. If anything happened to them, she didn't know what she'd do.

"Oh, my sweet little Dillon," she sobbed, "I'm so sorry I didn't take better care of you. I'm so sorry." She kissed her fingertips and then placed them softly on his cheek.

## The Blue Daisies

Each of them went about the business of living and healing, of pretending that things were getting back to normal, whatever that was. Eric never wanted to talk about Dillon, which frustrated Annie, because that's all she could think about. So she wrote in her journal endlessly, devoured books written by other bereaved parents and started reading not only the obituaries but the birth announcements in the newspaper every day. If there was a birth announcement for a baby weighing close to what Dillon had weighed, that validated his existence. If there was an obituary for an infant close to his age, that validated his premature death. One of her books said that mothers and fathers grieve in different ways -- that fathers weren't as close as mothers were to the unborn baby -- that they pictured themselves as the father of an older child, playing catch or shooting baskets, rather than changing diapers or nuzzling a baby's head, luxuriating in the newborn smell. So she did her best to leave him alone and taught herself not to expect too much. If he was hurting, he didn't want to share it with her. She was hurting, but kept it to herself, because of her love for Eric. He was doing the best he could; at least that's what she kept telling herself. Things wouldn't always be this way; it had to get better.

Annie had also begun to go to the cemetery every week. She needed to feel as though she was taking care of her baby, and bringing him blue daisies every Friday filled that need. It had been two weeks since the funeral when she had first decided to go. Eric had insisted that the headstone wouldn't be there yet, and that she should wait, but she wanted to go anyway.

She'd been shopping that morning and saw some baby blue daisies in the floral department at the grocery store. The idea of bringing them to Dillon immediately popped into her head. It was a beautiful, sunny Friday. While most new mothers would be excited to take their baby on an outing to the park, she couldn't wait to get her groceries home and put away so that she could go to visit her baby at the cemetery. She couldn't dwell on the cruel irony of it. This was her life now and there was nothing she could do about it.

When she pulled into the driveway, she was surprised to see Eric's car in the garage. He must have decided to take the afternoon off. Maybe he'll want to come with me, she thought hopefully. She parked her car in the garage next to his. In a hurry, she got out, opened the hatch and grabbed a bag of groceries to carry into the house. There were five bags in all, but this one was the heaviest. The others she could carry two at a time, or she'd ask Eric to help her.

"Hello!" she called in a singsong voice. "Yoo-hoo! I'm home!" She plopped the bag of food down on the counter. She knew she should get the frozen items into the freezer, but first pulled a vase from the cupboard and plopped the daisies into it with a flourish. She felt a little woozy and weak, but ignored it. Dr. Hayes had cautioned her to take it easy for a few weeks; she was on maternity leave, not vacation; but with no baby to care for, it was hard to take his warning seriously. She could sleep whenever she wanted to uninterrupted, so she shouldn't have been suffering from sleep deprivation as so many new mothers did, but sleep did not come easily.

What no one knew, however, was that every night at 1:30 a.m., the time that Dillon had been born, she awoke in a cold sweat and couldn't fall back to sleep because all she could see when she closed her eyes, was his face. This gave her some comfort at first, but after a few nights, just when she was drifting back to sleep, she'd see his face and he'd open his eyes and begin to cry. It haunted her because there was nothing she could do to help him. Night after night he'd cry and night after night she'd cry herself back to sleep because she couldn't make him stop. The first time he opened his eyes in her dream, she shook Eric awake, trembling and frightened.

"What is it?" he muttered as he forced an eye open to look at her.

"I had a bad dream," she told him. He'd reached out his arm and pulled her closer to him. It felt good to be held, to be comforted by him.

"You'll be fine," he assured her sleepily as he patted her arm. "Just close your eyes and go back to sleep." In seconds, he was sound asleep again, snoring gently.

She'd laid there for the longest time, next to him but so far away. She never told him what her dream had been about because he'd never asked her. She never told anyone, because there was no one to tell. After a while she got used to the dreams and while they disturbed her, the thought of them ending was even more disturbing because that meant that Dillon was really gone.

Shaking the thoughts from her head, she decided that she'd better ask Eric to help after all.

"Eric," she called, "can you help me with the rest of the groceries?" There was no response, no sounds from his office or from the family room where she thought he might be watching T.V. "Eric?"

She started to look for him, but then remembered the rest of the groceries out in the car, out in the very hot car in an even hotter garage. Trying to be careful, she made two more trips to get them. When she was down to the last two bags, she did a quick look around the garage for any signs of him. She sniffed as she looked, just in case he'd been out there smoking recently. Nothing. That was strange.

The groceries needed to be put away, especially the frozen items, so she went back into the house to take care of it. Surely Eric would turn up -- maybe he'd gone over to the neighbor's for a minute. It had been hard to shop for food when she had little or no appetite, but she'd forced herself. Now it was even harder to summon the energy to put them away. Everything was a struggle these days. The burst of excitement she'd had about going to visit Dillon was fading quickly and it made her angry; mostly angry at Eric, because she didn't know where he was. The anger fueled her with the energy she needed to complete her task, so it wasn't a wasted emotion. She was folding up the last of the brown paper grocery bags when she saw the yellow Post-it note stuck to the counter. It had been covered by the bags of food and wasn't visible until now. It read:

> Annie ~
> Went boating with clients. Sorry for the short notice. Don't wait up.
> Love,
> Eric

Annie stood with both of her hands on the counter and took a deep breath. Her anger was still close enough to the surface so that she could feel it bubbling up inside of her. Her face felt hot and her heart pounded in her chest as she took Eric's note and crumpled it in her hand. "Sorry for the short notice," she mimicked in a bitter voice. "Don't wait up."

She picked up the white porcelain vase that she'd placed the daisies in and hurled it across the room. The vase hit the corner of the table and broke into several pieces. The daisies seemed to float to the floor in slow motion, as she stood there, shocked at what she had just done. Water from the vase sat in little pools on the kitchen floor, reflecting the midday sun that shone in the windows. Ever so slowly, she walked over to where they had fallen and knelt down to pick them up, one by one, as though she was picking them out of a garden. Once she had gathered them back into a bouquet, she stood up, leaned against the counter and held them close to her heart, as if they were Dillon himself.

She was relieved that Eric wasn't there to witness her outburst. What would he think if he saw her acting like a madwoman? For that matter, what would anyone think?

As she walked over to the cupboard to find another vase, her gaze fell upon Eric's wrinkled Post-it note on the counter and the rage bubbled inside of her again. Who did he think he was, that such a cryptic scribble would suffice? She knew she hadn't been much fun lately, but couldn't he see that she needed him? Perhaps she'd been so unpleasant to be around that he was trying to steer clear of her. She arranged the daisies in the new vase, a cut glass one that had been her grandmother's, and made a mental list of examples from recent days to support her theory. As the light bounced off the vase and made prisms on the kitchen wall, she remembered how alone she'd felt in the days since Dillon's death. Dillon's death. The very thought made her realize how she'd been avoiding the painful reality of it all. She'd been thinking of how Dillon had been born, but couldn't quite admit that he had died. She didn't know if she was ready to do that. Maybe Eric was having the same problem, even though he'd told her that he was ready to move on. He said he was tired of the sadness and tears; he wanted his wife back the way she was before all of this happened. He wanted it to be fun again. Annie wanted to be supportive of his wishes, but she didn't know how to be fun right now. It seemed wrong, not to mention impossible. She hoped and prayed that she'd be "normal" again, but deep inside, at the very core of her being, Annie knew she'd never be the way she was before. It scared her to think of that because of how Eric would react. Would he be able to love the new version of Annie? Would he even like her? She needed him. Had she told him that? She couldn't remember -- all she knew was that he was awfully hard to talk to lately. Whoever he was with on the boat was probably a lot more fun.

Suddenly a disturbing thought popped into her head: Who else was on the boat? Was that blonde from the cemetery with him? A chill ran though her; a cold front clashing with the heat of anger. She felt dizzy and sick to her stomach and had to grab the counter for a second to get her bearings. She hated feeling jealous and insecure, but there was something about that woman that made her blood run cold. She felt it the first time she'd seen her, and then at the cemetery, and she felt it now. Annie took a deep breath and shook her head as if to make the bad thoughts disappear. She needed to keep her mind on the task at hand and that was to bring Dillon his blue daisies.

Seeing her baby's headstone for the first time had been painful. It made everything more real to see Dillon's name carved into the granite, with only one date to measure his life instead of two. She hadn't expected it to be there and was both pleasantly surprised and stricken with sadness at the same time. The grass had been recently mowed, leaving clippings scattered across the headstone. Some of them had settled down into the grooves, filling the curves and angles of his name. Annie knelt down and ran her fingers over the cold, smooth surface and lovingly traced the letters of his name. She patted it, as though she were patting his little back, soothing him to sleep. A tear ran down her nose and landed in a tiny splash in the center of the "o". What are the chances of that? She smiled to herself for a second and thought how if Eric were there with her, she'd point it out to him. She definitely knew that Dillon would find it funny and it occurred to her that perhaps he had something to do with it. Perhaps he was trying to make his mommy smile in spite of her tears. She wiped the tear away, patted the headstone again and whispered, "Thank you."

It was almost dinner time when she returned home to a still empty house. That was when she decided to open the bottle of Chablis. She'd been perfect throughout the pregnancy, never allowing a drop of alcohol touch her lips. A lot of good that did, she thought as she struggled to remove the cork from the neck of the bottle. The wine rolled over her tongue as she took a sip, tasting tart and sweet at the same time.

She ambled over to the refrigerator to see what there was to eat for dinner. There were fresh vegetables for a salad and two thick steaks, as well as juicy green grapes and succulent peaches. Nothing looked appealing even though it had earlier in the day when she bought it. Then she had been picking out food to make a special dinner for Eric that night, and now she would be eating alone. Again. She closed the appliance door, telling herself she'd eat later. Nothing appealed to her now anyway.

Annie took her wine glass and went outside on the deck. The late afternoon shadows stretched across the yard, making abstract shapes on the lawn below. She placed her forearms on the redwood railing and leaned forward, staring aimlessly past the trees. The distance that was growing between she and Eric worried her. She never thought she'd lose her husband, but now she wasn't so sure. She'd also never thought she'd lose her baby, but she did. She felt she was no longer immune to danger. Bad things could happen to her.

Eric didn't get home until well after midnight. He tried to be quiet, easing the bedroom door open slowly, but cursed under his breath when its hinges creaked, piercing the silent darkness. He undressed by the light of the small black and white T.V. that was perched on the chest of drawers in the corner. Annie had been falling asleep with it on lately, explaining that it kept her mind off her dreams. What she hadn't said was that it also helped her feel less alone since he was gone so many evenings. The low hum of the voices of Johnny Carson and Ed McMahon kept her company as she drifted off into the fitful slumber that had become her normal routine. Eric switched off the television and climbed into bed. The waterbed sloshed violently as he tried to rearrange the top sheet that Annie had clasped under her chin. He tugged at it gently at first and then more firmly when he couldn't loosen it from her grip. The noise and movement flickered in and out of the dream she was having about holding Dillon close to her chest as he sucked his thumb and slept contently. The commotion irritated her because it was finally a good dream, one that brought some peace to her heart and a smile to her lips. Because she didn't want to have the dream disappear, she pretended she was still asleep and let the sheet fall from her hands. She heard Eric let out a sigh of relieved exasperation as he pulled it over his shoulder and rolled onto his side with his back to her. With the sheet gone, Annie clasped her hands around each other, placed them under her chin again and hoped that Dillon had waited for her to come back to him.

Sunshine filtered in through the blinds early the next morning and fell across Annie's face. She opened her eyes and just laid there, waking as slowly as she could, taking in the day. Birds were chirping in the lilac bush outside the bedroom window. Hearing them as well as seeing the sunshine made her realize that she'd slept later than usual. She turned onto her side, and saw that Eric's place next to her was empty. Feeling it with her hand, she was relieved to discover that the sheets were still warm, that he really had been there next to her last night. Her mouth felt as though it was lined with cotton, a reminder of the wine she'd had the evening before. She swallowed and licked her lips a couple of times, happy to realize that she felt fine except for this. No headache, no nausea. Good. The last thing she needed was a hangover.

The aroma of fresh brewed coffee wafted from the kitchen and Annie followed it like radar. A cup of coffee would taste wonderful. Eric was in the kitchen with what appeared to be half the contents of the refrigerator on the counter. Bowls and frying pans and egg shells were strewn about haphazardly. He was humming a little tune as he used the wire whisk to beat pancake batter briskly. Sensing he was no longer alone, he looked up at her.

"Good morning," he said, smiling sheepishly. "Want some coffee?"

"Sure," she replied, still surveying the mess.

"Don't worry," he said as he handed her a mug of steaming coffee. "I'll clean up. Here -- why don't you sit down?" He rushed over to the table and pulled out a chair for her.

"Thanks," she said as she sat down slowly. He hurried back to his cooking project, barely making eye contact with her. She watched him add fresh blueberries to the pancake batter as she blew on her coffee to cool it off before taking a sip.

"What's all this for?" It hadn't been her intent to sound annoyed, but it sort of came out that way.

"I just wanted to make a big breakfast for us," he said as he poured a ladle of batter onto the hot griddle. He scooped the remaining batter from the ladle onto the newly formed pancake with his forefinger, and then licked it, smacking his lips. "Mmm -- now that's good!" Eric loved to brag about his own cooking and she almost smiled in spite of her anger.

"I guess I am a little hungry," she replied, sipping her coffee again. "Since I didn't have dinner last night." *Because you didn't come home,* she thought angrily.

"Why didn't you eat? It looks like you went shopping yesterday. The fridge is packed." He flipped the pancakes over as he spoke, appearing to have no idea what she was getting at. She watched him lay the spatula on the top of each pancake and press down, flattening them out firmly.

"I was all set to make a special dinner for you and after I read your note I didn't feel like it anymore." There. She said it. Then she added. "I thought you were going to be home yesterday afternoon." She was trying as hard as she could to control her emotions. Every time they had a disagreement, she'd lose her ability to sound reasonable because her mind would cloud up with emotion. She was determined not to let that happen now. Annie thought she saw Eric tense up a little as he transferred the pancakes onto a plate.

"Well, I was, but then the boating thing came up. Do you want bacon?"

"I want to know more about the 'boating thing.' Your note didn't say too much."

"One or two pieces?" he said impatiently, holding the tongs in mid-air.

"Whose boat was it?" Annie ignored his attempt to divert her attention.

"Do you want some bacon or not?" he was losing his patience now.

"Who all went?"

"Jesus, Annie. Just answer my question! Do you want bacon?"

"No. I don't want any damn bacon. I want to know about yesterday."

"Good God -- what's with you?" He loudly set a plate with two large pancakes and two pieces of bacon down in front of her. She stared at the fried pieces of greasy meat through cold, steely eyes. Remaining unusually calm, she surprised herself.

"I said I didn't want any bacon."

He strode over to the table and dramatically picked up both pieces of meat and shoved them into his mouth. "There, are you happy now?" His fingers were coated with bacon grease and he proceeded to lick them off as he had with the pancake batter.

Annie didn't know what to say. His question, 'Are you happy now?' was spoken with such sarcasm and disdain. Why was he acting this way? What had she done to deserve this?

"No, Eric, I'm not happy," she said in a firm voice. "I want to know more about yesterday."

"Fine. Yesterday." He paced back and forth in front of her. "Some new clients were in town and Kelly thought it would be a good idea to take them out on Lake Minnetonka. We bought them dinner at Lord Fletcher's, had some drinks, and came home. That was it. Now are you happy?" He folded his arms across his chest and glared at her.

"Kelly is the blonde?" Her stomach twisted into a knot.

"Yes, she's the district manager."

"So, she can have you work later just because some clients come into town?"

"Yes, she can. I report to her, you know. You weren't home anyway, which is why I left the note." He started to pace again. "Am I supposed to ask permission before I go anywhere now?"

She was trying so hard to remain calm. If she started crying he would completely tune her out.

"I need to spend some time with you," she added quietly, "but I feel like you don't want to spend time with me. You've been gone so much lately."

Eric ran his hand through his hair, and appeared to be searching for what to say to next. He walked over to the window and turned his back to her as he looked out into the backyard, silent.

Annie decided to give him all the time he needed to respond. The blueberry pancakes on her plate were getting cold, the butter and syrup congealed near the edge of the plate, a thin skin forming over the surface. Her appetite disappeared again, a dull ache taking up residence where the hunger had been. The clock on the kitchen wall ticked by the minutes in slow motion. Tick, tick, tick.

Eric took in a deep breath and exhaled loudly before he spoke. "I don't know what to do for you, Annie. You're always so sad." His voice was calmer than it had been just minutes earlier. She was thankful and frightened at the same time.

"Our baby died," she said softly, fidgeting with her fork. "Of course I'm sad. Aren't you?"

"Of course I am. I felt sad the night he died, but now I'm ready to move on. I can't think about it all the time like you do. I need to have some fun." He turned towards her a little bit, but was still near the window on the other side of the room. She so wished he'd come over to her and wrap his arms around her, but his arms remained folded tightly against his chest.

"But talking about it helps me, Eric. You're the only person I can talk to."

"What about that support group?" he interrupted. "Can't you talk to those people?"

"I've gone to that once -- and yes, I could talk to them, but I need you, Eric. I want to talk to you." Tears were starting to form and Annie did all she could to keep them at bay.

Here she was, reaching out to her husband, and he was pushing her away -- passing her off to a group of strangers in a hospital meeting room on the second and fourth Thursday of each month.

"I want the old Annie back," he said. "Maybe you'll feel better if you just try to go out and do something fun. Talking about it just makes you sad."

"And I feel as though talking about it will help me feel better and then maybe I'll feel like doing some things." She got up from the table and started to approach him. If he wouldn't come to her, she'd go to him. She was willing to meet him halfway and she wanted to demonstrate that.

He turned to face her and put his hands up as if to stop her. "I can't talk about this right now," he said. "I need to have a smoke." He disappeared into the sanctuary of the garage.

As the door slammed behind Eric, Annie turned and surveyed the mess that had been made in the kitchen; the mess that had been left for her to clean up. The white plastic mixing bowl full of pancake batter stood next to the electric griddle, globs of spilled, lumpy batter dripping down the sides of the bowl and dotting their way to the griddle. Dollops of batter were also covering the edges and handles of the griddle, the heat of the appliance cooking it just enough to make it as hard as concrete. A short distance away, there was a clean circle of countertop surrounded by a thin layer of flour, where the bowl sat when the ingredients had initially been combined. From the looks of the counter, it was difficult to believe that anything had made it into the bowl. Jagged halves of eggshells were piled in a jumbled heap, the slimy excess egg whites oozing out from underneath them.

The plastic from the bacon package was lying on the counter, greasy side down, in a puddle of flour and milk. It pushed Annie right over the edge she had been so precariously clinging to for the past few minutes. Angry tears sprung from where she'd been hiding them, as if in an ambush. The enemy, however, was not present amongst the aftershock of cooking supplies and ingredients. With nothing to attack, the tears trailed down her cheeks silently and fell onto the counter, adding a taste of salt to the recipe.

She decided right then and there that she was not going to clean it up. As thoughtful as it might have been of Eric to make breakfast, she just couldn't do it. This was going to come as a surprise to him she knew, because the unspoken arrangement was that when he cooked she cleaned up, and when *she* cooked, she also cleaned up. She tried repeatedly to convince Eric of the inequity of it all, but he refused to see it her way.

In spite of her anger, it was difficult for Annie to walk away from the mess. She was so used to doing things to avoid upsetting Eric, this new behavior did not come easily. *So what if he got mad,* she told herself, *what was he going to do? Leave me for not doing the dishes?*

Annie forced herself to leave the pancake disaster in the kitchen and walked down the hall to the bedroom. Her eyes fell upon another mess -- the bed. It had been a restless night. The sheets were pulled out from the mattress on every side, and were swirled into a tangled mess, much like the eggshells on the kitchen counter. She sighed and closed her eyes. She'd take care of this -- it would alleviate the guilt plaguing her for not doing the dishes.

As she pulled the sheets off the bed, she was struck by grief of a different kind. It used to be that when the sheets were this disheveled, it was because the night had been filled with passionate lovemaking. Annie had to stop and really think to remember the last time that had happened in their bed. It had been a very long time. The pregnancy had wreaked havoc with their love life. She had read that it often had the opposite effect, since the fear of pregnancy was eliminated, but that was not the case for them. The larger she became, the further away Eric became. It was as though her growing belly was pushing him away. *Maybe it was my growing thighs*, she thought as they jiggled when she put one of her knees on the bed as she reached for the corner of the bottom sheet. She grabbed the flowered percale fabric firmly and pulled it toward her, nearly falling off the bed in the process.

On her way to place the sheets in the laundry hamper, she passed the full length mirror and stopped in front of it. She glanced at herself quickly, almost afraid of what she'd see looking back at her. When the initial peek didn't prove to be too upsetting, she looked again, taking more time. Her shoulder-length brown hair was still unbrushed from the night before, framing her face with a halo of unruly curls. She tucked some loose strands behind her ears as she examined herself more closely.

Sad, weary eyes looked back at her. It reminded her of when she saw herself in the Polaroid picture of she and Dillon for the first time. It looked like someone else at first and then she realized it was her own blue eyes that were so painfully absent of joy. That was to be expected, but she was alarmed at how sad she looked. No wonder Eric was avoiding her. Who would want to look at that all the time? She made herself smile, just to see if she could. It felt foreign to force the corners of her mouth into an upward curve -- it seemed like an eternity since she had made that motion. Her face looked more pleasant, but her eyes remained haunted and lonely. *Maybe it will just take practice,* she thought. *Maybe it will get easier if I smile a little bit every day*. She was suddenly struck with guilt. How could she be thinking about smiling when her baby had just died? What kind of unfeeling monster was she? She put all thoughts of smiling or not smiling in the back of her mind. She couldn't think about that right now -- she'd wait until later.

Her eyes made their way down the rest of her body. She was wearing black knit shorts and a light pink tank top. The fabric of the tank top stretched over what used to be her wonderfully pregnant breasts and abdomen. Even if Eric had been turned off by her growing girth, she had loved every minute of being pregnant. She put her hands on her stomach now and her heart ached when she felt its flabby softness rather than the firmness of Dillon's little bottom or the protruding point of a tiny elbow that had been there before. Again, she forced away the sad thoughts -- she'd take them out later. She had no doubt that they'd be there waiting for her. She practiced her smile again.

Even though she was a little out of shape, she didn't think she looked unattractive -- or did she? Her thoughts drifted to Eric's whereabouts the day before and a frown immediately pulled the corners of her mouth down even further. Compared to Kelly, she looked like Two Ton Tillie. She turned and viewed her profile. No matter how much she sucked her tummy in, she still looked about four months pregnant. Her breasts were no longer swollen and engorged with milk as they had been -- they were almost back to their normal state. Eric had made favorable comments about how sexy she looked when they had been larger -- now she feared he wouldn't even look at her. She knew that if she had a baby to nurse and take care of, the way her body looked wouldn't matter so much. Both she and Eric would have been preoccupied with falling in love with Dillon instead her being preoccupied with the fear of Eric falling out of love with her.

She put fresh sheets on the bed. It felt good to smooth the cool fabric over the mattress and to make square corners with the top sheet. It was neat and orderly and perfect -- just the opposite of her life at the moment. It was good to have control over something.

Annie showered and put on a brightly colored sundress. It was light and airy and camouflaged the parts of her body that she disliked just enough so that she looked less disgusting to herself. She blow-dried and styled her hair and applied make-up for the first time in several days. She'd tried wearing make-up when she came home from the hospital, but she just cried it off almost as soon as she put it on. While she was at the store yesterday, she bought some waterproof mascara and eyeliner in the hopes of at least looking good through her tears. She felt prettier taking the time to look nice even though thinking of Kelly's perfectly applied make-up and her long, blonde hair made her cringe and feel queasy. What was it with the intense reactions to this woman? And why was Eric so irrational about her? Back in the old days, he would've scoffed about a woman who was that "high maintenance" but now he was enthralled. She was the exact opposite of what Eric found attractive -- or was she?

Annie emerged from the bedroom with new resolve to make more of an effort with Eric. She would save her tears for those times when she was alone. If being down in the dumps all the time was driving her husband toward another woman, she had better pay attention. She had to make some changes.

It had been an hour since she'd made the decision to leave the kitchen mess the way it was and nothing had changed in her absence, except that all the spills would now be even harder to clean. It would take a crow bar and brute strength to clean up this disaster now. Where was Eric? She was relieved that he hadn't come back into the house and blown a gasket seeing the mess still there, but at the same time it bothered her that he hadn't. Where was he?

Annie went out to the garage to see what he was up to. *Probably another cigarette,* she mused grimly. He had been smoking more than ever since Dillon had been born. He had promised her he'd quit when they first found out that she was pregnant, but as of yet no attempts had been made. It was understandable now, with the stress and grief, that it was not a good time for him to quit, and she vowed not to bring it up. A thick, heavy blanket of blue smoke assaulted her the moment she stepped into the garage. She wrinkled her nose in disgust.

"Eric?" She expected to see him there, sitting on the front step with a cigarette in hand, but he was not in his usual spot. "Eric, where are you?" She tried her best to keep her voice light and happy, but inside she was starting to panic. His car was there, so he hadn't gone anywhere, as far as she could tell. Her nose followed the trail of smoke outside and around the corner of the house to the backyard. He was sitting in one of the Adirondack chairs with his back to the house, cigarette in one hand, a beer in the other.

She approached him slowly, wanting to choose her words carefully. "Here you are," she said softly. "I wondered where you were." She came around the side of him and stood next to his chair tentatively.

He took a long, slow drag on his cigarette and held the smoke in his lungs for what seemed like forever. He looked up at her and slowly let it out through pursed lips, aiming it away from her. The wind was blowing toward her, so most of the smoke settled on her anyway. She tried to remain pleasant.

"Sorry," he said. "I didn't mean for it to get on you."

"Oh well," she started, "that's okay."

"You want some?" he pointed to the bottle of beer with his smoke.

"No thanks -- it's a little early." She glanced at her watch and saw that it was barely 11:00 a.m. This was new -- drinking before noon.

"You think? Well, I should have known that you wouldn't approve." He took a swallow and looked out into the yard at nothing.

"I didn't say that," Annie said, "I just know that if I have any, I won't get a thing done today." She decided not to point out that she had just gotten up not that long ago and that her stomach was still empty because of their argument. She had dodged the hangover bullet from the night before and didn't want to tempt fate.

"It's Saturday - what's there to do?" He took another drag.

"Well, for one thing, the kitchen needs to be cleaned up." Oops. She said it. It slipped out in spite of her intentions to be a good wife. Her stomach started to tie itself in a knot and she found a hangnail on her left hand thumb to pick at while she nervously waited for his response.

"That's no big deal," he said as he took another sip from his bottle.

"Well, it's a mess," said Annie.

"You better get going on it then," he said, chuckling. "What are you waiting for?"

"I'm waiting for you to do it," she said, injecting a small chuckle in her voice as she said it. Maybe if she kept the conversation "fun" he'd comply. She gave him a weak smile.

"You're kidding me," he said, still laughing a little bit.

"Actually I'm not. You said you'd clean it up." Annie's heart was pounding now, pumping adrenaline through her body. To keep her hands from shaking, she stopped picking at the hangnail and folded her arms in front of her.

"I did? As I recall, I was doing something for *you*." He said the words as though he deserved a medal and took another swig of beer.

"It was great of you to make breakfast, but having to clean it up kind of cancels it out. All I asked for was some help." It felt good to stand her ground for the second time that morning. She was surprised to see that it was easier this time. *Practice* must *make perfect*, she thought triumphantly. As good as it felt to stand up to him, she hated conflict and loathed every minute of this.

"Well, la-dee-da," the words rode out on a blast of smoke as he slowly shook his head. She hated it when he did that. It made her feel like an idiot. "This isn't about the dishes, is it?"

Annie thought for a second before she spoke. Of course this wasn't about the dishes -- it was about his going with Kelly on the boat trip yesterday, it was about his not wanting to talk to her about Dillon, it was about everything else in the world but the dishes.

Annie kept telling herself that she shouldn't hold any resentments against Eric. He had insisted that he'd take care of it, but when the mess sat untouched for hours, she found herself getting frustrated and angry all over again. She found him in front of the T.V. watching a baseball game.

"Who's winning?" she asked calmly, pushing down her anger until it cooperated and sat still.

"No one – it's tied," he replied as he reached for a handful of potato chips.

"Oh." She hesitated as she stood next to his recliner and then sat down on the couch adjacent to it. She scratched a small scab on her knee where there had been a mosquito bite. They sat in silence for a minute or two until she spoke again.

"I know you said you'd clean up the kitchen, but I just wondered when you were going to do it. It's almost time to start making dinner." She said it as pleasantly as she could although she wanted to chastise him for being so lazy. Her heart pounded; her anger had become a fist and was beating from the inside to be let out.

Eric sighed and rolled his eyes, shaking his head. "I said I'd do it ---" He let his voice drift off as his attention was drawn back to the television.

Annie seethed. Obviously he hadn't heard her when she said that it was nearly time for dinner. Or he had heard her, but didn't care. Either way, she was finding it difficult to breathe normally and she didn't know what would happen if she opened her mouth and tried to speak. For all she knew, fire would come shooting out of her mouth and burn him along with his ugly gold velour recliner, to a charbroiled crisp. Even though she couldn't think of one reason why that would have been a bad thing, she kept her mouth safely shut, hoping the fire within would extinguish itself quickly, without doing too much damage.

She stood up and started to leave the room and was already halfway down the hall when she heard him shout, "Besides, I won't be home for dinner, so don't worry about making anything for me." The words stopped her dead in her tracks. She could hardly believe it. She stood in the hallway, paralyzed by indecision, disbelief and exhaustion.

The attempts she made in the two weeks since Dillon had died, to convey to Eric how his behavior was hurting her, had apparently been made in vain. It had caused her an unbelievable amount of stress to challenge him, to veer off her path of compliance that had become the norm in their marriage, and for what? What good had it done? It had done nothing but add more pain to a heart that was already carrying much more than it was prepared for. What was she supposed to do?

Without making a conscious decision, she found herself in the kitchen, amidst the dried on lumps of pancake batter and the thick, white bacon grease that coated the bottom half of the electric frying pan. Annie released some of her pent up anger by banging the pots and pans as loudly as she could, even though she knew it would irritate her husband. She scrubbed the dishes and the counter with more energy than she'd had in weeks, and found great satisfaction in making everything in the kitchen sparkle and shine. She felt cleansed as she eliminated any trace of Eric ever having made breakfast or of there having been any mess at all. For the moment it gave her peace; for the moment she could breathe a little easier, but deep inside an old familiar feeling began to gnaw at her soul. Annie was oblivious to it because for the time being she was engulfed in grief. She was doing anything and everything she could to maintain her sanity and so the feeling went unnoticed -- or at least ignored.

When the game was over, Eric showered and put on a pair of khaki Dockers and a long-sleeved white shirt. He brought his empty beer bottles and chip bowl to the kitchen and placed them on the counter. The clean, shiny freshness of the room grabbed his attention and he made a little whistle through his front teeth in approval.

"Hey Annie," he called, "the kitchen looks awesome!" He listened for her to respond and when he didn't hear anything, he called out again. "Annie – where are you?" He busied himself putting his change, nail clipper and keys into the pockets of his clean pants. In his shirt pocket he placed a fresh pack of cigarettes and a new Bic lighter. He whistled as he waited for Annie to come from wherever she was. Even though he figured she was in the laundry room or something, he decided to leave her a note, just to be on the safe side. Already running late because the game went into extra innings, he reached for the stack of yellow Post-it notes and a pen. There, right on top, still on the stack, was a note with Annie's handwriting on it. He shook his head in amused frustration as he tore it off and slapped it on the spotless counter. How many times had he told her not to leave the grocery list or other reminder notes *on* the Post-it note tablet? He tore off another note and began to write on it, when his eyes fell upon the words that Annie had written:

Eric ~
Be back soon.
Annie

Annie had gone to the place where she found the most relief and comfort -- the cemetery. She'd stopped at the grocery store on the way and bought the usual bouquet of blue daisies. At least she could talk to Dillon and tell him what a jerk his dad was being without doing any permanent damage to anything or anyone. She had to tell someone or she'd go crazy. It seemed wrong to complain about Eric to any of her friends, because they were all his friends too. They'd probably think she was a monster for being so demanding of him at such a difficult time.

So, she'd tell Dillon. Her secrets would be safe with him. As she recounted the incidents of the boat trip and the dishes, she felt a little guilty, because everyone always said it was wrong to bad-mouth the other parent to your child. *Maybe I am a monster after all*, she thought as she sat by Dillon's grave, arranging the daisies in the cone-shaped cemetery vase. Her eyes traced the outline of the new piece of sod which had been recently placed over the hole that had been there. It wasn't very big, maybe only 2'x 3' – the size of the throw rug by her front door. She found herself smiling at the comparison. *Good. Now whenever I look at that rug, I'll think of Dillon.* It suddenly occurred to her how absurd that thought was – not because a rug in her front hall would remind her of her baby's grave, but because of the idea that she'd need to be reminded of him at all. He was on her mind every minute of every day and she couldn't imagine it being any other way.

Annie moved from the outside edge of the sod rectangle into the middle of it, and gently smoothed the lush, fresh greenness of the new grass. It hadn't rained much lately, and the shorter lawn surrounding it was becoming peppered with light brown and yellow sprouts. She hoped that the cemetery crew would take special care of Dillon's new sod and not let it die. Certainly they must have special guidelines for watering new sod. She didn't think she could bear to come and find a blanket of dead brown grass beneath her baby's name carved in blue-gray granite. *I'll just have to water it myself,* she vowed silently. *I'll be taking care of him.* Immediately she began to devise a plan for watering Dillon's sod. It felt good to use her brain to problem-solve. She'd been in such a heavy fog of grief for so many days, her thoughts revolved mostly around how much she missed her baby. This was still about him, but at least she was planning to *do* something, rather than just *be*. It felt like progress.

As close as Annie felt to Dillon, she had an urge to feel even closer to him. Looking around to see if anyone was watching her, she laid down on the new sod, letting the tall, green blades envelope her body in a gentle hug. She put her hand on the granite marker and felt its cool firmness against her palm. It soothed her in a way that nothing else had been able to and she closed her eyes and let out a long, deep sigh. Exhausted from the tension and events of the past couple of days, Annie's breathing soon became relaxed and rhythmic and before long, she was sound asleep.

While darkness fell over the rolling hills and curving roads of the cemetery, the air cooled and dew formed on the ground, covering the grass and granite with a thin sheet of glistening moisture. Overcome with fatigue, Annie hadn't been aware of the setting sun or the dropping temperature. Just as she did every night, like clockwork, she woke with a start. It was 1:30 in the morning. She opened her eyes and laid there, motionless. At first she thought she was dreaming that she'd fallen asleep on Dillon's grave and told herself to go back to sleep. As the dampness of the night dew soaked into the back of her shirt, her mind kept racing and she realized that she wasn't dreaming after all.

# The Broken Heart

A solitary tear ran down Annie's cheek and splashed onto the divorce papers on the counter in front of her. The notary's stamp was a blurry smudge, looming large. She remembered the last time they'd broken up with disturbing clarity. If she didn't know better, she would have thought it was yesterday. The distance between then and now had disappeared and all she felt was the pain. The pain had always been there – it had never gone away. If only she had known, so many years ago, that love didn't have to hurt to be real. If only someone had told her that there could be more happiness than hurt.

The red flags had always been there, but she had managed to ignore, deny, repress them, until the day that Dillon died. Looking back she realized this, but while she was in the moment, it had been much more difficult to see. She had loved Eric with all of her heart and soul. He had been everything to her and she had tried so hard to be everything to him as well, but it hadn't worked. She had always felt that something was missing -- that she didn't quite measure up. She never felt that Eric found her beautiful or sexy, even though sex was something they had plenty of in the early years. Feminists would have scoffed at her willingness to please him, but it was really all she wanted to do. Making him happy made her happy.

Of course, in all the wisdom and experience of twenty-three years, she thought she loved him. She *did* love him. However she soon found that love alone wasn't enough -- at least the kind of love that they had or the kind of love they could give each other. Because while she loved Eric, there was always an undercurrent of doubt whether he loved her. He said he did, but his actions told a different story. Annie always berated herself for doubting him; how could she be so disloyal? So she ignored the pain she felt when he'd stay out until the wee hours of the morning with his buddies or when he forgot the color of her eyes.

Once before they were married, Eric had wanted to go fishing. They were driving down a dusty, country road on the way to the lake, looking for a place to buy bait and a fishing license. Annie had planned on doing more reading and tanning than fishing and had assured him that she didn't need a license. They finally saw a run down building on the side of the road with a make shift sign that said "BAIT SHOP." It was connected to a liquor store that had a flashing Grain Belt sign that had half of the neon burnt out. Eric pulled his black Grand Prix into the parking lot.

"This is great!" he exclaimed. "We can get a fishing license and some beer. One stop shopping -- you've gotta like that." He turned off the ignition and turned to her. "Do you want to come with?"

"That's okay -- I'll wait here," Annie replied, smiling back at him. "But will you get me a Tab?"

"Alright," he said, and hurried into the store, extinguishing his cigarette before he went inside.

Twenty minutes later he emerged with a brown paper bag in his right hand, a carton of beer in his left and a white piece of paper between his teeth.

"Sorry I took so long," he said, dropping the paper from his mouth before he spoke. "It took a while to get waited on."

"No problem," said Annie. "I took a little nap."

"I got night crawlers and leeches for me, and worms for you," he announced as he set the bag of bait on the floor of the back seat.

"But I'm not going to fish," she reminded him, not that he couldn't put the worms to good use.

"Oh yes, you are!" With a flourish, Eric waved the piece of paper in front of her face. She blinked at the commotion and put her hands up to stop him.

"What are you doing?" she asked, confused.

"Well, I decided to get us a joint fishing license," he explained proudly. "Then if you want to fish, you can. Besides, it was cheaper than two single ones would be."

"But we're not married," she interjected, secretly pleased that he was even willing to pretend. She had been hoping for a commitment from him for a long time. Maybe he was finally warming up to the idea. "Won't we get in trouble if they stop us?"

"Oh you and your always wanting to follow the rules," he teased, dismissing her question. "It will be fine." He looked into her eyes a little longer than usual. She smiled back at him, ready to concede that it would be okay, when he muttered, "Damn!"

"What?" Annie was thoroughly confused at this point. "What's wrong?"

"You have blue eyes," he stated and then swore under his breath again.

"Yeah -- so?"

"I put down 'green' on the license. Damn it. I was so sure I guessed right."

Annie was stricken. He'd *guessed* her eye color? She couldn't believe he didn't know for sure. They'd been dating for four years, not four days. Her heart plummeted to her feet, but she was determined not to show it. How picky could she be to let something like that bother her? Besides, it was so sweet of him to get them a joint license. He'd actually put her down as his *wife*. That had to count for something; much more than getting her eye color right. But the fact that he'd gotten it wrong started to wear away at her heart, in one little spot way at the bottom, where she thought could ignore it.

"That's okay," she said, trying to sound cheerful. "Did you get my Tab?" She thought she'd change the subject to divert her attention from the sick feeling in the pit of her stomach.

"Damn," he said again. "I forgot."

Annie made a conscious decision not to say anything. It was better that way. She wasn't going to say it was alright and she wasn't going to get mad about it. It simply didn't seem worth the time or effort. Instead she found happiness in the fact that for the moment, she was a tiny bit closer to becoming Mrs. Eric Morgan.

As it turned out, being Mrs. Morgan didn't make much of a difference. Several years later, Eric came home from work one day and announced that he'd stopped at a sporting goods store during his lunch break and bought a fishing license. The state fishing opener was that weekend and he was going on the first of several trips he had planned for the summer.

"Guess what?" He waved the white piece of paper in front of her face as she cut up a red, juicy tomato for the salad she was making for dinner.

"What?" She reached for the dishcloth to wipe the juice and seeds from the tomato off the counter. She then ran the cloth under a stream of hot water from the faucet to rinse it off before she neatly folded it and placed it on the divider between the sinks.

"I got a joint license this year -- just in case you decide to fish."

"That's good, I guess," she replied. "We do have that family reunion to go to up at Breezy Point. It might come in handy." She wiped her hands on the blue terry cloth dish towel and reached for the license. Suddenly she was reminded of the first joint license he'd bought for them so long ago. She smirked a little as she wondered if he'd gotten her eye color right *this* time. Before she could get hold of it, he whisked it out of her hands.

"There's only one problem," he said, a sheepish look coming over his face. He put both of his hands behind his back, the license safely hidden from her. "I kind of had a little problem with one thing on the license. You're going to think this is really funny --"

"You didn't forget my eye color again did you?" She laughed as she took the cover off the pot boiling on the stove to stir the contents bubbling inside. As she removed the lid, a drop of spaghetti sauce made a leap for freedom and landed on the shiny white surface next to the burner. She frowned, grabbed the dish cloth and wiped it up without missing a beat.

"Not if they're brown," he said with a nervous chuckle.

Annie put the cover back on the pot of spaghetti sauce a bit too loudly and turned to face him. "You're kidding me, right?" she said, still smiling, but feeling her heart drop a few inches.

"Well, not really," he looked nervously at the floor, at the stove, out the window, anywhere but at her face. Or more specifically, into her eyes. *No wonder he doesn't know what color they are*, Annie thought angrily. *He never actually looks at them.*

"I stood there for the longest time, trying to remember, and I just couldn't," he went on to explain. "I just drew a blank. At first I thought *green* but then I remembered that's what I put down the first time. Remember how funny that was? Anyhow, I was holding up the line, and I had to put something, so I just said *brown*." He was folding and unfolding the license in his hands as he spoke. "But that's not right, is it?"

"You tell me," Annie closed her eyes and stood there with her arms folded across her chest. She leaned against the counter, crossing her right foot over her left, and waited.

Eric sighed heavily and rolled his eyes. "Come on, Annie. You're being ridiculous. You know that, don't you? Don't you have to get dinner on the table?"

"Quit trying to change the subject." She was losing her patience. "It shouldn't be that tough."

Eric was silent for a minute and then said," They're hazel, aren't they?"

She opened her eyes. "You tell me."

He did as she said and when their eyes met, she was stunned by the anger and coldness she saw as she looked into his eyes. He scowled and looked away.

"Your girlfriend must have the brown eyes, huh?" She tried to make a joke out of it, but neither one of them found it very funny.

Tears gathered in her eyes as she shoved the pages of the divorce decree into its manila envelope. It had been one of the moments in their years together that she'd never forget. It was the incident that woke her up; that made her pay attention. How could he not know the color of her eyes? What man who loves a woman doesn't remember a thing like that? The gnawing in her gut made her wince as she remembered more. If nothing else, it would confirm for her that they'd made the right choice; it had been the only choice, really.

It was a month after Dillon died when she'd found the note. It all happened innocently enough -- she was getting some of Eric's suits ready to bring to the dry cleaner's. Even though she hated the reason for being home from work, she found herself enjoying having unhurried time for household tasks. Usually she was hurrying to the dry cleaners to pick up Eric's suits or shirts on her way home from work when time was already cramped. It was a luxury to be able to be able to take her time, especially in the middle of the day, when everything wasn't so crowded with afterwork shoppers. Of course it would have been so much better to have Dillon along in his little car seat as she ran her errands, but she was trying to find the good in small things. It seemed to help her heal. Maybe if she told herself that enough, she'd finally believe it.

The T.V. in the bedroom was tuned to "Live with Regis and Kathy Lee". Kathy Lee was carrying on about her precious little dogs, Chablis and Chardonnay, her hand resting on her pregnant belly as she spoke. *Sure*, Annie thought jealously, ***her** baby will be okay*. No sooner had she thought it, when she reprimanded herself for being so horrible. She wouldn't wish her tragic fate on anyone -- even Kathy Lee. No one deserved this kind of pain.

"Oh, Reeg," Kathy Lee's voice droned on in the background as Annie went about emptying the pockets of Eric's suit coats and pants. He was usually good about taking everything out of them, but every now and then he missed something. Since she had the time, Annie was being extra careful to check every last pocket. The last time she'd brought one of his suits to be cleaned, a tube of lip balm had been left in the inside pocket of the jacket. The suit had almost been ruined because the dry cleaners had missed it too. Eric had been furious, more at himself than anyone, but Annie decided it was worth it to be more vigilant now, to prevent potential disaster later.

She was rooting around in the inside pocket of his dark gray suit jacket. No lip balm to be found, but there was a piece of paper or something there. *Probably a receipt,* she told herself as she removed it and looked at it. He had been searching for the receipt for a new tie he'd recently purchased and wanted to return, so she decided to open the folded piece of paper to see if that's what it was. He often shopped at an exclusive men's store near his office that had large, elaborate receipts, much larger than the usual cash register tape. Her heart stopped as she read the words:

Beth G. -
call anytime

Frantically, she turned the piece of paper over to see if there was anything on the back to indicate when it had been written. There was nothing; it was just a plain piece of white paper from a 4" x 6" notepad. There was a remnant of the red plastic binding on the top but that was all. Her hand shook as she stared at the carelessly scrawled words. She felt sick to her stomach as she sat down on the bed to get her bearings.

Annie closed her eyes and made herself take several very slow, deep breaths. What did this mean? She thought she only had to worry about Kelly. Now there was someone named Beth? Her heart pounded wildly, making it difficult to breathe. *Oh my God,* she thought, still trying to calm her upset stomach. *Now what do I do?* She had to talk to Eric -- she needed to confront him. As upset as she was, there had to be a reasonable explanation; there had to be. She tried to ignore the voice inside of her that told her that there could only be one explanation for such a note. She had failed at being a mother, she was determined not to fail at being a wife.

Furious tears nibbled at the inner corners of her eyes, but she pressed her fingers there to keep them from spilling out. She had to stay strong, to stay in control. This would not get the better of her. She could do this. Just then, Regis announced their next guest as a woman who had written a book about divorce. Annie's skin crawled as the words entered her brain and she bolted for the bathroom and vomited into the toilet.

*Enough of that,* she told herself as she tore off a length of toilet paper to wipe her mouth off. *Enough.* She stood up and looked at herself in the mirror. The tears she'd been fighting so hard to keep in, were running down her face. They'd snuck out while she was throwing up. *Okay, fine. Get it over with now, because you are* not *going to cry later.*

When Eric got home late that afternoon, she was sitting in the living room, reading a book and drinking a glass of wine. It had been a warm day, warm enough for air conditioning, but she'd opted to turn it off earlier in the day and had opened the windows instead. She heard the door open and then she heard his voice.

"Jesus, it's hot in here -- why isn't the air on?" He was unbuttoning the top button on his shirt as he entered the room. He stopped when he saw her. "Wow -- you look great."

Annie had taken extra care in getting ready that afternoon. Her hair and make-up were perfect and she'd put on Eric's favorite white sundress. She was pleased to discover that she could fit into it -- her pregnancy pounds were beginning to disappear.

She wanted to look especially good as she asked him about the note she'd found in his suit. She looked attractive and confident, even though she was terrified. The wine helped calm her nerves and gave her the additional courage she'd need for the task ahead.

"Thanks," she said as she reached for her glass and took another sip of wine. "Did you have a good day?"

"Yeah, it was fine," he said as he went to the refrigerator for the wine bottle. He poured himself a glass. "How was yours?"

"Well," she started, "it was all right. Nothing too exciting until I got your suits ready to bring to the cleaners." She took another sip and a deep breath. "And then I came across this." She held up the note between the first two fingers of her right hand.

Eric stood there, frozen in place, the color momentarily draining from his face.

"What's that?" he asked warily after a few seconds.

"Well," Annie started, "it's not the receipt for your new tie." She slowly unfolded the paper as she spoke. "At first I thought that's what it was, but then I read it." She looked at him squarely in the eyes and said, "But it's definitely not a receipt."

"What is it then?" he asked again. He reached out his hand toward her. "Will you give it to me please?"

Annie pulled the note close to her body and held it tightly. She looked at it for a moment and then looked back up at her husband.

"Annie –"

"It was really wonderful to be going through your suits before I brought them to the cleaners this morning and find something like *this*." She shook the note for emphasis.

She took another sip of wine, pacing herself. That afternoon, as she showered and primped for Eric's homecoming, she realized what a mistake she'd been making in trying to please him; in trying to be a "good wife." She was losing respect for herself – how could Eric not be losing it too? Why on earth should he respect someone who let herself be walked all over like an old rug? The area over her heart was getting particularly threadbare. At the rate they were going, he'd wear a hole right through it if she didn't do something.

"Annie – calm down. It's not what you think."

"No, Eric, I'm not going to calm down. " She stopped to catch her breath. Her heart was pounding like a sledge hammer. "Who is Beth G.?" She held the note out to him again. "What am I supposed to think?"

He sighed and slowly shook his head back and forth, "What do you want from me, Annie?" His voice was defiant and defeated at the same time.

"I want the truth." She said the words calmly and firmly. She was terrified inside, but was determined not to show it. She sensed she was heading to a place she hadn't been prepared to go, but there was no turning back now.

Eric felt his pocket for his cigarettes and fidgeted in his chair. "I need to go and have a smoke."

"No, you don't."

"It'll just take a minute," he sounded like a petulant, spoiled school boy.

"I want the truth," she repeated the words.

He stood there looking forlorn and subdued.

"Just tell me. Who is Beth?" Suddenly she wished she could take back the words. She wished she could turn back the clock to an easier, happier time, but had trouble remembering when that would have been.

Eric stood up and walked across the room to the window. He stopped there and looked out at the yard. His back was to her as he started to speak. "Beth is a family law attorney. One of the guys at work gave me her name."

She could barely hear him, but decided not to interrupt. Something told her to be still and wait. The only sound was the neighbor's dog barking, filling the awkward silence with a much needed distraction.

"I started to realize it while you were pregnant. All that mattered to you was the baby; I became less and less important to you. Now all we do is fight; I can never do anything to please you. I can't do this anymore, Annie. I want a divorce."

The floor seemed to shift under her feet and Annie reached down for the arm of the sofa to keep from falling. Suddenly she felt as though she was being pulled underwater by a violent, relentless current of disbelief and fear. She lowered herself down onto the sofa.

"A divorce?" The words left a bitter taste on her tongue.

He stood there like a statue, hands shoved in his pockets, his mouth a hard line.

"But I love you, Eric. We can work this out. We haven't even tried. This has been an awful few weeks. Maybe Dr. Hayes knows a counselor who can help us." Annie was desperate for him to listen to reason.

He shook his head. "No. No counseling. Let's just cut our losses and be done, Annie. It's pointless to keep up the act."

"What act? What do you mean?" Tears were now running down her face. "Doesn't our marriage mean anything to you?"

"I always wanted it to, I really did, but it's just not working." He sounded like a stranger. "It's never going to work. It's just too hard."

"I can't believe you're willing to just throw it all away." The words were getting caught in her throat, constricted by the torrent of emotions.

"Well, believe it."

"Is there someone else? That Kelly from work?" There had to be more to this than he was telling her. "Eric, are you having an affair?"

"No, there's no one else. You're so paranoid. Kelly has nothing to do with this. I just want life back the way it used to be." He looked away from her as he spoke.

He left her sitting there and went into the bedroom to pack a bag. When he came back out, she was still on the sofa, tears still running down her face.

"I'll call you," he murmured and then walked out the door, letting it slam behind him.

In the days that followed she couldn't remember what she'd been looking at when he left, if anything at all. The entire incident remained a blur, except for the words: 'I want a divorce.' It made her sick to think of it, but she kept repeating the phrase in her head over and over again. Each time she repeated it, it still sounded so foreign and unreal. How could Eric want a divorce? Had he really been that unhappy? How could this be happening to her? First her baby died and now her marriage was dying. Although according to her husband, it was already dead, and he wanted it to stay that way.

# The Scales of Justice

And so it went. Annie's aunt and uncle had just returned home from their trip to India and couldn't believe the news that Annie shared with them. Not only did they learn of Dillon's death, but that Eric wanted a divorce. They were shocked and saddened by it all.

Eric had suggested that they use only his attorney, Beth G., in order to save money and keep things simple. Sally insisted that Annie retain her own lawyer, a good friend, named Gwendolyn Jones.

"I don't know much about divorce law," Sally told her, "but one thing I do know, is that the outcome of this can effect your life for a very long time. It's wise to have someone who is looking out for your best interests. The lawyer Eric has hired will be looking out for him, not you."

As difficult as it was to face the reality of the situation, Annie listened to her aunt and retained Gwen. When Sally had shared Annie's story with Gwen over coffee one evening, Gwen offered to represent Annie at no cost, explaining that she took one pro bono case a year. With all of the heartache Annie had been through, not having to worry about lawyer's fees was a tremendous relief.

Gwen and Annie first met several months earlier at Sally's house. Annie had been about six months pregnant with Dillon at the time and they had all sat around chatting about how much fun it would be after the baby was born and Annie could bring him over to visit. Sally and her husband, Frank, hadn't been able to have children. They had always been close to Annie, and were living somewhat vicariously through her. When Annie announced her pregnancy, Sally rejoiced as if it was her own, and when a tearful Annie told her that Dillon had died, she grieved as only someone who has walked in those shoes can. It always made Annie sad to think about the many miscarriages that Sally had endured in the early years of her marriage. She and Frank would have made such wonderful parents. Even though they had suffered through four miscarriages, their devotion to each other never wavered. In fact, it became stronger. That was also why Sally had no time for Eric. She couldn't understand his treatment of Annie and she certainly couldn't tolerate it.

"It seems as though he's just trying to be as stubborn as he possibly can," Annie lamented during a telephone conference with Gwen. "He wanted to use one lawyer to save money, but now he's digging in his heels every chance he gets, just because he's angry that I've hired you." Annie cradled the phone on her right shoulder as she poured water into her coffee maker to brew a new pot.

"I don't like it, no matter what his reasons are," Gwen replied indignantly, "I agreed to take your case pro bono, so he can drag his feet until the cows come home and it won't put any more money in my pocket. He's making me angry because he's putting you through this hell. You have been through enough."

Gwen became not only Annie's legal counsel, but her friend as well. To have Gwendolyn Jones as your lawyer and your friend was a unbeatable combination – it didn't get any better than that. She was known in the legal community as having the loyalty and tenacity of a rotweiller --- no opponent came out of a settlement unscathed and every single one of them wished that they had hired her first.

"Well," Annie continued, "I appreciate your support, Gwen. I don't know where I'd be without you." She reached into the dishwasher for a clean mug and poured the freshly brewed coffee into it. A curl of steam rose and vanished in thin air when she blew across the top of the mug.

"What he doesn't realize, of course, is that he is the only one who is going to suffer financially from his selfish stupidity. He will be stuck with astronomical legal bills from Ms. Goldstein. I'll make sure that those expenses are his alone and not part of your marital debt."

"Gwen, I don't want to keep fighting with him about all of this --- I just want it to be over."

"I know you do, but as your attorney, I have to advise you as to what is in your best interests. Just because he wanted this divorce doesn't mean you have to give in to all of his demands. Your future is what is at stake here, my dear, and I'm not going to let you forget that."

On this particular day, the day on which they were supposed to decide upon the final details of the decree, Eric and Beth, or "Bambi", as Annie's lawyer had nicknamed the opposing counsel, arrived late to the meeting. Bambi bounced into the conference room and Eric followed. The swagger in his step disgusted Annie and she had to close her eyes and count to ten in order to control her breathing.

"Ms. Goldstein," Annie's attorney stood as she spoke. "This meeting was scheduled for 2:00 p.m. It is now 2:35 p.m. This is unacceptable. My client cannot afford to pay me to sit here and wait for you and your client. There is no excuse for such behavior."

Bambi set her briefcase on the shiny, mahogany conference table. Before she sat down, she unbuttoned the jacket of her tighter than professional espresso brown suit. She slid out of it with much more ease than Annie would have thought possible, given the way it had strained across her breasts and stretched over her shoulders. Under it she wore a white shirt, unbuttoned dangerously low. She draped her jacket over the back of her chair and then sat down, wiggling this way and that in an attempt to be comfortable. From where Eric sat, Annie observed that if he turned his head or even his eyes to the left, in Bambi's direction, he could catch a glimpse of the flesh bursting against the poplin fabric.

Annie's lawyer continued, pretending to be oblivious to the spectacle on the other side of the table.

"So, Ms. Goldstein, I'm assuming that your client has decided to comply with the terms of the decree that were discussed at our last meeting?" she peered at them over the rims of her tortoise shell glasses. Annie's lawyer was in her mid-fifties, a very successful, no-nonsense type of person. She had mentored Eric's lawyer at one time, but they had parted ways because of Bambi's unorthodox business practices.

"Well actually, Gwen --- " Bambi started.

"That is Ms. Jones to you," interrupted the older woman without missing a beat.

"Oh -- excuse me -- Ms. Jones," Bambi corrected herself. "Actually, my client has some issues with the details about the sale of the house."

Annie tensed up and shot a look across the table at her estranged husband. What issues could he possibly have? They had gone over this more times than she cared to remember.

"And what might those issues be?" asked Gwen tersely. She was getting as tired of this ordeal as Annie was.

"Mr. Morgan does not believe that he should receive only half of the proceeds of the sale of the house. He made more money during the marriage and therefore should get that much more when the house is sold." She looked over at Eric and gave him a little wink.

"Don't be ridiculous," Gwen sniffed. "The law says everything is divided equitably and that is all we will agree to. My client isn't requesting spousal maintenance as it is, so Mr. Morgan should consider himself lucky."

They hadn't been married long enough for Annie to be entitled to spousal maintenance, which was fine with her. She was young and able to support herself. She didn't want any monthly reminders of what had been, of how they had failed in so many different ways. She looked over at the person who she had fallen in love with so long ago and rather than anger boiling up inside, another piece of her heart was ripped off. When he glanced away from Bambi for a second, he caught Annie's gaze and for a moment his eyes softened and she thought she could see a hint of the old Eric -- the boy who had stolen her heart once upon a time.

A week later, Annie was on her way to another meeting with Eric and their lawyers. She was unusually nervous about what might transpire, because he had left several rather nasty messages on what was once "their" answering machine. She had changed the message from "Hi -- you've reached Eric and Annie ..." to "You have reached 555-0198..." She almost fell over when she hit the "Play" button one afternoon, only to hear Eric's voice emanating from the small black machine.

"So, you couldn't wait to take me off the message. You should think twice about that. I still own half of the house and everything in it -- including the answering machine. You can't get rid of me that easily."

His hostile tone of voice made the hairs on the back of her neck stand up and she swallowed hard. She stared at it and was almost afraid to reach out and touch the "Erase" button. If only erasing him from her life could be that easy. He was being so irrational. He had started the divorce proceedings, and yet he acted as though it had been her idea.

The last message started out even worse, but this time she was standing right next to the phone as it rang. "Annie, this is Eric - your husband, remember? I know you're home, so you ---"

She grabbed the telephone receiver from its cradle. "Eric -- what do you want?"

"I want you to return my phones calls, for starters."

"What do you want?" she repeated. She was trying to remain calm and strong, and had to sit down to keep her legs from trembling.

"I just want you to be prepared for the next meeting," he crooned.

"What do you mean?"

"Last time you weren't prepared to cooperate -- this time I want you to be ready to make it right." Here he was again, trying to call all of the shots, trying to be in control.

"What is it you want, Eric?" Sitting down wasn't helping, so she stood up as she spoke and started to pace the floor in the kitchen. The curly cord connecting the telephone receiver in her hand to the telephone on the wall kept her tethered and prevented her from spiraling out of control. Curling the cord around her finger for extra support, Annie could hear him taking a drag on his cigarette. She could also hear the clinking of ice cubes and concluded that he was having a cocktail.

"Once Dillon died, I thought I'd at least have you back to myself again, but he was still all you thought about. You were always so damn *sad.*" He said the word as though it were an obscenity and paused to take another drag. "You've ruined my life and it's all your fault."

She wanted to ask him why he had filed for divorce so quickly, but she decided to remain silent. It sounded as though Eric was divulging some powerful feelings and she felt that she needed to let him vent. It hurt her deeply to hear him blame her and Dillon for everything, but it was also very enlightening. Had she really shut him out so completely? Had her entire focus been on the pregnancy and then on their stillborn child? She hadn't meant to do any of those things. She had been trying to be a good wife and expectant mother who was then thrust into the role of a grieving mother. She had always wanted Eric to join her -- she had always tried to include him. Was he finally allowing himself to grieve? Is that what this was all about? She didn't know what to say to him.

"And what is it that would make it right?" her voice was barely a whisper.

"I'll tell you at the meeting," he said in a low voice. "Just be ready." And with that, he hung up.

The downtown traffic was horrific. One way streets, designated bus lanes, and bicycle lanes were all neatly spun into a web of tangled confusion. Navigating her way to Gwen's office was always an ordeal. This time she was totally preoccupied with her conversation with Eric. What did he have in mind that would "make it right"? She also had no idea about how she was supposed to be "prepared to cooperate". His warning had been menacing, almost threatening, but also very vague. His behavior had become so erratic and unpredictable, it was hard to know what to expect. What she really found confusing was that she was trying to cooperate. What was it that he wanted?

The traffic gods were kind to her that afternoon and she managed to make it to Gwen's office with no mishaps. The underground parking ramp was less crowded than the last time she had been there and she found a place to park without having to follow the downward spiral more than two levels. The parking ramp reminded her of what hell might be like. It was dark, desolate, and lonely. There were always quite a few cars, but she had never actually seen other people walking to or from their vehicles. For all she knew, people had parked there, but never returned safely. Perhaps they had all been to divorce meetings as well and had just shriveled up and disappeared, the way she hoped she could after an hour or two of sitting across a conference table from Eric. The previous meetings had each left her depleted, drained. It was a miracle that she could walk out of the room under her own power. She might have appeared healthy and unscathed, but inside she was shell-shocked and shaken. Each time Eric would lob an unexpected grenade of hurt at her and every time she was taken by surprise. This time, she told herself as she boarded the elevator, it will be different. *This time I'll be ready for him.*

The elevator doors opened and Annie stepped into the lobby of Gwen's office. It was beautiful -- compared to the parking ramp, it seemed like heaven. Annie always felt out of place here, not only because of the opulent decor, but because she never thought she'd be the client of a divorce attorney.

She was just about to walk over to the receptionist's desk to check in, when the next set of elevator doors slid apart to reveal none other than Eric. He appeared deep in thought as he exited the elevator, staring intently at the floor rather than where he was going. Annie felt trapped and it actually crossed her mind to sneak back onto the elevator to avoid a confrontation. She didn't want to begin the meeting this way, with him getting the upper hand, but then an amazing thing happened. Just as quickly as it occurred to her to run and hide, it occurred to her to stay and be strong. Who said he would have the upper hand anyway? She had the element of surprise going for her at the moment. He still wasn't looking where he was going. She decided to stand her ground, to completely fill the space she occupied.

"Eric." she greeted him confidently, and caught him off-guard. He stopped dead in his tracks, his head snapping up at the sound of his name.

"Annie." he said, nodding a little. He cleared his throat and stood there, half facing her and half facing the elevators.

"You're early," she observed.

No sooner had Annie spoken, when the elevator doors opened again and Bambi bubbled into the room. Her face lit up when she saw Eric and then clouded over when she saw that he was within speaking distance of Annie.

Bambi was wearing a red cashmere turtleneck that looked as though it had been painted onto her body. The young attorney's black wool pencil skirt was so tight that Annie wondered how she was able to do anything but stand in one place. Her questions were soon answered, because Bambi immediately started to make her way over to where she and Eric were standing. She took tiny little baby steps which were even more awkward due to the red stiletto heels she wore. When she walked, her knees knocked together and her hips wiggled from side to side, which caused the rest of her, the red cashmere part, to bounce and shift.

"Eric," Bambi whispered breathlessly as soon as she reached him, "what are you doing?"

Eric appeared mesmerized by the display he had just witnessed and was somewhat speechless. "Uh -- I just got here," he said, clearing his throat again.

"You haven't been talking to her have you?" she motioned toward Annie with her eyes.

Eric was about to answer, when Annie chimed in. " No, we just said "Hello", and I commented on how he's here so early." Bambi was visibly relieved. They were at the point in the divorce proceedings where they, as the parties involved, were not supposed to communicate directly with each other, but through their attorneys. Annie found some safety in that, but also found it a little ridiculous. Here she was, facing a person that she used to live with, used to sleep next to, used to make love with, and she was not allowed to speak to him. No wonder divorce was so painful and expensive.

He looked at Annie with guarded eyes. She wondered if he was worried that she'd mention his phone call from the night before as well as the rude messages he'd previously left on her answering machine. She had told Gwen about the messages, but hadn't had a chance to tell her about last night.

She knew better than to say anything. She was learning the "divorce game" quickly. It would be much more effective to wait and have Gwen bring it up in the meeting, where it would have the greatest impact.

"Oh good," Bambi sighed. "I'm glad you two are following the rules!" Then she tucked her hand under Eric's arm and smiled broadly. "Come on, mister. We have to have our meeting before the meeting!" And she led him off to a conference room down the hall, her red stilettos gleaming under the fluorescent lighting, as they went.

Annie let out a deep breath, shook her head a little, and walked over to the receptionist's desk. She was worn out already.

"Hi, Ms. Morgan," the young woman behind the desk said. " How are you doing today?"

"I'm okay, " Annie replied, smiling. "Can you let Gwen know that I'm here, please?"

"I already have," she replied. "she'll be out in a minute. Can I get you some coffee?"

"Or do you need something stronger?" Gwen's voice startled them both. She had come into the lobby from her office around the corner. "I couldn't help but overhear the excitement out here."

Annie turned and smiled, grateful for the warm, safe security blanket of her lawyer. "Oh, you heard that, did you?"

"I'm afraid so, but you handled it well. Let's go in my office and talk for a minute." She pointed at the coffee, "Do you want some?"

"Sure," Annie said. She went over and poured herself a large cup. "I probably don't need to get any more wound up, but why not?"

Annie followed her down the short hallway to her private office. Gwen's low black pumps allowed her to walk without the slightest chance of teetering or falling over. There was no chance of small animals becoming impaled on them, Annie thought. It was another meaning for "sensible shoes" that had never occurred to her until now. A unexpected grin spread across her face.

"What are you smiling about?" Gwen asked when they reached her office.

"Oh, I was just thinking about how different you and Bambi are -- and how glad I am that you're representing me." She decided to keep the stiletto thoughts to herself for now.

"Well, I'm glad I'm representing you too," she took Annie's file out of a wooden tray on her desk and held it as she spoke. "Let's go and sit over by the fireplace."

Annie walked over and sat down on one of the two overstuffed chairs that were arranged in front of the fire.

"It's so warm and cozy in here," she commented as she settled into the chair that enveloped her like a soft, puffy cloud.

"It helps me maintain my sanity," Gwen replied. "It's kind of funny. When I was choosing furniture for this room, the decorator insisted that I put a chair for me and a love seat for my clients here in front of the fireplace. I told him, 'I am a divorce attorney, Phillip. No one will be needing a love seat in my office!"

She picked up her china tea cup from the small, round marble table and took a delicate sip. Next to the cup was a square box of kleenex, because as she said, Gwen was a divorce attorney. The tears shed by her clients were measured in lost dreams and billable hours. If she thought about it too much, it could break her heart. What made Gwen special was that she made herself think about it often and when she did, she'd sit in front of the fireplace, curled up in one of the overstuffed chairs with the box of kleenex in her lap. Sometimes she shed the most tears of all.

"Anything new I should know about?" Gwen asked as she sat down.

"Well, actually, there is," Annie replied. "Eric called again last night."

"That's nothing new -- he's been doing that for a while now, hasn't he?" She had her pen poised over a blank yellow legal pad, ready to write.

"But last night I picked up during the message." Annie cringed, waiting for Gwen's reaction.

"Annie." Gwen peered at her over her reading glasses disapprovingly.

"I'm sorry, Gwen. I couldn't stand it -- I couldn't help it." She watched the flames dance in the fireplace, afraid to look at this woman who was doing so much to help her. Gwen had advised her against speaking to Eric when he called. It was obvious that Annie was under a great deal of stress. She had lost weight and and the circles under her eyes were getting more pronounced every day.

"It's okay, Annie -- you don't have to apologize. What did he say?"

"He said that he wanted me to be prepared to cooperate at the meeting today -- that he wants me to be ready. I asked him what he meant by that and he wouldn't say. He just said he wants me to 'make it right'. He also ranted on and on about how everything that's happened is all my fault." Annie looked down at her hands for a moment and then back at Gwen. "He sounded so angry, Gwen. It was scary."

"That's exactly what he's trying to do, kiddo. He's trying to intimidate you." She wrote a few words on her notepad.

"But what if he's finally starting to grieve? What if he's realizing ---"

Gwen straightened up, took her glasses off and leaned toward Annie. "What if he's realizing what? Annie -- listen to yourself. He is having exactly the effect on you that he's hoping for. Of course you can do as you like, but as your attorney, I have to advise you against this plan of yours to give Eric everything he wants. You don't even know what that is, and you're willing to give in." Gwen tapped her pen against her notepad.

"I just want it to be over. I can't stand all of this game-playing." Annie glanced at her watch and saw that it was almost time to go to the conference room.

"I know you do, sweetie. This whole ordeal is taking its toll on you." Gwen slid the cap firmly on her pen. "If you don't mind my saying so, you look like hell."

"Thanks -- good to hear before the big meeting."

"Sorry, but it's true. How much weight have you lost now? And those circles under your eyes are getting bigger each time I see you."

"I've lost a little," Annie acknowledged. "No appetite lately."

Annie didn't want to admit that she'd lost close to thirty-five pounds. Some of it was baby weight, but most of it had been lost since the divorce proceedings began. When she'd get a voice message or phone call from Eric, she could virtually feel the calories burning. Sleep was also fleeting, a collage of dreams about Diilon and the divorce. There was little, if any, refuge.

Gwen gave her a small hug. "Well, ok. We'll talk about that later. Now, let's go knock their socks off." She patted Annie on the back.

The meeting should have started on time since Eric and Bambi were in the building, but Annie and Gwen still had to wait fifteen minutes before they sauntered into the conference room. Gwen glared at her watch, one eyebrow raised in a disapproving slash.

"Glad you two could make it." Sarcasm dripped from her words. "There's a lot to cover today, so let's get started, shall we?"

"Sorry we're late." Bambi set her briefcase on the long, freshly polished table. She glanced at Eric and gave him a crooked smile.

"As I understand it, your client has been making some rather threatening phone calls to my client." Gwen barreled ahead with no hesitation. Eric and Bambi looked at her in shock, as did Annie. She had no idea Gwen was going to proceed like this. There was an extended moment of very uncomfortable silence. After everyone was squirming sufficiently in their seats, she added, "I expect it to stop immediately. Is that understood?" She folded hands on her legal pad, sat back and waited calmly.

Bambi cleared her throat with a nervous squeak. "Excuse me, please. I need to have a word with my client."

Gwen merely nodded, allowing the request. The two latecomers stepped outside the glass-walled room to confer. Gwen got up from her chair and reached behind the floor-length drapes. Once she found the cord, she pulled it, slowly closing the sheer cream colored curtains. With each tug of the cord, the fabric jerked, covering more and more of Eric and Bambi until they were no longer visible. She turned to Annie who was still trying to process what had just happened as she watched the frantic gesticulations of her husband and his lawyer, shadow puppets behind the fabric.

"Sorry to surprise you like that, but it had to be done." She returned to her seat. "There's no sense in beating around the bush. I want to get this show on the road."

Annie couldn't think of another bad cliche for a comeback, so she just shrugged and said, "Well, I think you've made that clear. So, now what?"

"That's up to them. Let's see what they have to say." She drew a solid black line across the middle of the yellow notepad. "This, my dear, is our new line in the sand. This is our new beginning." Annie looked at her quizzically but remained silent. Gwen continued. "Little do they know that whatever they come up with, the game-playing is over."

At that moment the door opened and Eric and Bambi returned to the room. Their cheeks were flushed from what appeared to have been a heated discussion, but their expressions were confident and assured. They settled back into their chairs and Bambi cleared her throat and straightened her posture, which made the red cashmere sweater swell out even more over the edge of the table.

"Okay," the young attorney started, "first of all, my client has not made any threatening calls. He doesn't deny that he's made phone calls, but they have not been threatening in any way. That is your client's perception." She looked smugly across the table at Annie and Gwen. Her fingers were laced together in front of her, the deep red manicured fingernails glistened under the lights.

Gwen didn't reply. She waited for Bambi to continue.

"And secondly, the only reason these calls had to be made at all, is because your client is refusing to cooperate with my client's requests."

The only clue to Gwen's rage was one tiny vein in her left temple that throbbed gently as her eyes narrowed ever so slightly. The corners of her lips curved up just a bit, not in a real smile, but more of an amused grimace.

"Really."

"Yes," insisted Bambi with an emphatic nod. " And his requests are very reasonable."

"Oh, I'm sure they are," Gwen sat up a little straighter. "But there will be no more phone calls. Period. These meetings are held to discuss all "requests", reasonable or otherwise. There is no need for your client to call mine. Now, what are these very reasonable requests?"

Bambi's eyes glittered as though she had just won the battle. She could hardly conceal her delight. "Well, he wants the house and everything in it, his car and his boat. He also wants his 401K in its entirety." She sat back with a triumphant flourish.

Annie's mind started racing and her heart started sprinting to keep up with it.

Eric had mentioned some of this on the phone, but she didn't think he was serious. How could he be so self-centered? Where would she go? What would she do without any money? Gwen's strong, assured voice interrupted the tornado of questions that were violently whirling around in her head.

"I need to consult with my client privately for a moment. Are there any additional requests we need to consider?"

Annie couldn't believe it! Why was Gwen behaving so calmly? Why wasn't she reading them the riot act? Had she decided to give up and let the game playing continue after all? She had to consciously take several long, deep breaths to slow down her heart rate and to keep her body from trembling. She had to appear calm and in control. She had to.

"No problem." Bambi and Eric prepared to stand. "We'll be in the lounge."

"No, we'll go to my office," Gwen insisted. She gently gripped Annie's forearm. "We'll be back shortly."

Annie wondered if she'd be able to even stand let alone walk, but she surprised herself with newfound strength from some hidden corner of her soul. She and Gwen walked down the hall and around the corner to her private office. Thankfully it was a short walk, so Annie didn't have to keep up the pretense very long. Once inside the warm, cozy confines of Gwen's office, she let down her guard and melted into one of the chairs.

"Oh my God," Annie exclaimed. "I don't believe it. He sounds serious. Can he do that?!"

"He can request anything he wants to, Annie. There are no laws against that."

"And you're ok with that?"

"The laws or his requests?" Gwen was seated behind her desk, pulling the rest of Annie's file out from a shelf on the credenza behind her. She spun her chair around to face her incredulous young client.

"His requests, of course! How can he just demand all of that?! What's going to happen to me? He sounds like he wants to throw me out on the street!"

"Annie. Pull yourself together," demanded Gwen. "We can't play hardball if you're acting like a sniveling lunatic." Annie was stunned by her harsh words and even harsher tone. Gwen had never spoken to her like this before. When had it become Gang Up on Annie Day? Afraid to utter another word, she waited for Gwen to keep talking.

"I'm sorry, Annie, but you've got to calm down and start thinking clearly. Eric thinks he "wins" if he gets everything he's asking for -- and at first glance it seems that way to you, doesn't it?"

Annie nodded. She was trying her best to focus on listening to Gwen as she brushed a pile of peeled clear nail polish from her lap absentmindedly. She sat on her hands in order to leave them alone.

"Well, I say, let him have it. He can have the house, the furniture, the car, the boat," she paused slightly. "And all of the debt that goes along with it. It's not all paid for, is it?"

"No, but I don't think that's what he's talking about," Annie offered quietly. "When he called the other day, he sounded as though he wants it all, free and clear."

"Well, honey, that *is* against the law -- unless you lose your mind and agree to it. You haven't been married long enough in this state to be entitled to alimony, but you are entitled to half of everything -- which means if he wants all of those things, he has to pay you for them." Now it was Gwen's turn to flash a smug grin.

"He'll never agree to that."

"Don't be so negative," shot Gwen. "You have to think positive. You're young and soon to be single. Do you really want that house and all of the responsibilities that come with it? Do you care about the boat or his car? Do you really want the bed you shared with him or any of the things you bought as you built your life together? Do you?"

The afternoon they'd discovered the house resurfaced in Annie's mind. They'd been looking for months, but had found nothing. The minute she saw it, Annie knew it was perfect. She could immediately picture children playing in the yard and imagined how sweet their childlike giggles would sound. Now she wondered if Eric had ever felt the same way that day. They had never really talked about it. He had been excited about the garage and how he'd finally have room for the speed boat that he'd always wanted, but had never mentioned children. It had been a happy day for them, each in their own way. Now, facing this crossroad in their lives, Annie was struck by how sad it was that they had possibly never shared the same vision and how it was all beginning to make perfect sense. Could there have been any other ending?"

"Annie -- earth to Annie," Gwen was waving her hand in front of Annie's face. "Are you still with me?"

"Yes, sorry. I was just thinking about the day we decided to buy the house --" her voice trailed off.

"I know you have lots of memories and emotions about this, sweetie, and I know it's not easy to let go of those things."

"Thanks for being so understanding, Gwen," Annie wiped away a runaway tear. "But it's ok. I did love that house and it was part of my dream. But it was *my* dream. And that's over now -- so, to answer your question, no, I don't want it. I don't want any of it."

Gwen got up from her chair behind the desk, walked over to Annie and gave her a big hug. "You, my dear, never cease to amaze me!"

"Now stop it or I won't be able to stop crying." Annie gave Gwen a shaky smile as she wiped away another tear.

"You're right." Gwen pressed on her eyes with her index fingers as if to hold her own tears in. "We don't have time for this now. We can cry later if we still want to." She gave Annie another squeeze. "Let's go get 'em. Poor Eric won't know what hit him!"

When Gwen and Annie strode back into the room to resume the meeting, they found Bambi sitting so close to Eric, it was almost impossible to tell where he left off and she began. Annie's stomach did a quick summersault, but she didn't skip a beat. She was ready to get this over with and nothing could steer her off course now.

"Sorry to keep you waiting," Gwen bellowed as she and Annie walked around the table to their seats. " I hope you were able to find something to do." Eric's face remained void of expression as she spoke, although Bambi's face turned as red as her cashmere.

The young attorney awkwardly attempted to regain her composure and professionalism, scooting her chair away from her client. Straightening her legal pad and pen, she ran a nervous hand over her long auburn curls as she prepared to speak.

"We're ready to present an offer," started Gwen. "It's good to know that you're well prepared, so you won't waste any more of *anyone's* time." She looked over the tops of her reading glasses. "You *are* ready, yes?"

During their walk down the hall, Gwen and Annie had briefly discussed their plan. Annie trusted Gwen with the details, all of which could be resolved later. The first hurdle would be to get Eric to agree to the general idea. Neither of them thought this would be a problem, however, since they were simply presenting his offer back to him, with a few twists.

The air in the conference room was thick with lust and tension, an odd combination for a divorce settlement meeting. As humiliating as it was for Annie to see her husband so enamoured with another woman, she also knew that this situation could work to her advantage. It was fairly evident that as long as Eric was in the vicinity of red cashmere, he wouldn't be thinking clearly. She did her best to maintain a somber, defeated expression, which wasn't hard to do if she reflected on the past year of her life for even a breath of a moment. Under the table, she nudged Gwen's foot, urging her to continue.

"Your client has requested ownership of the house and its furnishings as well as the speed boat and the 1986 Cadillac. He also wants to keep the entirety of his 401K. Am I right on that?"

Bambi and Eric nodded in unison, eyes bright and hopeful. It amazed Annie that neither of them seemed to comprehend how greedy and self-serving his demands sounded. In her wildest dreams it never would have occurred to her to ask for so much -- it just seemed wrong. When did he start hating her so much?

"My client agrees to these requests," Gwen went on, "with the understanding that Mr. Morgan gives her half the value of the house --"

"You've got to be kidding!" Eric shot up out of his chair, knocking his can of Coke over in the process. The fizzy brown liquid spread slowly across the table uninterrupted until Annie grabbed several paper napkins lying near her and tossed them on the spill before it reached her side of the table. He ignored this as he paced back and forth, shaking his head and running his hands through his hair, oblivious to the damage he had caused.

"No, I'm *not* kidding," Gwen replied sternly. " Mr. Morgan -- your wife is being extremely generous. Half the value of the home is all she wants. Legally she is entitled to and deserves half of *everything* but is willing to relinquish that right in order to make this easier on everyone. You are a lucky man, Mr. Morgan. You should be counting your blessings instead of your pennies." She leaned back in her chair and folded her arms solidly across her chest, waiting for his response.

He stopped in his tracks and glared at Gwen and Annie. Bambi turned her head toward him and waited too. His expression was frozen into a scowl, his eyebrows fused in an angry wedge in the middle of his forehead. The corners of his mouth which only moments ago had been tweaked up in a surly smirk, were now turned downward, dragging the lower half of his face toward the floor.

"Eric," Bambi's whisper was urgent. "Sit down." She flashed a tentative smile toward the opposite side of the table. Losing control of one's client was not a good thing.

"Do you need some time to confer?" Gwen asked, smiling back.

Bambi turned again and looked up at her client, who had resumed pacing, and then back at Gwen. She shrugged her shoulders and shook her head, her curls bouncing like springs on her shoulders. "Eric -- do you want to discuss this privately?"

He stopped pacing once more and looked at her angrily. "What is there to discuss? She wants to crucify me! And apparently it's even *legal.*" His eyes seethed with contempt. He turned his back on them and peered through the sheer drapes.

"Mr. Morgan." Gwen was losing her patience. " You are *far* from being crucified."

Eric swung around. "Oh really? Where am I supposed to come up with money like that?"

"Not our problem, darling," Gwen replied as she stood with a flourish. "Annie, let's go for a walk. I think these two need some time."

Annie was grateful for the opportunity to escape the intensity and frustration and quickly followed Gwen out into the hall. She had to nearly run to keep up with Gwen, whose stride seemed to get longer with every step she took. Before she knew it, they had taken the stairs up to the roof. Gwen led her out onto a small patio that held several wrought iron tables with matching chairs. The last, dried vestiges of an old petunia plant were draped over the sides of a forgotten bamboo planter. She walked over to the wrought iron railing that surrounded its perimeter and gazed down thirty-two stories to the city below. It was a long way down and she was thankful for the safety the railing provided. She hated heights.

"It's a good thing this railing is here," she said to Gwen. " It probably keeps a lot of clients from jumping, huh?" She followed the morose statement with a little laugh, so that Gwen would know it was meant to be funny.

"Or their lawyers," Gwen added with a scowl. She fished a cigarette and lighter out of her jacket pocket and turned out of the wind as she lit it.

"I didn't know you smoked."

"Normally I don't." She inhaled the cigarette smoke deeply. "I quit a long time ago, but sometimes, when I get really frustrated, I light one up. It calms me down." She slowly let the smoke escape from between her lips, taking care to direct it away from Annie. "Dumb, huh?"

"No, not at all." Annie rested her hands on the top of the railing. "I used to do that occasionally when I was in college while I was studying for finals. It never really worked, though, because I had never been a smoker. I had so much trouble coordinating the cigarette, the notebook and the textbook -- it stressed me out even more. Not to mention that I coughed my lungs out."

Gwen smiled and walked over to a sand-filled planter to extinguish her cigarette. She walked back to where Annie stood near the railing. "I've got to tell you, Annie, your soon-to-be-ex-husband is really something. I have never run across anyone like him -- and I've been doing this a long time. I'm actually starting to feel sorry for Bambi, as inappropriate and unprofessional as she is. She's got her hands full with him." She shook her head in disbelief. "I know this has all been hard on you, but your life is going to be *so* much better without him in it."

"I just want it to be over," Annie said wearily.

"I know you do, but you have to stand your ground. It will be worth it -- you have to believe me. You're not asking for the moon here -- you're giving up a lot of what you could have. You need something to start over with -- you deserve that, Annie."

"I know you're right, Gwen. He just wears me down so. That's his tactic; it always has been." She turned and leaned her back against the railing. The gentle afternoon breeze felt good as it softly blew her bangs back from her forehead.

"And he's good at it," agreed Gwen. "But his little guilt trips and games aren't going to work this time. If he insists on being so impossible, I'll threaten him with court. If we bring this case in front of a judge, there's a good chance they'll make him give you half of everything whether you want it or not." She put her hand up to stop Annie from interrupting. "I know you don't want it, but he knows that, Annie. He thinks he can run roughshod over you because you don't want to cause problems. But he's wrong -- and I'll be more than happy to point that out to anybody who wants to listen."

Just then Gwen's paralegal poked her head out of the door that lead back into the building. "I thought I'd find you out here. They're ready."

"Thanks Ellie. We'll be right there." Gwen turned and put her hands on Annie's shoulders. "Just trust me, okay? I know what I'm doing."

"I *do* trust you."

"Alright then -- let's go back and finish this, shall we?"

This time when they came back to the conference room, Eric and Bambi were nowhere near each other. In fact, they were on opposite sides of the room. Both of their faces were flushed, but their expressions were tense and angry, not the mischievous ones from earlier in the day.

"I hear you're ready to continue," Gwen stated as she and Annie entered the room.

Eric and Bambi seemed to be having a stare-down. Neither of them responded to Gwen's remark, but stood there, glaring at each other. Gwen cleared her throat abruptly, not once, not twice, but three times. Finally, Eric spoke.

"Yes, *I* am," he said firmly.

"Well, good. Glad to hear it," Gwen plopped down in her chair and motioned for Annie to do the same. Annie couldn't stop looking back and forth between Eric and Bambi. Something had happened here -- something major. The electric current that had charged the air between Eric and the young attorney had changed. Before it had been flirtatious and playful. Now the playfulness was gone and a more serious mood had settled over them.

"Alright then," Gwen said, "let's continue, shall we?" She looked from one to the other and back again. "Are you two going to join us at the table or should we all stand up?"

No response.

"Hellooo --" Gwen rose her voice and octave higher and twenty decibels louder. "Are you two going to join us or not?"

It was Bambi who finally broke the stare-down and spoke. "I'm sorry, Ms. Jones. Yes, my client is ready to continue -- but I'm not. I've just been fired." She turned her angry eyes back at Eric. "He thinks he can do a better job of representing himself than *I* have been doing -- so, I guess I'll be leaving." She strode over to the table and began stuffing papers and files back into her briefcase.

Annie and Gwen turned and stared at each other, mouths ajar, utterly speechless.

"You can't be serious!" Gwen sputtered after she was able to express a coherent thought.

Bambi continued to shove papers into her briefcase with all the vengeance of a woman scorned. It looked as though she was using every ounce of determination she possessed not to lose control. In spite of everything, Annie felt her heart going out to the young woman. She knew first-hand how infuriating Eric could be. Although, given the circumstances, on a certain level, she enjoyed the way things were playing out. The old saying, "What goes around, comes around" was finally proving to be true.

"Hey, wait a minute," Eric interjected suddenly. " You can't take those files. Those are mine."

The head of lustrous curls snapped up and glared at him with angry eyes. Her hands were shaking every so slightly and her chest was heaving with every breath. It was obvious by the rhythmic motion of the red cashmere, that Eric's now ex-lawyer was counting to ten. Annie and Gwen stood mesmerized, hanging on every breath, ...7, 8, 9..... 10...Wham!!!

The briefcase and the papers she was holding tipped over onto the table in a jumbled mess. The thud made by the black calfskin leather case was muffled by the sound of red stilettos marching over to where Eric stood by the window. Each step unleashed a burst of energy so volatile, even the potted plant in the corner seemed to curl up and cower as she passed by. Eric stood there, chest puffed out, ready for battle.

She marched up to him, her cashmere tantalizingly close to his torso. She put her hands on her hips, using every inch of her anatomy, God-given and otherwise, to make her presence, as well as her wrath, known. She thrust her chest toward him as she jutted out her chin and did a little swivel with her hips as she planted her heels on the terrazzo floor. They stood almost nose to nose. Bambi was a tall woman to begin with, and her high heels brought her close to Eric's height.

"There is no way I'll *ever* give you those files," she spat, her chest still heaving.

"But you have to. They're mine. I've paid for those!" Eric's face turned a deeper shade of red; he appeared not to be breathing at all.

"Really."

"Yes, *really,*" he sneered as he exhaled deeply into her face.

She blinked hard a couple of times as she struggled to maintain her composure as well as her stance. "That is where you are wrong. You haven't paid me a penny of my retainer yet and gosh -- I no longer represent you, do I? So no, Mr. Morgan, I don't have to give you anything." She held his furious gaze for a couple of seconds before she drew her shoulders back even more and turned her back on him to leave. She strutted over to where her briefcase was propped on the table, stopping once to adjust her skirt. Her hands ran up and down her hips, smoothing the black fabric, giving special attention to her curves. She shot a withering glance back at Eric and then licked her pouty lips slowly before they curved into a satisfied simper. Then she turned her attention to packing the coveted documents into her leather satchel.

Eric stood there, seething. Annie could tell by the look on his face that he was balancing precariously on a tightrope between embarrassment and anger. She knew that anger would win out. He had a surplus of pride and did not take well to anything less than being right and what he considered respected. She waited for the fireworks.

"Where do you think you're going?" he demanded. His breathing was still heavy and his face was still red.

Bambi ignored him and continued to gather her belongings. A cascade of hair worthy of a L'Oreal commercial hid her face, the rise and fall of her shoulders revealing her irritation.

Eric stood with his hands on his hips, waiting for an answer. When she continued to disregard him, he walked over and stood behind her. "Don't ignore me."

Bambi turned around and looked at him with wide-eyed innocence. " Oh -- were you talking to *me*?"

He just stood there, glaring at her. His nostrils flared in and out and his foot tapped with each breath, waiting.

Annie grimaced inwardly at the imminent train wreck. When he got to this point there was never an elegant, dignified finish. She began to simmer herself, at the spectacle he was making of himself, and their divorce. After all, she did have *some* pride of her own.

"You know I was," he sneered.

At first Bambi leaned away from him, appalled, but then she ricocheted in his face. "No one talks to me that way. No one."

"Oh yeah? You think I'm afraid of you?" He grabbed her wrist when she started to turn away.

Before she had a chance to struggle or even react, there was a loud crash, startling everyone in the room.

"Eric!" Annie was on her feet, her chair tipping over in the process. "That's enough. Let go of her."

Eric stood there motionless, a tight hold still on Bambi's wrist.

"Now!" Annie said and then calmly sidestepped the upturned legs of her fallen chair and made her way over to where he stood. He let Bambi's wrist drop from his grasp, his hand frozen in midair. His irate eyes were fixed on his wife.

"I just-- "

"You *just.*" She cut him off, as he had done to her so many times in the past.

He looked at her, thoroughly befuddled, and slowly returned his hand to his side.

"I've had it, Eric." Annie faced him squarely. "Look at yourself. You're out of control. Do you think this is all a joke or do you just think that it's all about *you*?" She didn't wait for an answer. "Well, guess what? It's not."

"That's right. It's all about *you!*" He shot back at her. "If anything had *ever* been about me, we wouldn't be here. None of this would be happening!"

Annie reeled at the statement. "What?"

"You heard me." He took a few steps back from her and turned to face the windows.

Gwen looked as though she was going to intervene, when Bambi discreetly stopped her by putting her forefinger up to her lips. Gwen caught the hint and unassumingly took a seat at the table. They exchanged intentional glances and then turned their attention back to their clients.

"So, as you said on the phone that day, this is all *my* fault."

Eric turned back toward her and shrugged, raising his hands in the air, as if to say, *'I told you.'*

It was a gesture full of bitterness and contempt and it grabbed Annie and shook her to her core. She had tried to take the high road, but now the road was too steep. Its terrain was littered with jagged pieces of her heart and mangled bits of hopes and dreams that had once held so many expectations. There was no longer a decent place for her to get her footing. Each time she tried to find a higher niche to climb to, Eric figured out a way to pull it out from under her. The cruel irony was that traveling the high road hadn't helped at all. Why had she even bothered?

"Okay," she conceded. "Blame me. Will that make you happy? Just please stop playing these games. Please."

He looked at her warily, peering out from a worried brow. He paced back toward the window and paused to look out at the city below.

"Why should I believe that?" he asked, his voice drenched in defiance.

"What do you mean?"

"Well, sure -- you *say* you'll take the blame, but then you'll turn around and blast me later," he grumbled over his shoulder.

Now it was Annie's turn to raise her hands in disbelief. *Would nothing please this man?* She folded her arms across her chest and looked at the floor, breathing slowly and deeply as she searched her soul for a response. Her stomach was trying to tie itself into a knot, as it so often had a tendency to do where Eric was concerned. She made a deliberate effort to take in oxygen, hoping to relax and regain her foothold. Nothing would get accomplished if she faltered now. She had to be strong.

"No, Eric -- I'm going to do that *now.*"

His head snapped around, bringing the rest of his body with it in a whirl. Before he could speak, she continued.

"And you know why? Because I hope that once this divorce is over, I'll be able to move on. I don't want to spend the rest of my life or even one small part of it being angry or vindictive."

"That's --"

"Stop," she cut him off. "It's my turn. You have made a mockery of our marriage, of me and of yourself, Eric. How can you have the nerve to behave the way you have with *Bambi* here, and still expect to get everything you want besides?" She shot a glance over at Gwen, suddenly horrified at having said their secret nickname out loud. To her surprise, Bambi was trying to conceal a smile and Gwen gave her a sly wink. She let out a sigh of relief and forged ahead. Everything she had been holding inside for months was spilling out of her and she couldn't stop it.

"You can blame me for Dillon if you need to, but he was not an accident, Eric. I thought he was conceived intentionally and in love. Why didn't you tell me how you felt, if you didn't want to have a baby?"

"You would've freaked out if I'd told you that and you know it," he said in a tired voice.

" And this is better *how*?"

He was silent, at a loss for words. He turned away from her and looked out the window once again.

"I'll tell you how," she continued solemnly. "We found out that we don't belong together before we brought another child into the world."

It was so quiet in the room that they could hear the chain from the drapes jingling against the wall as the breeze from the heat vent blew past it. Eric pivoted toward her, the floor length window behind him.

"Annie, don't say that." His voice was gentler now, the hostility ebbing.

"Well, it's true, isn't it? I have to believe that Dillon died for a reason -- "

"The reason isn't that we didn't love each other." He interrupted, his voice ragged with fatigue and frustration.

"Then what was it?"

They stood transfixed, quietly facing one another, each waiting for the other to speak. A cumbersome silence hovered over them like a storm cloud, threatening to burst forth with thunder and lightening at any moment. Gwen and Bambi began to fidget uncomfortably in their chairs. As with any storm, sometimes the watching and waiting was the most difficult part.

"It doesn't really matter what it was," Gwen interjected carefully. They simultaneously turned their heads in the direction of her voice, as though it was the beacon from a lighthouse.

"What matters," she continued, "is that you two don't destroy all the good things that you might have had and destroy each other in the process." She got up from the table and slowly walked toward them. "You have experienced a horrible tragedy in the loss of your son. No one can argue that. I don't know how either of you is getting through it and I'll never pretend that I know how you feel. But I do know this -- marriages fail for many, many reasons -- and often for something much less than what you're dealing with. The only reason it's good to understand why, is so it doesn't happen again. If you continue down this path of blame and destruction, you'll do more damage than is necessary." She looked at Eric as she said the final sentence.

"That's right," added Bambi cautiously from her place at the table. "Enough damage has been done. And Eric, whether you represent yourself or not, keep in mind that dragging this out longer than you need to, isn't healthy and its definitely not worth it. You are both young enough to start over --"

"How am I going to be able to start over if I have to give her half the house?" blurted Eric, the vein in his forehead throbbing. Annie turned and stared at him, incredulous. She couldn't believe what she was hearing. Before she was able to say a word, Bambi catapulted from her seat.

"Oh my God! You are incredible! Have you not heard a single word? Have you no sense of decency? Oh, but wait -- I should know the answer to that, shouldn't I? No, you don't, and shame on me for ever taking your case!" She stood there, fuming, her hands gripping the edge of the table. She took several deep breaths and then turned to Annie. "Annie, I want to apologize. I have behaved like an idiot and I am so sorry if I've contributed to your pain in any way. I don't know what I was thinking."

It took a moment for Annie to catch her breath. She was caught completely off-guard by everything that was happening, especially Bambi's apology.

"Thank you," she said, her voice shaking, her throat dry. "I'm sorry I called you Bambi --"

The young attorney waved her hand nonchalantly in the air and laughed. "Oh, don't worry about that. It was actually pretty funny." She was relaxing a bit now, her blood no longer boiling. "But just so you know, my name is Beth."

Annie smiled, happy not to have caused more problems by her earlier slip of the tongue. As both lawyers had pointed out, enough damage had already been done.

Beth reached for her briefcase and pushed her chair further from the table with the backs of her shapely legs. She strutted around the end of the table as daintily as she could in her red stilettos and paused in front of Eric, Annie and Gwen.

"It's been a pleasure working with you," she said, extending her hand toward Gwen.

Gwen took the perfectly manicured hand into both of her own and shook it firmly. "It's been an experience, I must say. I will miss seeing you in court, though."

"Oh," snickered Beth looking in Eric's direction. "You'll still see me in court. I wouldn't miss seeing *Mr.* Morgan represent himself." She readjusted the shoulder strap of her purse with a little wiggle.

And with that, she sashayed her way out of the room.

Annie, Gwen and Eric stood frozen like statues, staring at the flurry of bouncing curls and cashmere whirling away from them. She seemed to have taken a large amount of the energy that had been unleashed with her in her dramatic exit, and for that Annie was grateful. Afraid to move, she shifted her eyes in Eric's direction. Even though she didn't want to bestow any power on him, his reaction to this series of events was monumental. It could mean the difference between moving forward or stagnating in the squalor of insinuation and blame that surrounded them. If she had been holding a feather, she probably could have knocked him over with it at that moment. She always knew that he could be bullheaded and unreasonable and she said a little prayer that he'd rise to the occasion and be sensible. That, more than anything, is what they needed right now.

Gwen was the first to thaw. "Eric," she started slowly, "it's not that I don't have every confidence that you can represent yourself in court, because I certainly do." She ambled over to him from her place next to Annie. "But for the sake of time and of course, money, I urge you to reconsider."

"And find a new lawyer? You've gotta be kidding. How would that save time or money?" He jammed his hands into his pockets, his lower lip folded over in a sullen pout and peered out the window.

"I'm not suggesting you start over. I'm suggesting you work with Annie and I to settle this. There's no need to hire another lawyer *or* go to court. That's what you wanted in the first place, isn't it? One attorney?" Gwen returned to her place near the table, giving him an abundance of space.

Annie found herself holding her breath, her stomach churning. Gwen was being very logical. There was no way that Eric would ever agree to that -- especially now that he had been abandoned and humiliated in front of them. She could see what Gwen was trying to do, but was afraid that he would see it too and dig in his heels even further.

"Oh -- and have *you* handle it? Yeah -- I'd come out great in *that* deal." He spewed belligerent sarcasm as he defiantly planted his hands on his hips.

"Actually you would, Eric." Annie finally spoke. "If you hire a new attorney, that means another retainer. Then we really would be starting over."

"So?"

"So, don't you want this to be *over?* So you can have your life back again? The way it was before?"

"Yeah, well, you still have *your* lawyer. Who will look out for *my* interests? I'm going to get destroyed in this deal for sure if I agree to that." He started pacing back and forth in front of the window.

Annie's patience was as worn and frazzled as a taut, fraying rope, ready to snap at any moment. "You should have thought of that before you fired Beth." She folded her arms across her chest, each hand grasping the flesh of her upper arms to keep from putting him in a choke hold. "This is *not* going to become my problem."

The room was quiet, except for the occasional voices of people in the hall as they passed the closed door of the conference room. Annie wished that she could be out there with them, going to get coffee or checking the fax machine. She wanted to be anywhere but here, doing normal everyday things, living her life instead of watching it hang in the balance. It occurred to her that she was wishing a lot of time away, wanting the divorce to be final. Life could be short, shorter than one would ever imagine. She'd witnessed that first hand when she buried Dillon. Rage began to stir deep inside of her at the thought of wasting any more life, especially due to Eric's stubborn attitude. He could do whatever he wanted with *his* life, but she'd be damned if he was going to bring her down with him.

Gwen leaned against the mahogany conference table, and observed the stalemate before her. The blasé expression on her face camouflaged any emotions she might have been experiencing. She looked from Eric to Annie and then back at Eric again. It seemed to be his turn, but he remained silent, as he stood quietly seething.

"Eric? Do you have anything to say to that?" She asked, her voice an oasis of serenity and strength.

He stopped his pacing and faced her, his face burned with anger and frustration.

"Does it even matter what I think? You two are going to do whatever the hell you want to anyway." He turned his back to them once more, his shoulders heaving up and down with each labored breath.

Annie sharply took in a breath to speak when Gwen put up her hand in the air to stop her.

"All right, Mr. Morgan, have it your way. We certainly don't want you to feel as though you haven't had a fair chance to represent your case. I will file a petition to appear before a judge as soon as possible -- so I suggest you start working on putting your case together -- however you choose to proceed." She reached for her leather portfolio that was lying on the table. "Annie? Shall we be going?"

Annie looked over at Eric, waiting for a response. Time was standing still as she stood there watching him.

Gwen cleared her throat as she paused near the door. The sound quickly jarred Annie to her senses and she jumped a little as she reentered the moment. She knew he was suffering and part of her wanted to reach out to him and make it all better. Her heart tap-danced in her chest, skipping several beats as it returned to its normal rhythm. She smiled wanly at Gwen and walked over to her and then glanced back at Eric as she stepped out of the room. He turned his head to look at them, silent and unmoved, his face a mosaic of arrogance, pain, and disbelief.

# The Cardboard Box

Boxes of various sizes lined the perimeter of Annie's living room, their flaps standing open, waiting to be useful. A large, black magic marker laid on the end table, along with a roll of clear packing tape in a bright orange plastic dispenser.

Some of the boxes were partially full, others were completely empty. Only two of them had been filled and taped shut. These were labeled: ***Eric.*** It had taken Annie the entire morning to pack them, agonizing over every item as she went. When Eric had so abruptly moved out, he'd returned to get some essentials, but had left behind the less important things, such as gifts Annie had given to him over the years.

She picked up a picture frame in which she'd placed a picture of the two of them, and smiled. She'd searched high and low for just the right frame and just the right picture for it, so afraid to send the wrong message. They'd been dating only a few months at the time, and while she was helplessly in love, his feelings were less clear. She hadn't known if it would be too personal a gift, too presumptuous of her to assume that he'd even want a picture of her, let alone the two of them. She'd given it to him in spite of her fears, and while he'd acted pleased, she'd never seen it displayed. Now she found it in the bottom drawer of his dresser, some old sweatshirts piled on top of it. She smirked as she thought of the irony -- she'd put so much thought into it and it had never even mattered. It was a metaphor for their relationship -- she putting in the effort, while he did his best to ignore it. Sighing, Annie placed the picture in the box labeled: ***Misc.*** She wasn't sure who should get it. If Eric hadn't really wanted it then, what made her think he'd want it now? Especially now? She reached into the box to retrieve it when the telephone rang, a welcome diversion from an unpleasant task.

"Hello?"

"Annie? It's Gwen. What are you up to this afternoon?"

"Nothing too exciting, I'm afraid. Packing."

"Packing? Going somewhere?"

"Well, yes, eventually," Annie explained, laughing a little. "Why wait until the last minute?"

"You are something else, my dear," remarked Gwen. "Always on top of things, even though it's probably the last thing you feel like doing."

"Actually it's kind of therapeutic -- you know, thinking about getting out of here...." She surveyed the walls around her, and wondered if Gwen could tell that she was lying through her teeth. While she had said she wanted to move on, that the house held too many painful memories, she really did love it. Leaving it was going to be another one of the most difficult things she'd ever have to do. A frown settled on her face as she realized that the list of those things was getting longer and longer -- much longer than it should be.

"Well, hang in there. It will all be over soon," Gwen encouraged and then added, "I just got off the phone with Eric."

There was a pregnant pause worthy of a set of quintuplets. Annie heard something in Gwen's voice but couldn't determine what it meant.

"And?" she prompted.

"Well, let's just say that I think Mr. Morgan has finally figured out that he's bitten off a tiny bit more than he can chew..."

"Meaning?" she probed further.

"Meaning that I think he's going to settle soon, my dear. He was in such a snit when he called -- saying he wasn't going to be ready to appear in court and all that. It was a joy to behold! I was just sorry that you weren't in my office, listening to it on speakerphone. It was quite a moment."

"Are you sure? What exactly did he say? How do you know we can believe him?" Annie fired the questions at her, one right after the other. It would be just like him to act as though he was going to settle, to lure her into a false sense of security, and then pull the rug out from under her when she least expected it.

"Calm down, calm down. Of course I'm not 100% sure, but everything indicates that he's ready to be reasonable. Once I talked some sense into him, that is."

"What do you mean?"

"He told me that he was going to call Beth and rehire her!"

"What?"

"Yes! Well, once I stopped laughing, I told him that I didn't think that was such a good idea. That was when he came to his senses and he decided to talk turkey."

"Wait a minute, Gwen," Annie interjected. "This doesn't make sense. Eric is more stubborn than that. There's something you're not telling me. What else did you say to him?" She stretched the phone cord over to the dining room and sat down at the table.

Gwen sighed audibly into the phone. "I'm afraid I played some dirty pool, Annie. I told him that if he approached Beth, it was very likely that she'd slap him with a sexual harassment suit. I reminded him of the "compromising positions" we'd seen them in, and well, inferred that she'd use that against him. That took the wind out of his sails *very* quickly. I also gently reminded him of the fact that if we went to court, *and* that if Beth didn't take his case again, I might be forced to use her as a character witness -- or should I say a *lack* of character witness?"

It took a minute for Annie to digest what she'd just heard. Gwen had managed to play hardball without even going to court, without hardly batting an eye, and it had worked. Amazing. It was disappointing that Eric might concede out of self-centeredness, but at this point it didn't matter. She would be foolish to expect anything else at this point.

"Annie? Are you still there?"

"Yes, Gwen -- sorry -- I'm here."

"I threw a lot at you all at once, didn't I?"

"I'll say you did. Yeah -- I don't quite know what to say." She drew circles on the tabletop with the index finger of her left hand. "Thank you?"

Gwen chortled. "Let's save that for when he actually decides, ok? I just wanted to let you know there's some light at the end of the tunnel -- and the tunnel appears to be getting shorter."

"That's good to know."

"And Annie -- I'm sorry if I overstepped my bounds with this. I just followed my instincts -- and that's what happened."

"No, that's fine, Gwen. Whatever works, right?"

"Right. We'll be in touch, ok?"

"Yep -- sounds good," replied Annie quietly. "Thanks for calling."

"Bye sweetie -- and remember, hang in there."

Annie sat there for a moment after she heard the click of Gwen disconnecting the call. The telephone receiver laid heavy in her hand. She stared past it, at the jumble of boxes and the assorted belongings in the living room. If what Gwen had told her was true, she'd soon be packing for real, not just "in case", and suddenly she was terrified. She hadn't thought much past the divorce becoming final. That was her beacon, the carrot dangling in front of her. Eric coming to his senses seemed to be such an insurmountable hurdle, that lately she'd put the next step on hold. She didn't dare to start making plans or even think about it, for fear that she'd have to abandon them, or worse yet, actually have to move forward. Gwen's call made everything seem more real and it scared her to death.

A tinny voice spoke to her from the receiver: *If you'd like to make a call, please hang up and dial again. If you need help, please dial your operator...* It annoyed her back to the moment. She hated that recording. The woman's voice sounded so pinched, as though she really was being inconvenienced by whoever left the phone off the hook this time.

"Okay, okay," Annie said to the recorded voice.

No sooner had she placed the receiver in the telephone's cradle, when it rang again.

"For Pete's sake," she muttered. "Now what?" She cleared her throat and then picked up the phone again. "Hello?"

"Annie?" It was Eric. His voice still held some residue of the contempt it had been saturated with the last time she'd heard it.

"Oh -- hi." She was guarded, remembering their last encounter.

"How's it going?"

"Okay." There was no way Annie was going to be too candid with him. Even though she wanted the game-playing to be over, there were no guarantees where he was concerned. She had to be careful.

"Have you talked to Gwen?" he asked.

"Yes, she just called."

"What did she tell you?" his voice was guarded, yet condescending.

"Why don't you tell me, Eric?"

She heard an exasperated sigh and the unmistakable clink of ice cubes. The next sound was that of smoke being pulled through a cigarette and then exhaled slowly. She could almost smell the smoke through the receiver.

"Well, if you must know," he started," I've given it a lot of thought, and decided that what Gwen said about working together makes sense."

"What happened to representing yourself?" Annie asked, even though she already knew the answer.

The silence was palpable. It sagged between them, ready to cling to the next word that was spoken. Annie decided that she was going to give him plenty of time. There was no hurry tonight.

"Well," he said the word with hesitation in his voice. "Things are really crazy at work right now and I just don't have the time to devote to it. I'm up for a promotion, too, so that's taking a lot of my energy."

*I'll bet it is,* mused Annie. His voice interrupted her thoughts. "....so, if I get it, the promotion, that is, things have to start moving faster than they have been."

"Why is that?" Annie found this a strange comment from him, considering that he had been the one to slow down the process all along.

"Because a VP of marketing can't live in his mother's basement." He said with a mixture of pride and disdain. "I need to live somewhere better -- and that's our house."

"Really." She couldn't keep the sarcasm out of her voice, but he didn't hear it anyway.

"Really. Don't you remember, Annie? I thought we should buy it because it's such a great place to entertain. The bar, the surround sound -- it's perfect."

Suddenly she felt deeply wounded, her breath catching in her throat. The differences between them glared with all the painful brilliance of looking directly into the sun. *He* had dreamt of entertaining important clients and colleagues in the house in which *she* had hoped to raise a family. Had they ever shared the same vision? Her heart ached with the realization that she had been more alone than she'd ever known.

"Yeah -- so, we need to get the ball rolling. Gwen said that if we *both* cooperate, we could be finished in about a month. Oh -- and one more thing. Since I'm going to buy you out, I think that I should live there instead of you. It's only fair." He took another drag on his cigarette.

Annie remained silent, almost afraid to breathe. Her stomach twisted into a tight pretzel and she thought she was going to be sick. *Fair? How was* any *of this fair?*

"It'd work out best for me to move back next weekend," he continued.

"Next *weekend*?" she nearly choked on the lump in her throat. "That doesn't give me much time --"

Anger churned inside of her, coiling itself around her stomach tighter and tighter. She started pacing back and forth, stretching the telephone cord to the limit. Her heart pounded so loudly she could feel it throughout her entire body. *Breathe*, she told herself. *Breathe. Don't let him get to you.* She closed her eyes and inhaled deeply several times as she tried to get her bearings. She knew that she'd be moving eventually, but in a *week*? She didn't have a clue as to where she would go.

"Annie -- you still there?"

"Yes."

"So, will that work?"

"Let's let Gwen handle this. Good-bye, Eric." She hung up the phone before any more damage was done.

She stood there for a long time, her hand still on the receiver, replaying the conversation in her head. So he was in line for a promotion. Vice-president of marketing for the accounting firm. Amazing. She suspected that Kelly was involved somehow, but also knew that Eric was very talented at what he did, so it was possible that he had earned at least some of it on his own. It really didn't matter. In fact, it was a good thing. If he got a substantial increase in pay, he'd be able to pay her for her half of the house and everything in it more easily. Perhaps he'd even be less likely to squabble over little details. Maybe he'd even be generous.

"Yeah, right," she said aloud, as she poured herself a glass of Chablis. "Like *that's* going to happen." She took a sip and let it glide down her throat. One sip wouldn't erase all of her tension, but it helped ease it a bit.

The cardboard boxes seemed to mock her now. Before talking to Gwen and Eric, she'd felt pretty good about the prospect of moving and all that it represented, but now it just seemed absurd and surreal. Annie was a planner -- she needed to figure out what was going to happen next and she liked to feel organized. The boxes with their contents neatly labeled in the upper corner of the right hand flap looked ridiculous now. If she cooperated with Eric's request and was out in a week, there's no way she could even think about packing with a plan. She pictured herself throwing things in boxes with no rhyme or reason and standing in the middle of them on a street corner, alone and homeless. Panic enveloped her. She finished her wine in three quick gulps and made her way through the boxes to the refrigerator to get some more. They probably didn't serve wine in homeless shelters, so this was going to be the last chance she'd have to enjoy it for a while, she reasoned as she poured.

Nestled back amongst the half-empty boxes, she set her glass on the coffee table and started to sort through a shoebox full of photographs. The first picture she saw was one of her, taken the week before Dillon had been born. She was wearing her favorite maternity dress, a blue eyelet sundress with a big ruffle around the hem. Eric had commented once that it made her look "as big as a house." She took it as a compliment, although she wasn't sure that was how he meant it. As far as she was concerned, she was supposed to look big -- she was pregnant. In the picture, she was turned sideways, her hands holding her belly. Her expression was radiant and proud, as if showing the whole world how happy and excited she was to become a mother.

A sharp pain suddenly pierced her heart, the same pain she'd felt so often in the first days after Dillon had died. Tears filled her eyes and she let out a shrill wail as they ran down her face. It had been nearly eight months since that picture had been taken, nearly eight months since he died, and it felt like it had just happened. Annie hugged her knees, buried her head in her arms and sobbed inconsolably. Her heart was breaking all over again, only this time she wasn't numb or in shock. She could feel every wretched pang, and as each spasm of grief washed over her, she wondered if she would survive it.

"Oh Dillon," she cried, "why did you have to die? I'm so sorry. Mommy is so sorry."

There seemed to be no end to the tears and she cried until sheer exhaustion made them stop. She leaned back against the front of the couch, totally drained. Her eyes had become narrow slits, her face red and puffy. With the back of her hand, she wiped her nose, when sniffling no longer worked.

"What am I going to do?" She said to the disheveled living room. "What's happened to my life?" Hearing her voice articulate her fears started another bout of crying, new tears having had a chance to form during the brief respite. In between sobs she heard the doorbell ring.

"Shit," she muttered and looked around in a panic. "Who could that be?" As soon as she said it, she remembered that Sally was coming over that evening to help her pack. Relief splashed over her and she hurried to the door. As soon as she opened the door it took less than a second for Sally to gather Annie in her arms.

"Oh sweetie," whispered Sally as she gently patted her head. "I'm here now. There, there." When there was a break in the sobbing, she steered Annie into the foyer and closed the door behind them. They walked together, Sally's arm around Annie's shoulders, into the living room and sat down on the couch.

"Want to talk about it?" Sally asked, her voice quiet and calm.

"Oh Sally -- I don't know where to start," Annie sniffled loudly and reached for her wine.

"Got any more of that?" Sally nodded toward the glass. "Am I going to need it?"

Annie managed a weak smile and started to get up. Sally patted her knee and stood up.

"I know where the glasses are -- if you haven't packed them, that is."

"I guess I'm having a little panic attack," Annie explained. "It started with a call from Eric, telling me he's going to 'work with us' but then telling me he wants me out of the house in a week."

Sally's head shot up as she finished opening another bottle of wine. "He can't do that to you! Who does he think he is?! There's no way he can make you do that." She tip-toed around the boxes back to where Annie was sitting. "Oooh -- that Eric just makes me so mad!" She took a swig from her glass.

"There, there," said Annie, patting her aunt's knee. Sally smiled sheepishly and gave her niece a hug.

"Sorry. I'm the one who should be calming you down. I just lost it for a minute there. So, tell me the rest." She gave Annie her full attention.

"Well, then I saw a picture that Eric had taken of me just before Dillon was born and it all just hit me, you know?" Tears sprung from her eyes again. "He'd be eight months old now. Crawling, getting into things. And if he hadn't died, the divorce wouldn't be happening. Sally, what am I going to do? Why did all of this happen to me?"

"Oh honey --" Sally rubbed Annie's arm. She didn't say anything. She just waited until she was finished, and then said,"Do you want to know what I think?"

"Of course I do," Annie answered quietly as she dabbed at her tears with a Kleenex.

"First of all, I'm so sorry that any of this has happened to you. It is so unfair. Even though I've had miscarriages, I'll never know what you've gone through. It's the worse kind of awful. But you know what? I'm not so sure that if Dillon were here he wouldn't be teething on one of these cardboard boxes right now."

Annie looked at her, perplexed.

"What I mean," Sally continued, "is that I'm not so sure the divorce wouldn't be happening anyway. Losing Dillon might have caused Eric to show his true colors sooner than he would have otherwise, but you never know. What makes you think that having a baby in his life would have turned him into 'Father of the Year'?"

As much as it hurt to hear it, Annie nodded in agreement. In the months since Eric left, she had done much soul-searching and had faced the fact that she had never felt as though she was a priority to her husband -- at least not the way a wife should be. Even while they were dating, she always felt as though she was never good enough, that she could be replaced at the drop of a hat. She had suspected it then, but loved him in spite of it and tried harder because of it. Sally was right. There was no solid proof that things would be any different had Dillon lived. The only thing that might be different, was that she'd be facing all of this as a single parent. To put her child through this agony would have broken her heart in ways she couldn't begin to count.

"Maybe things *do* happen for a reason," she murmured.

"Well, honey, I don't know about that. If anyone is meant to be a mother, it's you. Dillon was a lucky little boy to have been growing inside of you. Eric, on the other hand, didn't deserve either one of you."

Annie hugged her aunt and started crying again. "Thank you, Sally. That means a lot to me."

"Well, it's true. But you know what? Even though I think Eric is a major league jerk for asking you to be out in a week, maybe it would be a good thing."

"But --"

"Uh,uh,uh!" Sally stopped Annie from interrupting her further. "My turn!"

"Sorry."

"Look at it this way. You've already started to pack, right? I could come over every night this week and help you. As we fill boxes, Frank can bring them over to our house, which is where you can stay for the time being."

"It's just so sudden --"

"Annie -- it's not sudden. It's been six months since Eric left. We knew this was coming. How long did you think it would take? How long do you want to drag it out?"

"Well, it's just that there are so many memories here -- it's the only place that Dillon ever 'lived'."

"I know, sweetie, but Dillon lived in *you*, not in this house."

Annie nodded again, a sob catching in her throat. She'd always remember the way it had felt when he kicked her or when he rolled from side to side, no matter where she lived. She didn't have to stay in the house to have those memories.

"There has been a lot to take care of, living here alone," she admitted. "Eric hasn't exactly been great about helping with any of it. It would be a relief to not have to worry about that so much."

"See?" said Sally, encouraged. "Less yardwork, less housework. You could spend more time doing what *you* want to do."

"And what's that?" Annie laughed as she wiped away a few straggler teardrops.

"That, honeybunch, is moving forward and being *happy* again someday!" She raised her glass and clinked it with Annie's. "To the future!"

# The Butterfly

Six days after she talked to Eric, Annie left the house that had once held so much hope. Frank and Sally had just driven off with the last load of boxes. She was going to go to their house, her new home for the time being, as soon as she said one last "goodbye." She looked at her watch. There wasn't much time until Eric would be there to move back in. She had to hurry. Even though she knew she'd have to see him again at Gwen's office next week, he was the last person she wanted to see right now.

It wasn't hard to say good-bye to the pain and disappointment that had become as much a part of the house as the shingles and floorboards. Now she knew that she could never be happy there. Pain permeated every recent memory and lurked around every corner. Would it find Eric and make his nights restless and his days unbearable? Or would he carry on as he always had, living for the moment, doing whatever made him happy with no thought to tomorrow?

"I hope not," Annie said to herself as she got into her silver Honda Civic and wiped a tear from her cheek with her fingertip. She looked back toward the house. It was hard to see it clearly, since the sun had set nearly an hour before. Crickets chirped an evening song as darkness settled on the neighborhood.

In spite of everything, she really did hope that Eric would find his own happiness someday. This was not an entirely selfless wish. Annie didn't want her future to be compromised by the poison that harboring old resentments could generate. She needed to begin again, to be the person she was always meant to be; strong, happy, loving and someday, to be loved back.

It was then that she put her hand over her heart and gently patted the cradle of memories that were Dillon. Eyes closed, she leaned her head against the headrest in her car. So much had happened since she'd last held him in her arms. Her life had taken a path that a year ago, she never would have imagined. She had been happily pregnant, expecting not only to have a baby, but a family as well. Now she had neither. The thought made her heart ache sharply, and her eyes blinked open, surprised by the actual pain of it. The first thing she saw as she looked up through the sunroof was the moon, a dim sliver of light. The tears filling her eyes made the night sky hazy; it was hard to focus. She closed her eyes, making the tears spill out and run down her cheeks. Opening them, her vision was clear again and she was able to see the heavens above her. There it was -- a star shining brightly and twinkling just for her. Dillon. A feeling of warmth spread over her, a comforting embrace from the inside out. For the first time in months she felt some peace. Dillon would always be with her, in her heart and peeking down at her from his perch on the star, sparkling so far above.

Smiling, she turned the key in the ignition and started the car. A lilting melody wafted through the radio speakers, a violin and piano playing "Schubert's Lullaby." Annie turned up the volume and sat back, gazing up at Dillon's star.

"This one's for you, sweetie," she whispered softly. "Now, let's get going. Sally and Frank are waiting!"

Annie's car turned the last corner and there was Sally and Frank's house, lights glowing warmly from the windows, awaiting her arrival. Before she could even turn off the engine, her aunt and uncle were coming out to greet her.

"You made it!" squealed Sally as she gave her a big hug.

"We just saw her a half hour ago," laughed Frank, as he opened the back door of Annie's car and reached in for an armful of clothes.

"I know that, silly," replied Sally. "I'm just so happy she's finally here! We're going to have so much fun!"

"Well, I don't know about *that*," Annie cautioned her as she opened the hatchback and grabbed a laundry basket full of shoes. "I'm not that much fun to be around these days."

"Oh baloney!" said her aunt. "You're just perfect however you are! Are you hungry? I've just warmed up a big pot of soup."

Once inside, she brought the basket of shoes to the room that would now be hers, and sat it on the bed. Annie could smell the delicious aroma of Sally's chicken noodle soup all the way from upstairs and her stomach gurgled in response. She hadn't eaten yet that day, having given the contents of her cupboards and refrigerator to Frank and Sally to bring to their house the day before, and she was starving.

She looked around the room. Sally and Frank had remodeled the lower level of their home into a separate apartment for Frank's elderly mother, Edna, who could no longer live alone. Shortly before she was going to move in, she had a heart attack and passed away. No one had lived in it until now, which was one reason Sally was so anxious for Annie to stay there.

"It even has its own little kitchen," Sally said enthusiastically as she'd tried to persuade a hesitant Annie to live there. "Of course, we'd love you to join us for meals, but at least you could cook for yourself if you wanted to."

They had done an excellent job with the decorating. It was beautiful -- cozy and elegant at the same time. Annie could picture herself curling up on the chocolate brown chenille sofa with a cup of tea and a good book on a cold winter evening. There was a gas fireplace in the wall between the living area and the bedroom, so that a fire could be enjoyed from either room, with just the flick of a switch. The little kitchenette in the corner had a small refrigerator, a little stove and a microwave as well as a sink and a small dishwasher.

"This is wonderful!" Annie had seen it before, but was looking at it through different eyes now.

"Thanks!" Sally grinned proudly. "It was a labor of love, so I'm glad that someone I love so much gets to finally use it."

"It's too bad Grandma Edna never made it here -- she would have loved it."

"Yes, she would have," agreed Sally. "I like to think that she's probably rocking Dillon to sleep this very minute." The two women exchanged sad smiles. "Let's get you something to eat. We can unpack all of this stuff later."

After filling their stomachs and replenishing their souls with large bowls of homemade chicken noodle soup and crusty French bread, Sally, Frank and Annie lingered around the kitchen table, talking. Frank nursed a beer while Sally and Annie sipped on wine.

"I was going to crack open a bottle of bubbly," Frank mused, "but we'll save that for another day."

"Yes, like when --" Sally was interrupted by the loud jangle of the phone. She sighed, clearly annoyed, and got up to answer it. "Hello?"

Her face clouded instantly. "Just a minute. I'll see if she's available." She loosely put her hand over the receiver and shouted. "Annie! Can you come to the phone?"

Frank and Annie looked at each other, confused that Sally was shouting for her when she was sitting inches away. Annie started to stand up when Sally shook her head and motioned to her to stay put and took a deep breath before hollering again. "Annie!"

Sally stood there and tapped her foot for thirty seconds or so before she motioned Annie to take the phone, mouthing *"It's Eric."*

"Hello?" Annie said, pretending she had no idea who was calling her.

"Annie." Eric said. "Where did you put your key for the house?"

"I'm fine. Thanks for asking." Annie couldn't squelch her sarcasm.

"What the -- never mind. Where did you put your key?"

"It's in my purse. Where else would it be?"

"I thought I told you to leave it *here*."

"You did, but then how would I have locked the house?"

"Goddamn it, Annie. I told you to put it under the mat," he scolded.

Annie could feel her pulse quicken and her blood pressure rise. "Don't you still have your key?"

"Of course I do," he said.

"So, what's the problem?"

"*So*, I don't want *you* to be able to get in. *I* live here now."

"For God's sake Eric, what do you think I'm going to do?"

"I don't know -- but if you don't live here, you don't need a key, do you?" his voice was harsh.

"Go to hell, Eric." Annie slammed the phone down, shaking with anger.

"You go, girl!" Sally jumped up and tried to give her niece a 'high-five.' "I don't know what he said, but good for you!"

Annie tried to calm herself down by breathing deeply, ignoring Sally's outburst for the moment. She couldn't believe she had just done that. Hanging up on people was one of the things she detested most. Swearing made it even worse.

"Well, I guess I can't always take the high road." She sank back down into her chair.

You haven't fallen off the high road, Annie," Frank tried to reassure her. "Everyone's entitled to lose it now and then."

Sally raised her glass in a toast. "To Annie! That was wonderful to witness! I'm honored to be here!"

Annie blushed and rolled her eyes. "Good Lord, Sally!"

"I'm serious," continued Sally. "You surprise me every day with how much you're growing and changing. It's amazing. It's like watching a butterfly break out of a cocoon. That's something most people never get to see." She dabbed away the tears forming in her eyes. "I want you to know that I don't take it for granted."

Annie got up and went to hug her aunt. "I love you."

"Okay, ladies," sniffled Frank as he blinked away a tear of his own, "we'll all be bawling our heads off in a minute at the rate we're going." He stood up and pushed in his chair. "What do you say we tackle those boxes downstairs and get you settled in?"

They all got up to clear the table when the phone rang again. This time Frank picked it up. "Hello?"

He waited a moment as he listened to the voice on the other end of the line before he spoke again. "She's busy, Eric. Can I take a message?" Frank maintained a cool but cordial tone of voice. He shot a *"Calm down"* look at Sally, as she took a deep breath to protest. "I'll tell her. Good-bye," he said and hung up the receiver.

"What did that jerk want?" Sally demanded, holding a plate in midair. "Why were you so *nice* to him?"

"He wanted to tell Annie that he's having the locks changed tomorrow."

"He told you that and you were still nice to him?!" Sally was hyperventilating.

"Relax, Sally," Frank put his hands on his wife's shoulders. "It will be fine."

"But --"

"But nothing. Listen to me, please? You have everything out of the house that you need, right, Annie?"

"I guess so," replied Annie.

"Then it doesn't matter, does it?"

Sally and Annie looked at each other and shrugged their agreement.

"I think the guy is as much of a jerk as both of you do, but antagonizing him is only going to make it harder for Annie in working out the settlement. Believe me -- it's going to be fine." Frank's voice had the calming effect of a mild tranquilizer on the situation.

"Alrighty then," Sally said as she squeezed Frank's hands on her shoulders. "Let's unpack."

They spent the next couple of hours deciding which boxes to open and which to store. Frank stacked the stored boxes in another part of the basement where they'd stay until Annie found a place of her own. The only boxes she opened contained clothing and assorted personal items, so it didn't take very long to get settled. She got her clothes hung up in the closet and folded neatly in the dresser before she plopped down on the bed, exhausted.

"I can't believe it's already 11:00 p.m." she yawned, looking at the clock on the nightstand.

Frank had gone to bed hours earlier, when the conversation turned to reminiscing about Annie's childhood. It was always hard for him to talk about those years, because that was when he'd lost his best friend, Annie's father, in a freak boating accident. He and Sally had taken Annie and her mother, Sally's little sister, under their wing the best they could after that. Annie had only been eight years old and had adored her dad -- they had called themselves "The Dynamic Duo." They had done everything together -- camping, fishing, cooking breakfast on Saturday mornings while Annie's mother slept in. He taught her how to ride a bicycle, how to skip stones, and how to tell ghost stories while holding a flashlight under her chin. The hole torn in her heart by her father's sudden death had left a part of Annie unfinished and hurting. Nine years later when her mom was diagnosed with breast cancer, Annie was terrified that she would lose her too, which she did, only a year later. It had been a time of turmoil and vulnerability in her life, which made it a perfect time to fall in love. With Eric. Looking back, it all made so much sense.

"Oh Sally -- if only I had known then what I know now. Everything would have turned out so differently." She leaned against the headboard and hugged one of the pillows to her chest.

"What would be different?" asked her aunt.

Annie thought for a minute. "I don't know, but I have to believe I would have made better choices."

"That may be," started Sally, "but who knows how *those* would have turned out? You don't get to call *all* the shots, you know."

"You've got that right." Annie frowned, smoothing the soft fabric of the pillowcase with both of her hands. "I guess I have to stop the 'what-if' thinking, don't I?"

"That would be good," agreed Sally. "Easier said than done, but I know you can do it." She reached over and gave Annie a hug. "It's time for me to call it a night. Are you as exhausted as I am?"

"Yes, and then some," Annie covered her mouth as another yawn escaped.

"See you in the morning. And sleep in, ok? You deserve it."

The next week Annie and Eric had another meeting with Gwen. As painful as these meetings could be, Annie was looking forward to it, hoping that it would bring them closer to the end of the ordeal, one she hadn't chosen. The three of them sat around a conference table. Gwen was at the head of it, with Annie and Eric on opposite sides. Annie sensed a shift in Gwen's attitude as well as her choice of seating. Before, when they each had an attorney, Gwen always sat next to her. She liked that -- the feeling of having an ally, someone on her side. Now her lawyer seemed to be straddling the abyss of heartbreak and disillusionment between Eric and her, and it didn't feel right. She could understand it intellectually, but emotionally it threw her off balance. It was as though she'd misplaced her security blanket, or more accurately, had it torn in half by Eric, who had grabbed hold of it and wouldn't let go. She knew this was the sensible way to go about things, but was it the best way?

"So, Eric, as I understand it, you had the locks changed on the house last week," stated Gwen at the start of the meeting.

"Yes, I did." He was smug and self-righteous.

"And may I ask why?"

"Annie moved out and took her key with her. I told her to leave it under the mat and she didn't do it. Then when I called to ask her about it, she said told me to go to hell. I don't have to take that kind of shit, so I had them changed. Oh -- and here's the bill." He slid the receipt from a locksmith across the table toward Annie. "You need to pay me back."

Annie looked at the piece of paper without touching it. The amount was over $300.00. She looked back at Eric. "You expect *me* to pay this?"

He folded his arms across his chest, leaned back in his chair and nodded. "That's right. If you hadn't kept the key, I wouldn't have had to have them changed. It's the least you can do."

Annie straightened up in her chair, her heart pounding. "This is ridiculous! I am *not* reimbursing you for this or anything else! Even if I *had* left the key, I could've had more made. Yes, Eric, all I want to do is to sneak back into that house and -- and, do *what?* Why would I want to go back there? It's the last place I want to be." She turned to Gwen. "I don't care that he changed the locks, but I shouldn't have to pay for it, should I?"

Gwen straightened the papers in front of her and reached for the receipt. She put her reading glasses on and examined it closely before speaking. She looked at Annie and then at Eric. "No, Annie, you don't have to pay for it. Eric, it was your decision to change the locks. Since you're still married, the cost will come out of your marital assets anyway, so it's really a moot point. Now, what's next?"

"What do you mean it's a moot point?" Annie was confused. "If it comes out of our marital assets, then I *am* paying for it, aren't I?"

"Not really. Eric will just get $300.00 less when you split things up, or we can add that amount to his buy-out for the house."

Eric shot up out of his chair, sputtering. "What the hell? That's not fair!"

Gwen sighed heavily, leaned back in her chair and waited for him to calm down. "Are you finished?" she said.

He scowled at her, his face red with embarrassment and anger, and sat down again. The sun shining in the window from behind him cast a menacing shadow on the table. From the length of it, Annie could tell that it was getting later in the afternoon without even having to look at her watch. This was taking much too long.

"I've explained to both of you before that the marital assets will be divided fairly, but not necessarily 50-50. Now Eric, if you have a problem with that, go and get yourself another attorney and blow through even more of your money. We're trying to negotiate a settlement here so that we can save you both some money and time, is that not correct?" They both nodded. "So let's get back to work and get this finished."

She glanced at Eric, who continued to frown. He was rifling through his stack of papers, finding numbers and scribbling them down on another sheet of paper. Whatever he was up to, she was quite sure he wasn't giving the task at hand sufficient attention. Gwen was summarizing the next issue on the agenda when he interrupted again.

"Okay, listen up. I've added up everything I've spent on the house since we bought it and I have *way* more into than she does, so I want *that* taken off the buy-out amount." He looked at both women and shook his head up and down like a cocky rooster who had just walked into the hen house. His arrogance made Annie want to scream. Instead, she did something else that surprised everyone, herself included.

In a very quiet, calm voice she said, "Eric -- why are you so angry?"

Both he and Gwen were caught off-guard by her question. Gwen looked pleased and Eric sat there, seething. His face turned a darker shade of red, and beads of perspiration popped out on his forehead and upper lip.

"What do you mean?" he asked, his voice indignant. His eyes darted fro Annie to Gwen and back to Annie again.

"I just don't understand your anger. You're the one who wanted the divorce and yet you're acting like such a victim.You also refused to see a counselor with me. Can you explain it to me because I'm really getting tired of this. Everything becomes an issue of how unfair this all is to *you*. Well, guess what? It's not fair to me either. Losing Dillon and then having you leave -- none of those things were fair, but you seem to forget that. I want to cooperate, but I'm not going to be a fool. I loved you so much -- I wanted you to be happy -- so I ignored the problems. Obviously that didn't work very well, because here we are. I just don't get it. You're getting everything you want -- no wife, no child to tie you down. You're free to see whoever else you want. You can do whatever you want to your heart's content and have no one to think about but yourself. So why the anger, Eric?"

He was silent, looking down at the table for a very long time. The fingers of his right hand were fiddling with the corner of the legal pad in front of him, bending its pages back and forth, back and forth, until they resembled a stack of dry, yellow leaves, curled up at the edges. He seemed to be deep in thought, as though he were searching the innermost recesses of his soul for the answer. Annie continued to watch him, her expression detached yet sincere.

Finally, he looked up at her, his eyes an essay in contradiction; cold and hard, but moist with tears. "Because I miss you. There. I said it. Are you happy now?"

Annie sat there, barely breathing. Of all the answers she expected him to manufacture, missing her was not even on the list. She couldn't believe her ears. Silence seemed to be the best response. She could see Gwen out of the corner of her eye and saw that she was also dumbstruck, waiting for the next shoe to drop.

Eric took a deep, ragged breath and continued. "Going back to the house and not having you there was terrible. It's not the same without you. What makes me so mad about all of this is not having *you* anymore." He grabbed a Kleenex from the box on the table and loudly blew his nose. "What can I say?"

"I still don't understand," she whispered. "That might explain the anger today, but what about the rest of the time?"

"I'm angry that everything has changed. I had a plan for my life and now it's different. I want our old life back -- our life before Dillon," he explained, his voice sober. "And what makes me the angriest, is that you *don't* want that anymore." His gaze shot right through her. "Do you?"

"No, I don't."

"I knew it."

"Like it or not, everything *is* different now. We can't go back. The damage has been done." She stopped for a second to gather strength. "We don't belong together, Eric. The past few months have made me see that more and more. I can't give you what you need to be happy -- and you can't give me what I need either. It's no one's fault, it's just the way it is. I'm a different person now than I was before Dillon was born. I can't change that." She waited a second and then continued. "I don't *want* to change it."

She didn't know where the words came from, but every single one was spoken directly from her heart.

The three of them sat there, letting the meaning of what had just been said, settle over them and sink in. Annie's heart felt lighter than it had in years. She was amazed to find that the nagging feeling of self-doubt that had been part who she was for so long was all but gone. She didn't fear Eric's reaction as she had in the past. She was no longer worried that he'd be mad at her or worse yet, leave her. All of that had already happened and she had emerged from it, a stronger person than she'd ever imagined possible. She knew she was going to be alright.

A week later, during the second week in March, Gwen sent both Annie and Eric copies of the draft of the divorce decree for them to examine. To Annie's surprise, Eric found nothing to dispute, and so in short order, the final papers were ready to be signed. They decided it would be easiest to meet at Gwen's office to sign them and then she could walk across the street to the court house to file them.

Each page required both of them to place their initials at the bottom. He put "E.R.M." for Eric Robert Morgan and she carefully scrolled "A.E.M." for Anne Elizabeth Morgan. It brought her back to the first time she'd signed it. This time was nothing like the first, for now she was only filled with a disappointing sadness that pervaded the moment. The first time, on her wedding day, she had hoped the future would bring happiness. Now she knew all too well that the future holds no guarantees, only the promise of the unknown. Now she knew that happiness was something that you had to choose -- it didn't choose you. As she signed "Morgan" for one of the last times, she promised herself that she would no longer wait for happiness to find her -- she would live her new life in a new way, to purposefully make every day count, to make every moment the best it could possibly be. In spite of her good intentions, however, the pain and enormity of the situation was overwhelming and she had to focus in order to maintain her composure.

Eric, on the other hand, appeared to be more light-hearted, doing his best to hide his feelings. There had been a brief glimpse of them at their last meeting, but those glimpses were few and far between. It had been one of her downfalls, always hoping for more from him and making him feel inadequate in the process. She could see that now, hindsight being 20/20, but found odd comfort in knowing that she couldn't have gone back and made it work. To deny the part of her that needed to feel deeply and share those feelings with someone else, would have been to commit emotional suicide. She had nearly done that once; she would not let it happen again.

Two weeks later, Gwen called Annie to tell her the judge had signed the decree and that the divorce was final. At first Annie wondered if she was playing some sort of bizarre joke.

"I have a pretty wicked sense of humor," Gwen said when she heard what Annie suspected, "but this is one thing I don't joke about."

"I appreciate that, Gwen. It's just that it seemed as if this day would never happen."

"I can see where you might wonder. You probably feel like life has been playing some pretty cruel jokes on you this past year, don't you?"

"I don't know if I'd say that," Annie replied quietly. "I can't think about it that way, or I'd be paranoid about what's coming next. I don't know what to call it -- bad luck?"

Gwen sighed. "Life is rarely perfect, Annie. More rain certainly falls into some lives than others, doesn't it? Once we know why, all of the mysteries of life will be solved. Then what fun will it be to get up every day?"

"Exactly. Even though it hasn't been fun to get up a lot of days this year," Annie started. "I'm still looking forward to what's to come. It can only get better, right?"

"Oh, I hope so, Annie. I most definitely hope so!" exclaimed Gwen. "Not to change the subject, Ms. Stanford, but you have some name-changing to keep you busy for the next few days."

"Yes, I guess I do. It's going to be strange to be called that again, but I'm ready!"

Annie looked at the clock on the microwave to see what time it was. Two o'clock. She would never forget the significance of this date, at this time. It was when her life started over.

# The Coffee Cup

The grief support group meeting at the hospital was supposed to start at 7:00 p.m. and Annie only had a few minutes to get there or she'd be late. A phone call had delayed her on her way out the door and then traffic was worse than she'd anticipated. Not wanting to be late, she'd already decided that if she was going to have to walk into the room after the meeting had started, she wouldn't walk into it at all. From what she'd remembered from the one time she had been there, the leader got down to business right away. There were so many people and so much grief to support, wasting time in idle conversation seemed inappropriate. Besides, what kind of small talk can there be in a group of near strangers whose babies have died?

The elevator was not moving. She stood and watched the numbers, willing them to light up in the descending order, from Floor 12 down to Floor 1 where she stood. She folded her arms across her chest and impatiently tapped her fingers on her upper arm. Glancing down at her watch, she saw that it was 6:56 p.m. Her heart thumped and her mouth was dry as she pictured herself walking into the small conference room and having all the tear-filled eyes turn toward her as she looked for a place it sit. What was taking so long? Annie looked around a little bit to see if the door to the stairs was nearby. She didn't want to go on a wild goose chase looking for them, but it they were right there, she'd take them, two at a time if need be. She didn't see the stairway, but she did catch the eye of a flustered looking man who had just hurried to a spot in front of the elevator next to her. He sort of nodded at her and then hurriedly pressed the "Up" button several times.

"I'm almost ready to find the stairs," Annie said as they continued to wait. "Do you know where they are?"

The man, who looked to be around her age, appeared surprised that she had spoken to him. He looked at her for a moment and hesitated before he replied.

He cleared his throat briefly and said, "I'm afraid I don't know. I've never been here before."

Just then the elevator bell rang and the doors opened.

"Finally!" Annie said and checked the time again. 6:58 p.m. She only had to go to the fourth floor and the room wasn't far from the elevator. She was pretty sure she could make it. They stepped into the cubicle. The panel of numbers was on the left and she quickly pressed "4."

"Which floor do you need?"

"Four."

Annie smiled at him and then looked up at the numbers above the door as they went up. One, two, three....four. The doors slid open and they both stepped out. Just as she was going to hurry off to the conference room, the man said," Do you know where Room 406 is?"

"Yes, I do," she answered, "That's where I'm going too." Their eyes met again, this time with the realization that they had something in common – Room 406.

They rushed down the hall and around the corner to the conference room. Thankfully the door was still open and people were still getting settled. Annie let out a relieved sigh. She and the man nodded and smiled at each other and her eyes searched the table for an empty chair and a kind face sitting next to it.

She found her place next to a woman with short auburn hair and a friendly smile. The first time she had attended the meeting had been when she was still in a fog of grief so fresh and thick, she couldn't recall if she'd seen the woman before or not. It seemed as though she must have, because she felt like she was being greeted by an old friend.

"It's good to see you again," the woman said. "I wondered if you were coming back."

"I'm sorry," Annie replied, her face turning red as she spoke. "I don't –"

"You don't remember me, do you? That's okay – I'm Lora." She smiled at Annie again. "The first time I came I was in such a state I couldn't remember driving home, let alone any names."

Annie felt reassured by Lora's friendly compassion. It was good to know that she was normal, that maybe she wasn't losing her mind after all. It also impressed her that this stranger remembered her, especially since it had been months since she'd been there the first time.

"How long ago was that?" Annie asked quietly. "If you don't mind my asking."

"I don't mind at all – that's what we're here for – to talk about it. I started coming a few months after my baby died – almost two years ago." Her voice cracked as she spoke and a tear ran down her face. She managed a smile for Annie in spite of it. "Sometimes it still feels like it happened yesterday. Other times it feels as though it's been eons."

The reassurance she had felt a minute ago was replaced by a sudden feeling of panic. It had been almost two years since Lora's baby had died and she was still feeling this sad? It was a shocking revelation. She had no idea how long it would take to get over her feelings of grief and loss, but for some reason, she thought that by two years she should be further down the road to recovery. It was frightening to think that many months from now, she'd still feel so bad. Lora noticed her reaction and patted her hand gently. "It surprises me too."

Annie looked toward the end of the table, where Jane, the group leader was sitting. She was surprised to see the man from the elevator sitting next to her. Jane walked over to close the door and began to speak.

"Excuse me everyone," she started, "It's time to begin. It's good to see all of you tonight. I hope you've all had a good couple of weeks." She paused and smiled kindly at the faces seated around the table.

One of the reasons Annie had decided to return to the support group was because of the genuine concern that Jane had for every person who was there. She had experienced the stillbirth of her own baby as well as several miscarriages and an ectopic pregnancy, so she knew of what she spoke. As each person told his or her story, Jane would sit and listen silently, a single tear coursing down her face.

"As some of you may recall from last time, we have a guest with us tonight." She tilted her head toward the man from the elevator. He nodded back at her and smiled briefly.

Since Annie hadn't been at the last meeting, she was confused as to what Jane was talking about. Everyone else was smiling at the guest who seemed to be looking directly at her. She smiled a cautious smile back at him as she wondered who he was and what he was going to speak about.

"I'd like to introduce all of you to Matthew Preston. As I told you last time, Matthew is writing a book about loss and grief and has asked if he could spend some time with us. I want you to meet him before that decision is made, because after all, this is your group." As Jane said this word "your" she offered an outstretched arm toward the bereaved parents sitting around the table and smiled warmly. She then nodded at Matthew as she took her seat.

Annie observed the guest speaker with interest. She had momentarily thought that he was a psychologist or a minister and was already putting up her defenses. The last thing she wanted to hear was some "expert" giving advice. He was a writer -- or that's what it seemed. Then it occurred to her that this guy was just intending to use these parents and their raw grief to get material for his book. *How dare he?* She thought, her anger growing. *Who does he think he is?* She looked around the table again and saw only acceptance on the faces of the others. She wanted to nudge Lora to ask what she'd missed when the guest began to speak.

"Hello everyone," he started. "First, I want to thank you for allowing me to be here tonight. Grief can be a very private thing and I want you to know that I don't take this privilege lightly." As he spoke his eyes scanned the faces around the table. He had kind blue eyes and a very pleasant smile. His approach was tentative and gentle -- not authoritative or condescending in any way. Annie recalled how distraught he seemed when she first encountered him by the elevators and it piqued her curiosity. She was surprised by the level of interest she felt for this man.

It had been months since the divorce was final and she had been operating under the assumption that all men were worthless and out to hurt her. Well-meaning friends had cautiously attempted to introduce her to eligible men, but it never seemed to work out they way they hoped. It just wasn't the right time. Annie knew that they felt bad for her; losing her baby and then her marriage. She was well aware of the tragic figure she had become, but no one understood that she was healing on her own, in ways they couldn't see. Living at Frank and Sally's had been a Godsend, giving her time to regroup and heal, but even they couldn't break down the barriers that she had constructed to protect her heart.

During that first support group meeting Matthew Preston attended, something happened to Annie that she hadn't expected. She felt an attraction, a connection to him, unlike any that she had ever known. During the many times she and Eric had broken up before they were married, she had dated other guys, but it had never amounted to very much. She had still been hopelessly smitten with Eric. Now it was different; the feelings for Eric were gone and had made room for some happiness, and the happiness was taking the form of very preoccupying thoughts of Matthew Preston.

The group had agreed to let Matthew visit their meetings and he had been observing them for a couple of months when one evening he took longer than usual gathering up his notebooks. Annie chatted with Lora for a couple of minutes as the rest of the group was saying their good-byes and preparing to leave. Lora could see him over Annie's shoulder as he tried to look busy and inconspicuous at the same time.

"Don't look now, but I think someone's waiting to talk to you," Lora whispered to her out of the corner of her mouth.

"Really?" Annie was careful to remain still.

"Don't act so innocent with me, girlfriend," Lora teased. "You know who I mean. He's only been making eyes at you for the past month."

"Do you think so?" Annie smiled and blushed. Matthew had seemed to have been flirting with her very subtly lately -- or at least she was hoping that's what his attentiveness meant. It made her nervous to think of getting to know someone new, but she wanted to live again. She had a lot of life ahead of her.

"Yes, I do," Lora replied. "And because I like you so much, I'm going to get out of here." She put her hand on Annie's shoulder and squeezed it. "Good luck!" Lora causally waved at Matthew as she breezed out of the room.

Annie's heart was racing as she turned to get her coat, but it was gone. Matthew had already taken it from the back of her chair and was holding it out for her to put on.

"Oh -- thank you, Matthew," she said, surprised by his action.

"You're welcome," he said. "And you can call me Matt. Only my mother calls me by my full name. I keep looking for her hiding in the corner or something each time someone calls me that," he laughed nervously at his own remark.

"Okay -- Matt it is." She finished sliding her arms into the sleeves of her coat and started to button it. Her fingers were having trouble matching the right button with its corresponding buttonhole.

"What did you think of the meeting tonight?" she asked as she kept fumbling with her coat. Why couldn't she just be confident and calm in these situations? No, she had to become a bumbling idiot in front of his very eyes. He wouldn't be flirting with her much longer at the rate she was going.

"I thought it was very interesting," he replied, watching her struggle. "Every week I learn something important," he paused, his eyes trained on her. Finally she completed her task, a triumph, even though the buttons were off by one. She smiled at him, happy to be finished. "Good," he said, smiling at her, "that was driving me crazy."

She rolled her eyes, shrugged her shoulders, and laughed, "Thanks. I'm usually not this klutzy. You wouldn't know it to look at me, but I've actually been buttoning my own coat for years now."

"Really," he chuckled. "Now why don't I believe that?" He smiled at her with happy eyes.

Laughing, Annie blushed some more and shook her head. "I don't know -- but I appreciate the concern." She picked up her purse from the table and adjusted the strap over her right shoulder.

"I was wondering," Matt started, his voice wavering a little, "if you'd be interested in getting a cup of coffee. There's a coffee shop around the corner or we could just go to the hospital cafeteria ..."

Annie was pleasantly surprised, but tried to act calm. She had been hoping for something like this to happen, but now that it had, she was terrified. She couldn't even talk and button her coat at the same time -- how would she be able to talk and drink coffee without making a total fool of herself?

They sat across the white Formica cafeteria table from each other, sipping bad hospital coffee out of Styrofoam cups. Annie blew across the top of her cup and smiled at Matt through the rising steam. As soon as she took off her coat, she realized that she'd buttoned it all wrong. She made a snap decision not to mention it -- why draw attention to her weaknesses? Maybe he hadn't even noticed.

"So, what brought you to this support group?" he asked. "I mean, why this particular one? Didn't you say that you lived in Minneapolis?"

Annie had just taken a sip of coffee and was waiting for it to cool off a little bit before she swallowed it. She could only nod and point helplessly to her mouth. Matt waited patiently for her to speak.

"Well, it's kind of a long story," she started, "but basically my doctor recommended it to me."

"Isn't it kind of a long drive all the way to downtown St. Paul?"

She crinkled her nose and shook her head from side to side. "I don't mind it too much. Now if there's ever a blizzard or an ice storm, I might feel differently, but for now it's ok. Do you live very far from here?" As soon as she asked the question, she regretted it. What if he thought she was trying to pick him up? She couldn't believe she had said something so stupid.

"I'm sorry," she continued, "I'm really not trying to be nosy." The burning in her cheeks told her that she was blushing furiously. She hated it when that happened.

Matt laughed and grinned at her. "Don't worry -- I didn't take it that way -- but yes, I do live sort of nearby. Over off Grand Ave."

"That's such an interesting area," Annie replied. "Have you lived there long?"

"A little over two years. After my wife died, I decided to sell our house and start over. Everyone told me not to make any big changes during that time, but I didn't listen to them."

He looked sadder and older just at the mention of his wife. He had shared his story with the group shortly after he began attending the meetings. It was the saddest story Annie had ever heard. His wife had not only been killed in a car accident, but had also been expecting their first child. No one had known she was pregnant, not even Matt. She had been on her way home from a doctor appointment to tell him the news, when a drunk driver crossed the center line and hit her head on.

"Did you ever regret it?" She was really prying now, but it seemed like the natural question to ask, especially since she had just moved as well.

Matt had a far off look in his eyes. "Yes, sometimes I've been sorry I sold it so quickly, but for the most part, it was a good thing. Too many memories there, you know." He took a quick gulp of his coffee.

"I had to move out of my house because of the divorce," explained Annie. "Eric wanted to stay there."

"How do you feel about that?"

"It doesn't really matter how I feel about it. I didn't have much of a choice." Now it was her turn to gulp her coffee quickly. Fortunately it had cooled down so that she didn't burn her throat. What did burn were the tears that sprang to her eyes when she thought about everything that had happened. She blinked and looked away, not wanting Matt to see. He reached across the table and covered her free hand with his and gave it a gentle squeeze. Her heart skipped a beat and she slowly looked back at him. He had tears in his eyes as well.

"I'm sorry you have to go through this, Annie," he said, his voice quiet and steady. "I can't begin to imagine how hard it must be." His hand was like a gentle blanket over her hand.

She looked at him through the tears that were threatening to run down her face, amazed. Here was a man who had been to hell and back, and here he was, saying that he couldn't begin to imagine how hard it was for her.

"But after all you've been through --"

"I still don't know how *you* feel." He finished the sentence for her. She just looked at him, confused.

"You don't get it, do you?" he finally said.

"No, I don't."

"Yes, Sara died and she was pregnant, but I didn't know she was pregnant until after the fact. As much as I wanted to be a father, it was different than living through eight months of a pregnancy and then losing the baby. You actually held Dillon in your arms. You felt him move and grow inside of you. He was with you every minute of every day."

"But you lost Sara --"

"And you've lost Eric."

"That's not the same. Eric didn't die -- he wasn't taken from me the way Sara was from you." Annie couldn't hold her tears back any longer. "You were *happy*."

"Yes, we were -- but at least I had that and I have all of those wonderful memories. I'll always be grateful. To me it's more tragic that you didn't have even that."

Annie contemplated his words for a moment and then studied the man across the table from her. A couple of hospital personnel dressed in blue surgical scrubs passed behind him and sat down at a nearby table. They were nothing but a blue blur moving slowly in the background. This sensitive man with tears in his eyes, his hand placed so tenderly over hers, was all she could see.

He had been through so much but he still would not assume anything about her journey through grief. Even though his wife and unborn baby were taken from him, he managed to find the strength from within to be thankful. He sat there looking at her with kind blue eyes that in spite of what they had seen, were willing and able to look into her heart at even more pain and sadness. "You are amazing," she said quietly.

"Not really," he replied, shaking his head.

"Yes, you are," she insisted. "Usually when people go through something so awful, it leaves them either bitter or arrogant or both -- like they've suffered more than anyone else. You aren't like that at all, and you have every right to be."

"What would that accomplish?" He glanced around the room and then fixed his gaze directly on her. "If I can't use my experience to help someone else, then Sara and the baby died for nothing. And really -- there are so many others that have suffered so much more. It's not a competition."

"No, it's not -- although when it's your loss, it's always a ten."

"You've got that right," he nodded. "The days after the accident were some of the darkest days of my life. Believe me -- I wasn't at this point back then. I was miserable to be around. I even thought about suicide."

Annie didn't know what to say, so she remained silent. He looked as though he was going to say more, so she sat quietly and waited for him to continue.

"That would've been such an insult to Sara and the love we had for each other. I just couldn't do that to her. So, I went to a counselor for a while and then started to write about it. And now here I am -- talking to you and holding your hand." He smiled at her and gave her hand a squeeze.

She blushed again and wasn't exactly sure where to look. There was more to this than just a cup of coffee between acquaintances, but it had been a long time since she'd been down this road or one even remotely like it. This new terrain was unfamiliar but also comforting and exciting. She felt such a connection with this man across from her. It transcended the fact that their hands were literally touching, physically connected. He felt like an old friend, a kindred spirit -- someone who really understood her.

"I hope I'm not overstepping my bounds here," he said, and started to let go of her hand.

"No," she said quickly, while she tightened her grasp, "it's okay. Really, it's fine. You're not overstepping anything."

Matt grinned from ear to ear. "Good. The last thing I want to do is cause you any more stress."

"It's just the opposite," she assured him. "Really, it is."

"Really?" he said, teasingly. They just sat there and smiled at each other for several minutes.

Finally Annie said, "I'm afraid to even look at my watch. It's got to be getting late." When she saw that it was after 10:30 p.m. her heart sank. She frowned and said, "I suppose I should get going. Morning comes early."

"Wow -- that time sure went fast. It seems like we just sat down."

Nodding in agreement, she started to gather her things. Matt hurried to her side of the table and helped her with her chair and then once she was standing, with her coat.

"Thank you," she murmured. "And thanks for the coffee too. I had a nice time."

"So did I. Um -- maybe we can do it again some time."

"That would be great," she answered quickly and then internally kicked herself for sounding too eager. She had done that with Eric when they met -- been too eager -- and she wasn't going to make that mistake again, no matter how wonderful this man was.

"Okay, then. Good." Now it was Matt's turn to blush and he smiled at her in spite of it. They threw away their coffee cups in the large plastic trash can and lingered by the door.

"Well, good night then," Annie said hesitantly. "I'll see you next time."

"Where are you parked?" he asked suddenly. "Can I walk you to your car? It can be dangerous around here at night, you know."

"I'm in the ramp," she replied. "And yes, I'd like that. Good idea."

They walked side by side to the elevators around the corner from the cafeteria. Matt pushed the "Down" button and then glanced toward Annie and said, "I just realized that this is the same place we first met. At the elevators here."

"So it is," remarked Annie, although this time she wasn't in a hurry for the elevator to arrive. She wanted this evening to last as long as possible.

## The Cello

With the divorce behind her, Annie was finally able to settle in to life at Frank and Sally's. She no longer felt as though she was walking a tightrope between what used to be and what lay ahead. She was living her new life now, not waiting for the moment she had permission to do so. Annie would have been the first to admit that this new life was a bit on the quiet side, but that was fine with her. Some of her friends had tried to persuade her to go out to singles' bars with them and had even brought up the subject of a blind date or two, but she wasn't interested. Not yet. What she needed was time to heal, first from the loss of Dillon and then the loss of her marriage. Both events were tragic and life-changing in themselves, but to have them both happen, only months apart, was hard for most of her friends to grasp. They tried to be supportive, but being young and idealistic, didn't want to be reminded of how lives could be shattered so unexpectedly. It was almost as though they worried that her bad fortune might be contagious. After the initial rallying-around period, most of them went back to tending their own gardens of hopes and dreams, afraid to divert their attention for even a second. What Annie longed to tell them, was that sometimes things happen no matter what you do, but she knew they'd never believe her and that they'd grow to hate her for her honesty. Sometimes she felt so much older than her twenty-nine years and other times so young, for here she was, living in her aunt and uncle's basement with nothing to show for all the life she'd just lived. Nothing, that is, but the scars and bruises that a broken heart can bring.

She sat on the couch in her little basement apartment, with an afghan she'd made as a teenager snuggled up around her shoulders, her journal in her lap and a cup of chamomile tea on the end table. The late afternoon sun was peeking in through the wooden blinds, making horizontal stripes on the notebook in front of her. Her pen was poised over the paper, ready to form words, but her attention was focused elsewhere.

She was looking across the room, at her cello, leaning in its case in the corner next to the steps. It had been untouched, for months. The day Dillon tried to make an early entrance into the world had been the last time she had played it. Each time she'd looked at her beloved cello since then, painful memories came flooding back; memories of how she'd spent hours playing lullabies to her unborn child, the melodic tones of the instrument vibrating against her pregnant belly. The music always seemed to make him calmer, which she took to mean that he had been lulled to sleep. She'd always felt so complete then, making the music that she loved, so close to the child she loved more than life itself.

The orchestra had been more than understanding, giving her an extremely generous leave of absence, but she knew that if she wanted to retain her position as the cello section's newest member, she couldn't stay away much longer. She just didn't know if she had the energy to go back yet. As much as she loved her career, it was very demanding. The orchestra performed three to four nights a week, usually Thursday through Sunday, with the week's music being distributed each Tuesday. That meant hours of practice on her own as well as with the rest of the musicians. It also meant being at the concert hall for four to five hours the evening of each performance. It was a huge commitment, but one that Annie had been passionate about making. To be granted an audition, let alone actually getting the position, was unheard of for someone her age. She knew how lucky she was and took her responsibilities seriously. Unfortunately, it had been one of the things that she and Eric had argued about the most while she was expecting Dillon.

Finally there had been a positive pregnancy test, only two months after starting with the orchestra. What timing! She hadn't felt well during her audition, but had chalked it up to nerves and stress. They had been trying to conceive for a little over a year with no success, so Annie had decided to accept the invitation to audition. It made no sense to turn it down, just in case she were to become pregnant. She had to live her life, not put it on hold for something that may never happen. There were plenty of professional musicians who had families and lives outside the concert hall. If they could manage it, so could she and Eric. The problem was that Eric wasn't so sure.

"Who's going to watch the baby while you're at work?" he asked one night while they were eating dinner.

"*You* will." Annie replied, her tone very matter-of-fact as she took another bite of green beans.

"But I can't be home four nights in a row every week," protested Eric. "I have meetings and events to go to for work. I told you that when you wanted to take that job."

"When I took the job I wasn't pregnant and didn't know if I ever would be. This is a great problem to have, Eric," she said excitedly. "We're going to be parents! We can figure the rest out as we go."

She reached across the table and took his hand. He seemed to flinch a little when she touched him. At the time she thought nothing of it, but looking back after all that had happened, she could see that it was a huge red flag. Of course, by that time, Dillon was already alive within her and growing bigger every day. There was no turning back, whether he was ambivalent about parenthood or not.

"Are there day care centers open at night?" he pulled his hand away and poured himself another glass of wine.

Annie couldn't stifle the giggle that bubbled up inside of her. "Now that's an oxymoron if I've ever heard one! A *nighttime* day care center! I guess they'd call that *night care*, huh?" she smiled at him, amused by the idea. Eric grimaced.

"It's nothing to joke about, Annie. What are we going to do?" His face had oozed into a frown, his eyes dark and his frown getting longer by the second.

"What do you mean, what will we do? You'll see your clients the nights I'm home. They're usually quite flexible -- and besides, they'll understand that you're a father now."

"Not yet," blurted Eric. "The baby's not here yet."

"Well, yes he is!" Annie patted her stomach and beamed happily. "He reminds me of that every time I throw up!" Morning sickness wasn't pleasant, but it was reassuring. It meant that the hormones were still coursing through her body, that the baby was still there and growing.

"Do you have to talk about that when we're eating?" he said and took a large swig of wine.

Annie looked down at her plate, and found it difficult to swallow the food in her mouth; it had trouble making its way past the lump in her throat.

Each time they discussed it, he had become more adamant about how inconvenient it would be for him to "babysit" when Annie had to be at work. She kept gently reminding him that when a father takes care of his own child, it's not called 'babysitting,' it's just part of being a parent. He'd scoff and mumble and stomp out to the garage for a cigarette. After a while, Annie started to dread the topic as well as the day when she would have to leave the baby home alone with Eric. He seemed so set against it, and it made no sense to her. Hadn't he thought about any of this while they were trying to get pregnant or had he only living in the moment, happy to be having sex so frequently?

"If you didn't have that *job*," he complained again one day, "*that's* the problem here."

"Eric, you keep saying that, but I could say the same thing. If only you didn't have that *job* that has you working day and night. You leave at 7:00 in the morning and don't get home until after midnight at least three nights a week." She imitated his whiny voice as she spoke.

"Well, that's the way my job is!" he said angrily.

"And that's the way *my* job is!" she shot back at him. "There aren't too many orchestras that perform from 9:00 - 5:00!"

They stood there, seething and glaring at one another. Finally, Eric spoke.

"You haven't been there that long. You could quit."

Annie drew her breath in sharply. "I can't believe you just said that. You know how long I've wanted to be in an orchestra. It's been my dream for as long as I can remember. Besides -- we need the money, don't we?"

"I'm not saying you shouldn't work. You could get a day job. Teach or something. You say that playing in an orchestra was your dream, but isn't having a baby more important?" He was not only pushing her guilt buttons, he was playing "Flight of the Bumblebee" on them.

That evening before the concert, she sat on stage after running through the final piece of that evening's program, and reviewed a section she was having trouble with. Jen, the woman who played first chair in the cello section, came over and put her hand on Annie's shoulder.

"Is everything ok, Annie?"

Startled by the touch, Annie jumped slightly and then smiled. "I'm fine, Jen. Don't I seem fine?"

"Well, you just seem a little preoccupied. I know how overwhelming it can be to be the "new kid on the block," I just want you to know that I'm here to help."

"Thank you. I appreciate that. Actually, can I ask you a personal question?"

"Sure." Jen sat down in the chair next to her.

"Do you have kids?"

"Yes, I have two. Why do you ask?"

"My husband and I want to start a family, but he's a little worried about how it will work for me to be a mom and play in the orchestra." Annie hadn't told anyone she worked with about her pregnancy yet -- it was still too new and it seemed too soon the share the news.

"Actually, it works out great," Jen said enthusiastically. "I can be home during the day, and can usually get my practicing done while the kids are napping. My husband is home in the evenings when I have to be here. He absolutely loves having his own time with the kids without me hovering around. It's been wonderful."

"That's good to know," Annie replied, feeling queasy as she spoke, not because of morning sickness, but because her gut was trying to tell her something she didn't want to hear.

When Annie's pregnancy was no longer a secret, she had confided some of her concerns about Eric to Jen, wondering if Jen's husband had worried so much about becoming a father.

"Oh, I think he probably did," Jen had assured her, "although he didn't talk about it much. I think it's fairly normal -- especially when the pregnancy is a surprise. We had been trying for quite a while, so we were both really excited. Eric will feel better once the baby's here -- he just doesn't know what to expect."

Annie had smiled on the outside, but inside, that queasy feeling reared its ugly head again. This pregnancy had not been a surprise -- it had been very much planned in the sense that they were trying to get pregnant. The surprise was Eric's attitude and apprehension -- she hadn't anticipated that.

"I'm sure you're right," she told Jen. "He'll be fine."

Looking back, she could see that he hadn't been fine. She had tried to rationalize, ignore, and downright deny the fact that Eric was not as excited about parenthood as she. Even if he was nervous, he still could have been excited, couldn't he? Lord knows she was apprehensive about all the unknowns that were ahead of them, but she was happy beyond belief at the same time. At the time she had tried not to dwell on it, but now, sitting in Sally's basement alone, it all made perfect sense.

How could she have been so blind? So stupid? What else could she have done? She had been living her life the way she thought she was supposed to. Things hadn't always been great, but she loved Eric and wanted their marriage to work. Eric was the one who switched gears mid-stream. He was the one who changed his mind once Dillon was no longer a wish but a real, live baby growing within her. And as painful as losing Dillon had been, she never wished he hadn't existed. Every moment he had been snuggled up inside of her had been precious and magical. No, she'd never trade that for anything, not even to have her marriage back. Anger flared deep within her. And Eric had the nerve to blame her for all of this. *How dare he!* she thought, her grasp tightening on the pen. *How dare he!*

Annie lowered her eyes to the notebook in her lap and saw that a big tear had plopped onto the ink and was making the words written there run together until they were no longer legible. This unexpected crying was getting old. How much longer would this go on? What phase of grief was she in now and for what? Her baby or her marriage? It was exhausting. She had to focus on something else.

The instrument in the black case on the other side of the room beckoned to her, quietly at first and then with increasing intensity. At first Annie did her best to ignore it.

After taking a sip of tea, she rearranged the afghan around her legs and repositioned the notebook in her lap, ready to do some more writing. Staring at the paper and clicking the button on the top of her ballpoint pen repeatedly, she waited for some coherent thoughts to flow from her mind through the pen to the paper. Writing about her anger toward Eric, about grief, about fear, might be helpful but she was so tired of it all.

Again, her eyes rested on the cello. It had been so long since she'd held it or even looked at it. Surely it would need to be tuned. That would be a good place to start; tuning it. Then if she felt up to playing it she would and if not, it could go back in its case. As far as she knew, she was home alone -- no one would have to know.

She stood up and kicked the afghan from around her feet. Bending over, she picked it up and draped it over the arm of the couch, patting it gently into place. Her heart was pounding as wildly as it had before her first audition. *This is silly*, she told herself, *get a grip. This is no big deal.* Annie grabbed the handle on the side of the case and lifted it gently from its place in the corner. She laid it carefully on the floor and knelt down to open it. It mortified her to see just how dusty the case was and she promised herself (and her cello) that she'd pay more attention to such details from that point on.

The strings were suspended loosely on the neck. Annie set about the business of turning the pegs to wind and adjust them to their correct notes. First the "A" string, then "D", "G" and finally "C". Sliding the bow over the strings, she lingered on the "C" string, her favorite. Its melodious depth was a sound that had always stirred something deep within her soul. Smiling, she closed her eyes, played another scale and then her favorite Bach concerto. This helped her remember why she played the cello -- it centered her and sustained a part of her in a way that nothing else could. It felt good to lean its neck against her shoulder and rest its body between her legs again. The firmness of its strings as she pressed her fingers on each of them sent shivers throughout her that ended in her heart. Satisfied, she sighed and smiled again.

"This is a sight for sore eyes if there ever was one!"

Startled, Annie opened her eyes at the sound of Sally's voice. "I didn't know you were home!" She was embarrassed to have her private moment of bliss witnessed by her aunt.

"It sounds beautiful. Don't let me interrupt, though. I was just passing through to the laundry room. Forget you ever saw me!" Sally said as she scooted around the corner and down the hall.

She closed her eyes and dragged the bow across the strings again, letting the sounds fill the emptiness she'd been carrying with her since Dillon had died. The rich, bass tones swirled around within her, making her tingle from the inside out.

Sally knocked on the open door to the hallway coming from the laundry room, a basket spilling over with clean laundry balanced on her hip. "Just me again. Sorry."

"Don't apologize, Sally. It's fine," assured Annie, resting the bow on her knee.

Sally hesitated for a second and then set the blue plastic basket on the floor. "Do you mind if I say something?"

"My practicing is going to bother you, right? It's more distracting than you thought it would be?"

"No, not at all, sweetie. It's incredibly beautiful. I know it's been a while, but I don't think I've ever heard you play so well."

"Really?" Annie was surprised. "I'm just doing what I've always done."

"Well, I'm no expert, but it sounds different to me -- in a good way. Whatever you're doing, keep it up! I love it and I'm sure Frank will too." She picked up the basket and headed for the stairway and then stopped before going to the upper level. "Does this playing your cello mean anything?"

Annie chuckled. "As in: am I going back to work anytime soon?" She knew that her aunt and uncle were worried about her. They had assured her that she could live with them indefinitely, but were concerned with how much time she was spending alone, wrapped in the afghan on the couch.

"Well, you know..." Sally fumbled with her words.

"Yes, it does mean something," Annie admitted. " Even though I'm nervous about it, I think it's time I go back."

"What are you nervous about?" Sally put the basket down again and sat down on the arm of the couch.

"I don't know -- just the whole thing. I was just getting comfortable being there when Dillon died. Everyone has been very kind, but there's a lot of politics that go on. I'm a little worried I'll be "punished" for being gone so long..."

"They'll have me to answer to if they even *think* about giving you a hard time," declared her aunt. "Besides, once they hear you play again, they'll be putty in your hands!"

"Oh, you think so, huh?" Annie laughed as she unfolded the black cello stand that had been stashed under the couch.

"I *know* so, my dear! I'm serious -- your music has a different tone. It's more -- I don't know what word to use -- *emotional*, than it used to be. I think everything you've gone through has made your music better. Does that make any sense?"

Annie cocked her head to the side as she contemplated Sally's observation. She'd heard of that happening to artists before; that they were able to transform their pain into beauty. She had never thought of herself as an artist, but perhaps it was time she started. One thing she knew for sure, was that she didn't think she could live without her music -- and if that didn't define her as an artist, nothing did.

Annie felt as though an entire percussion section was pounding within her chest as she tried to summon the courage to pick up the telephone receiver. As her hand reached for the phone, it jangled loudly announcing an incoming call, piercing the uneasy solitude. The ring made her jump from her seat on the plump, chenille couch.

"Stanford residence," Annie said into the mouthpiece, her heart still imitating a snare drum.

"Annie? Hi -- it's Jen from the orchestra."

"Hi Jen! How are you?"

"Forget about me-- how are *you*?" There was genuine concern in her voice.

"I'm doing well. It's sort of a one day at a time thing, I guess."

"I can't imagine how hard it must be. You've been through so much."

"Yeah, well...." Annie wondered when she'd come up with a good response to that well-meaning comment. Yes, she'd been through a lot, but others had been through so much more.

"I don't know if you got my message, but I called last week to let you know that we're going to be starting section practices for the new season soon. I'm hoping I can convince you to come back to us. We miss you."

Annie's heart skipped a beat. "Really?"

"Of course, *really*!" laughed Jen. "We've been doing okay with subs, but it's just not the same. Everyone feels just awful about what you've been through, so if you're not ready, they'll understand, but ...."

"But they won't wait forever?" Annie attempted to fill in the blank.

"No one has said *that* ..."

"It's ok -- I get it," Annie assured her. "Actually, I've been thinking about it more and more lately. I'm not sure if I'm ready, but I'd like to give it a try. It's the only way I'll find out."

"Oh good! I'm so glad!"

"Well, wait until you hear me play before you say that!" warned Annie, "I'm a little rusty."

"No worries! It will come back to you quickly. You just don't know what a relief this is! If you had decided to resign, Conrad was going to hire the latest sub -- and just between you and me, she's a bit *strange* -- so this is just wonderful! I'm going to call and tell him right this minute!"

Before she hung up, Jen told Annie she'd drop off the music she'd need to work on before the section practice, as well as the exact times and dates. Looking at the information she'd jotted down, Annie realized that this was really happening -- she was going back to work in two short weeks. She closed her eyes and said a little prayer to Dillon, "Please understand, sweetie. Mommy still misses you, but I miss my music too."

She couldn't have her son, but she could have what made life feel worthwhile and valuable. Nothing could replace Dillon or what being a mother meant to her, but music was all she had right now, and Annie was determined not to lose it as well.

The weeks of rehearsals leading up to opening night were fraught with tension and stress for Annie, but they also filled her with a sense of purpose and a feeling of competence; a reason to get up each morning. Jen had been right; it all came back very quickly. It wasn't long before her fingers were dancing up and down the neck of her cello, forming each note without her having to think about it. Frank and Sally were her biggest cheerleaders, encouraging her when she needed it most, as well as leaving her alone at just the right moments. For never having had children, they certainly knew how to be excellent parents.

Finally, it was opening night. All eyes were riveted to the stage as the musicians played the final chord of the last piece, a Mozart concerto. A silver cloud of silence hovered over the audience just long enough for them to absorb the splendor and harmony as it fell over them like delicate snowflakes. They broke out into thunderous applause. The conductor turned and took a bow and then fanned his outstretched arm toward the musicians sitting on the stage behind him. Joy soared within Annie's entire body, accompanied by much welcomed relief. She had done it!

After the curtain closed, she sat back in her chair and let out the huge sigh that she'd kept bottled up during the applause. Jen came over and gave her a hug.

"Good job, Annie! You were great!"

"Thanks, Jen -- I was so nervous!"

"Yeah -- I could tell by that 'deer in the headlights' look that you had on your face before the concert."

"Oh -- so you could tell?" Annie was so sure she had put on a facade of total confidence and tranquility.

"Just a tad!" laughed Jen. "But we've all been there. I didn't say anything because the last thing you needed was for someone to draw attention to it."

"I appreciate that!" The two women made their way backstage to the rehearsal room where they had stored their instrument cases. It helped Annie feel better to know that she wasn't alone. She felt welcomed by her fellow musicians and was so grateful for that camaraderie. There were always such horror stories about what prima donnas orchestra musicians could be and how newcomers were often put through hell before they were accepted. Annie wasn't sure why they were being so kind to her, but she decided not to overanalyze and just enjoy it.

Just then, one of the stagehands stuck his head around the corner. "Is Annie Stanford back here?"

Annie waved in his direction.

"Someone's here to see you," he announced and then scurried off to his next task.

Annie excused herself from the huddle of musicians packing up their instruments and hurried across the room and out into the semi-dark hallway, curious and excited to see who it was. She thought she'd caught a glimpse of Matthew Preston, the writer from her support group, in the audience, and was hoping that it was him. He'd hinted at the last meeting that he'd like to hear her play, but she hadn't let herself think about it too much.

With so much on her mind about just getting through the performance, wondering if Matt would be there would have thrown her into a complete tailspin. She had put it out of her mind, deciding that if he came, she didn't want to know about it until after the concert.

The backstage hall was dimly lit so that no superfluous light could sneak out onto the stage during a performance. Single light bulbs hung suspended within black wire cages, each impersonating a prisoner trying to outshine all the others. She wasn't even looking up at first, not wanting to appear too excited, so when she heard the familiar voice and then snapped her head up to see the familiar face, she froze in her tracks, unable to move or speak.

There stood Eric, looking particularly handsome in a black suit, holding a gigantic bunch of red roses arranged in a presentation bouquet, a wide ribbon of ivory satin tied around their long, elegant stems.

"You looked great up there tonight," he said quietly. "I was so proud of you."

Annie finally found her voice. "Eric -- what are you doing here?"

"What kind of welcome is that?" he chided her teasingly. "Aren't you happy to see me?"

Her heart was racing, beating wildly in her ears. "What are you doing here?"

"Can't a guy come to hear his beautiful wife -- I mean ex-wife -- make beautiful music?" He flashed an extra charming smile at her.

"You never wanted to hear me play when we were married. Why does it suddenly matter?"

He ignored her question and handed the flowers to her. "I thought you might like these."

When she didn't reach out to take them, he pushed them into her arms. The razor sharp thorns scratched her arm and she winced in pain. Reaching down to where the ribbon was tied, she carefully wrapped her fingers around the bouquet.

"Here," she held it out to him.

"What are you doing?"

"I don't want these. You shouldn't have wasted your money."

"Aw, come on Annie. Don't be like that." He kept his hands slung in his pockets and kept smiling at her. It was making her angry. She wanted him gone.

He reached out and put his hand on her arm that wasn't holding the flowers. "I thought we could go out for a drink or something --"

They hadn't had any physical contact for nearly a year -- since the night he'd left -- and it made the hair on the back of her neck stand up. She raised her arm in an attempt to remove his hand, but he tightened his grip, making it difficult to move.

"Let go of me," she hissed at him. The shadows from the lights above them cast a sinister grid across Eric's face. "You're hurting me."

He continued to grip her arm as he moved closer to her. Raising his other hand, he caressed the back of her head, then moved it down to her neck, "Aw, come on, Annie. It's so lonely in that big house." He kneaded her neck the way she'd always liked, but now it only filled her with disgust. The more she struggled, the rougher his touch became. For the first time in her life, she was afraid of him.

Before she could shake him off, the backstage door opened, throwing a rectangle of bright light into the hallway. She looked past Eric's shoulder to see Matt standing there, holding a bunch of white tulips. The moment he saw her with Eric, she could see his arm holding the bouquet drop slowly to his side.

"Matt! Wait!" she called out, shrugging out of Eric's grip. Eric was so startled, he loosened his grasp and his hands fell away. She quickly shoved the roses into Eric's arms and ran down the hall toward the sliver of light in which Matthew stood.

"Matt!" she exclaimed again when she reached him. "It's so good to see you!"

"Hi, Annie," he started, "I didn't mean to interrupt." He gestured toward the hallway and Eric standing there holding the roses, dangling by the ribbon. "I can talk to you later if it's a bad time..."

"No, it's a perfect time. Excellent. Your timing could not have been better!" she smiled at him in a panicked sort of way. He was a welcome sight. Not as dressed to kill as Eric, which made him look even better. A brown tweed sports coat worn over a white button-down collar shirt with no tie and khaki pants made him look irresistibly sweet and unassuming. He'd mostly worn jeans and sweaters to the support group meetings and seeing him this dressed up made Annie's heart dance a little minuet.

"These are for you," he said as he handed her the tulips. "They're not as impressive as those roses, but I thought you'd like them."

"I love them, Matt. They're my favorite." She gazed at them tenderly, a smile forming on her lips. She gave him a gentle hug.

"I'll let you get back to your friend --"

"No!" she responded quickly and then lowered her voice to a whisper. "That's Eric."

A knowing look settled over Matt's face. Annie had talked about the death of her marriage in the support group, so he had heard all about Eric. She didn't need to say another word.

"Would you like to go somewhere for coffee?" he asked as he looked past her down the hallway. Eric was leaning against the concrete wall, looking impatiently in their direction.

"I'd love to. I need to get my purse and pack up my cello, though, which unfortunately means I have to walk back down *there*." Now it was her turn to glance toward Eric, who was beginning to pace a bit. She knew that he wouldn't be able to last much longer without a cigarette. Even if he'd gone out to smoke at intermission, that was well over and hour ago. He may have become a stranger to her over the past year, but this was one thing that hadn't changed.

"Do you want me to go with you?" offered Matt, always the gentleman.

Annie thought about it for a second. If she had Matt accompany her, she'd either appear weak and helpless in Eric's eyes or give him an incentive to be even more cruel to her, or worse yet, to Matt. Who knows what he'd do or say in an attempt damage her budding friendship with this wonderful man? The fact that he'd shown up with that awful bouquet of roses, and had basically propositioned her, had shocked her. Touching her as roughly as he had, scared her into believing that if there hadn't been an interruption, he would've taken it further, which made her queasy to even think about. Was she making too much of it? This evening was forcing her into uncharted territory -- there was no doubt about that. *The old Annie would have been indecisive and timid,* she thought. *Not anymore. Those days are over.*

"Thank you, but I need to do this by myself. It will only take me a minute or two."

"How about I wait right here for you?" He smiled at her with blue eyes that melted the wall around her heart more with each blink. His gaze was so intent, so reassuring, it was difficult to look away.

"I'll be right back."

Matt gave her hand a little squeeze as she turned to go. Annie smiled at him and hurried back down the hallway. Eric stopped pacing when he saw her running in his direction.

"Who's *tha*t?" he demanded, nodding toward Matt, clearly annoyed.

*"That* is none of your business," she replied, her eyes blazing.

"So, is that your new *boyfriend*?" He said the word with disdain. "You can do better than that, Annie. I mean, come on -- *tulips*?" He chuckled a little. "After all, you've got *roses* right here." He opened his arms as if to say *Here I am*, roses and all.

Laughing voices trickled out of the practice room, reminding her of her fellow musicians and what she had just accomplished with them onstage that evening. A newfound strength bubbled up within her.

"And I've always *hated* roses," she declared, her voice firm and strong. "Go home, Eric. Give your roses to someone else. Just leave me alone." She pivoted on the ball of her foot and disappeared into the rehearsal room.

When she came out several minutes later, Eric was gone, but the roses remained, their soft, red petals peeking out from the trash can next to the door. One single rose lay across the cover of the trash can, its stem stuck through the program from the concert. On it was scribbled, "To Annie, with love, Eric."

Annie picked up the flower, avoiding the thorns, and inspected it with detached curiosity. Eric's audacity had angered her, but now, looking at the familiar handwriting on the program, she felt nothing but pity for him and even that seemed like a waste of energy. She brought it to her nose to smell its fragrant scent and then thrust it into the trash can with the others.

# The Tulips

Another white petal fell to the nightstand in a soundless descent. Annie saw it from where she sat propped up against her pillow and sighed. Putting down the book she was holding but not reading, she reached over to pick up the fragmented blossom. She smiled when she looked at it, remembering the night after her concert when Matt had given her the tulips. It had been nearly two weeks, and she was nursing the flowers along the best she could. The trouble with tulips, was once they bloomed, they didn't last very long. She wanted them to last forever. It was probably time to put the last of the wilting stems out of their misery, but she just couldn't bring herself to do it. Every time she saw them, her heart swelled with a feeling that she was beginning to recognize as happiness.

The petal felt smooth and delicate as she held it to her cheek and closed her eyes dreamily. She felt like a schoolgirl, swooning and fantasizing about the new boy who had asked her out on a date. Matthew Preston made her heart race and her palms sweat in a way that no one ever had before, but he also spoke to her soul, which was an entirely new experience for her.

After her concert they'd started out drinking wine and switched to coffee after only one glass, since they each had to drive home. Time seemed to stand still as they talked for hours, not even noticing when the waiter warmed up their half-empty coffee mugs. Eventually it was closing time and they had to go their separate ways.

"Well," said Matt as he glanced toward the bartender who was wiping down the bar, "it looks like they're getting ready to close for the night."

Annie pushed up the edge of her sleeve to peek at her watch and frowned when she saw how late it was. Matt grinned at her, "Time flies when you're having fun, doesn't it?"

Blushing, she smiled back. "You've got that right! It feels like we just got here." She fidgeted in her chair, not sure of what to do next. Obviously they'd have to leave, but then what? It became apparent that all the coffee she'd had to drink was making a trip to the rest room the first item on the "to do" list.

"Do you know where the rest rooms are?" She hated to admit that she even *had* bodily functions. "It's a long drive home..."

"Yes, I think they're right around the corner." Matt pointed toward the opposite side of the room. "I better stop in there too, now that you mention it."

Once in the rest room, Annie looked in the ornately framed mirror above the sink to see if she could still recognize herself. Yep -- there she was. Same blue eyes, same brown hair, same mouth, but somehow she was different. Her eyes were cheerful and vibrant, even though it had been a very long day, and she should have been exhausted. Her hair, which she had been so frustrated with earlier in the day, looked just fine to her now. And her mouth, well, that was the same too, but she discovered that she couldn't stop it from turning up at the corners in a gentle smile. Looking at her lips, she wondered what it would be like to be kissed by Matt, and then smiled even more. Her heart beat a little faster at the thought and when she glanced in the mirror again, a pink blush had covered her face. *Good Lord*, she thought. *Get a grip!* But it was *fun* to think about first kisses again, and she decided not to feel guilty about it. She took a couple of deep breaths as she washed her hands and then went back out to where Matt was waiting for her.

He was leaning against the wall just outside the little alcove where the rest rooms were located. His head was down, looking at a City Pages newspaper, but when he heard the door shut, he immediately looked up and smiled. He pushed himself off the wall, and walked over to meet her.

"I was just thinking," he started somewhat cautiously. "Would it be okay with you if we exchange phone numbers? If you don't want to I'll understand, but I just really like talking to you. I don't want to wait until the next support group meeting..."

"Sure." Annie tried hard to sound nonchalant, but was having difficulty keeping her joy from bursting from every pore.

"Are you *sure*?" His eyes lit up and he grinned from ear to ear.

"Yes, I'm sure! I've had a wonderful time tonight, Matt. I like talking to you, too. It's like we've known each other for years." She dug in her purse for a pen.

"I think so too. I felt that way when we had coffee a few months ago after the support group meeting that time, but figured you had enough going on without *my* complicating your life...but now, well, it's just hard to ignore it. So, if you're really sure it's okay, can I call you?" He handed her his phone number which he'd already jotted down on a square white cocktail napkin. As she reached out to take it, he blushed a little as he nodded his head sheepishly. "I was hoping you'd say 'yes.' Wishful thinking, I guess.."

Annie was touched by the emotions that were emanating from Matt. It was sweet, the way he was so concerned about her feelings; so afraid of being too forward. She took the napkin from him, knowing that she'd tuck it away in a safe place once she had written the number in her address book.

"Thank you," she said, smiling as she looked at it. "Here's mine." She grabbed a napkin from an empty table and quickly wrote down Frank and Sally's number. "I'm still at my aunt and uncle's house," she reminded him. "So don't be surprised if they answer." She suddenly felt embarrassed not to be living by herself. This was more like being a teenager than she'd planned on.

Matt seemed to sense the shift in her mood and stepped closer to her as he took the napkin from her outstretched hand. He very gently took her hand in his, raised it to his lips and gave it a kiss as delicate as the whisper that followed it. "It's okay, Annie. It's okay."

He then covered her hand with his as he looked into her eyes so deeply she was sure he could see every little thing she was thinking. Tears sprang to her eyes at feeling so transparent and yet so understood. Her cheeks burned as she felt a tear run down her face. He slowly reached out to catch it and then ever so softly ran the side of his index finger along her cheekbone. The tenderness of his touch was too much for her, and the tears kept falling.

"I'm sorry," she sniffled, "It's been an emotional night..."

He reached into an inside pocket in his jacket, pulled out a crisp linen handkerchief, and offered it to her. Annie had never seen a man in real life who carried a handkerchief and accepted it from him hesitantly. "Do you really want me to use this? I'll get it all messed up!"

"That's what it's for, silly!" His teasing voice broke the tension and lightened the moment. They both laughed a little. "Come here," he murmured as he wrapped his arms around her in a comforting hug.

The tweed of his jacket was soft against her cheek and his arms were strong and solid. Annie let herself melt into the moment. His embrace was reassuring and safe; she felt accepted. A long sigh escaped from deep within her as she somewhat painfully realized that Eric's arms had never felt like this. Whenever Eric held her, it had been a perfunctory sort of action that indicated that he had more important things to do, so let's get this over with, type of thing. It had never been this slow or prolonged. It had never provided this much peace.

"Thanks, I needed that," she said as she gently leaned back to look at him.

"My pleasure," he replied, his eyes shining. "I'm always willing to help."

The moment became increasingly awkward. Neither one of them seemed to know what to do. Every fiber in her being wanted Matt's arms around her again, but the voice in her head that was her common sense, was shouting out all sorts of warnings. It wasn't quite a year since the divorce was final. Everything she'd read stressed the importance of letting enough time pass before starting any new relationships, that to rush into a romance was the worst possible thing to do. Tell her heart (and the rest of her body) that, though. There was nowhere to put all the feelings that had blossomed within her; she couldn't hide them much longer. Spending time with Matt made her want to loosen the padlock and chains she had so securely placed around her heart. He seemed to appreciate and respect who she was as a person and what her life had become. His life had also taken some tragic turns, and if the trench that had been forged by his pain was as bottomless as the one that had been carved within her, their combined capacity for joy could be infinite. Annie believed that suffering made more room in her heart for happiness; that she couldn't truly experience one without the other. It was such a fine line that separated the two, if they could even be considered two different things. She had learned to think of them as two sides of a coin or better yet, two threads in a tapestry, good and bad woven together, side by side, over the course of time.

"I'll walk back to your car with you," he stated, "since mine's in the ramp too."

Nodding her agreement, they set out for the short walk to the orchestra hall's parking ramp. He held the door for her and she whispered her thanks. This was so unlike anything that Eric had ever done. He had usually led the way and let the door slam in her face, if she didn't pay attention. Matt's chivalrous actions made her feel special, not in a helpless way, but respected.

They walked down the street in semi-darkness, the only lights being the streetlights that punctuated each city block. There were other people leaving the bars and restaurants along the Nicollet Mall, some deep in conversation, some giggling and laughing, and others walking along silently side by side, together but alone. A half block into the walk, Annie felt Matt reach for her hand. She let him find it and their fingers laced together as though they'd been holding hands for years. She smiled at him and he gave it a playful squeeze. Her heart soared although she tried to leash it in by telling herself that of course this was exciting and wonderful, but that feeling this good wouldn't, *couldn't* last forever.

Eventually they made it to the ramp where their cars were parked. Hers was on the ground level, his was one level up. Annie reached into her purse and felt for her keys. Her hand was shaking a little, and when she found the jumbled set of keys, she clutched them, attempting to calm down.

"Well, here we are," she said, as they approached her car. "Thank you for a wonderful evening."

"It did turn out to be pretty wonderful, didn't it?" He looked at her intently. "Thank *you* for agreeing to go out after the concert. You made it all possible." His eyes twinkled when he smiled, which Annie was finding terribly sweet and delicious. It also totally unnerved her.

"Well, I don't know....," she fumbled for the right words and then decided that it didn't matter. The words didn't have to be right. "How about another hug?"

His face brightened and he beamed at her as he opened his arms to encircle her within them. This time she hugged him back, not as a crying woman needing comfort, but as an equal counterpart, who liked, respected, and was really attracted to this incredible man who seemed to feel the same way about her. His embrace was different than it had been at the bar. The caution was replaced with deliberate emotion that enveloped her completely. They held on as though they never wanted to let go, now that they had found each other. It crossed Annie's mind that this must be what it feels like to find your way back home after you've been lost for a very long time.

She knew that if she looked at him, she'd want to kiss him. She hadn't even wanted to kiss anyone for so long and it had been so long since she had -- would she remember how? If she initiated a kiss, would he think she was a floozy? If he kissed her first but she kissed him back, would that be too brazen as well? She hadn't gotten so lost in the moment that she wasn't able to think straight. Then she remembered that one of the problems with Eric had been that she had hidden her feelings more than she had expressed them. Good or bad, feelings are feelings, and it's okay to have them *and* to share them. To care too much about what someone else thought of her had not served her well *ever*, so why was she worrying about that now? Why was she even thinking about all of this while being held in the arms of the most amazing man she'd ever met? What was wrong with her?

Her crazy, random thoughts were brought to a screeching halt when Matt's arms were no longer around her, but instead, his hands were gently framing her face, his gentle gaze resting on her like a whisper. Before she could analyze the situation, she felt his lips upon hers, as soft and silky as the petals from the tulips her had given her earlier that evening. She allowed herself not to think, or worry or wonder about anything, but to be transported for that moment, to a place so new and different that surely they had to be the first two people to ever travel there. As quickly as it had begun, it was over, ending with Matt kissing her forehead as though she were made of delicate porcelain. He then rested his forehead against hers and they smiled into each others eyes.

The spell was broken when the car alarm of a minivan parked at the other end of the ramp started shrieking incessantly, startling them both so that they knocked foreheads as they jumped. Simultaneously they dissolved into laughter, each rubbing their heads as they tried to catch their breath.

"This is definitely one of my smoother moments," laughed Matt. "Talk about first kisses going bad!"

"I wouldn't say that," said Annie, still giggling, "I'd say it ranks right up there at the top of the list!"

"As '*Most memorable due to head injuries*'?" Matt chuckled, and then turning serious, he gently touch her forehead. "Are you sure you're alright?"

"I'm fine. How about you?" She ran her fingers over the red spot above his right eyebrow, a cautiously intimate gesture.

He smiled, took her hand, kissed her fingertips and then held it to his cheek. "I'm just wonderful, Annie Stanford. Just wonderful."

# The Stained Glass Windows

Annie took an absentminded sip from her coffee mug as she studied the classified ads, circling the possibilities with a black Sharpie. The choices looked promising: $550/ 1 BR/ HW floors/Security and $650/ 1 BR / New carpet, were just two of many. She was finally looking for a place of her own. As the months ticked by, she felt more like an intruder at Frank and Sally's, as well as a freeloader. They refused her offers to pay them room and board, which left her frustrated and embarrassed. After all, she was an adult; a gainfully employed adult at that. There had also been a fairly large settlement in the divorce, since Eric had to buy out her half of the house. She was more than able to contribute financially, but Sally insisted that she save that money for her own place, whenever the time was right, and that time had arrived.

Matt was becoming a frequent visitor, and while they were taking things slowly, every time he came over, she felt more like a teenager than the grown woman she was. In many ways it was a good thing -- sort of like a built-in chaperone. It kept her from taking her relationship with Matt to a more intimate level; something she wanted to do, but at the same time the thought terrified her. Lora, her friend from the support group, had just spoken to her about it the night before, after the group met. Matt had hurried out of there right after the meeting, since he had a deadline looming, and needed to get home to write.

"He certainly is devoted, isn't he?" Lora mused after having watched Matt say good-bye to Annie. "It's as though he couldn't bear to leave you. I don't think my husband has *ever* looked at me like that."

Annie blushed from the tips of her toes all the way to her hairline. She shrugged and smiled as if to imply, *"What can I say?"*

"So," continued Lora as she put an arm into the sleeve of her jacket, "exactly how close *are* you two, if you know what I mean?" She gave Annie a covert wink.

"Lora!" Annie exclaimed in mock outrage and then added. "Well, I *do* live with Frank and Sally, you know...."

"Sort of cramps your style, does it? I can see that. What about his place?"

"A little nosy, aren't we?" Annie was more amused than offended. "To be honest, though, it's sort of a relief, making it less convenient, to, um, you know --"

"Have *sex*?" Lora said in a hushed voice. "Oh honey -- what are you waiting for?"

Annie and Lora made their way down the hall to the elevators. They had lagged behind enough so that they were alone, the other group members already gone. Annie pushed the "Down" button and turned to her friend.

"To be honest, I'm scared. I'm afraid that once we get to that point, everything will fall apart; it will all be ruined. Or, if that *doesn't* happen, then what?"

"Then you'd be happy?"

"But I'm happy *now*."

"Then you'd be happi***er*** ?"

"But as wonderful as Matt is, should I depend on him to make me happi***er***?"

Lora looked at her, shaking her head slowly, her eyes softening with understanding.

"Listen to me. You're responsible for your own happiness. You've been through hell this year. You've worked hard at healing; you're doing a great job of getting back on your feet. What's wrong with being with a man who obviously adores you? What's the harm if you're happy when you're with him? Matt is not *anything* like Eric. And he *gets* it. He's suffered losses of his own. He respects you, Annie. He's not going to bulldoze his way into your life and then break your heart. I just know that he'd never do that."

"What if it's too soon? Even you admit that I've been through a lot. What if I'm not ready and I break *his* heart?"

The elevator finally arrived. It was full of people leaving the hospital after visiting hours. On the silent ride down, Annie observed the various passengers, crammed into the elevator car like a can of sardines. An older couple, with white hair and deeply lined faces, stood in the corner, holding hands. Knobby, bent fingers were laced together like a shoe. It was difficult to tell where one of them started and the other ended. Their expressions were serene, content. What a wonderful picture they made, she thought as she studied them. They were a powerful advertisement for marriage. Next to them was a couple in their late teens, clearly in the throes of young love. The boy rested his hand on the girl's hip and she in turn had tucked hers into the back pocket of his jeans. His thumb moved back and forth, grazing the skin exposed at the top of her low-rise jeans. Both of their mouths were curled into dazed, intoxicated smiles, their eyes glassy with hope and lust. The young girl sighed softly and rested her head on the boy's chest. It was a moment ripe with sweet tenderness and unbridled passion. The air around them almost sizzled with the heat they generated.

Annie found herself feeling jealous of both couples, coveting what they had that she never did and possibly never would. Then it occurred to her that she *had* felt similar to how they both looked, in the time since she'd met Matt. Their first dates and the high she reached just talking with him was like nothing she'd ever known before. When his fingers brushed hers, it was as though an electric current traveled through her entire body. The first time he kissed her in the parking ramp was a moment that she replayed over and over again in her mind. Each time the memory became more delicious, just as each subsequent kiss had been. At other times, she felt like they were a pair of old shoes, broken in just right, that had been side by side forever.

"You look like the cat that just swallowed the canary," commented Lora as the elevator bounced to a stop. "A penny for your thoughts."

"Oh, nothing," lied Annie, looking down at her feet.

"Yeah, right," teased her friend, nudging her with her elbow as they exited the elevator. "I wish thinking of nothing made *me* glow like that!"

"Yeah, well...."

"Well, nothing, my dear. I hate to tell you this, but you look like someone who's in love, whether you're ready or not." She gave her a quick hug. "I've got to run. See you next time!"

"Okay. Bye!" Annie gave her friend a little wave, and hurried to her car.

Annie's mind was whirling on the drive home, with images of the people in the elevator intertwined with thoughts of Matt, and peppered with Lora's comments. What if Lora was right? What if love had found her, even if she hadn't been looking for it? She didn't have to be jealous of what anyone else had, because she could have it too, if she was just willing to accept it. What *was* she waiting for?

As she signaled her lane change to get off the freeway, she was hit with the realization that the main thing holding her back was fear. She was afraid that the happiness would run out, just as it had with Eric. There had never been this much happiness, ever before in her life. She had been happy while she was pregnant, but it had been contaminated with Eric's ambivalence and infidelity. So much of that time had been filled with insecurity and doubt that the good feelings had been hidden in a shroud of fear.

Matt was slowly but surely showing her that there didn't have to be fear or insecurity anymore. He was helping her remember how to live in the moment, how to laugh and be silly, but most of all, how to trust. That, she admitted, was the hardest part. Her trust in just about everything had been shattered, and in many ways, so had Matt's. He knew what it was like to have the rug pulled out from under his world, and he knew what it was like to start over. He was more than willing to help, but she also knew that she had to do it herself. It was time to start.

"There's a six or a twelve month lease option," explained the landlord as he led Annie down the hallway to the apartment. "The rent's a little higher for the shorter lease, but everything else is the same."

Annie followed behind him, taking quick strides to keep up with him. He was an older man, a cantankerous yet affable type, his plaid flannel shirt straining across his broad shoulders. The lines from where he had raked the comb across his hair made an intricate design on the top and sides of his head. Salt and pepper hair swept from a part above his left ear, up and around to the other side, ending squarely above his right ear. A generous application of Brylcreem or some other type of hair tonic kept it all in place. Annie vowed to herself that no man of hers would ever have a comb over, if she had anything to say about it. A smile came to her lips as she imagined what Matt would look like with his hair like that. Her heart fluttered a little as she realized what she'd just done; imagined Matt in the future, a future that she hoped to be a part of. The amazing thing was that she'd like him no matter what he did with his hair.

"Well, here we are."

They stopped in front of the door to the apartment. It was an older building, with two stories and four apartments on each level. They were looking at Apt. E. Annie hoped that the inside was as nice as the beautiful mahogany door with the stained glass transom above it.

"This is a gorgeous door," she said as the landlord fumbled for the correct key on his keyring. "I love the stained glass."

"Yeah, that was my wife's idea, God rest her soul. She thought it would add some *'charm,'* as she put it." He smiled wistfully.

"She was right. It's wonderful."

He turned the key in the lock and turned the glass doorknob carefully. "She wanted these fancy doorknobs too, which I thought was a little much, but what do I know?"

"They remind me of the doorknobs that my grandma's house had when I was little. They're lovely."

"She was all about lovely. Well -- here it is." He opened the door dramatically and gestured for Annie to enter. "Since it's empty, take as much time as you want looking around. I've got to run downstairs for a minute. Just close the door if you leave before I come back up."

"Okay -- thanks Mr. --"

"Jacobsen. Everyone calls me Jake for short." And with that, he bustled back down the hallway to the stairs.

It was nice to be able to explore the apartment by herself. Sally had offered to come with, as had Matt, but she wanted to do it alone. It was important to her to make a decision based solely on what *she* wanted. Once she found a place she really liked, she might bring someone else to see it, but she had to trust her instincts. She was the only one who had to live here and she was the only one who had to like it.

"I only have one request," Matt told her the evening before. "I just want it to be safe. I can't imagine having you live somewhere dangerous."

This building was on a nice, well-kept street in a fairly quiet neighborhood. It had a good security system and a small parking lot adjacent to it. The fact that there were only eight units made it feel safer as well. Less people coming and going, and easier to get to know everyone.

One glance inside, and Annie was ecstatic that it would pass the safety test, because it was everything she hoped it would be. The hardwood floors gleamed in the afternoon sunlight that shone through the stained glass transoms above the bay window in the living room. The living room and dining room were adjoined by a graceful arch of oak woodwork, giving it a charming, old-fashioned feel. The kitchen was next to the dining room. It was small, but adequate. The appliances were older, but clean, and if they worked, that's all she really cared about. The bedroom and bathroom were on the other side of the dining room, separated by French doors. The bedroom was larger than she expected, with a little sitting area off to one side. The bathroom was at the end of a short hall just inside the french doors. It had a claw foot bathtub with a shower in it, and an old-fashioned pedestal sink. It was charming.

Annie could see herself living there, but had trouble imagining the details. Since she had little or no furniture, she'd be starting from scratch. Eric had insisted on keeping all the furniture and when she moved to Frank and Sally's she had no need for it anyway. Her stomach sank a little at the thought of furnishing an entire apartment, but it was also kind of exciting. She had the money from the divorce, but wanted to spend as little as possible. For the first time in her life she had money in the bank and she wanted to keep it there. As she walked from room to room, it occurred to her that she could go to thrift shops to find what she needed; it didn't have to be brand new. *It sure would be great if people threw divorce showers,* she mused as she listed the things she'd need to buy in her head.

She sat down in the middle of the living room floor, drawing her knees up to her chest and hugging them tightly. Looking around the room, she pictured an overstuffed sofa with flowered pillows and a large comfy chair and ottoman. She imagined a round wooden table and chairs in the dining room, maybe on top of a large area rug. She *could* see herself living there, even if she had nothing. It felt right; it felt as though she belonged. So many questions came flooding in: Six months or twelve? When should she move? When could she show Matt, and Sally and Frank? Curtains or blinds? Would Mr. Jacobsen let her paint the bedroom walls a soft shade of blue? Where would she put her cello? Would the neighbors be annoyed when she practiced?

"So, what do you think?" It was Jake. He appeared out of nowhere, a friendly grin on his face. "You look like you feel right at home!"

"Oh -- hi!" Annie felt her face turning pink, wondering how long he'd been standing in the open doorway.

"Any questions about the place? Like I told you, utilities are covered. You just have to pay for the phone. The neighbors are all real friendly. Most of them have been here a long time. It's a good bunch."

"How soon do I have to let you know?" Annie asked as she stood up, self-consciously brushing off the seat of her pants.

"Well, another couple just called to come and look at it, but if it's already been spoken for -- then I'll tell them to never mind coming. So, the sooner the better. If you're interested, that is."

Annie knew she had to make a decision. On one hand, there was no rush. Sally and Frank weren't evicting her, but she had a sense of urgency about this. It was as though all the forces in the universe were cheering her on, encouraging her to move forward. She wanted to get another opinion, but why shouldn't she trust her gut? There wasn't a thing she didn't like about this place. It was clean and in great condition, it had off-street parking, it was close to Orchestra Hall and the rent was in her comfort zone.

"I'm very interested, Mr. Jacobsen. In fact, I'd like to rent it." The moment she said it, she felt weightless, as though she might float away.

"Okay, but there is one problem I can see right now." His forehead was furrowed in concern. "And if we can't fix it, then I'm not so sure it's gonna work out." He scratched the five o'clock shadow on his chin.

Annie gulped. "What's that? I can get you extra references if you'd like. I know I don't have any rental history, but I did own a house --"

"If you're gonna live in my building --" He hesitated, peering out from under his massive eyebrows streaked with gray. "No more of this 'Mr. Jacobsen' business. You've gotta call me by my real name. Jake." He squinted at her, trying to look serious.

The knot that had formed in Annie's stomach untied itself as she let out a deep breath of relief. "Oh -- yes -- of course! Jake. I can do that!"

"Okay then! You're in!" He beamed as he shook her hand vigorously. "I'll need some paperwork filled out, and a small deposit in order to hold it for you. It's not that I don't trust you, but I've been burned a few times. People say they're gonna move in so I take the ad out of the paper and then I never hear from 'em again. I started doing this a while ago. I hope you don't mind."

"No, of course not," said Annie. "I don't mind at all. Is it ok if I bring a couple of friends by to see it? Oh -- and when can I move in?" Having never done this before, she wasn't sure how to handle all of the details.

"Seeing as it's vacant, you can move in as soon as you'd like."

"That sounds great!" Annie's heart was thumping wildly, the way it did when she was either really nervous or really excited. This time she was both. It wasn't like her to make decisions so quickly, but then again, maybe it was. She could do anything she wanted; she only had herself to answer to, right?

Annie went down to Jake's first floor apartment office with him to fill out the rental agreement and to give him the deposit to hold the apartment for her. His place was very cozy and more than a little disheveled. In the corner of the dining room was a small desk, stacks of paper covering the calendar desk blotter. Annie could see beneath the piles that the calendar was from the previous year, June to be exact. Her breath caught in her throat for a second, because that was Dillon's month. Jake caught her looking at the desk.

"Yeah -- I haven't gotten around to changing that calendar yet."

"Oh -- I hadn't noticed." Annie was ashamed of herself for staring.

"That's when Maggie passed on." A sad look washed over his face. The Mrs."

"Oh, Jake. I'm so sorry."

"Thanks. Yeah -- Maggie was the business person in this setup. She'd have a fit if she could see how I've messed up her desk here."

"I don't think she'd mind that much." Annie didn't have a clue as to what type of person Maggie Jacobsen was, but she didn't know what else to say. She just knew that Jake seemed like a good person and she wanted to help him feel better

"Oh, I don't know about that." He smiled sadly. "She was a stickler for details. Everything always had to be perfect. I'm sure she'd find plenty wrong with how I'm doing things." He fiddled with a blown glass paperweight in the shape of a fish, keeping his eyes on the desk.

"Well, things look good to me. After all -- I want to live here, don't I?"

"You got a point there!" He glanced toward her, smiled and took a deep breath. "So, let's get down to business."

Jake cleared a spot on the dining room table for Annie to fill out the paperwork. He busied himself with some chores out in the kitchen and listened to his off-key whistling while she filled in the blanks. Relieved to have brought her checkbook, she carefully wrote out the check for the deposit and got up to bring everything to Jake.

"I think I'm finished with this," she said, handing him the paperwork and the check.

He looked it over quickly. "Yep. It looks good. Let me give you a receipt."

Annie's eyes surveyed the room as he hunched over the desk, writing on a small pad of paper. There were doilies on the backs of the chairs and on the end tables under the clay pots of African violets, no doubt put there by Maggie. On a small table near the front door was an old photograph of a bride and groom in a silver frame. Annie sauntered over to it to get a better look. The couple in the picture were very young and looked to be very much in love. It had been a simple wedding; simple but elegant. The bride wore a long, white dress with no train and held a bouquet of tulips and daisies. The groom wore a military uniform. The bride was smiling at the camera as the groom gazed lovingly at her, his hand holding hers. It was clear from the expression on the man's face that he was utterly devoted to his bride and that it was the happiest day of his life. Annie was startled by Jake's voice.

"That's my Maggie there, on our wedding day."

"She was beautiful. And you were quite handsome yourself." Annie turned to look at him and thought she saw a tear in his eye.

"It was a great day," he said as he reached in his back pocket for a handkerchief. "Her parents weren't too keen on the idea of her marrying me, but eventually I won them over."

"Well, how could you not?" Annie smiled at him. "What year did you get married?"

"It was 1945. Times were tough because of the war, but we made it okay."

They stood in silence, looking at the picture a while longer. Jake seemed to have been transported back to another time, a small smile softening his face. Annie tried to imagine how Maggie must have felt on that special day that signaled the first day of her new life with this man next to her. Suddenly the grandfather clock in the corner of the dining room chimed one, two, three, four times, bringing them back to the moment.

"Holy cow -- would you look at the time?" Jake said, not even having to look at the clock.

"Yes, I better get going." Annie adjusted her purse over her shoulder. "Is it alright if I bring one of my friends over to see the place tonight or tomorrow?"

"Sure. No problem. I'm always here. Just give me a call when you're on your way."

"Thank you so much, Jake. I'll talk to you soon!" Annie shook his hand and hurried out to her car.

Once in her car and ready to leave, she surveyed the building again before driving away. A warm, cozy feeling bubbled up inside of her as she realized that this was a very special day for her, as it signaled the beginning of her new life, just as Maggie's wedding day had back in 1945. As Annie turned the key in the ignition, she smiled as she realized that there were many kinds of new beginnings; that new lives didn't have to start with a wedding or with a baby. A new life could start anytime, anywhere, just as long as someone was ready to start over. She was ready. *This is it*, Annie thought. *My new beginning!*

## The Calendar

The calendar pages ruffled in the warm evening breeze from the open window. The heading still read "May" even though that month had been over for nearly a week.

It had been a busy month. Annie had moved into her new apartment, and had been working tirelessly to furnish and decorate the place in addition to her job with the orchestra. Things were coming together nicely, and while she enjoyed poking around thrift stores and antique shops for unique items for her new home, she also was anxious to be done. Her job was demanding; she needed to practice daily, and she found that the music required her undivided attention. If her mind wandered while she played, contemplating which type of lamp would look the best next to the rocking chair, she often found herself either lost in the piece or playing the same stanza repeatedly. She was also spending more and more time with Matt. Lora had been right; she was in love. Matt was becoming a bigger part of her life. Each and every day was brighter because of him, even when they did nothing more than ordinary things, such as going for a walk or reading the newspaper together. There just didn't seem to be enough hours in the day to be with him; quite a contrast to what her life had been like earlier in the year.

"Dinner was wonderful," Matt said as he brought their plates over to the sink.

Annie was standing at the sink, lost in thought. Her mind had wandered back to the week before Dillon died, when he was still safely cocooned within her. Eric had been out with a client, and so like so many evenings before, she was home alone. Normally Annie wouldn't have liked the solitude, but the pregnancy had been a gift in that way. Eric's erratic work schedule felt more tolerable as long as she had the baby to keep her company. She'd spent the evening working on a counted cross-stitch birth sampler for the baby and watching T.V. With her feet propped up on an extra pillow on the ottoman, she mostly listened to the rerun of "Newhart" that droned on in the background as she concentrated on stitching perfect x's to make a little brown teddy bear. Every so often she would feel a kick or a stretch from within her belly and every single time it made her smile. She'd pat the place where the movement had been and decided that she had to be the luckiest person on the planet to be this baby's mother. After one particularly energetic punt to her pelvis, she realized that she had to go to the bathroom yet again. It had only been fifteen minutes since the last time.

"This is getting old, little guy." She hoisted her swollen body out of the chair. "I know it's not your fault," she patted her tummy, "but can't you let me sit a little while longer?"

Part way down the hall, she felt a strange twinge in her lower back and an unusual tightening around her belly. *Braxton hicks,* she thought. The feeling went away but then came back minutes later with more of a vengeance. *Weird,* she mused. *Is this what I get to put up with now?* Annie contemplated calling Eric, but she knew how irritated he got when she disturbed him at work, especially in the evening. Instead, she went to the pile of books stacked on the nightstand by her bed and plucked the one from the top: What to Expect While You're Expecting, nestled it under her arm and lumbered back to her spot in front of the T.V.

The book had become her bible during the previous seven and a half months and she knew it inside out. She didn't even have to look in the index to find the chapter she needed. The section on "Labor and Delivery" was well-read and the corners of the much-turned pages had become dog-eared and ragged. She glanced over the paragraph on how to know if you're really having labor pains or not. It said that if you put your feet up, rest and the sensations stop, then it's not the real thing. The theme song to the next sitcom was starting to play, and Annie decided that if the twinges didn't go away by the time the first commercial was over, she'd call Eric. As she waited for the minutes to pass, she paged ahead in the book, skimming through the chapters. The pages stopped rippling and laid open on "Complications: Stillbirth." Her eyes closed quickly, as if to protect herself from seeing the word. Slowly, she pried open one eye and then the other, to read the words printed there. She cradled her unborn baby with both of her hands, willing it to kick her again. "Go ahead, Baby, let me have it. Right in the bladder." A swift kick was delivered seconds later and she laughed out loud. "Oh thank you! Thank you,

God!" She shivered and closed the book with a thud. *Stillbirth. How did anyone survive* that?

She had survived, and three hundred and fifty-nine days later, some days were still a struggle. With all the progress she had made, she was still in survival mode. Today was one of those days.

Matt put his arms around her and kissed the back of her neck. "Earth to Annie."

"Oh -- I'm sorry." Annie put her hand to his cheek. "What did you say?"

"You okay?"

"I'm fine. I was just day dreaming for a second."

"Okay," Matt rubbed her neck and shoulders. "Can I ask you something?"

"Sure." Annie got back on task and continued to rinse off the dinner plates.

"It's about the calendar."

Annie stiffened a little. "What about it?"

"Well, it's still on 'May'."

"So?"

"It's June." He gave her arm a gentle squeeze.

"It is?" She pretended to be surprised. "Boy, that month went fast." The plate in her hands nearly had its design rubbed off, she was scrubbing it so hard. "Where did the time go?"

"Annie, look at me." Matt turned her to face him.

The moment her eyes met his, the tears that had been forming spilled over and ran down her cheeks. He wrapped his arms around her and pulled her closely to him. Feeling the strength and comfort of his embrace, Annie let all the grief and sadness flow out of her, and sobbed into his shoulder, making a big, round tearstained spot on his shirt. He put a protective hand on the back of her head, and kept it there until the first ragged gasps of breath were needed.

"Dillon's birthday is next week," she sniffled.

"I know." Matt took out his handkerchief and dabbed her tears as he spoke.

"I'm not trying to avoid it or anything. It's all I can think about. God, Matt, a year ago tonight I went into the hospital. A year ago tonight he started to die." A new wave of pain washed over her and she buried her face in his chest and sobbed.

The timing of Annie's move had been both a curse and a blessing. It made her think about something besides the upcoming anniversary, but also left her unprepared to face the month or the day. Unbeknownst to Matt, she'd sat with the calendar in her lap after she bought it before Christmas, staring at the date of Dillon's birthday, June 10th. It would be on a Wednesday this year. She would sit and gaze at it; touching the solitary square lovingly, as though it were Dillon himself. It had become such an obsession that she had to force herself not to look at it, which was silly, because she knew it by heart. How ironic that now, when the calendar pages had been flipped over, month by month, and it was finally "his" month, she couldn't bring herself to face it.

"It all feels pretty raw again, doesn't it?" Matt ran his hand over her hair, smoothing it as he spoke.

Annie nodded, unable to speak. She wiped her nose with the back of her hand.

"The first anniversary of Sara's accident was almost worse than the day it happened. I wasn't numb or in shock anymore; the reality of it hit me hard. It was tough, because even though everyone expected me to remember it, they didn't expect me to feel so bad. Hell -- *I* didn't expect it." Matt blotted her hand with his handkerchief.

"I'm so sorry you had to go through that." She reached up and moved a strand of hair away from eyes that were seeing unspeakable pain all over again.

"*I'm* not. If I hadn't gone through that, I wouldn't know how you're feeling right now. And I still don't know *exactly* --- I'm just guessing." He gathered her into his arms again and they stood there, trying to absorb each other's sadness.

Annie took a deep, shuddering breath as she pulled back to look at him. "I am convinced that God sent you to me. I am so blessed."

He planted a gentle kiss on her forehead. "No, *I* am the lucky one. You are why I'm still on this earth, Annie; why God didn't want to take me when I thought I should go."

That comment brought more tears to both of their eyes and they clung to each other, rooted to the square of tile under their feet. The connection she felt to this man never ceased to amaze her. Even when she tried to downplay or second-guess it, something like this happened, where it seemed as though he could peer through her eyes into her soul, and know exactly how she was feeling. The beautiful part was that even though he already knew so much, he never tired of listening to her. He treated every word she uttered as compelling and important. There were times when she actually felt uncomfortable, because his attention was so riveted on her. However, as uncomfortable as she was, she was also flattered and pleased to know that he cared; that he was that interested.

Annie sniffled and shimmied out of Matt's arms to reach for a Kleenex from the box on the counter.

"You can use my handkerchief, you know," he reminded her.

"I know, but why get it dirty when there's a perfectly good box of Kleenex right here?" She pulled two tissues out and blew her nose. "God, I hate it when I cry. Now I'm shot for the night."

Matt shook his head and rolled his eyes toward the ceiling. "You look wonderful."

"Are you crazy? Look at me. My nose is all red and my eyes are all puffy. I look pathetic."

He took her hand and led her over to the burgundy velour couch. Very gently, he plopped her down on the velvety cushion and sat next to her. He put his arm around her and she settled into him, holding his free hand in both of hers. She laid her head back against his shoulder and closed her eyes. The intensity of the last few minutes had exhausted her. She felt as though she was made out of lead.

"This is nice," she murmured, her eyes still closed.

"It is, isn't it?" Matt raised her hand to his lips and gave it a soft kiss.

She sighed and snuggled into him a little more. "Thank you for being so understanding."

"You're welcome." His voice had become a whisper and he squeezed her hand.

They sat there for a few minutes, savoring the silence. The only sounds were the animated voices of neighborhood children playing outside. It made Annie's heart hurt to listen, knowing that she would never hear Dillon's voice call out to his friends while he played with them on a warm summer evening. A part of her worried that she'd never even have children, that she'd never know the joy that childbirth could bring, not just the sorrow.

A heavy sigh, laden with a labyrinth of regret and longing, escaped her throat with an intensity much stronger than she intended. Matt untangled himself from her grasp and shifted to face her, his eyes shrouded in concern.

"You okay?"

Annie closed her eyes as if to gather strength. She took in another deep breath and let it out slowly, hesitating before she answered him. "No, I'm not. It seems as though everything reminds me of Dillon these days." A shiny new tear slid down her cheek.

"That's to be expected, honey. His birthday is coming up. It's normal." Matt rubbed her arm tenderly.

"But Matt, don't you see how unfair this is to you? This is no way to act. You deserve so much better than this."

Matt's expression clouded. "What's this about, Annie? It's not just about Dillon, is it?"

"Well, it is and it isn't," she started. "I don't know how to say this."

"It's ok. Just say it. I'm listening." He patted her hand in encouragement.

"Ok. Promise you won't be upset."

"Annie, you're scaring me now. What is it?"

"You know how we haven't spent the night together yet; how I didn't feel comfortable doing that while I lived at Frank and Sally's?" she hesitated. It was impossible to pick at her nail polish while he held her hands.

"Go on," he urged.

"And you know how I've always stopped us before we go too far ---"

Matt grimaced. "Uh -- yes. Yes, I *do* know that." He squirmed uncomfortably.

"Well, how do you feel about that?" she blurted.

Matt looked like he'd been knocked over. He drew back from her a little, although never letting go of her.

"How do I feel about that? Is this a trick question?" He looked at her out of wary eyes.

"No, it's an honest question. How do you feel?"

"You really want to know."

Annie nodded, trying not to look too closely at him; to give him time to compose his answer. He was a writer. The words had to be in there -- he just had to put them in the right order. She was so afraid of what he'd say, but she had to know. For some reason, the meltdown she'd just had suddenly pushed her to her limit. There was no turning back.

"Let's see -- how do I say this without it sounding all wrong?" He let go of her for a second, running his hands through his hair. Clearing his throat, he reached out for her again, grasping her hands tightly. "Annie, there is nothing more that I want in this world than to make love to you. I've wanted you from the first time I saw you in front of the elevators. There was just something about you. And it's not just how you look -- it's how you are. *All* of you." He gripped her hands firmly before he let go of them and stood up and walked to the other side of the room. "There -- I said it. Do you think I'm a complete jerk?"

"No, not at all --"

"I understand why you stop us -- at least I think I do. I don't want you to do anything you're not ready for. I want the time to be right. As much as I want you, I can wait. It's killing me, but I can wait." He looked across the room and gave her a smile.

"Then let's not wait anymore."

"What did you say?"

"Let's not wait." She got up and walked over to him. "I'm ready." She put her arms around his neck, raised up on her tiptoes and kissed him seductively.

Whoa," he exclaimed as he prematurely ended the kiss. "Hold on a minute, here."

She looked up at him, hurt and confused. "What?"

"Are you serious? As recently as last night you weren't ready -- and that's fine. You're not changing your mind because of what I just said, are you? Because really, Annie, I don't want to rush into this."

"We've been dating for over three months -- it's hardly *rushing* into anything."

He dissected himself from their embrace and paced around in a little circle, running his hands through his hair and shaking his head as he walked. Concern and frustration were etched on his face as he turned toward her. Annie wasn't sure what to think or what to say, but she felt that they were reaching a crossroads, an impasse. She would have expected that they'd be in her bedroom by this time instead of standing here debating it. Most men would welcome the desire to take things to a new level, so why wasn't he? Instead he stood there like a statue, staring at her, speechless.

"Why are you looking at me like that, Matt? Did I do something wrong?" He was making her nervous as well as angry.

"No -- you haven't done anything *wrong,* it's just that you've blindsided me. One minute you're feeling sad about Dillon, and the next you're trying to seduce me. I especially don't want to take advantage of you when you're so vulnerable --"

"I am not vulnerable!" she cut him off. "My God, Matt. I am not a fragile little creature!" Annie's heart was pounding and her face turned red with anger. "You're confusing me too. One minute you say you've wanted me from the first time you saw me and in the next breath you reject me. How do you think that makes me feel?" Tears stung her eyes. She folded her arms across her chest and turned away from him.

"I'm sorry. I didn't mean to hurt your feelings." Matt apologized, and took a tentative step toward her. He reached out to touch her shoulder, but she shrugged him off.

"Why does this have to be such a big deal? Why can't we just let our feelings take over?" She still kept her back to him, the rejection she felt hovering over her like a big, black cloud. It had taken a lot of courage for her to approach him in that way. She never thought he'd turn her down. What had she been thinking? Whoever said that men liked it when women initiated things, hadn't known Matt. Leave it to her to find a man who was old-fashioned and chivalrous; who had morals and a conscience. Just because she wanted to seduce him didn't mean that she *didn't* have morals or a conscience, did it? She was just so tired of being careful, of doing the "right" thing. Since when was following your heart's desire so wrong?

Matt sighed heavily before he replied. "Because it *is* a big deal, Annie. I don't want either one of us to get hurt."

She rotated to face him. "So you think I'll hurt you? I would never do that, Matt." Her voice was calmer, but filled with sadness and disbelief. "This isn't just about satisfying urges. I hope you know that."

His eyes were guarded and forlorn. "I know."

Suddenly it was clear that this wasn't only about her. Matt had as many fears and insecurities as she did -- maybe even more. Now he probably thought she was sex-crazed and reckless on top of it. If she had just waited until after Dillon's birthday to bring up the subject, then he wouldn't think of her as being so fragile. She looked at Matt as he stood there before her, his own fragility displayed over every inch of his six foot frame. As strong as she knew he was, he seemed utterly breakable at the same time. His forehead was creased with worry, his mouth set in an uneasy line. She cared about him so much. Apprehension washed over her in a wave of remorse as it suddenly became clear what she had to do.

"Matt, I love you. But I love you too much to risk hurting you." She paused for a second to get her bearings. This was so hard. "I think we're both afraid of being hurt. Each of us has been through a lot. You've been such a big help to me in the past few months. I am so grateful to you." She stopped and swallowed. The words were getting caught in her throat.

Annie, what are you saying?" Matt's voice was a whisper.

"You're right - I *am* confused and it's not right to drag you into the middle of it."

"I want to be here. You're not dragging me anywhere."

Annie sighed. "I know. But don't you see? I have to be strong on my own. I have to trust myself. I've been wrestling with this for a long time -- to tell you how I feel about the physical part of our relationship. It's a big deal, but it shouldn't be, if it's really right. I'm just so tired of being afraid."

He took her hands in his. "What are you afraid of?"

"Everything. I haven't really been on my own, *ever*. Right after my mom died I was with Eric, and Frank and Sally rescued me after the divorce --"

"And then you met me," he finished the sentence. "Do you feel like I rescued you?"

She cocked her head to one side and considered his question. "Sort of."

"What would you say if I told you that you rescued me too?" He kissed her hands, which were still entwined with his.

"I'd say that's wonderful. It's nice of you to say that."

"I'm not trying to be nice, it's the truth. You want to be strong and independent, but you already are. Don't you see that?"

"No, I don't." She shook her head. Giving his hands a squeeze, she wiggled her hands free and stepped back from him. "I need to figure that out for myself." Her heart was thundering in her chest. This was so hard.

"I'll do whatever you want me to do." Matt's voice was barely a sigh. "Just tell me."

Annie took in a deep breath and let it out, a slow, deliberate stream of air. "I don't know what I want! In so many ways I don't want to do this, but I think it's best if I have some time alone. I just need to know that I can stand on my own two feet."

She couldn't believe this was happening; that she was eliminating this extraordinary man and this promising relationship from her life. That morning when she'd awoken, she'd had no inkling that tonight she would be making such a painful decision, but here she was, making it, and as difficult as it was, it felt as if it was the best thing.

Matt stood there, quiet and somber. "I sure didn't see this coming." His voice was rough with emotion. "Is it because I want to wait to have sex with you? Because if that's the case, I can change my mind --" He managed a crooked smile.

"No, that's not why, but I appreciate the offer." A joyless smile was pasted on her face. "To be honest, I didn't see it coming either, but I've felt, what's the word -- *anxious* -- for a while. I thought that taking the next step would help, but it won't. Not right now, anyway. It's just that I feel so dependent on you -- and that bothers me. I need to be able to depend on *myself*. Does that make sense?"

"As painful as it is to think about being without you, yes, it does make sense. I don't want you to have doubts about us in any way. Annie, my intent isn't to cause you anxiety, it's to make you happy. You mean the world to me, you know." He closed the distance between them with a long step and embraced her gently. "Is this alright?"

All she could do was nod her head, because speaking would allow the torrent of tears building inside of her to burst through. She had to hold herself together for him. He was being so understanding, so kind. Resting her head on his chest, she closed her eyes and breathed in the scent of him. She tried to memorize this moment, so that in the days ahead when she felt alone, she'd be able to remember what comfort felt like. Matt's embrace did feel like "home" to her; the best place to be in the world. She let out a small shudder and he laid a gentle hand on the back of her head. Her heart rate finally began to slow down, gradually returning to normal.

"So," Matt loosened his arms as he spoke, "now what?"

"Now the hardest part." Annie didn't want to let him go. "I've never done this before -- stopped seeing someone I'm in love with. How does that work?"

"Well, I guess I leave and don't come back." He put one hand up to her cheek, touching it as though it was made of the most delicate silk.

His eyes explored her face, as though some answers to the mysteries within her would be hidden there. She fought the urge to avert her eyes and let him look past her brave mask, and into her heart. He placed his other hand on her face and gently leaned down to kiss her good-bye. At first Annie's lips met his with uncertainty, but once she felt the soft curve of his mouth, any qualms dissolved, disappearing into the darkening corners of the room. The heavy night air outside the open window became ominous and still as Annie and Matt came together with an intensity born of the desperate need to make this moment one that would sustain them indefinitely. When it became clear that stopping would be next to impossible, Matt took the initiative and extricated himself from her all too tempting embrace.

You're not making this any easier, you know," his voice was hoarse with restraint.

"I could say the same for you."

"I know -- I'm sorry."

"It's okay."

They stood there, not knowing what to do next. Matt finally gathered the courage to speak. "Well, I guess I better be going."

"I guess." Annie couldn't say anything more without sobbing.

"I love you, Annie Stanford." He moved closer to the door. "Take care of yourself."

Annie stayed where she was, afraid that if she moved any closer, she'd grab onto him and never let go. "I love you, too."

"Good night, Annie." And with that, he stepped over the threshold and out of her life.

The door remained unlocked until she heard his car drive away and only then did she make herself walk to it and turn the deadbolt. She broke down at the thought of locking Matt out of her life and leaned against the door for support as the tears began to flow. What had she been thinking, to send him away, especially so close to Dillon's birthday? What had seemed like the only choice just moments ago felt like a monumental mistake as she sank to the hardwood floor and sat with her back against the wall. What had she been thinking to send him away at all?

She sat on the floor of her apartment, weeping at the thought of it all. Huddled in a ball, she felt as though she was falling apart; that all of her body parts were going to disconnect and evaporate into thin air. All that would be left of her would be the round splotches of tears on the floor in the remnants of dust she'd missed with the mop.

Tears could be shed without having to explain or apologize. They each became a healing salve for the other, knowing just what to be until the moment passed, until a smile could form where the tears had been.

# The Birthday Candle

The orchestra conductor swirled his baton through the air to signify the cutoff and all of the instruments became quiet, their notes silenced.

"Good work, everyone. That sounded much better. See you tonight!" He put his sheet music back into the folder on the music stand as he hummed the last stanza, an absent-minded smile on his face. "Oh -- and please remember to give the European tour some thought. We need to make a decision on that soon."

"How many members do we need to have?" A French horn player emptied the spit valve on his instrument while he waited for an answer.

"It'd be great to have thirty or forty. And again, I apologize for the short notice on this, but it's a wonderful opportunity."

Jen turned around and grinned at Annie, her eyebrows in high arches. "Doesn't that sound great?"

"I guess so -- maybe." Annie's voice was noncommittal and bland as she loosened the tension on her bow.

"You don't sound very convincing. Everything okay?"

Annie sighed and looked over at her friend. "It's just been a bad week."

"I'm all ears. Talk."

"Tomorrow is Dillon's birthday." Annie's voice cracked a little.

"Oh honey -- I'm so sorry. That's got to be so hard." Jen came over and sat next to her, placing a kind hand on her shoulder. "Is there anything I can do?"

"Thanks, but I'll be fine. It's just something I have to get through."

"You're missing Matt a lot too, aren't you?"

Annie's head snapped up in surprise. How did Jen know? She hadn't told anyone at work about her and Matt yet; it was too painful. It was all she could do, with Dillon's birthday on the horizon, to get out of bed every day and drag herself to rehearsal. Talking about it just made it more real and she preferred to live in denial this week.

After Dillon's birthday was past she'd deal with her feelings about Matt, if she could even feel anymore by then.

Jen smiled at her. "I know that look. What happened?"

"I'd rather not talk about it, Jen. It's a long, stupid story."

"Okay, but I'm a great listener."

"I know you are. It's just a bad time." Annie readjusted her cello and leaned it against her thigh.

"Exactly. A very bad time for him to do this to you." Jen's voice was harsh.

"No, no -- it wasn't Matt's idea. It was mine," she explained. "He never would have done that to me so close to Dillon's birthday."

"So, why did you do it to yourself then? I thought you two were doing so well."

Annie did her best to explain even though it was draining every last bit of energy she had left. By the time she finished, she and Jen were the only two musicians left on the stage.

"I don't know what to say," said Jen. "You are one tough lady. I don't think I'd have the guts to send someone so wonderful away. Gems like Matt don't come along very often, you know."

"I know that, but that's exactly why I have to do this. I have to be sure that *I'm* ready. He's too important to me to risk hurting him. I have to be sure that I love him for the right reasons."

"Well, more power to you, but can I tell you one thing?"

Annie nodded her head, waiting. Jen continued.

"I adore my husband. He's a wonderful man and a fantastic father. Before I met him, though, there was someone else; someone I wasn't sure I was ready for, but who made me the happiest I'd ever been in my life. I decided we needed to take a break. He decided to enlist in the Army as a medic. I don't know why, to get away, I guess. Anyhow, long story short, he ended up getting killed in Viet Nam, right before the end of the war."

"Oh Jen, I'm so sorry."

"Thanks. It's just that I'll always regret taking that break. He'd managed not to get drafted since he was in med school, so he would have been free and clear. I'll never know what might have been, but I'll always wonder. I'll always feel some responsibility.

I know that things happen for a reason, but it's hard to find the reason for that. So just be careful. Don't throw something good away."

Annie didn't know how to respond. The regret and pain in Jen's eyes was very tangible and hard to witness. Jen was always so upbeat and happy. Who would have guessed that her heart held so many painful memories? She reached over to give her friend a hug.

"I'll remember that. Really, I will." She wiped a tear away. "I appreciate your telling me about that."

"I just don't want to see you lose this chance at happiness. I'm proof that you get more than one chance to be happy, but as you know, it can be a rough journey."

"You've got that right," Annie said. "And I promise I won't join the Army, the Navy *or* the Marines."

"Good!" Jen laughed a little and then her eyes lit up. "Hey -- I just had an idea! You should go on that little spur of the moment trip to Europe! It's only for a month or so. You'd get some time away without joining any branch of the military, and maybe it would give you some perspective. What do you think?"

Europe. It *was* appealing. She'd been there for a brief time while she was in college and had always longed to go back. This would be a good opportunity to do so. A change of scenery might do her some good.

"How much did he say it will cost?" Annie hadn't been paying very close attention to the conductor's sales pitch for the trip.

"I thought he said it's be about $2000.00 a person -- and that would cover everything. Five star hotels and *everything*."

"It does sound good. He wants to know soon though, doesn't he?" She was busy calculating how much she could skim off of her savings account as she spoke. With the money from the divorce she could make it work. It was definitely worth thinking about.

"Well, I've got to get going." Jen stood to leave, cello in hand. "Are you going to be alright?"

"Yes, I'll be fine. I'll see you tonight, okay?"

Once she emerged from the darkness of the parking ramp, Annie could see that the morning rain and clouds had dissipated and the sun shone brilliant in a cloudless sky. She was thankful for the warmth and brightness, since the dreary weather that had greeted her that morning had done nothing to help her somber mood. It struck her as ironic that as the sky brightened, so had her spirits. At Jen's urging, she had signed up for the trip to Europe after the morning's rehearsal. She had given it some thought when the conductor had first mentioned it a couple of weeks ago, but had been reluctant to leave Matt. Now there was no reason not to go and as Jen said, the change of scenery would do her good. All things considered, the trip couldn't have come at a better time.

Traffic was light and she made her way out of downtown without any delays, a blessing, considering her distracted frame of mind. The parking lot at the grocery store was crowded, but she found a parking spot close to the entrance in spite of it. She made a beeline to the floral department and grabbed the last bouquet of blue daisies, and then on an impulse, hurried back to the bakery. The choices were limited, but sitting amidst the sweet rolls and muffins, was one lone cupcake, with brightly colored sprinkles on vanilla frosting. It was perfect. After having the cupcake placed in a small white bakery bag, she headed to the baking aisle. Every birthday cake needed candles, and for this cake, she'd need only one. Of course, she had to buy a whole box of them, since single candles were rarely needed. Even if you started out needing just one candle, you'd always need more the next year. It became difficult to swallow and her chest burned with suppressed emotion. Technically she had no use for *any* candles. She wasn't celebrating a *real* birthday. People would think she was crazy if they knew what she was doing, but Annie didn't care. She even decided to go one step further and returned to the floral department to pick out a mylar birthday balloon. There was one that was particularly cute, with a teddy bear holding a cupcake with one candle stuck in it. How could she not buy it? She got the attention of the woman working in the department.

"Hi - can I help you?" The woman had short hair dyed too dark for her age and a big, toothy smile.

"Oh hi. Yes. I'd like the balloon with the teddy bear on it, please." Annie was finding it more difficult to speak than she'd expected. The words felt dry and chalky in her mouth.

"That's a darling one, isn't it? I just got that one for my grandson's first birthday last weekend. He just loved it!" She flashed a grin at Annie. "From the looks of it, you've got someone's first birthday coming up too!" The helium tank made a squeaky sound as the balloon was inflated into a shiny, swollen pancake.

As Annie watched the balloon grow, the lump in her throat grew right along with it. She observed the store employee who was helping her, and while the comment about her grandson broke her heart, she couldn't blame the woman for saying it. Why shouldn't a proud grandma share her joy? Sally would have definitely been like that about Dillon, especially since Annie's mom wouldn't have been there to brag. It was what grandmothers were supposed to do.

"Yes," Annie finally said. "My son's first birthday is tomorrow." Her throat felt like it had been rubbed raw with a coarse piece of sandpaper. She fought back tears.

The woman saw the difficulty she was having and she placed a gentle hand on her arm as she handed her the balloon. "They grow up so fast, don't they? But just remember, he'll always be your baby."

Annie entered the cemetery gates and pulled her car up next to the curb. She put it in park and left it idling while she hurried to the large wire basket overflowing with a mountain of green metal flower vases. Reaching down into the jumbled mess, she rooted around for one without any obvious dents or too many lumps of dried dirt clinging to it. The third one was the charm and she retrieved it from the basket, triumphant. She inspected it on her way back to the car, flicking the leftover traces of dirt off with her fingers as she walked. Back in the car, she placed it on the passenger seat, alongside the flowers, the cupcake and the balloon.

The afternoon sun created dappled shadows from tree branches that were laden with early summer leaves. A gentle breeze made the shaded images hop and dance in between the stately rows of granite and stone. She had the route to Babyland memorized by now, having made the trip every week since Dillon's funeral. It occurred to her that a year ago today, she had no idea that she would ever have to visit her baby's grave. She knew that such things happened, but of course she never thought that it would happen to her. A year ago if someone had told her that today she'd be driving around the winding curves and gentle hills of a cemetery to bring her baby blue daisies, a cupcake and a balloon, she would have told them they were crazy. She would have been certain that she'd never be able to handle such a tragedy. But here she was, feeling lucky to have found a dent-free cemetery vase in which to put her baby's birthday flowers. She had been thrilled to find the perfect birthday balloon, even though in reality she had no little boy to give it to, only his headstone with a lamb carved on it, on which to place it. The cupcake with the sprinkles had nearly made her giddy, even though there was no one year old safely strapped into his highchair, who would be smearing his adorable face with its frosting once "Happy Birthday" had been sung. There would be no pictures in the photo album of a happy, loving family, no party hats, no presents. There would only be a mother visiting her baby's grave all by herself, on the day before his first birthday.

Lost in thought, Annie maneuvered her car around the last curve in the road, and then slammed on the brakes. Parked on side of the road in front of Babyland, was a blue Honda Accord. Her eyes went from the car to the grassy area dotted with tiny headstones and there she saw him, kneeling on the ground, oblivious to everything going on around him. It was Matt. Her heart fluttered as she removed her foot from the brake and eased her vehicle forward, inching closer. He turned and caught her looking at him. With shaky fingers she reached around to unbuckle her seat belt, gathered Dillon's birthday gifts into her hands and got out of the car. She walked toward him, her heart thumping with each step. Her journey was made shorter as he strode over to meet her. They stopped about three feet from each other.

"I thought it would be okay to come today. I didn't think you'd be here until tomorrow." He sniffled a little as he spoke, his eyes moist and red. "I just wanted to say 'Happy Birthday' to the little guy. I hope you don't mind." He shifted his gaze to the lush grass blowing softly in the wind.

Annie was overwhelmed with emotion, her heart breaking for Dillon, Matt, and herself all at the same time. The fact that he took the time to come here on his own, in itself explained why she loved him so much.

"I don't mind at all. I came today so that he'd have something the minute it's his birthday." A bouquet of blue daisies were arranged carefully in a green metal vase stuck in the ground by Dillon's headstone. She looked up at him and smiled. "But you've already done that for him. Thank you, Matt."

He shook his head slightly and blushed. "I'll never see blue daisies and not think of Dillon." He nodded toward the items she held in her hands. "I see you brought some too."

"Among other things." Annie gave the ribbon on the balloon a slight tug and held up the bag that contained the cupcake. "Would you like to join me for a little birthday party?"

"You're sure you don't want to be alone? I don't want to intrude."

"I can't think of anyone I'd rather be with right now."

"I've missed you, Annie. I hope it's okay to say that." Matt stood with his hands shoved in his front pockets.

"I've missed you too." They stood there in an awkward stance; neither of them seemed to know what to do next.

"I'll get some water." He reached for the vase she held in the crook of her arm and strode over to the water spigot on the other side of the road before she could answer. Moments later he was back at her side, the water sloshing around inside the cone shaped vessel. "Here you go."

"Thanks." Annie took the vase from him and pushed it firmly into the ground next to the one he had placed there. She knelt down, the bouquet of daisies resting on her lap, and set about removing the cellophane wrapper that protected them. The ends of the stems needed to be trimmed, and when she was ready to break them off with her hands, Matt offered his Swiss Army knife to do the job. They worked together to trim the stems, neither of them saying a word. Once trimmed, Matt handed the flowers to Annie one at a time, and she placed each of them in the vase with the tender concentration. After she placed each daisy, she paused and touched it as though it was Dillon's tiny cheek, as silent tears slid down her own. When she was finished, she sat back on her feet and admired her work.

"There," she said. "How does that look?"

"It looks great."

"Now I have to get this balloon to stay on there somehow." She caught the end of the curly blue ribbon that was waving in the breeze and tied it around the lower part of the vase down near the ground. "That should work." She patted it with her hand and leaned back to observe it.

"Nicely done." Matt smiled at her.

"Thanks." Annie grinned back through misty eyes. "It's my first balloon -- or should I say it's *his* first balloon."

"It's perfect." Matt was fighting back tears of his own.

"And then, of course, I saw *this*." She took the cupcake out of the stiff white bag. "How cute is that?" She stuck the candle in it and held it out for Matt's approval.

"You are such a good mom, Annie." Matt reached for her free hand and cradled it in both of his.

That was all it took. Annie closed her eyes and let herself cry. It was so good to have Matt there, to have him holding her hand as she felt her heart splinter apart and shatter all over the ground. She handed Matt the cupcake, because it suddenly became too heavy to hold, making her hand ache with the painful reality that her little boy would never have a birthday cake; he'd never blow out the candles. All of his candles had been extinguished on the day he was born.

She patted the grass he lay beneath, letting her grief water it as her tears fell and disappeared amidst the blades of green. There had been so much lost the day Dillon died -- her baby, her marriage, her dreams. It was impossible not to wonder what life would have been like if all of that hadn't happened. Would she and Eric have made their marriage work for the sake of their little boy? She couldn't deny the fact that their marriage was broken. Dillon's death didn't cause the crack in the foundation; that had been there for years. The tragedy did make it crumble, however; there was no denying that.

Matt sat nearby, keeping the cupcake safe, as she wailed and sobbed and pounded the ground with her fists. When she stopped for a breath he put a gentle hand on her back until she gathered the strength to cry and rage some more. He didn't tell her to calm down or that everything would be okay. He was simply there for her and with her, and for that gift she would be eternally grateful.

The third time she paused for a rest and felt Matt's hand on her back, she turned and looked at him. She didn't speak right away, but instead just took in the sight, sound and feel of the moment. He hadn't been looking directly at her, but was staring at the ground near his foot. It felt as though he was trying to give her some privacy, some shred of dignity as she mourned the day her life fell apart, the day it was forever changed. As though she had willed him to, he raised his eyes and focused on her. His smile was sad but drenched in understanding.

"You okay?" He patted her back.

"I think so," she said. "I didn't know I had that many tears left."

"And anger and grief?"

"Yeah. I don't think I've ever let go like that before. Especially in front of anyone."

"How'd it feel?"

She paused for a second. "Good. Great, actually. Thank you."

"For what?"

"For staying. It helped a lot. Especially after I sent you away last week. I'm being real strong and independent, aren't I? Talk about a contradiction." She brushed some loose blades of grass from the palms of her hands as she shook her head.

"Annie -- a person can be strong and independent and still turn to others for help. There's no shame in that."

"But still --"

"But still nothing. Yes, it's a contradiction, but you are a walking contradiction -- and that's a *good* thing. That's one of the things I love about you."

"Really."

"Yes, *really*."

They sat there in silence for a few moments. Annie glanced over at him, not sure what to do next. Her gut was telling her to go over to him and wrap her arms around him, but the last time she'd done that things hadn't gone so well. If only there was an instruction manual for relationships; that would make life so much easier.

"A penny for your thoughts," Matt said, interrupting her reflection.

"Oh -- I was just thinking about everything that's happened."

"You've had quite a year."

"We both have. Finding you was a miracle."

He looked at her, surprised. "You think so?"

"Of course, I do." The tuft of grass she had been playing with became dislodged from the dirt. Embarrassed, she tried to pat it back into place, like a divot on a golf course.

"I feel the same way about you, Annie. You've made my life better in so many ways." He smiled at her feeble attempt at landscaping, and then doubt clouded his expression. "That's why your decision about us surprised me so much." He looked at her with cautious hope. "I've missed you."

He was such a sight for her red, bleary eyes. Sitting there a few inches away from her, his hair disheveled from the afternoon breeze and his eyes glistening with the remnants of tears shed for Dillon, he stirred so many feelings within her. Her heart twisted with affection and confusion. She reached her hand out to him. "I've missed you too."

Before she knew what was happening, he caught her hand in his and placed a tender kiss on it. In less time than it took for a smile to form on her lips, they were in each other's arms. They held each other with a combination of restraint and passion. Annie's confusion was replaced with the certainty of feeling as though she was where she belonged.

Matt drew back just enough to see her face. "What's going on here?"

"We're hugging each other. In a cemetery, no less." She smiled at him.

"Do you know what you're doing? Because honestly, Annie, I don't want to go through another week like this past one. I don't think I could stand it."

She leaned her forehead against his and looked into his eyes. "I couldn't either."

They wrapped their arms around each other and held onto the moment as long as it took to make it a precious memory. Annie's head was reeling with thoughts of the past week, the past month and the past year. So much life had happened in such a short amount of time. For the most part, time had slowed down and at some points, stood still. She was a different person than she'd been a year ago; a better person. Losing Dillon had taught her not to take the good things or people in her life for granted; that she had to hold everyone and every moment dear. If Dillon's short life was to be worth anything, she had to open her heart and let all the goodness in. Finding Matt here was not a coincidence. She couldn't help but think that her little boy had a part in this. He brought them together at the support group and he was bringing them together again, in this very special place, on the day before his birthday.

# The Picnic Basket

Matt's breath was steady and warm on her neck and his embrace both comforted and enlivened her. She gave him a squeeze and whispered, "Do you have time for a walk?"

They followed the winding road out of the cemetery, to nearby Lake Calhoun. The paths and beaches were crowded with joggers and sun-worshippers, eager to soak up every possible bit of summer. It was 3:00 p.m., which gave them plenty of time to walk around the entire lake at a leisurely pace. Annie didn't have to be back for the concert until 6:30 p.m.

"It's a gorgeous day, isn't it?" Annie took in a deep breath of sunshine and suntan lotion as she looked out onto the wide expanse of sand and water. Several small sailboats bobbed and darted out in the middle of the lake, their sails colorful triangles on the horizon.

"I'd say it's just about perfect." Matt smiled and grasped her hand as they walked along the blacktop path. "Can I ask you something?"

"Sure." She braced herself for a barrage of tough questions, something she fully deserved. Her split-second decision to break up with him had been one of the less brilliant and more impulsive moves of her life. She hoped she'd be able to help him understand.

"What do *you* think just happened back there? I have some ideas of my own, but I need to hear yours." He let go of her hand, planting his own hands in the front pockets of his jeans as they walked.

"Well, I think that Dillon had something to do with it." She looked at him out of the corner of her eye. He didn't flinch or laugh or look at her as though she'd lost her mind.

"I think you're right." Matt said. He wore an earnest expression on his face.

"Really?" Annie was surprised. "You don't think I'm crazy?"

"No, I don't." He took her hand again. "It makes perfect sense. Why else did I wake up this morning with an overpowering urge to go to the cemetery? You and Dillon's birthday were on my mind, I won't deny that, but it hadn't really occurred to me to go to the *cemetery*."

"I do have to admit that I didn't expect to see you there, but it makes sense." They stepped around a little boy weaving across the path on a tiny bike with training wheels. His harried mother pushed his baby sister in an umbrella stroller, struggling to keep up.

"How so?"

"Because you care. Going to the cemetery was a way to show it." She smiled at the tiny cyclist who made his wobbly way between them again. They raised their hands, making an arch for him to pass under. "Why did I have an overwhelming urge to go there a day early? All week I was planning to go tomorrow, but after rehearsal this morning, I decided to go today. Strange."

Matt nodded but remained silent. They continued to walk, both deep in thought, until they spotted a bench near the lake. As if reading each other's minds, they veered off the path and headed toward it. The bench was under the canopy of a weeping willow tree, providing both privacy and shady relief from the heat of the sun. Matt leaned over and brushed some bird droppings off the bench with his handkerchief and then he motioned for them both to sit down.

"You know, don't you, that if we ever tell anyone else our ideas about this, they'll lock both of us up in *separate* institutions?" He nudged her with his elbow and she gave his arm a playful punch.

"I won't tell anyone if you don't. Mum's the word." She pretended to lock her lips and throw away the key.

"I'm glad we can joke about this," said Matt. "Although I really am serious."

"So am I. That and the fact that seeing you today made me realize how stupid I was last week."

"You weren't stupid. I could have been more understanding."

"How could you understand someone so irrational and confused? No, you were wonderful. *I'm* the one who wasn't very understanding. To throw myself at you and then send you away when you were only being decent and kind? That was a terrible thing to do. Can you ever forgive me?"

"Well, let me think about it for a minute." He paused and gazed out at the lake, a stern look on his face. "I will on one condition."

Annie swallowed her apprehension, expecting the worst. "What's that?"

"That you forgive me too. I behaved like a jerk. You had every right to kick me to the curb." He turned to face her, putting his hands on her shoulders. "I am so sorry, Annie. To cause you pain, especially this past week, was inexcusable. I never wanted to hurt you."

Annie threw her arms around his neck. "Oh Matt. I'm so sorry too."

They held that pose for a moment, their arms around each other, and then as though a hidden orchestra started to play, Matt's lips found Annie's and he gave her a long, tender kiss. When they both came up for air, they just sat there and grinned at each other, like a couple of teenagers.

Annie cleared her throat. "I made another spontaneous decision today."

"Oh really? You're just full of surprises, aren't you?" He beamed at her.

"Yes, well, the orchestra is going on a short tour of Europe and I signed up this morning to go."

"That's great! When do you leave?"

"In a month." Her heart sank. Part of her hoped that he'd be upset that she'd be leaving. Instead, he seemed glad about it.

"How long will you be gone?"

"About six weeks." The magical mood of a few minutes ago was beginning to vanish. She looked at him, her smile fading.

"You don't sound very excited."

"I *am* excited. I will miss you, though." Her eyes searched his for a clue as to how he really felt.

He gathered her into his arms and held her tightly. "You have no idea how happy it makes me to hear you say that."

"I was just hoping *you'd* be a little more disappointed."

"Oh, way to care about how *I* feel." His voice took on an exaggerated "Valley Girl" tone. He folded his arms across his chest and his bottom lip stuck out in a dramatic pout.

At first Annie was mortified that she had been so insensitive and then she saw the hint of a smile tugging at the corners of his eyes. She flipped her hair over her left shoulder and then the right one. “Well, it *is,* like, all about *me*, you know!”

Neither one of them could keep a straight face and they burst into giggles, both of them having to wipe away tears again, only this time, tears of laughter. A teen-age couple walking by on the path looked at them as if they were crazy, rolled their eyes and kept on going. Annie and Matt caught a glimpse of their reaction and that started another fit of giggles.

“Oh my God!” Annie had trouble catching her breath. ‘Did you see the look on their faces?”

“It was priceless. I’d say it’s unanimous; we *are* a couple of goofballs.” He wiped the tears from his eyes and then smiled at her.

“Well, there’s no one I’d rather be goofy with than you.” Annie took his face in her hands, brought it closer to hers, and kissed him.

The kiss started out as a light and playful peck, but once their lips met, the desire that had been smoldering beneath the surface all afternoon was sparked and they lost all sense of time and place. Matt’s arms were around her, his hands moving up and down her back, pulling her closer to him with each breath. Realizing that too many people might see them, Matt took Annie’s hand and they moved from the bench to a spot further under the curtain of branches provided by the willow tree. First they sank to their knees and then tumbled to the ground, their arms and legs entwined, their mouths finding each other once again.

Annie’s emotions overwhelmed her and she clutched Matt close to her as she tried to catch her breath. Her heart felt as though it was going to burst with all the feelings it contained. Finally opening her eyes, she was surprised to see that Matt was already looking at her. She returned his steady gaze, willing to lose herself in the warmth and passion she saw there.

“Something’s different,” he said, brushing her hair back from her face.

“What do you mean?”

“This is the first time you haven’t looked away.”

Annie smiled, knowing what he meant. Until this moment, true intimacy had made her uneasy and self-conscious; remnants of her days with Eric. He had shut her out so many times, spurned her attempts at closeness, that she’d ended up feeling ashamed and needy. No one had ever accepted her so fully or had offered themselves so completely, until now.

"I know. I'm not afraid anymore."

They continued to lie silently together underneath the tree, neither one wanting to be the first to come back to earth. A soft breeze blew the branches of the willow, carrying the sounds of the afternoon to their private little haven. Strains of classical music floated from someone's radio or cassette player, serving as a gentle nudge into reality.

"You have a concert tonight?" Matt finally spoke.

Annie nodded and frowned as she peeked at her watch. It was nearly 5:00 p.m. "I have to be there in an hour and a half." She wished she didn't have to break the spell. "Which means I'd better get going."

Matt let out a heavy sigh. "I know." He cupped her face with his hand, rubbing his thumb along her chin. "Do you think there are any tickets left?"

"I'm sure there are. It's a Tuesday night." She continued to hold his free hand in hers, and gave it a squeeze.

"Would you mind if I'm in the audience?" His voice was quiet and cautious.

"I'd love that." Annie's face crinkled into a smile. "And if you're not too tired after the concert, maybe you'd like to come over?"

"Well, I'm not the one who will be working all evening. Maybe if *you're* not too tired."

Annie knew she wouldn't be tired. The thought of spending more time with Matt filled her with excitement and hope. There would be no problem staying awake tonight. Driving home from the lake, she felt twinges of guilt for feeling happy for herself instead of feeling sad about Dillon. In the support group she'd learned that it's normal for feelings of guilt to interfere with healing during the grief process. She also learned that it's healthy to acknowledge them and then continue to do whatever is responsible for the happiness. Dillon would want her to move on and be happy, and even if he didn't, it did no good to live in misery. Seeing Matt today made her realize how much she cared about him and how much happiness he brought into her life. She wasn't going to throw that away again.

After the concert, Annie quickly packed up her cello and hurried out into the hallway, excited to meet Matt. There he stood waiting for her, holding a bouquet of tulips, just as he had the first time he'd come to hear her play. The smile on his face and the look in his eyes reached into her heart and held it, melting it with the warmth he exuded.

"Hi." He held out the bunch of assorted colored tulips toward her. "I thought you might like these."

"They're beautiful! Thank you, Matt." She put her cello case down as she took the flowers. "Did you like the concert?"

"Very much. You were spectacular, as usual." He gave her a small hug.

Just then the practice room door opened and Jen came bustling through, carrying her cello case, her purse and a Dayton's shopping bag.

"Oh, go ahead and kiss her!" she shouted on her way down the hall, "You know you want to!"

Annie turned to look at Jen and when she turned back toward Matt, he surprised her by grabbing her, bending her back in a dramatic dip, and planting a big kiss directly on her open mouth. He popped his head up, grinning at Jen.

"Is that better?" he called down the hallway.

"Yes!" hollered Jen. "Much, much better!" She gave Annie a wink and a smile and hurried out the side exit, dragging her things behind her. The heavy door closed with a thud.

"Wow!" Annie steadied herself against Matt's shoulder. "Talk about being full of surprises."

"And I've got more where that came from," he said, doing his best Groucho Marx impression.

"I'll bet you do." Annie said, a seductive smile on her face. "Just remember, two can play that game." Their eyes locked and while humor still percolated close to the surface, the intensity of their feelings simmered underneath.

Matt let out a deep, ragged breath. "So, I'll follow you home?"

"Sounds perfect." Annie took his hand, squeezed it and then raised up on her tip-toes and kissed his cheek. Hand in hand they walked to their cars.

The drive to Annie's apartment was a short one but it seemed to take forever, since they managed to hit every red light the entire way. Normally waiting at red lights didn't bother her, but tonight they made fifteen minutes feel like an eternity. At each light, she'd peek back at Matt in her rear view mirror and her heart would begin accelerating faster than her car's engine. It had felt so good to kiss him and feel his hands on her that afternoon. The thought of it still elicited a strong reaction over every inch of her body, even though it had happened hours before. She couldn't stop smiling.

When they reached her apartment, their paths diverged; Annie turned into the parking lot in the back of the building and Matt went around the corner to park on the street. She had just removed her cello from the back of her car, when she turned to find Matt coming around the corner of the building. In his left hand, he carried a large picnic basket and his face carried a huge grin.

"What have you got there?" Annie eyed the basket he was toting as she slammed the trunk shut.

"I thought we'd have a picnic. You haven't eaten dinner yet, have you?"

"No, I was a little busy before I went to work tonight." She winked at him.

"Well, not to worry. I have a veritable feast here." He lifted the basket. "Shall we go in?"

They went in the back door and climbed the steps, Annie leading the way to her door. She fumbled with her keys, leaning the cello against her hip while she cradled the bouquet of tulips between her elbow and her body. The keys slipped from her fingers and fell, landing on the faded Oriental rug that ran down the middle of the hall.

"Allow me." Matt set the picnic basket down and stooped to retrieve the keys.

"Thanks. Could you hold these a second?" She handed him the flowers. "I'm kind of klutzy tonight." Her heart was racing and butterfly wings fluttered inside her stomach.

The energy that radiated between her and Matt would have sizzled if a drop of rain had fallen between them. She tried to take a deep breath and relax, but it wasn't working very well.

The door swung open and Annie felt on the wall next to the door for the light switch and flipped it up. Immediately the glow of the Tiffany lamp bathed the room in a warm, inviting light. She walked in and set her cello on the floor next to the dining room table and then changed her mind.

"Oh, this will be in the way when we eat. I'll put it in the bedroom."

"It won't be in our way at all." Matt had opened the picnic basket and was unfurling a white tablecloth. "It's a picnic, remember?"

"I'll still put it away." She hurried into the darkened bedroom next to the dining area. "I need to change my clothes anyway."

"Sounds good. I'll get things ready out here." Matt smoothed out the wrinkles in the tablecloth as he spoke.

Her heart started racing again. Closing the French doors behind her, she brought her cello over to the alcove where she practiced. She set it on the floor and then went into her closet. From the moment she had known he'd be coming over tonight, she'd been trying to decide what she should wear.

The jeans and t-shirt she had worn that afternoon were draped over the side of the wicker hamper and she felt a rush of excitement when she saw them. A grass stain on the back of the shirt made her smile as she remembered how it got there, lying with Matt on the grass under the willow tree. She hadn't had a grass stain on her clothes since she was a child. As her thoughts roamed, she peeled off her black knit concert dress and plopped it in the hamper. Hanging in front of her was a pink sundress with spaghetti straps that tied at the shoulders. It had an empire waist and the bodice was softly shirred with narrow rows of elastic, forming gentle folds that made the skirt fall like a whisper. She pulled it off the hanger and stepped into the dress, pulling it up over her hips. When she reached her waist she hesitated for a moment and then in a deliberate motion, unhooked her bra and threw it in the hamper. She felt warm as she tugged the bodice over her breasts. Glancing in the mirror, she saw the telltale blush covered her face and neck. The last time she'd worn the dress, she'd tied knots in the shoulder straps before she'd formed the bows, just to make sure they wouldn't become united. Fingers trembling, she loosened the knots and was going to retie them but decided instead to tuck them inside the bodice, making the dress strapless. *Annie, Annie, Annie,* she said to her reflection. *You're going to go to hell, you know.*

The woman looking back at her had a knowing gleam in her eye. *Mind your own business,* she scolded. Just to make sure it knew who was in charge, she looked her reflection straight in the eye as she fluffed her hair and smoothed her dress. There was a sharp rap on the glass pane of the bedroom door. She jumped in surprise.

"Annie?"

"Just a second." She rolled her eyes at her image in the mirror as if to say, *'See what you're doing?'* For a brief moment she thought she saw her reflection talking back to her, saying, *'So, what are you waiting for?* Annie took a deep breath and tried to clear her head. What *was* she waiting for?

Reaching up, she found the cord hanging from the light on the closet ceiling and gave it a yank, turning off the light. She tiptoed over to the French doors and peeked around the edge of the lace curtain that stretched across the center of the glass. A small sigh escaped from her lips at what she saw. Matt looked so handsome and sweet as he sat on her floor, the white tablecloth neatly set with two ceramic plates and cloth napkins. There were two glasses of white wine poured, a loaf of French bread, a block of cheese and a bowl that had red and green grapes tumbling over its sides. An assortment of candles were arranged on the floor, on the dining room table and the coffee table. Their flames danced flirtatiously with each other, casting lively shadows on the curtains and walls. He had gone to so much trouble. No one had ever done anything like that for her before and her eyes stung with happy tears. She turned the crystal doorknob, opened the door and shyly entered the room.

"This is beautiful." The words came out in a whisper. The moment he heard her, Matt jumped to his feet. It took one step for him to reach her.

"I'm glad you like it." He took both of her hands in his. "You look wonderful, Annie." His eyes sparkled in the candlelight as he smiled at her.

All she could do was smile back. Words escaped her at the moment. Still holding her hand, he steered her over to the tablecloth and helped ease her to the floor. He reached for the glasses of wine, extending one of them to her. He raised his glass in a toast.

"To a very beautiful, wonderful woman. I am so lucky to know you and even luckier that you're giving me another chance. To you, Annie."

"To *us*." She gently touched her glass to his and they each took a sip, not taking their eyes off of each other.

"Would you like something to eat?" Matt glanced at the food he had so painstakingly arranged for their picnic feast.

Annie's eyes scanned the tablecloth and her hand shook as she raised her glass to her lips for another sip. The sip turned into more of a gulp and she coughed and sputtered in surprise. In an instant, Matt was patting her back as she tried to catch her breath.

"I'm sorry," she said, her hand covering her mouth as she coughed again.

"Do you want some water or something?" Matt's hand ran up and down her back as he spoke.

"No, I'm fine." She took a deep breath and let it out slowly. "See? No more coughing." A few tears had snuck out of the corners of her eyes and she quickly brushed them away with her free hand. She didn't want to ruin this moment or this evening. She wanted it to be perfect and it was fairly clear that he was hoping for the same thing. Matt was too quick for her and saw the tears. Out came the handkerchief. For the first time she accepted it, blotting her face carefully.

"What can I do? I've overdone it, haven't I?" Panic radiated from Matt's voice.

Annie put down the handkerchief and smiled at him. "You have *not* overdone it." She scooted closer to him on her knees and put her arms around his neck. "This is the nicest thing anyone's ever done for me."

He enveloped her in his arms and they knelt there for what seemed an eternity, melting into each other. Annie ran her fingers over his shoulders and back, and felt that she had never touched anything so precious since she held her son for the first time. Leaning back, she searched for Matt's eyes and when she found them, she could not look away. In his eyes she saw everything good and safe and right. She saw peace and passion, and most of all, love.

At that moment, all of her doubts and fears disappeared and were replaced with a joy unlike any she'd ever known. The food was never eaten and the rest of the wine was never poured. As they walked hand in hand to Annie's bedroom, they blew each candle out, one by one, until the last one glowed bright and alone in the darkness. Annie carried it carefully into the room and set it on the dresser, it's warm flame flickering and bouncing off the mirror and sending sparkling stars throughout the room. The candlelight glimmered against Annie's skin, deepening every curve and outline so that she seemed to glow from within.

Matt stood in front of her, his hands on either side of her face, and gazed at her, an intoxicated expression on his face. "Are you sure about this?"

"I've never been more sure of anything." She put her arms around his neck, pulled him close and gave him a long, slow kiss. Still kissing, they were just about to tumble onto the bed, when the telephone rang loudly, slicing through the sensual hush with a razor-like jolt.

"Should you get that?" Matt whispered and froze, his fingers just about to inch down the top edge of Annie's dress.

"I don't know who'd be calling so late," Annie muttered, her fingers unbuttoning his shirt. "It's probably just a wrong number. That's been happening a lot lately. Let's not worry about it." She kissed the newly exposed portion of his chest.

"Oh -- okay. Good. Now, where were we?" He nuzzled the curve of her neck and skimmed his lips along her shoulder. Annie tilted her head back and a satisfied moan escaped into the candlelit darkness. They dropped onto the bed, clothes askew, reveling in being alone together. Unlike that afternoon by the lake, they were now able to express their feelings for each other without restraint, without anyone else around to interrupt them. There was no hurry, no schedule to follow. They had all the time in the world and it was all for each other. Entangled in each other's arms and legs, their pleasure and passion increased with every kiss.

Annie couldn't remember ever feeling so powerless and powerful at the same time. Matt's kisses were turning her inside out, weakening any resolve she might have had to resist him. If someone had told her that she had to stop, she wouldn't have had the strength to remove her mouth from his, to shift her body away from his loving touch. It was as though a magnetic force was drawing them together, their bodies molding to each other as though the other was the missing part.

At the same time, she was beginning to understand for the first time in her life, the power she had to attract a man. During her years with Eric, she had never felt so attractive that he had trouble keeping his hands off her.

She had always compared herself to other women and had always come up short. Over time her insecurities grew, dwarfing her confidence in the process. She had become inhibited and unsure of herself as a woman, always wondering what was wrong with her.

Motherhood had appealed to her in so many ways, one of them being the opportunity to love and be loved without worrying about how desirable she was or wasn't. Babies didn't judge or reject their mothers based on the size of their breasts or bottoms; they loved them no matter how big the bags under their eyes became or how flabby their thighs. Life with Eric had been so lonely. She had convinced herself that being a mother would have made up for all the nights huddled alone on her side of the bed, for all of the times an absent-minded peck on the cheek was the extent of his passion.

Now, with Matt planting a row of gentle kisses along her collarbone, she found it hard to believe that she'd actually believed that she could have lived the rest of her life without experiencing such feelings and worse yet, that she didn't deserve to have them in the first place. Needs that had lain dormant for too long were not only being discovered, but met. Her heart trembled wildly as she stopped trying to contain all of the happiness that filled it and she closed her eyes and smiled.

# The Eiffel Tower

The rich black liquid was a stark contrast to the white porcelain of the delicate cup into which it had been poured. Its pungent aroma stung rather than satisfied and Annie pushed the cup and saucer across the white linen tablecloth, so that its swirling steam would be further away.

"Mademoiselle, is there a problem with the coffee this morning?" The waiter who had served her the beverage seemed to appear out of nowhere. "And you have barely touched your croissant. I saved it especially for you."

Annie smiled up at the portly man who was bent over the small table of the sidewalk cafe. His face was a portrait of worry and consternation, his dark brown eyebrows furrowed in a deep "V" over his eyes and the corners of his mouth pulled down into an exaggerated frown.

"No, Pierre, it's *très bon.*" She knew that Pierre would be pleased if she attempted to use his native language. It was the end of her second week in Paris, and she was feeling bolder about dusting off the remnants of high school French rattling around in her brain and used them when it felt appropriate.

"Then why do you push it away?"

"I'm just not very hungry this morning." With clammy hands, she smoothed the linen napkin that had become a jumbled heap on her lap.

"You will let me know if there's anything else I can bring you? Some *fromage,* perhaps?"

"No thank you. But I promise to let you know if I change my mind."

"Very well. I will check back in a little while." He nearly did a little pirouette as he turned to leave her table. She imagined him in a pink tutu and had to squelch a giggle.

"Merci, Pierre." Annie smiled at him again as he bowed slightly and glided away to tend to his other patrons.

The sidewalk cafe was right next to her hotel and going there for breakfast had become a morning ritual. Because she had been the last one to sign up for the tour, the travel agent had scrambled to find her a room at all, let alone in the same hotel as her fellow musicians. Annie's hotel was a bit off the beaten path, and that suited her just fine. She loved the romantic Old World charm that oozed from every nook and cranny, preferring it to the stuffy atmosphere of the Plaza Hotel where the rest of the group was staying. Her walk to the symphony hall was somewhat longer than it would have been from the Plaza, but she didn't mind. To be able to amble along cobblestone streets lined with quaint little flower shops, mouthwatering bakeries, and enchanting cafes made every day a new adventure. People were usually very kind to the American carrying a tattered canvas cello case on her back, and she was beginning to recognize many of them and waved as they called *"Bon jour!"* or *"Bon soir!"* as she walked past. Aunt Sally had warned her about the French being rude to American tourists, but she hadn't found that to be the case at all.

Annie was enjoying her time in Paris. The rehearsals were long and grueling, but all the hard work paid off when the strains of the notes she played bounced off the walls of the Cathedral of Notre Dame or the Basilica Sacrè-Coeur. As the music reverberated within her, she couldn't believe that she had nearly missed this opportunity. It *was* the chance of a lifetime and she felt so grateful to be able to experience it. She loved the idea of performing in the massive churches that were hundreds of years old. It added another level of reverence to the music which she could never find in a regular concert hall.

The only thing missing was Matt. It would have been so wonderful and romantic to be able to explore the city with him. Perhaps they could come back another time, together. Matt would love Paris. Being a writer, perhaps he'd want to investigate the old haunts of Hemingway, Fitzgerald, and Faulkner and try to absorb the inspiration that infused the atmosphere so long ago. It was fun to imagine the two of them pursuing their art together, she her music, he his writing, in a place where so many gifted artists had created before them. Every day Annie saw something that she wanted to tell him about, and every day she became increasingly frustrated with not being able to do so.

Communication had been difficult. Airmail delivery was slow and long-distance telephone calls were expensive. The itinerary consisted of three weeks in Italy and three weeks in France. The seven hour time difference and their work schedules made even the shortest of phone calls difficult to execute, but that didn't stop them from trying, at least at the beginning. After many interrupted sleep cycles and even more phone messages left on either Matt's answering machine or with the hotel concierge, the frequency of attempts began to decrease. The insecure part of her kept worrying that perhaps Matt wasn't as devoted to her as she'd thought; that he'd gotten tired of waiting. She kept reminding herself that it was only a six week tour, not that long to wait. That's when the strong, feisty part of her would interject that she was being ridiculous to ruin this incredible experience by pining away for a man, no matter how wonderful he was.

Oscillating between worry and anger, she kept busy. Her days were filled with rehearsals and sightseeing, her evenings filled with concerts and fitful sleep. It wasn't until she turned off the bedside lamp and collapsed on the fluffy featherbed in her hotel room each night that she let herself dwell on it. As the nights turned into weeks, the time spent obsessing about Matt became shorter and shorter, as she became more and more exhausted. Soon she was falling asleep the moment her head hit the pillow, any worries about Matt lost in some hidden corner of her mind.

That morning in the cafe, she had been surprised and a little irritated by Pierre's concern. Certainly people left untouched food all the time; she was no different than anyone else. She did have to admit that she was always ravenous first thing each morning and had never left one of the delicate, buttery croissants uneaten. In fact, on more than one occasion, she'd asked for another. She'd also sung the praises of the cafe's coffee and drank so much of it that Pierre had begun to leave a carafe of it on her table, to save himself the trouble of having to refill it every ten minutes. So it made sense that this sudden shift in behavior might be somewhat noticeable, especially to a professional like Pierre.

"Mademoiselle Annie!" A dismayed Pierre approached her after he'd given the check to a nearby table. "You will not have the strength to carry your cello if you do not eat. What is wrong?" He pulled out the chair across from her and sat down.

"Pierre, aren't you going to get in trouble for sitting down on the job?" Annie looked around for the ill-tempered maitre d'. She'd seen him berate other waiters and didn't want Pierre to fall victim to that because of her.

"No, Mademoiselle. No worries." He waved a dismissive hand. "Henri is away at his mother's today. And while *le chat* is away..." A mischievous grin slid across his face.

"You look as though you're working pretty hard," Annie said, trying to divert the subject away from her lack of appetite. "Is it always this busy?"

Every table was occupied and there was a line of waiting people, which curved out of the restaurant and around the corner. Even though Pierre insinuated that he was playing while Henri was away, Annie could see that he took his work very seriously. He was working just as much as he would have if his boss was there supervising him. The only difference was that today Pierre was having more fun than he did when Henri's nasty glare followed his every move and managed to find fault with most everything he did.

"*Mais oui,*" he said. "Our croissants are the best on the Left Bank. People come from all over Paris for them." His chest puffed out with pride.

"I can see why. They *are* delicious."

Pierre frowned again. "Which again brings me to my question: What is wrong? Why do you not eat the delicious croissant?"

"I'm just not very hungry today, Pierre. I don't know why. My stomach feels, sort of sick-- you know, *malade* ."

A look of genuine concern clouded his face. "*Mon Dieu*! I am so sorry to hear that, Mademoiselle. Is there anything I can get for you? How can I help?"

Annie patted his hand and smiled. "It's fine, Pierre. It's probably just something I ate -- not *here*, of course."

"You must go and lie down until the feeling passes," said Pierre. "The orchestra can do without one cello this morning."

Annie shook her head. "I wish that were true, but I'm afraid I'll get in trouble if I miss rehearsal. We have a concert tonight."

"Well, take it easy. Do not push yourself too hard." He reached into his pocket and took out a business card from the restaurant. "Here. Take this. If you need anything, you call."

Annie took the card from him, thinking that he was very kind, but knowing that there's no way she'd ever call him. It's not as though she was in Paris alone; her fellow musicians were there for her if she needed help. But what sort of help would she need? She'd be fine.

"*Merci*, Pierre. I'll be sure to do that." It wouldn't do any harm to make him think she'd call; she didn't want to minimize the parental concern he was showing her. He seemed to have taken her under his wing during the past couple of weeks and she didn't want to hurt his feelings.

Annie eyed the uneaten croissant on the small plate in front of her. Perhaps she would feel better if she had something in her stomach. As if her stomach knew what she was thinking, it growled, reminding her that it could be a very long morning and an even longer rehearsal if it wasn't properly fed. She picked up the delicate pastry and broke off a piece. Golden buttery flakes floated to the pristine tablecloth. Before she could brush them away, Pierre was there with his shiny, silver crumb sweeper, neatly removing the flaky remnants in a discrete, fluid motion. He placed the slender tool back in his pocket with deft fingers, a broad grin on his face.

"I am so happy to see you are going to eat after all!"

"I'm going to try." Annie smiled up at him and popped the broken portion of pastry into her mouth. She chewed it while Pierre watched, anxiously anticipating her enjoyment. As excellent as the cafe's croissants had been in the past, today it tasted like slimy Styrofoam, and the thought of having to swallow it made her stomach lurch in rebellion. Pierre's eager gaze didn't make her task any easier and she gestured for him to go back to work. Beaming with pride, he scurried away.

As soon as his back was turned, Annie grabbed the napkin from her lap and spit the contents of her mouth into it. Embarrassed, she balled up the napkin and shoved it into her bag, all the while vowing to her conscience to bring the napkin back another day, freshly laundered and pressed. The crisp morning breeze made her shiver, and a clammy sheen erupted on her forehead as the queasiness intensified. Annie closed her eyes and inhaled deeply in an attempt to chase away the feeling of impending doom. Just a few deep breaths and she'd feel better, she told herself, as her heart hammered an erratic rhythm in her chest. She'd be late for rehearsal if she didn't get going, so she brushed the crumbs from her lap and stood up. The sudden movement made the tables, chairs and people spin around her head like a kaleidoscope and before she could grab the table for support, she fell to the ground, hitting her head on the bumpy cobblestones.

Water trickled down her face from the cold, wet bar towel that had been placed on her forehead. She intercepted a drop of water right before it ran into her eye, blinking it away as her eyes fluttered open. Her head was on a makeshift pillow of folded white terry cloth towels, and as she floated up into consciousness, she became aware of the cool, hard stones that were beneath her, and she shifted slightly. There was a firm pressure that enveloped her right hand, squeezing it at regular intervals. Without warning, the pressure increased and her hand was raised to something soft and warm.

"Oh, mon Dieu, she's waking up!" Pierre said after he took his lips from her hand, which he continued to clutch and shake as he spoke.

Once her eyes were able to focus, Annie could see the wrought iron legs of the cafe's tables and chairs surrounding her, her cello propped up in the midst of them. Pierre knelt on the ground next to her, holding her hand. Not too far behind him she could see a hungry pigeon pecking at half a croissant that had fallen from a table, probably her own. At least someone was eating it. With her free hand, she felt the top of her head and then the back of it. The large bump that protruded felt sticky and warm. Pierre reached for that hand with another towel before she could see the blood.

"What happened?" The words came out muffled and thick. She squinted up at the frenzied waiter.

"You collapsed, Madamoiselle. I turned to bid you "Adieu" and saw you fall to the ground. I couldn't reach you before you hit your head. I am so sorry!" His grip on her hand tightened as he recalled the incident.

"Don't worry, Pierre. I'm sure I'm fine. Low blood sugar or something." She moved to sit up, but a new wave of nausea and dizziness washed over her and she eased back down to her terry cloth pillow.

"You are *not* fine." A female voice declared. It was Jen, bent over her like a pretzel.

"What are *you* doing here?" Annie craned her neck to look at her friend.

"What do you think?" Jen's sarcasm was laced with genuine concern.

Annie was now thoroughly confused. Jen hadn't been able to go on the tour with the group, and seeing her suddenly appear seemed like a hallucination or a dream. Sensing Annie's disorientation, Jen repositioned the towel on her forehead and patted her shoulder.

"It's a long story, which I'll tell you later. Right now we have to get you to a hospital."

The expression on Jen's face was serious enough to make Annie abandon any arguments and she simply closed her eyes and nodded. She was relieved to have Jen there and would be even more relieved to find out what was wrong with her.

"What is taking so long?" Jen was pacing back and forth next to the gurney that Annie was lying on in the hospital's emergency room. "This is ridiculous!" She blew a strand of hair off of her forehead with an angry humph.

Annie rolled her eyes and craned her neck to get a better view of her friend. "Calm down, Jen. I'm sure they're taking care of people who actually need to be here."

It had seemed like overkill to be taken by ambulance to the hospital, but Jen had been adamant, so Annie kept her opinions to herself. Even though the lights and siren weren't used, she still felt like a spectacle. She was thankful she didn't have to hear the shrill sound of the two note siren which reminded her of World War II movies. Why did European sirens sound like that anyway? They sounded so harsh and military. It was a scary enough sound as it was, without throwing in visions of enemy soldiers occupying every other street corner.

Jen had ridden along in the back of the ambulance, watching nervously while the paramedics took Annie's vital signs. They applied a cool compress to the bump on the back of her head to keep it from getting any larger. She'd probably need a few stitches when she got to the hospital. As the paramedic explained, 'The head bleeds so *abondamment*.' Jen had looked at Annie, her eyebrows arched as if to say, '*What does* that *mean?*' Annie shrugged; she had no idea. Her tenuous command of the language didn't extend to bleeding of any kind and she'd prefer to keep it that way.

Going by ambulance did get her into the emergency room more quickly than if she had taken a taxi, but once it was determined that she wasn't in any imminent danger of dying, she was relegated to a lower place in the lineup. It was a very busy place. The paramedics had wheeled her past many people who appeared to have been waiting a long time; a very long time. Some of them slept, slumped down in the hard plastic chairs in an attempt to be comfortable. Others paged through outdated, dog-eared magazines and still others, like Jen, paced back and forth liked caged animals.

A young woman in a white lab coat appeared at the slender opening in the curtain that separated Annie's cubicle from the rest of the chaos. Her dark brown hair was cut in a short bob that framed her large eyes and wide mouth, which curved up into a curt smile. Annie half-expected her to break into "Singing in the Rain" and dance over to her side. It was uncanny how much she looked like the French actress who had been in that movie with Gene Kelly. Instead she stood at Annie's feet, a medical chart in her hand. For a moment Annie had a flashback to that day in the hospital when the young female resident had told her that she'd have to stay on bed rest until Dillon was big enough to be born. She hadn't even been near a hospital, except the one where the support group had met, since Dillon had died. The sounds and smells brought to life memories that made her heart hurt and her head pound in response. The incessant beeping of the blood pressure monitor accelerated. The young woman walked over to it, looked at the display closely and jotted the numbers down on the chart.

"*Bon jour,* Mlle. Stanford. I am Dr. Caron." She extended her hand to Annie, who gave it a weak shake. "It's nice to meet you. I have your preliminary test results. As you know, some blood was drawn to help us determine why you collapsed."

Annie's eyes widened in disbelief when she realized that the doctor's name was the same as the actress. What were the odds of that? She caught Jen's eye, and realized that she must have been thinking the same thing. They gave each other a quick smile, which helped Annie relax a little. The beeping on the monitor slowed down a bit.

Dr. Caron glanced at Jen. "Would you like your friend to leave the room?"

"Oh no, she can stay." Annie glowered affectionately at Jen. "She's the one who made me come here."

"Are you certain, Mlle?" Dr. Caron's large eyes held a hint of disapproval.

"Yes, I am." Annie's voice became stronger, more emphatic with each word.

"Very well then." Dr. Caron took a deep breath. "The test results indicate the probable reason for your episode."

Annie and Jen held their breath, waiting for the serious young doctor to continue. The ticking of the clock on the wall filled Annie's ears with deafening gongs, marking the time to the much awaited announcement. A parade of various maladies trudged through her brain -- brain tumor, cancer, stroke, rare mystery disease. Wasn't this just her luck? She was in love with a wonderful man, had a dream job, was on the trip of a lifetime and now some fatal illness was going to ruin it all.

The doctor's wispy yet businesslike tone continued. "You are pregnant."

"Excuse me?" Annie said, thunderstruck.

"Well, you appear to be pregnant, but the hormone levels are very low, so it is very likely that the embryo will spontaneously abort within 24-48 hours."

The room started to spin again. Annie squeezed her eyes shut, willing the motion to stop and for this all to be a bad dream. This couldn't be happening for so many reasons. She opened her eyes one at a time, first in narrow slits, to see if she was back in her bed in the hotel after all, or even better, in her bed back home. Once it was clear that she was in a hospital, she opened them the rest of the way. The first thing she saw was Jen, her face contorted with emotion, talking to the doctor, her hands gesturing in wild circles. They were just outside the curtain, thinking she wouldn't see or hear them there. She couldn't hear what was being said and she didn't know what difference it could make anyway. She was pregnant. With Matt's baby.

As surprised as she had sounded, it confirmed a fear she'd had since the first night they had made love. They'd been so consumed with passion they'd all but forgotten about the concept of birth control. After the telephone rang and interrupted them that night, Matt had raised the question, but she'd hushed him and urged him not to worry. Now it occurred to her that perhaps the phone ringing had been fate trying to intervene, but they had ignored it. Many months of trying and the use of fertility drugs had been required to conceive Dillon, so Annie was convinced she wasn't all that fertile. Besides, the odds of her conceiving the very first time, had to be next to impossible. At least that's what she told herself, especially when her period hadn't come on time, or at all, after that night. She was supposed to get it the day she left for Europe and when it didn't come, she attributed it to the stress and excitement of the trip. Now here she was, pregnant with a baby that was going to die. Another one. She didn't know if she could live through it again.

"Annie, sweetie?" Jen was suddenly at her side, smoothing her hair with a gentle hand.

Annie turned her head toward the familiar voice and gave her friend a blank stare.

"I was just talking to the doctor."

"I saw."

"I asked her what the chances are --," her voice was choked with tears.

"The chances of what?" Annie couldn't keep the cynicism out of her voice. She didn't even try.

"Of the baby being okay. Of course, first I read her the riot act. I couldn't believe how incredibly insensitive she was being. I wanted to slap her."

"It's not her fault, Jen. She's an ER doc and she's never seen me before in her life. She can't become emotionally invested in every patient."

"I know, but still. Anyway, she said that they could run another test, just to be sure. She also said that sometimes, if you're very careful, the baby will make it and everything will be just fine." Jen wiped away a tear with the tip of her index finger.

"So why isn't she telling *me* all of this?"

"I don't know. I told her I thought you'd want another test run. I hope you don't mind."

Annie let out a deep sigh only to realize that she'd been holding her breath. She didn't know what to do. If she was going to lose this baby anyway, she wanted to go ahead and lose it; not even try to give it a chance. To get emotionally attached to a new baby, to fall in love with it only to have it taken from her; she wanted no part of that. Then she thought of Matt; dear, sweet Matt. Should she call him with the news or wait and tell him only if there was something to tell?

"Are you going to call Matt?" It seemed as though Jen had read her mind.

"I don't know --"

"What do you mean you don't know?" Jen pounced on her.

Annie drew back from her a little, startled by the intensity with which she answered, "I mean I don't know."

A lab tech who looked even younger than the doctor slipped through the opening in the curtain. In her hand she carried a light blue plastic caddy which held an assortment of needles, clear plastic test tubes and shiny metal syringes.

"Bon jour," she said in a silky voice. "I am here to draw some blood." She then proceeded to tie the stretchy rubber ribbon around Annie's arm. It took her only a second to choose the vein that she wanted to poke, and did so with impressive skill and speed. Annie barely had time to react and she was finished, affixing a flesh colored Band-aid over a folded up square of gauze in the crook of Annie's arm.

"Merci." Annie said as the lab tech left the cubical.

"So, what do you mean?" Jen's voice was a whisper, brimming with urgency.

"I mean, I'm not sure if I should even tell Matt about this. If I'm going to miscarry anyway, what's the point? I mean, if he were a few minutes away, I'd call him in a heartbeat, but he's thousands of miles away. What can he do?" Her eyes examined the pattern of holes in the ceiling tiles, afraid to look at Jen because she knew she'd start to cry.

"But wouldn't he want to know?" Jen left the second part of her question unspoken, trapped behind her lips. It was the part that said, *Especially if the baby dies?*

The lump in Annie's throat burned, threatening to ignite into a shower of sobs the moment she opened her mouth and let even a smidgen of oxygen in. She turned her head toward the side of the room where her friend was not.

"He's been hard to get a hold of lately." Her voice was so quiet, Jen had to strain to hear her, and even then she couldn't make out the words.

"What did you say, sweetie?" Jen's tone was cautious. "He's been hard to get a hold of?"

"I've left messages on his answering machine, but he hasn't called back. What if he's lost interest, Jen? Out of sight, out of mind, you know?" The tears started to flow. "I can't call and tell him I'm *pregnant*. I'm so *embarrassed*. I'm too old to make a mistake like this."

"Whoa. Hold on a minute." Jen strode over to her, hands on her hips. "Correct me if I'm wrong, but I don't think you got pregnant all by yourself, did you?"

Annie shook her head.

"Alright then. If any *mistakes* were made, and I'm not sure that's what I'd call this, he was just as much a part of it as you were. You were *both* there; you *both* decided to throw caution to the wind. Am I right?"

Color rose in her cheeks as she remembered that first time with Matt. It had been such a crazy, magical, emotional evening. It was a night she'd never forget.

"Yes, I guess so, but I never thought I'd get pregnant. I've been a little worried about it since my period was late, but I figured it was just the excitement of traveling and everything. I do not get pregnant easily, Jen. With Dillon ---"

"This isn't Dillon, sweetie. Different baby, different daddy," Jen said in a gentle voice.

Annie shivered. "When you say it like that, I sound so slutty."

"I don't mean it like that, silly. What I mean is that with *Eric* you didn't get pregnant easily. Matt is a totally different story, in *so* many ways. Maybe this baby is supposed to be born; maybe God has a different plan for you."

"Let's not bring God into it right now."

Annie hadn't written God off since Dillon had died, but she felt a bit jaded about religion. She had prayed everyday while she was pregnant with Dillon; prayers for a healthy baby. It hadn't mattered whether it was a boy or a girl; besides, it would have been greedy to put in a specific gender request. After Dillon died, she felt that God was trying to tell her that even asking for a healthy baby was unreasonable, too much to ask.

"You never told me why you're here," Annie said, trying to change the subject.

"Well, you know how I didn't think I could arrange child care and all of that?"

Annie nodded.

"I figured it out the day all of you left. I called Conrad and begged him to let me meet up with all of you here. He said that I could; the more the merrier, as long as I could arrange my own hotel accommodations. As luck has it, I'm in your hotel. I just got here today." Jen told the whole story without taking a breath.

"It's strange how things work out, because now you'll probably end up taking my place. I don't know how I'm going to play tonight. I'm supposed to be at rehearsal right now." Tears welled up again.

"Don't worry about that. I can fill in tonight, but once everything settles down, we'll just both play." Jen glanced at the clock on the wall. "I should try to get to rehearsal, but I hate to leave you here all alone."

Annie hated to be left alone too, especially in a hospital where the command of the English language was shaky at best. It was a miracle that Jen appeared when she did. If she hadn't, Annie would be here alone anyway; it wasn't right to keep her friend from an important rehearsal.

"It's okay. I'll be fine. You go ahead." Annie did her best to sound confident and strong. No one could answer the difficult questions for her or solve the tough problems. She had to do that on her own.

# The Ruby Slippers

The droning voice of the French meteorologist floated across the room and tip-toed into Annie's ears. She stirred a little as the voice became more precise instead of a hazy tangle of words. It occurred to her that the French could even make a weather report sound romantic, as her eyes flickered open. The television was on the other side of the room, partially hidden by a length of fabric covered with brightly colored circles. The circles were overlapped and linked, their individual colors blending to make new ones. The red and blue converged to become purple. The yellow and blue became green. Annie squinted at the curtain, trying to make sense of it all, when she felt a cool hand on her forehead, followed by a gentle kiss.

Closing her eyes again, she smiled, hoping to go back to sleep. In her dream, it had been Matt's lips that were kissing her forehead. She had been so happy that he was finally there with her. The lips were there again, brushing her cheek, and she felt a light touch on her shoulder and then a more insistent squeeze.

"Annie, honey, are you awake?"

Annie frowned and pried her eyes open. This voice was louder than the one from the television, and sounded very familiar. Her eyes opened wider and worked hard to focus on the face so close to hers.

"Matt?" Either she was still dreaming or her dreams were finally coming true.

"Hi, sweetheart." He held her hand in both of his, and laid his cheek against it.

When she saw the I.V. catheter taped onto the back of her hand, she began to remember where she was and what had happened, but she was still a little foggy on some of the details. It was light outside, the kind of early morning light that's full of dew and promise.

"Are you really here or am I dreaming you?"

"I'm really here. My plane landed about an hour ago." He kissed the palm of her hand. "I came the minute I heard."

Annie didn't remember calling him or asking anyone else to notify him. The last thing she remembered was Dr. Caron telling her that she was indeed pregnant and that the hormone levels were more promising than the first test had indicated. The next 48-72 hours were critical however, complicated by the concussion that she'd suffered in her fall. That still didn't explain Matt at her bedside.

"What exactly did you hear?"

From the look on his face she could see his writer's mind working hard, trying to put the words in just the right order. His eyes never wavered from hers, and the long, silent pause expanded and filled the space between them with a softness only the two of them could feel.

"Well, I heard that you had a fall and ended up in the hospital. You hit your head and have a concussion. You also have about eight stitches in the back of your head." He looked down for a second to maintain his equilibrium and then continued. "I also heard some other rather amazing news."

Annie put her hand up to his lips, to stop the words. She searched his face for a hint of how he was feeling. His forehead was creased with worry, his eyebrows arched over wide eyes that were watery, with either tears or jet-lag. His mouth was relaxed in a pleasant line, neither a smile or a frown, but leaning more towards a hopeful grin.

"That I'm pregnant." The words swirled in the air, revolving between them in a slow, expectant dance. They both seemed to be waiting for the dancing to stop, for the words to find a comfortable place to rest.

"That *we're* pregnant." Matt said as he brought her hand to his face. His cheeks were wet with tears and she dabbed at them with her thumb.

"So, this is good news for you?" Annie's voice was cautious.

"It's *great* news, Annie. I am *so* happy." His voice wasn't enthusiastic or excited, but it was genuine. She could tell by how his eyes never left hers. That is what Matt did when he meant it; he never looked away.

"You're not upset? I thought you might be, because I hadn't been able to get a hold of you for a week or so. I thought that maybe you were tired of waiting for me or had met someone else." The fears that had been building up inside of her spilled out. She couldn't stop them.

Matt put his arms around her and gave her a steadfast hug. He didn't say anything, but just held her until the squall had passed. When her breathing returned to close to a normal cadence, he pulled back and looked at her.

"You don't have any more faith in me than that?"

"I do, but I didn't want to assume anything; I didn't want to take you for granted."

"Having faith in someone is not the same as taking them for granted, Annie. I *love* you. That means that even if you're thousands of miles away, that even if our phone calls don't connect, you're still in my thoughts every moment of every day. I've been counting the days until you come home; crossing them off on my calendar like a kid waiting for Christmas."

His words felt warm and cozy around her uncertainty. The events of the past day had been unsettling in so many ways. She closed her eyes and took in a deep breath.

"Have you heard the rest of the news?" She was afraid the possibility of losing the baby would devastate him. How could she take away his joy so quickly?

"Yes, sweetie, Jen told me and the doctor spoke to me as well." He smoothed her hair back from her forehead. "It's going to be okay. No matter what happens, it's going to be okay."

"But what if --?"

"The baby dies?" Matt finished the sentence for her.

She nodded, so sorry that he had to go through another loss because of her.

"If the baby dies, at least I've had the chance to know it and to love it for a little while." He placed his hand on her stomach and bent over to plant a kiss there. "But until that happens, I'm going to be happy and love that little munchkin as much as I can."

She gave him a guarded smile. "I've been so worried that this would be so hard for you."

"Annie, it will be very hard for both of us. To be so happy and then to have it taken away would be horrible. Honey, don't you see? We've made a miracle. A real, live miracle that's here right *now*."

"What if there's something wrong with *me*? Maybe *I'm* the reason Dillon died and if this baby dies too, it will be my fault. I don't want you to ever have to go through something like this again. I'm so sorry, Matt." She started sobbing again. Her head throbbed, especially the place where the stitches were neatly sewn. Each beat of her heart stretched the black silk sutures, punctuating the pain.

"Annie, please calm down." His voice was emphatic, just this side of harsh. "You are not the reason. You're not God. Not that you aren't the center of *my* world, but everything doesn't begin and end with you. It's not your fault. *None* of it is all your fault. Do you understand?"

His words struck a nerve and at first she felt annoyed. Who was he to say that she wasn't to blame; that she wasn't responsible for her babies' lives? That's what mothers were for, wasn't it? To be responsible for the well-being of their children? Maybe God created life, but it was up to the mother to nurture them in her womb until birth and then after that until they grew up and had lives of their own. Even though all babies have fathers, it was usually mothers who got blamed for everything. Why shouldn't she think it was all her fault?

Looking at him, at the genuine concern in his eyes, the full meaning of what he said hit her. It wasn't her fault that Dillon had died. It wasn't her fault at all. She had been carrying around a backbreaking load of guilt ever since it had happened. Eric didn't do anything to ease the burden, by blaming her for everything that had happened. It was no wonder that she had taken on the task of berating herself. She didn't have to do it all over again. Suddenly she felt lighter and the pain behind her eyes diminished. The knot tied around her heart began to loosen its chokehold, allowing Matt's joy to flow in and chase away the shame and regret that had been there for so long.

If this baby died, she would be okay. She prayed with all her heart that she didn't have to find out, but she had to face the possibility squarely, to stare it down and let it know that it had no power over her, in order to move forward. It was a bizarre way of trying to be happy, but it was the only way she knew. To know that she could survive the worst case scenario gave her the courage to face whatever happened. Of course she had no idea if she'd be fine or not -- she knew full well that if this baby died, or if Matt stopped loving her, she'd be teetering on the brink of God knows what, but she had to convince herself that she'd be alright. She had no choice.

"Does it hurt a lot?" Matt looked anxiously at her head.

"It's not too bad. Seeing you has helped take my mind off of it. That and thinking about the baby." She tried to sit up so that he could get a better look at her stitches.

"Whoa," he said as he ran his fingers over the goose egg laced with a black dotted line. "This is huge. Are you sure it doesn't hurt?"

"I'm sure." She averted her eyes as she spoke.

He looked at her closely. "I don't believe you, Annie."

"Well, I can't take any pain meds, so I'm trying not to think about it. Let's talk about something else." She paused, her lips pursed in concentration, and then said, "How was your flight?"

"To be honest, I don't remember too much about it. I was a little distracted." He kissed the tip of her nose.

"Did Jen tell you about the baby when she called you?" Suddenly Annie was ravenous for details.

"No, she just told me about the fall. She didn't tell me anymore than that. I was so worried about you being okay. It felt so much like the call I got from the hospital after Sara's accident. All I could think about was that I might lose you." His voice broke, sobs hovered in the back of his throat, threatening to escape. "I couldn't stand that. *That* is what I couldn't handle." He burrowed his face next to her leg on the bed, burying it in the white cotton hospital blanket.

Annie placed her hand on the back of his head and gently stroked his wavy brown hair. "Shhh, sweetie. I'm right here. I'm not going anywhere. I promise."

The was a soft knock on the half opened door. It was Dr. Caron, her stethoscope hung around her neck like a scarf, her hands shoved deeply into the pockets of her lab coat. She cleared her throat. Even that sounded better in French.

"Excuse me. May I interrupt for a moment?" She lingered in the doorway which made Annie like her even more. The doctors she was used to back home would have simply barged in, giving no thought to the patient or what they might be doing. The young doctor who had been so coarse at the beginning seemed to be softening around the edges.

"Of course, doctor," said Annie, as she gave one of Matt's curls a little tug, pulling his head up in the process.

She gave him a sheepish smile as he now rubbed the back of his head where her hand had been.

"Hello Dr. Caron." Matt stood up as she entered the room. He extended his hand to shake hers, but she gave him a friendly nod instead.

"Please sit down, Mr. Preston." Her tone was pleasant but professional. She came closer to the bed. "May I sit down?"

Annie struggled to raise herself to a more upright position, but a wave of dizziness washed over her. Resting back on her elbows, she hesitated until the feeling subsided. Matt leaned over and helped her ease back down onto her pillows.

"No, no, Ms. Stanford. Please stay where you are. May I?" She gestured toward the edge of the hospital bed.

"Of course," said Annie. She started to have a bad feeling about this. Doctors usually didn't come in and sit on the patient's bed unless something was very, very wrong. At least that's what happened in movies and on T.V.

"How are you feeling?" The doctor was now holding her stethoscope in her hands, preparing to put the earpieces in her ears. "Mr. Preston's arrival makes you feel better, no?" Her eyes had the beginning of a smile that never made it to her lips.

Dr. Caron placed the round disk of the stethoscope on Annie's chest and listened intently. She moved the instrument to a different spot and listened some more. The expression on her face never changed, although her large eyes framed with black lashes looked at various places on the ceiling as she listened for heart and lung sounds.

"Yes, I'm very happy that he's here." Annie said. "When can I go home?"

Dr. Caron shifted her weight on the bed as she hung the stethoscope back around her neck. "You mean to the United States?"

"I don't know. To the United States, to the hotel. I just meant when can I leave the hospital?" She tried to disguise the irritation in her voice by making it a question.

"I understand that you want to be discharged, but we have serious things to consider here; your head injury and your baby." She reached into her pocket and retrieved a small penlight. "Look at me, s'il vous plait."

Annie obeyed the command and gazed at the doctor while she shone the bright light into each eye to see if and how much the pupils dilated or contracted. The light was so intense that when Annie looked at Matt, he had small spots all over his face. She blinked and rubbed her eyes to make them disappear.

"Good. Your pupils appear to react normally to stimulus. That is very good." Her dark head bobbed up and down as she made notes in Annie's chart.

"So, I can leave?" Annie was hopeful.

"I'm sorry, but it is too soon. You must stay for observation a while longer. We need to keep a close eye on you and the baby. Sometimes the effects of a head injury don't surface until days after the event." Her voice was businesslike but her eyes conveyed unspoken concern.

Annie's shoulders slumped. She'd have to miss the rest of the tour, but there were only a handful of performances left, and Jen could take her place. There were no worries about that, not with the more critical concern about the baby. The tiny new life inside of her deserved all of her attention; she was committed to do whatever she needed to for the baby to survive. Munchkin. That's what Matt had called it and it made her smile. Munchkin.

"Will traveling be an issue once she *is* discharged?" Matt said.

"We'll evaluate that at the time. Your baby won't have to be born in Paris, unless you want it to be." Dr. Caron said, smiling for the first time.

*Your baby won't have to be born in Paris.* The phrase had a bittersweet ring to it that started out as music to her ears and then became a funeral dirge. At first, it sounded so ordinary, so *normal.* It didn't take long for Annie to hear the change in the melody. Dissonant chords ridiculed and mocked her for thinking this baby would be born at all. Born alive, that is. Who did she think she was that she could just become pregnant and actually plan to bring a baby home? It was something that millions of people did every day as easily as they ate breakfast or got dressed for work. Everyone thought birth was miraculous, but it was a miracle that they took for granted, something she and Matt could never do.

"We don't want to seem uncooperative," said Matt. "This is just a little scary for us."

"I know, Mr. Preston. Ms. Stanford's friend, Jen, told me about both of your experiences. That is why I want to take even greater care to make sure everything is done correctly. Normally we would perform a CT scan after a head injury, but because of the pregnancy we cannot do that. So we must wait and observe for just another day or so. Do you understand?"

Annie nodded. "Yes, Dr. Caron. We appreciate your being so careful. I'll try harder to be a patient patient." She groaned at the lame joke before anyone else had a chance.

Matt promised the taxi driver an exorbitant tip if he made the trip from the hospital to the hotel a smooth one. The abundance of cobblestone streets made it a challenge. It became a longer ride than usual in his attempt to avoid them, which also increased the fare along with the tip. None of that mattered to Matt, who cradled Annie in the back seat as though she were made of delicate French crystal. He anticipated every bump, by gently bracing her body against his, as he closed his eyes and held is breath as if he expected her to shatter into thousands of pieces.

"If I didn't know better, I'd think you were doing this just to get your hands on me," Annie said as she snuggled closer to him, nibbling his neck.

He looked at her, raised an eyebrow and smirked, twirling an imaginary mustache between his thumb and forefinger. "Mademoiselle, one as precious as you must be protected and held very, very carefully." He ran his hands over her shoulders and arms, finally resting them on her stomach.

Well, sir, I must say, you are making this the most sensual taxi ride I've ever had." She pretended to fan herself and laid her head back on his chest. As soon as the back of her head made contact with him, she flinched, the bump on her head, throbbing in pain.

"Sorry." Matt stopped kidding around. His expression changed from happy to terrified in a split second.

"It's just a little tender." Annie tried to downplay the discomfort and plastered a brave smile on her face. "I'm sure it will be like that for a few days. Don't worry."

"You're kidding, right? If you think I can stop worrying, you've got another thing coming." He patted her hair as though it was made of gossamer. "It's what I do; for now and for the rest of your life."

Did he just say what she thought he did? *For the rest of your life?* Annie knew that the new life within her meant that they'd be in each other's lives from that point forward, but she hadn't allowed herself to think beyond that. Whether this baby would survive the pregnancy was still unknown, and she couldn't trust that it would, until she was holding the squalling newborn in her arms. Until then no one would be able to reassure her enough. Of course she had thought about a life with Matt in it, but didn't dare dream about it, afraid that it would be taken from her, much like the baby. Not wanting to appear too anxious, she tried to act as though his words hadn't flown directly into her heart and taken root there. She directed her eyes toward the sights outside the cab for a second until she regained her composure.

"Annie honey?" Matt's voice was filled with a quiet urgency.

She turned her head to look at him, and saw the black velveteen box, sitting in his outstretched hand. He opened it in what seemed to be slow motion, exposing its contents; a breathtaking solitaire diamond set in a warm, honey gold band. The sunlight bounced off the many facets of the stone, making it sparkle and simmer unlike anything she'd ever seen.

"I wanted to ask you at the top of the Eiffel Tower or along the Seine," he started, "but I can't wait." He repositioned himself, settling on one knee before her, balancing on top of the jump seats on the floor of the cab. "Annie Stanford, will you marry me?"

Annie looked at him and then at the ring and then back at Matt again. "Are you serious?" She looked back at the ring. "Is this for real?"

It was the first marriage proposal she'd ever had. When she'd thought about their future together, she'd never thought about *how* it would happen. Back when she'd been dating Eric, there hadn't been a proposal. The decision to get married was unspoken; it just seemed like the next step, the next thing on the list of things to do. This was romantic and unexpected and she was completely caught off guard. She looked back at him, trying to steady himself on one knee as the cab swerved to miss a stray dog that was crossing the street, and her heart skipped a beat. His expression was a Picasso, a mixture of fear, longing, and love, all rolled into one.

"Yes, I'm serious and yes, it's for real." He put out the hand without the ring and held onto the edge of the seat to keep from falling as the cab hit a particularly large bump. "Will you spend the rest of your life with me?"

Annie threw her arms around his neck and gave him a fierce kiss.

"Is that a yes?" He asked when the kiss ended, his voice tentative.

"Yes, yes, yes!" She hugged him tightly.

"Well, I wasn't so sure, with all the questions you were firing at me," he said as he took the ring out of its soft, satin nest.

"I'm sorry -- I'm just so surprised! I never expected this!"

"But it's definitely a "yes"?" He still sounded unsure of her answer.

"She said 'oui', monsieur," said the cab driver, exasperated with Matt's uncertainty. "Put the ring on her finger before she changes her mind!"

Annie and Matt both looked toward the driver and then started to laugh, realizing how silly they must have sounded. Annie held out her left hand to Matt, and grinning from ear to ear, with trembling hands, he slipped the ring onto her finger. Holding her hand away from her, she gazed at it, admiring how beautiful it was and how it radiated his love for her. She looked back at Matt, and seeing the tears rolling down his face, started to cry.

"I just can't believe this," she said, sniffling. "Things like this don't happen to me. It's just too perfect."

"It is?" Matt sounded incredulous. "I thought I'd blown it, especially when you didn't give me an answer right away."

"I was just so surprised. I had no idea you were going to do this. I hoped you would, but hadn't let myself think about it very much." She sank back into Matt's arms, once he settled himself back on the seat.

"You really hoped I would?" He brightened at the thought.

"Yes, silly." She gave him a playful elbow to his ribs. "I've thought about it since I first met you. We just hadn't discussed it at all."

"I knew from our first cup of coffee in the hospital cafeteria that I wanted to spend the rest of my life with you." He kissed her hand and then held it, admiring how it looked with the diamond ring sparkling on it.

Annie was silent, savoring the moment and making it a precious memory. She would tell Munchkin about this someday, about how romantic his or her daddy was, and about this wonderful time in Paris. Thinking about the baby, the happiness that had been pulsating through her body was replaced by nervous apprehension. There were so many unknowns, so many things that could go wrong.

She felt Matt tighten the protective circle of his arms around her and she gave him a reassuring squeeze. The question that kept taunting her was which one of them needed the reassurance more.

"There no place like home," he whispered into her ear. "And home is wherever we are. You, me, and," he patted her stomach, "Munchkin."

# The Shooting Star

Impatient footsteps echoed down the hall, each step a brusque staccato. They had been waiting for Dr. Caron for nearly an hour and Matt was consumed with worry and frustration. Annie had sent him out in the hall to walk if off because he was wearing a hole in the fabric of her patience with all of his pacing. Each step snagged another thread until she felt ready to unravel.

"Is she here yet?" He poked his head in the examination room door.

"Have you seen her come in? You're the one out in the hallway." Annie's voice snapped with irritation.

"You're the one who sent me out here," Matt said and backed out of the doorway. He continued to pace.

Annie could just see him, hands shoved in his pockets and a scowl on his face as he measured the floor tiles with anxious, petulant steps. Dr. Caron had instructed them to come in for an appointment to determine if Annie was well enough to fly home to Minnesota. They had extended their stay another week and while Paris was a lovely place to be detained, they were ready to go home. She had called Frank and Sally with the news of their engagement, but had decided to wait to tell them about the baby, to keep them from worrying. They had embellished the truth and told them that they were staying in Paris to celebrate. Sally had been green with envy and had scolded Frank for his lack of romanticism, making him promise to bring her there for their 25th wedding anniversary. Annie felt guilty not being completely honest with them, but it seemed like the right thing to do, especially to Matt.

Matt and Annie had been having breakfast of croissants, tea and coffee on the balcony of their hotel room. Ever since Annie discovered she was pregnant, she would not allow coffee to cross her lips. It didn't make her as queasy as it had at first, which was lucky for Matt, because she could now tolerate its aroma. The week before, the slightest whiff of coffee was enough to send her running to the bathroom or looking for the closest waste basket. It hadn't been easy for him to refrain from drinking it although Annie had insisted that she'd be fine. He'd refused, patting her tummy and telling her that she and Munchkin were more important to him than a cup of coffee. Now that it didn't bother her as much, the reappearance of a coffee pot on the table that morning had been a pleasant surprise.

"I still think we should wait until we get home to tell them about Munchkin. It just seems safer," Matt said, his nose perched on the edge of his ceramic mug, inhaling the rich coffee aroma.

"What's not safe about telling them we're pregnant?" Annie dunked a tea bag up and down in her tea cup and then stopped. "Unless." Her eyes grew big and filled with tears.

"Unless what?" Matt looked up from his plate, suddenly aware that he'd done something wrong, but he didn't know what. That happened a lot lately.

"Unless you only proposed because I'm pregnant." She finally uttered one of the fears that was gnawing away at her and kept her awake while she laid in Matt's arms each night, looking out over the sleeping city as he snored softly beside her.

"Annie. How can you say that?" Matt's wounded voice grated on her already fragile nerves.

"Because." Annie had reached the point where if she said one more word, the weeping would be uncontrollable. Her bottom lip trembled as she struggled to gain command of her erratic emotions.

"Because?" Matt tried to jog her memory, as though she had forgotten what she was going to say.

"Because," she started again, her throat was choked with frantic tears, "I don't know. It's just that so much happened all at once. I'm afraid that if the baby dies, you'll feel trapped or something."

"You really don't give me much credit, do you?" Angry and hurt, Matt stood up, went to the railing and looked out over the city. "How many times do I have to tell you that I love you? Baby or no baby, I love you!"

She sat at the table with her hands in her lap, trying to avoid contact with the anguish in his eyes. Hurting him was the last thing she wanted to do. Her throat ached with the sobs that were trapped there, fighting to be freed. Afraid to make matters worse by saying something even more stupid or cruel, she chewed on her lower lip and twisted her napkin into a knot.

"It doesn't strike you as odd that I just happened to have an engagement ring with me?" His tone was less angry but there was still an edge to it that made Annie cringe. "Didn't you ever realize that I came here ready to propose before I had any idea there was a baby?" He turned to face her, waiting for a response.

The cobwebs that had been draped like a veil in her mind, obscuring what was real and true, began to disappear, one sticky strand at a time. She got up and stood next to him by the railing and put her hand over his, which was gripping the wrought iron like a vice on a workbench. When she felt his hand loosen, she laid her head against his arm.

"I'm sorry. I guess I hadn't thought about it like that." She rubbed his arm. "You were planning to propose all along?"

"I'd been thinking about it since you left on this trip. I even found a ring. Every day was just so long without you near me; I missed you like crazy."

"I've missed you too," Annie murmured.

Matt's small smile faded from his face. "When Jen called and said you were in the hospital, I booked a flight as soon as she hung up. I stopped at the jewelers on my way to the airport and got the ring. The thought of losing you made me realize just how much I love you. Then I found out about the baby and it was even better; like a miracle." He wiped away a tear that escaped down his cheek and turned to face her. "Annie honey, I know that you've been through a lot this past year that makes it hard to trust, but I promise you, I'll always be here for you. If you don't want to get married until after Munchkin is born, I understand. It's your call. I don't want to rush you. But I have to tell you, even if you had decided that you never wanted to try to have another baby, I'd want to marry you. It's not about babies, it's about you and me together for the rest of our lives."

A cool breeze ruffled the collar of her robe and she shivered as she pulled it closer to her body. Matt's hair had blown into his eyes and she reached up to smooth it over to the side. He blinked through tears as he looked at her, and she brushed them away as well. The early morning sunlight bounced off her diamond. The sparkles caught her eye and left her momentarily speechless.

A year ago she had been overwhelmed with more pain and sadness than she had ever known. If anyone had told her that she would be this happy ever in her life, let alone a year later, she would have scoffed at them and told them they were insane. Sally had tried to tell her, as well as others, and she'd shaken her head and told them she didn't see how that could ever be. They meant well and by saying those things they helped themselves feel better. It must have been awful to watch someone they cared about be so wrapped up in sorrow. She would have done the same thing, even knowing that it wouldn't make much of a difference. But here she was today, remembering their words of encouragement, as they were coming true.

"I *do* trust you, Matt. I'm just not used to being loved so much. It's a new experience for me." She looked into his eyes. "You had this with Sarah, didn't you?"

He turned his head and looked out over the menagerie of rooftops dotted with chimneys. "Sara and I had a good marriage. We loved each other very much, but it was different." His gaze returned to her. "I'm not the same person I was then."

"Because of the accident?"

"Yeah, that had a lot to do with it." He held her hands tightly. "Annie, I have to tell you something."

"What?" The miserable expression on his face was making her nervous. His hands felt clammy as they gripped hers.

"I wasn't always a very good husband to Sara. I was pretty wrapped up in my work, trying to get established, you know. She tried to be patient, but it couldn't have been easy for her."

"Every relationship has challenges. That doesn't mean you weren't a good husband."

"I could have been better."

"And I could have been a better wife to Eric. Matt, you don't have to confess anything to me. You've been nothing but wonderful to me. That's what I know and trust; that's all that matters now."

"No, Annie. I have to tell you this. I have to."

"Okay then. Go ahead." Her stomach was starting to hurt. "Should we sit down?"

"Sure."

As they walked back to the bistro table on the balcony, Annie tried to imagine what it was that Matt was struggling to tell her. Had he cheated on Sara during their marriage? Was he no better than Eric had been? Panic began to spread over her like a prickly rash.

"Okay." He took a deep breath. "This is harder than I thought it would be. If you decide not to marry me, I'll understand."

"Matt, you're scaring me now. Please just tell me."

"On the day of the accident, Sara and I had a huge fight. I left the house angry and said some awful things to her on my way out. The next time I saw her was when I identified her body in the morgue."

Annie's heart ached for him. As furious as she had ever been at Eric, if he had died in a car crash after one of their fights, it would haunt her as well.

"That had to have been so hard."

He nodded. "And our baby died along with her." Tear-filled eyes looked across the table at her. "The baby I didn't want."

"But you didn't know about the baby, did you?"

"No, but that's what we'd argued about. She wanted a baby; I thought we should wait. It was a recurring fight. I had no idea she had a doctor appointment that day. I didn't know she thought she was pregnant already." He buried his face in his hands.

"Matt, why are you telling me this?" Annie kept her voice calm.

"Because I don't want you to hear it from somebody else. And I want you to know how much I've changed. I'm not the same self-centered jerk I was back then. Now I know how important it is to be there for the people I love and who love me. I know it's not something that can be taken for granted." The words were a torrent spilling out of his mouth. When he was finished he sat there, trying to catch his breath, as if he'd just run a marathon.

Annie got up and went to him. She put her arms around his shoulders and cradled his head against her stomach. He held onto her and cried, his sobs coming from deep inside.

"She died thinking that I didn't want the baby she just found out about. She was probably afraid I'd be mad about it."

"You don't know what she was thinking," she said, her hand on the back of his head. "You need to stop being so hard on yourself."

He looked up at her. "You don't think I'm the worst person on the face of the earth?"

"Uh, no, sweetie. Not even close." She kissed the top of his head.

"I worked through it in counseling, or thought I had, but when I heard that you were pregnant, it all resurfaced. I'm sorry you had to see me like this." He wiped his nose with his napkin.

"I'm glad you told me about it. It's not good to carry things like that around inside of you. It only does damage."

"Well, I just wanted you to know, before anymore time passed. I wanted to, you know, give you a chance to change your mind."

"This just makes me want to marry you more," she said as she scooted onto his lap. "It shows what a caring, sensitive person you are. The fact that you took the risk to tell me means a lot."

"I love you so much." He took her face in his hands and gave her a deep, penetrating kiss.

They forgot where they were; that they were out on a balcony just three stories up from the bustling street below. The neighborhood was in full swing by now. Shopkeepers were opening their shutters and propping open their doors, ready for business. Kissing Matt awakened feelings in Annie that had been somewhat dormant and they returned with a flourish. When the front of her robe fell open slightly, the morning breeze floated across her skin.

"Um, sweetie," she said as his hand slid inside her robe. "Maybe we should go inside."

Matt stopped kissing her and looked at her through half-opened eyes, an almost drunken grin on his face. He glanced down at the street below, his hand still roaming and then returned his gaze to her. Her eyes were closed, a blissful smile on her well-kissed mouth.

"You don't look like a woman who wants to go inside," he teased her. "You look like you want to be kissed again."

"Mmmmm. And I do," she said. "I'm just afraid we'll cause a scene if we stay out here."

"You're probably right. We better be careful." He pulled the lapels of Annie's robe closed, overlapping one over the other very properly. "There. Last one to the bed is a rotten egg!"

The few frenzied steps it took to get to the bed was enough to bring them to their senses. The doctor had advised Annie to take it easy, to rest as much as possible. She wasn't supposed to do anything that would "cause excitement." And so they wisely gave each other a long hug, a quick kiss and tried to ignore their unsatisfied longings. For so many reasons they both hoped that the doctor would give her a clean bill of health that afternoon.

Matt came back into the exam room to wait with Annie. He came over to where she sat on the exam table, a white sheet draped over her lap.

"Sorry, honey. I'll try to be more patient." He kissed her cheek.

"Relax. I'm sure she'll be here any minute." She swung her bare feet back and forth.

"Are you getting cold under there?" He playfully lifted the corner of the sheet and peeked beneath it.

"Matthew!" she hissed. "Stop it!" She couldn't stop her giggles as his hand grazed her leg. Somehow it seemed wrong to be having so much fun at a doctor appointment, but it felt so good to laugh.

At that moment, the door opened and Dr. Caron strode in, huffing and puffing from her hurried walk down the hall from the hospital. Annie smiled and pushed Matt's hand from under the sheet.

"Hello, Dr. Caron!" She hoped her cheerful greeting would divert the doctor's attention from Matt's shenanigans.

"I am so sorry to have kept you waiting," the doctor said as she walked over to the desk in the corner. She pulled a manila folder from under her arm and flipped it open. "I wanted to have your lab results before I saw you and the lab was very busy."

That explained why they had been waiting so long. When Annie and Matt arrived at the medical center that afternoon, they first had to go to the lab for Annie to have blood drawn. The doctor wanted to check the hormone levels for the pregnancy. This was the third test in a little over a week. The desired result was for the hCG, the pregnancy hormone to double every few days. If the levels decreased or stayed the same, the chance of a miscarriage or ectopic pregnancy was more likely. Several days before, Dr. Caron had told them things "looked good" and if the results today were adequate, they could possibly go back to the States.

"How have you been feeling, Annie?" Dr. Caron was shining the penlight in Annie's eyes as she spoke.

"Better. The past couple of days I haven't felt as queasy. Matt can even have coffee in the same room with me now." She gave him a little wink. "I've been able to keep more food down, too. I'll start expanding before we know it!" She patted her stomach, grinning at Matt.

The doctor inspected the chart in her hand, her mouth in a solemn line. She took a deep breath and looked up at them.

"The lab results were not what I'd hoped. The hormone levels have dropped significantly since the last test."

Matt moved from his place on the chair near the desk to be closer to the exam table. Without even seeing him there, Annie reached her hand out and he grasped it in his.

"What exactly does that mean?" Annie said, her voice much quieter than it had been a minute ago.

"There is no easy way to say this. It means that the pregnancy is failing."

Dr. Caron's voice was assertive, but kind. "It is only a matter of time before the fetus spontaneously aborts." She averted her gaze to the floor.

"But the levels were low before, weren't they? Isn't there a chance they could go back up?" Matt's voice sparkled with hope.

"If they had only gone down a small amount, perhaps, but they dropped significantly. We were hopeful when they started to increase shortly after Annie fell, but even then the increases were very small; not the typical doubling every couple of days and not where you should be at eleven weeks of gestation. That explains why you have been feeling less nausea the past few days."

"So, what happens now?" Annie felt as though her voice was not her own; that it was coming from somewhere across the room. She held onto Matt's hand as he became her tether to sanity. He drew closer to her and put his other arm around her shoulders.

"Well, there are two options. I can schedule you for a D&C immediately, or you can wait for nature to take its course. If you do that, I do not recommend traveling until the event has passed. Either way, we can do an ultrasound first." She looked from Annie to Matt. "I will give you some time to talk it over. You may get dressed now." She put a gentle hand on Annie's arm and then left the room, closing the door softly behind her.

Matt wrapped Annie in his arms and buried his face in her hair. She raised her hand to his head and held him close. The place in her heart where tears were born began to hurt but she breathed deeply in an attempt to stop them. She had to be strong, if not for herself, then for Matt.

"Can you grab me my clothes, honey?" her voice cracked.

Matt unfolded his arms from around her, and without speaking, reached over to the chair and retrieved her jeans and underwear. He handed them to her and helped her down from the table so that she could put them on. Once she was dressed, standing before him, she took his hands in hers. She looked at him, unable to speak. He gathered her into his arms again, holding her as if he'd never let go.

Resting her head against his chest, she let herself dissolve into him. The hollow gorge inside of her that Dillon's death had created was larger now, holding the lost dreams of two tiny lives within its cavernous walls. She could feel it filling with memories that would never be made and hopes that would never be realized. Pain surged inside of her, spilling over the edges of the emptiness. She let the tears come, soaking the front of Matt's cotton shirt. There was no handkerchief large enough to collect them.

"It's just so sad," she said. "We didn't even get a chance to know him. I'm so sorry to put you through this."

"You aren't 'putting me through' anything, Annie. We're going through this together. No matter what happens, I'm here for you. Understand?" His voice was full of quiet caring. He held a protective hand on the back of her head.

"Yes, but --"

"But nothing. I love you. I thought we discussed this earlier today."

"I just don't know how strong I can be. I don't know if I can do this again." Once she uttered the words she feared the most, a new wave of tears were upon her.

Matt tightened his embrace and then cried with her; cried for the son or daughter they'd never get to hold in their arms, cried for the loss of their little Munchkin. When he was able to gain his composure, he drew back and placed his hands on her forlorn shoulders.

"I don't blame you for feeling that way. We just need to get through right now. Can you do that?" He traced a tear down her cheek with a gentle finger.

She nodded her head, appreciating his understanding. He had told her shortly after they'd met, about how he felt when he'd been told that Sara was dead, and so she knew he'd walked in her shoes. He wasn't patronizing her, he was doing what he'd promised; he was there for her.

"Good," he continued. "We have a decision to make."

"I know."

"Whatever you want, honey."

"I definitely want the ultrasound. We have to know for sure. We never got to hear the heartbeat, so maybe we can *see* it, if -- if it's still beating."

"Okay." Matt's tone was hesitant. "I know I said it's your call, but is that going to be too hard for you?"

"Yes, it's going to be hard, but I have to be sure. If there's still a heartbeat at all, we wait. If there isn't one, well, then we'll cross that bridge when we get to it." She was determined that this was the best course of action and drying her tears, she put on a brave face.

There was a soft knock on the door, and Dr. Caron came in. From her red eyes and blotchy complexion, it appeared that she'd shed some tears of her own. Annie extended her hand, and the usually stoic physician caught it in hers and gave it a compassionate squeeze.

"What have you decided?" Her voice was a little hoarse and she cleared her throat.

They waited in the darkened room for the technician to perform the ultrasound. It felt surreal to Annie; it was as though someone had rewound her life, and she was living the worst part of it all over again. Had she not done things right the first time? Was God trying to teach her a lesson in tolerance or forgiveness? She tightly clutched Matt's hand as cold jelly was squirted on her skin and the instrument crisscrossed across her belly. All eyes were on the small black and white screen, watching and waiting.

"There it is," the technician said and held the instrument still as she clicked on a button that would freeze the image and take a picture.

On the screen was the pie-shaped picture of Annie's uterus. In the middle, was the shadowy outline of their baby, lying on its back. They could see a perfect profile; a forehead, nose and mouth, as well as the trunk of a little body and tiny curled up legs. The room was silent as they all watched the screen, transfixed, as a small, dark spot in the chest pulsated in a slow, faltering rhythm.

"Look!" Annie pointed at the screen. "It's the heartbeat. Isn't that the heartbeat?" She was nearly frantic with hope.

"Yes," said Dr. Caron from her station behind Annie's head.

Matt was staring at the screen, a look of awe on his face. He leaned down and kissed Annie's forehead, never taking his eyes off the screen.

"Can you tell if its a boy or a girl?" Annie asked anyone who would answer.

"It might be too soon to see, but we'll try." The technician moved the ultrasound wand around a little bit, and as if it suddenly became a magic wand, made a small gasp. "It looks like a girl."

Annie and Matt held each other as they watched their little girl on the screen. They soaked up every second they could, committed every nuance and shape to memory.

"Since there's a heartbeat, we wait," Annie said, her voice exuberant. "Look at how strong she is. Maybe the lab tests were wrong. Look at her!"

The four sets of eyes in the room were trained on the tiny image, her heartbeat a faint blip on the screen. Everyone was rooting for her, praying for Annie to be right. As the moments between each beat of her little heart became longer, no one seemed to breathe, holding their breath until the next beat occurred. Then, ever so quietly, the beating stopped; the screen was still.

A reverent hush settled over the room. Annie laid in the darkness, gazing at her little girl on the screen, a silent, still portrait of what might have been. She and Matt didn't even notice that the doctor and the technician had left the room.

"We just watched our baby die." Matt's voice was a whisper, ragged with emotion. He and Annie were still holding onto each other, their arms entwined, their hands clasped.

"Yes, we did." Annie brought his hand to her face. "Do you know how blessed we are?"

"Blessed?"

"Yes, blessed. We might have watched our baby die, but we also got to watch an angel being born." She looked up at him, suddenly filled with peaceful grace.

Dr. Caron had urged Annie to have the D&C so that she and Matt could then go home and begin to heal both physically and emotionally, but Annie disagreed. Matt understood how she felt, but also saw the doctor's point. He had been deemed with the task of trying to change her mind.

"I'm sorry, Matt, but I can't just let them tear her out of me like that. After seeing her on the ultrasound, after seeing her alive inside of me, I just can't do that." Her voice was strong with conviction.

"I know, but according to Dr. Caron, it could be a danger to you not to have the D&C. It's been hard enough to lose Munchkin; I don't want to lose you too."

"I want us to see her and hold her. We'll never be able to do that if they do the D&C." The peaceful grace that Annie felt less than an hour ago had been replaced by simmering agitation.

Matt had moved from his perch on the bed next to her, to pacing back and forth again. Annie's distress was contagious. He took a few steps and then stopped to make sure she was okay, and then took a few more.

"Remember the Franklins from the support group? They had a situation similar to this, didn't they?" He crouched down next to the bed so that he was at eye level.

"Yes, they did. After three miscarriages, they finally asked if the last one could be induced. They were finally able to see and hold one of their babies."

Annie's eyes filled with new tears as she remembered all that couple had gone through. As much as her heart ached right now, she felt as though God was being easy on her, compared to so many of the others whose stories she'd listened to week after week.

"Let's ask Dr. Caron if we can do that," said Matt.

"Okay," said Annie.

Dr. Caron agreed to induce labor the next morning if Annie didn't "spontaneously abort" on her own. Annie hated that term -- it was so technical and cold. She found that for the most part, the medical community was eager to wash their hands of a fetus, or the "products of conception" once there no signs of life. Again, very technical and cold.

The Pitocin drip started at 7:00 a.m. and by 7:45 a.m. the contractions were in full swing. As with Dillon, she was told she could have all the pain medication she wanted, but again, she wanted to be fully present at the moment the baby was delivered. Matt marveled at how in control she was, breathing through each contraction and remaining calm. He stayed right by her side, holding her hand, counting contractions and wishing he could take every last bit of her pain away.

By 9:55 a.m. it was over. Even though Dr. Caron had warned against seeing the fetus, Annie and Matt had insisted, knowing the closure it would provide. As painful as it was, it helped them both to know that their baby was at peace.

"Should we give her a name other than Munchkin?" Matt asked as he stared at their little daughter. She was only two and a half inches long.

"I don't know. Maybe," Annie said as a tear trickled down her cheek. "We can decide later."

Matt nodded in agreement, his eyes still gazing at the tiny baby.

Annie remained in the hospital until the next day, to ensure that everything was okay physically before they flew home to the States. Matt stayed with her that night, cradling her in the narrow hospital bed, mourning their loss together. They laid awake, talking late into the night, sharing the hopes and dreams they'd had for Munchkin, even though they'd only known her for a very short time. Finally she felt Matt's embrace relax and felt the soft, measured breaths of sleep on her neck. She patted his arm gently, happy that he could get some rest.

The night sky was an inky black. The minuscule sliver that was the moon shed only a tiny bit of light, making the stars seem even brighter. As Annie looked out at it, she couldn't help but think about how different this was than the last time she'd looked out a hospital window late at night. Feeling Matt's heart beating so close to her gave her comfort and strength, something that Eric had never even tried to provide. They had a difficult road ahead of them; they both knew that. Annie prayed that she would be able to comfort Matt as well. She'd come to realize that she might have let Eric down in that way, too wrapped up in her own grief to even notice how he felt. Her ex-husband hadn't even acknowledged that he had many feelings about Dillon, so how could she have helped him? He wouldn't let her in. How ironic that she was being given another chance to prove her love, by having another child taken from her. She hoped that she would get it right this time, not so much to ensure that her next baby would live, but because she truly loved this man sleeping next to her and wanted to see him happy.

A blanket of contentment settled over Annie when she saw Dillon's star. She smiled, because seeing it always made her feel closer to him. Suddenly the most wonderful thing happened. From out of nowhere, a shooting star appeared, streaking high above Dillon's star and then ending right next to it. Annie blinked, rubbed her eyes and blinked again. Even her tears couldn't suppress the smile that spread across her face. She snuggled into Matt's arms deeper and settled down to sleep, knowing that tonight both of her babies were resting in God's hands.

## The Wedding Bells

"A Thanksgiving wedding!" Sally clapped her hands and bounced up and down. "It's just what we need to cheer things up around here!"

Annie suppressed a giggle as her aunt reacted to the news. When Annie and Matt had told them of their engagement while they were still in Paris, no date had been set. They had intimated that the wedding would take place at some vague date in the future. Sally had been disappointed by that, wanting to start making plans right away, but Frank had worked his magic and calmed her down before the long-distance call ended.

"It doesn't give us much time, though, does it? It's already the end of September!" Sally had a spiral notebook opened on the patio table in front of her, ready to start making lists. "I knew I should have started making plans sooner."

"Don't worry, Sally," said Annie. "We've both been married before. We want to keep it simple."

Sally let out an exasperated sigh. "Okay, fine. But simple can still be complicated."

Frank and Matt had been talking in the living room. Snippets of their conversation floated out to the deck on the unseasonably warm evening breeze from the open windows. Annie smiled as she heard Frank's voice.

"I don't know what to do with her," he said to Matt. "She's so excited you two are getting married. Neither of us were very happy about her first marriage." There was a slight pause. "He just wasn't the right person for our Annie."

"And how do you feel about me?" they heard Matt ask quietly.

Annie held her breath as she strained to hear her uncle's response. Frank hadn't seemed as excited as Sally had been about the wedding. His reaction had been a guarded one and it bothered Annie to think that he had any objections. Frank was the closest thing she had to a father and his opinion meant a lot to her.

"A penny for your thoughts." Sally patted her hand.

"Shhh. I'm trying to hear what they're saying," said Annie.

"It's not polite to eavesdrop, Missy," Sally pretended to scold her.

"I know, but I can't help it. I'm just not sure how Frank feels about all of this." She wiggled her foot nervously under the table.

"He's thrilled, Annie!" Sally's eyes sparkled as she spoke, her voice lowered to a loud whisper.

"You're kidding me. He sure doesn't act like it."

"He's protective of you, that's all. He doesn't want to see you get hurt again. At first he thought it was too soon for you to get married, but it's obvious that you and Matt belong together. He realized that the minute you got off the plane."

"What do you mean?"

"Oh Annie," Sally said, squeezing her hand. "It's just the way he was with you, especially when you told us about the baby." Her eyes were bright with tears. "It erased any doubts that either of us had. The "old Annie" has come back to us. That's how we know he's the one for you, because he appreciates the *real* you. As for it being too soon, why wait? That just makes no sense at all."

Annie couldn't help but smile at her aunt. There were so many unspoken words, so much understanding between them. To hear Sally say that the "old Annie" had come back, made her heart skip with unexpected joy. The memories of who she had been back when she'd had both of her parents were so hazy; it was difficult to recreate them in her mind. Even though there were photo albums and videotapes of birthdays and holidays that helped her remember what her life had been like before her father died, it was the way she felt when she thought of those days that she found the most precious. Loving Matt made her feel that way again.

"It's funny you should say that, Sally, because that's how I've been feeling lately; like I did when I was young, when I was happy. I just hope I can love him enough."

She watched Matt through the window as he told an animated story to Frank. He caught her eye and his entire face lit up as he waved to her.

"Oh, I don't think you need to worry about that," said Sally. "You know the way he takes care of you? You do the same thing for him."

"You think so?"

"Of course, silly. You two are just a 'mutual admiration society'. I think it's wonderful! So, let's get this wedding planned, shall we?"

It was a very small wedding, the day after Thanksgiving. Sally made Annie's dress, which was a simple floor length ivory silk sheath. Annie had insisted that it be knee length, but Sally challenged that she was still the bride and the bride's dress should be long. It was pointless to argue with her aunt once her mind was set on something, so Annie let it go. Deep down she liked the idea of a long dress anyway. This was her second marriage, but in so many ways it was more significant than her first. It deserved to be every bit as special, even though she now knew that so much of the fuss wasn't as important as the people getting married. This time there was more intention to the decision; it wasn't just the next thing on the list of things to do. She and Matt already knew each other more completely in less than a year than she and Eric had in all of their years together.

Frank and Sally acted as her parents, and Matt's parents made the trip from their home in Florida to be there for the event. Jen was Annie's matron of honor and Matt's best friend, Jason, was the best man. The rest of the guest list consisted of a handful of their closest friends, around twenty people in all.

The ceremony and reception took place in a French restaurant that was in an old train depot downtown. Annie and Matt had eaten dinner there on one of their first dates, and had both been mesmerized by its history. The atmosphere was romantic and just a little exotic, with the gauzy memories of journeys, both past and future, hanging like wisps of promise amidst the chandeliers and abandoned ticket windows. It was the perfect place to begin the adventure of their new life together.

"I'd like to make a toast to the bride and groom," said Jen as she raised her glass of champagne.

Conversation slowed to a stop as everyone gave their attention to the matron of honor. The string quartet, all friends of Annie's from the orchestra, ended their piece with an exaggerated flourish and tipped their bows in Jen's direction.

"I was honored and a little surprised when Annie asked me to be her matron of honor. Annie and I have only known each other for a little over a year, but in that year I have seen her go through a sequence of events that would have put many people out of commission. She fought her way up from the depths of despair and found this beautiful man, Matthew Preston, during her ascent. Matt has had tragedies of his own and so when they met, rather than turn away, he held out his hand to her in friendship, respect ,and love. In Paris, I watched these two exceptional people weather a new tragedy together. I was blessed to have been in their presence, because I was able to witness what true love is. I have no doubt that they will make the world a better place because their love is so big and so wonderful that it can't help but spill over on all of us who know them and those they have yet to meet. So, here's to Matt and Annie Preston. I love you both!"

The tears that had been building in Jen's eyes trickled down her cheek as Annie gave her a big hug. Matt also gave her a hug, as well as his crisp, ivory handkerchief. She looked at it and shook her head. Annie took the handkerchief from her new husband's outstretched hand and dabbed her friend's tears away.

"One thing you have to know about Matt, is that he *wants* you to slobber all over his hankies!" Annie said, laughing.

"It's a *handkerchief*, not a hankie," corrected Matt, acting appalled. "Next you're going to say it looks good with my *outfit*." He rolled his eyes and folded his arms across his chest.

"Well, it *does*!" said Jen. "*Very* lovely!"

Everyone was emotional yet festive and a good time was had by all. Matt's parents, who had been devastated by Sara's death and how it had nearly destroyed their only son, welcomed Annie into their family with grace and warmth.

"Annie," said Donna Preston as she took Annie's hands in hers. "This has been the most wonderful day! I am so glad we were able to be here."

"Thank you, Mrs. Preston," said Annie.

"Uh, uh, uh," interrupted her mother-in-law. "Call me Donna. We're family now!"

"Okay, Donna." Annie smiled at her. " And I'm happy to be in your family."

"We want you two to come and visit us in the Keys just as soon as you can," chimed in Matt's father, Ed. "We have to get to know Annie better."

"We will, Dad," said Matt.

Since the trips to Europe had depleted their budgets, the newlyweds decided to postpone a honeymoon trip until they could better afford it. Instead, they spent the weekend at the hotel in the depot, in the penthouse suite, courtesy of Frank and Sally. That night, after they said their good-byes to their guests, they walked hand in hand to the elevator. As they stood waiting for the elevator to arrive, they looked at each other and smiled.

"Does this remind you of anything?" Matt said.

"When we met before the support group meeting." Annie said as she gently twirled her shoes in her free hand.

"Who would've thought that we'd end up here?" Matt pulled her into his arms. "Who would have thought that we'd ever be this happy?"

"It's pretty fantastic, isn't it?" Annie smiled up at him.

"I love you, Mrs. Preston. God, I love saying that."

"And I love hearing it." Annie wrapped her arms around him and put her mouth on his, giving him a long, deep kiss.

The elevator arrived and they barely stopped kissing as they stumbled into it, not wanting to take their hands off each other. Alone once the doors slid shut, they allowed their passion to fully ignite. Matt slipped his hand inside the back of her dress, which was a deep V that plunged almost to her waistline.

"I've wanted to do this since the minute I saw you in this dress," he said as he kissed her neck.

"And I've been wanting you to," said Annie breathlessly. "It's good thing this is a private elevator."

"You can say that again," Matt said, as he slipped the silk dress off her shoulders.

"It's a good thing --" she started to say, but soon became speechless, as Matt's kisses followed the ivory silk as it fell onto the floor and pooled around her bare feet.

The moon shone in the floor to ceiling windows, bathing their bodies in a cool, pale light as they lay tangled together on the bed. Annie laid her head on Matt's chest, as he ran his fingers through her hair and then lazily down her back. She looked out at the night sky, a contented smile on her face.

"What are you thinking about?" Matt whispered softly.

"I'm just thinking about how happy I am and how much I love you." She raised her head enough to kiss his chin and then plopped it back down again.

Matt bent his neck and kissed the top of her head. "The stars are bright tonight, aren't they?"

"Yes, they are."

"Does that make you sad?" He wound a strand of her hair around his fingers.

Annie paused and thought before she answered. Looking out at the stars she saw that they really did seem brighter than usual. It had been a wonderful day, the happiest day of her life, but to pretend that the babies that had left them weren't on their minds would have been ludicrous. She loved that Matt wasn't afraid to talk about them tonight. Suddenly it occurred to her that there were three stars shining in the midnight sky for them. One for Dillon, one for Munchkin and one for Matt and Sara's baby.

"The stars will always remind me of our babies -- all three of them."

He raised himself up on his elbow and looked at her, a puzzled expression on his face. It only took a second for the full meaning of her words to sink in. His mouth wavered between a frown and a smile, as the mix of feelings swirled beneath the surface. Finally he spoke.

"This is one of the reasons I love you so much," he said, his voice breaking. "Thank you for giving me permission to include him -- or her."

"Memories don't need permission," she said. "Memories are part of us, Matt. They help make us who we are."

He ran his thumb along her cheek, his face crumpling under the weight of unexpressed emotions. It broke her heart that he still felt so much pain at the thought of all that he had lost, but she also knew that the depth of his feeling was one of the things that made her fall in love with him. They laid back on the fluffy down pillows, arms around each other and remembered their babies as they gazed at the night sky, without saying a word. The only sound was the quiet hum of their breathing as they found their rhythm and became one.

# The Christmas Tree

The snow began to fall just after midnight, covering everything with a thick, fluffy blanket of white silence. Annie got up to go to the bathroom and peeked out of the bedroom window with eyes that were still heavy with sleep. She gasped at the snow globe beauty of the winter wonderland below. It never ceased to amaze her how peaceful and enchanted a normal neighborhood could appear once it was covered with snow. All the local meteorologists had dire predictions for a brown Christmas, and since it was only days away, it seemed that they were going to be right.

Annie hadn't cared whether it snowed or not. With the excitement of the wedding behind them, she couldn't seem to be able to chase away the sadness about little Munchkin. She counted the weeks on her fingers. It had been sixteen weeks since she had died. Her hands cradled her flat, empty stomach, trying to imagine how big it would be if she was still inside of her. She would be in her twenty-sixth week, a little over six months along. Where had the time gone? After Dillon had died, time had gone in slow motion; each day felt like an eternity. Time was moving faster and she wondered if that was because she was becoming more calloused, more jaded. Perhaps she was building up a tough layer of scar tissue around her heart to keep it from aching so much. As much as she didn't want to keep hurting, she didn't want to stop feeling either.

The glistening snowflakes reminded her of the tiny stars that twinkled for each of the babies and she couldn't stop the tears from slipping down her cheeks. She curled up on the window seat in the living room and quietly watched the snow falling, growing deeper by the minute.

"Annie?" Matt put a gentle hand on her shoulder and whispered, not wanting to startle her.

She reached for his hand and brought his arm around her shoulders. He encircled her with his other arm and snuggled behind her on the narrow cushion. Together they watched the snowflakes fall from above, sparkling and swirling as they danced like tiny ballerinas to the ground below. Annie leaned back against Matt and sighed, kissing his hand.

"I didn't think I cared if it snowed, but I'm glad it did," she said. "It makes everything prettier."

"I woke up and you weren't there." He tilted his chin to nuzzle her neck. "I missed you."

Annie reached back with her left arm and put her hand on his head. She derived so much strength from just being near him. They sat there a while longer, mesmerized by the wintery scene, saying nothing, huddled together in a cocoon of love and longing.

"This is harder than I thought," said Annie quietly.

"I know," Matt said, his breath warming her cheek. "I can't begin to imagine how much you miss Dillon, because I miss Munchkin more than I ever thought possible. Right now all of that crap I said about knowing her for a little while doesn't help very much, does it?"

"It's okay, sweetie." Annie stroked his arm. "You were right; sometimes it helps. And sometimes it doesn't."

"Like now?"

"Sort of." She gave him a sad smile. "I keep thinking about how big she'd be; how big I'd be."

"It must be hard because you were that pregnant with Dillon so you know what you're missing." He kissed the top of her head and rubbed her shoulders.

"Yeah. I think that's why this is so difficult. It's strange -- it's like there's more to miss, even though we lost her sooner. Does that make any sense?"

"Yes, honey, it does. It helps to talk about it, though. It helps me anyway." His embrace tightened gently, giving her a loving squeeze.

"It helps me too. Just having you here makes me feel better. Last time I was so alone. Thank you, Matt." She kissed the back of his hand that was resting below her chin.

"Should we go back to bed?" Matt said, looking at the clock on the wall.

"It's only a little after 2:00 a.m. There's a lot of night left."

Annie yawned and stretched against him like a cat. "Okay."

Arm in arm they sauntered back to their bedroom. Annie hoped that she'd be able to find some solace in her dreams as the snow fell upon the silent night.

Rehearsal was especially grueling the next day. Annie's eyes were heavy with fatigue from the sleepless night before. There were only two more concerts left before the Christmas break, a matinee and an evening performance, all Christmas music. She knew all the music, but found it difficult to put her heart into it. Every song was about the birth of a baby, which only made her miss her little ones even more. She looked at her watch and sighed. There was only a half hour until the 2:00 p.m. concert began. Her head wouldn't be able to hit the pillow for at least 10 hours.

"Alright people, listen up," said Conrad, tapping his baton on his music stand. "As you know, after the first show you and your families are invited to partake in the holiday buffet sponsored by the orchestra auxiliary. It's their little holiday gift to us, so it would be wonderful if all of you can attend. Let's have a great show!"

An enormous yawn escaped from Annie's mouth as she applied some rosin to her bow. She wondered when she'd be able to love the holiday season again. Two years in a row with baby grief was beginning to take a toll. This year was better because of the happiness she'd found with Matt, but her arms still ached with emptiness.

"I saw that yawn, missy!" Jen swooped down from behind her and squeezed her shoulder. "Are you hanging in there?"

"Oh, I guess so," Annie smiled at her friend. "How about you?"

"Barely. Is Matt coming to the concert? More importantly, is he coming to the buffet?" She rolled her eyes. "It is an amazing buffet, but sometimes it's just nice to have some downtime, you know?"

"Yes, he's coming. How about your family?" Annie was intent on steering the conversation in Jen's direction. If she dwelled on her feelings, she'd never make it through the evening.

"Yeah. It's gotten to be a tradition." She glanced at her watch. "I've got to pee. I better hurry!"

Jen kissed her cheek and then hurried off in a frenzy. Annie shook her head and smiled. Jen was always in a hurry but with her busy life it couldn't be any other way. It took some effort but Annie managed to shrug off the avalanche of doubt that threatened to descend upon her. Would she ever be busy with children to chauffeur to and from activities? Would there ever be a holiday season where she was frantically trying to fit everything in or would she never become a mother?

Annie sensed an increase in the activity level around her and realized that all the musicians were taking their places, preparing for the first piece of the concert. She wrenched her thoughts from the sad route they were on and tried to think happier thoughts. When she tried to conjure up an image of what made her happy, a smiling, laughing Matt popped into her head. She was ashamed of herself for thinking that her life would be empty without a baby. Even if God never gave them children, He had given her Matt. While babies were miracles, finding love with a wonderful person was also a miracle; possibly an even greater one. Babies were easy to love and loved you back. It wasn't always that easy with people.

The next two hours flew by, as the orchestra kept the audience captivated with unique musical interpretations of almost every holiday song ever written. There was a sing-a-long portion of the concert, and Annie swore she could hear angels singing, as the tiny voices of children floated back to her on the notes she had sent out to them. She became so engrossed in the music, it felt as though her heart had become the strings of her cello, each vibrating and resonating with every Christmas memory she'd ever had. By the end of the performance she had been infused with the Christmas spirit. Matt beamed when he saw her backstage. He wrapped her in a big bear hug and lifted her off the floor.

"That was fantastic!" He plopped a happy kiss on her smile.

"Thanks, sweetie. So we sounded okay?"

"Everyone sounded great. The audience was really into it, too. I loved the sing-a-long part. I sang and no one even told me to stop!" He smiled and waved at some of the musicians that he recognized as they passed by.

"Well, it definitely put me in a Christmasy mood. There's nothing like music, is there?" She gave him a big hug. "Are you ready to head over to the buffet?"

"Sounds good. Is this one of the fringe benefits of being married to a member of the orchestra?"

"Yes, it is, my dear sir. Just one of many." She smiled and gave him a mischievous wink. "You'll have to wait until I get home for the rest of them."

Hand in hand they made their way down the hall to the buffet. The orchestra auxiliary had transformed what was usually a very drab corner of the backstage area into a bright, festive Christmas feast for the eyes and well as the stomach. A long banquet table stretched from one wall to the other. It was laden with platters of meats and cheeses, salads, desserts and mouthwatering breads and pastries. The decorations were elegant. Larger than life ribbons and ornaments graced fragrant evergreen boughs that ran the length of the table. Annie felt as though they had stepped into Fezziwig's feast and wondered when The Ghost of Christmas Present would pay them a visit.

"This is amazing," said Matt, as he laced his fingers between hers.

"It's beautiful! It almost looks too beautiful to eat," Annie said as she surveyed the variety of goodies.

"Well, what are you waiting for?" a voice said from behind them.

They turned their heads and saw Jen, her husband and kids standing behind them. They were an adorable family and Annie fought to suppress pangs of envy as she admired them. Jen's son was six years old and was dressed in a Christmas sweater that matched his three year old sister's, making them look like they just stepped out of a Christmas catalog.

"Mommy, let's go eat!" the little boy was pulling on Jen's arm.

"I want a cookie!" his little sister chimed in as she danced around in an excited circle.

"No cookies until you eat something healthy," said Jen, her patience wearing thin. "Mike, can you help Alexander? I'll take Emma." She flashed an embarrassed grin at Annie and Matt as they moved toward the buffet.

Annie and Matt joined the rest of the musicians and their families as they ate and visited with one another. Since Annie was the newest member of the group, there were a lot of people who wanted to meet Matt and congratulate them on their marriage. It was a relaxing, jovial event and everyone hated to see it end. Before long, however, Conrad was circulating through the crowd, announcing that it was time to prepare for the next concert.

"Thank you all for coming and making some holiday memories with us," he said. "Right now I must get these people back on stage for the next performance. I hope everyone has a safe and happy holiday break."

Everyone murmured their "Thank you's" and Christmas wishes as they bustled around, finishing up their meals. Families gave hugs and kisses as they prepared to leave, some going home, some staying for the concert.

"I'll be waiting for you at home, Mrs. Preston." Matt gave her a long, lingering hug. "Have a good second show, okay?"

She nodded, every inch of her feeling the love in his embrace.

"I love you, Matt."

"I love you, too, Annie. See you soon." He kissed her forehead, turned and strode down the hall toward the parking ramp.

Annie looked after him, a tender smile on her face. She couldn't wait to get home.

The second concert was even better than the first, the audience giving two standing ovations. The final song was a rousing but short "We Wish You a Merry Christmas" ending the show on a lively, jolly note. Backstage was a whir of activity, musicians packing up their instruments and wishing each other well, all in a hurry to get home. It had been a very good, but a very long day.

"Wait a second, Annie," Jen said as she clicked her cello case shut. "I have something for you."

"Jen, I --"

"Hush. This is just a little something I wanted you to have." She handed Annie a small package wrapped in gold paper with a bright red bow as they walked to their cars.

"I feel bad that I don't have one for you," said Annie as she accepted the gift.

"Please don't. This is just something small. I saw it and thought of you, that's all. I have to run. You have a wonderful Christmas, promise?"

"You too, Jen. Thank you for everything." Annie gave her a hug.

"It's been quite a year, hasn't it?" Jen's voice was choked with tears. "1988 is going to be great! I can just feel it!"

"I hope so!" Annie sniffled as tears filled her eyes.

"It will! Well, bye!" Jen gave her an extra squeeze and dashed off, her cello bumping on her hip with each step she took down the ramp toward her car. Her breath marked her trail with frozen white puffs that looked like word balloons above her head.

The frigid December air made the parking ramp feel like it was made of blocks of ice instead of concrete. With cold fingers, Annie unlocked the hatchback and placed her cello inside, and then scrambled into her car. While the engine ran, warming up the car, she decided to unwrap Jen's gift.

Her hands were too stiff to be careful with the wrapping paper, so instead of making it an intricate procedure, she ripped it open. Inside she found a small nondescript white box. Upon removing the cover, she found iridescent gold tissue paper. A sticker held the edges of the tissue together and Annie carefully peeled it apart. Inside were three white porcelain Christmas tree ornaments; teddy bear angels, one with Dillon's name, one with Munchkin's and one with no name at all. The letters of their names blurred together as tears formed in Annie's eyes. Jen was such a good friend. As she ran her fingers over the smooth surface of the ornaments, she regretted her decision not to get a Christmas tree this year. There would be nowhere to display these as they were meant to be. Matt had wanted to get a tree, but relented when she insisted she wasn't in the mood for it. Now she was sorry she'd been such a Scrooge. After all, it was their first Christmas together; that was worth celebrating, wasn't it? Wiping the tears away with the back of her hand, she decided to go home and ask Matt if he still felt like getting a tree. Christmas Eve was only three days away; hopefully there would still be some good ones left.

The drive home was peaceful and quiet. It was a Sunday night, so the city streets were empty, except for a random car every so often. Snowflakes began falling, covering everything with a frosty layer of white lace. Christmas lights outlined windows, doors and roofs of many of the houses she passed, glowing warmly in the winter darkness. It brought back childhood memories of when her parents would drive around with her to look at the elaborate holiday light displays. They would "ooh" and "aah," declaring that each house was better than the one before. At the end of the night they'd agree that every house had been the best; each one was a masterpiece. After her father died, Christmas had never been quite the same, even though her mother, Frank, and Sally had done their best to make it a happy holiday. She had learned from an early age that it was people who made Christmas special, not the presents. Now, as she drove home, the teddy bear ornaments on the car seat beside her, she realized that the person who made this Christmas special was waiting at home for her, and suddenly it seemed she couldn't get there fast enough.

Driving past the apartment to the parking lot, she could see the faint glow of the television illuminating their living room. Her heart still beat faster at the thought of seeing Matt and she wondered if that's what it meant to be a newlywed. She hoped the feeling lasted forever, that she'd never take what they had for granted.

The bitter wind whipped around the side of the building, and she squinted and shivered as she lowered her head to avoid the chilly onslaught. Her mittens slipped on the brass doorknob of the main door of the building as she tried to turn it and she muttered curses under her breath that turned into icicles on her wool scarf. Before she could turn it again, the door flew open, a blast of warm air burst out from the entryway to envelope her. She looked up in surprise, and there stood Matt, a Santa cap on his head and a red and green striped scarf around his neck.

"Welcome ho-ho-home!" he said as he held the door open for her and gathered her into his arms.

"What a nice surprise!" said Annie as he took her cello. "I thought you were watching T.V. up there."

"I was, but I was also watching for my wife. You haven't seen her, have you?" He winked at her and then planted a long, deep kiss on her mouth.

"You are such a dork!" she said, giggling and kissed him back.

"How was the second show?" he asked as they plodded up the stairs to the second floor.

"It was good, but I'm glad it's over. I'll have to show you what Jen gave us." She fumbled around in her bag as she spoke. "It made me change my mind about -- "

"Okay, but wait just a minute." They were outside the door to their apartment. "Close your eyes."

"Why?" Annie looked at him, confused. The box that held the ornaments was in her hand.

Matt set her cello case down in the hall, and stood behind her, his hands on her shoulders. "Are your eyes closed?"

"Yes, but why?"

"I have a little surprise for you. On the count of three, you can open your eyes. One, two, three!"

Annie heard the door creak open and felt Matt guide her into the apartment. She opened her eyes, and there before her was the scrawniest, most scraggly evergreen tree she'd ever seen. Multi-colored lights adorned its branches, making it shine and twinkle in the shadows of the living room. Annie gasped with delight.

"I know you said you didn't want a tree this year, but after the concert today, I got to thinking and --" Annie silenced him with a kiss.

"This is the most beautiful tree I've ever seen. I love it!" The lights reflected and sparkled in her eyes.

"You're not mad?" Matt sounded sheepish.

"How could I be mad? It's perfect! In fact, I was going to tell you that I changed my mind about getting one."

"Really? I'm so relieved! The last thing I wanted to do was upset you, but it just didn't seem like Christmas without one. I hoped it would make you feel a little better; a little more Christmasy." He grinned at her but then turned serious. "What made you change your mind?"

"Well, Jen gave me these and I realized that we had nowhere to hang them." She held the box of ornaments out to him.

"That was so kind of her," said Matt as he examined the teddy bear angels. "They even have their names on them." He touched the letters of Munchkin's name as he spoke.

"They can be the first ornaments on our first Christmas tree." Annie put her arms around his waist, resting her head on his chest.

"At this point, they're the only ornaments," he said, rubbing her back. "But that's okay." He handed her Dillon's porcelain angel. "Shall we?"

They walked over to the tree, holding the angels gently in their hands. Annie found a branch near the middle of the tree and gently placed the ornament on it.

Matt did the same with the nameless angel, giving it a little kiss before hanging it on a nearby branch. Together they placed Munchkin's angel on the tiny tree with extra care.

"Merry Christmas, kiddos," he said, his voice cracking with emotion.

"We love you," Annie added.

They stood there, arms entwined, making a new Christmas memory as the snow continued to fall.

# The House

Fingers poised over the strings, Annie took a deep breath and started to play the measure again. It was a beautiful piece with an abundance of arpeggios and key changes and an especially challenging cello part. Her fingers flew up and down the strings rapidly and the bow in her other hand glided lightly until she hit the sour note again. She came to an abrupt stop and pounded her feet on the floor.

"Careful, sweetie," said Matt looking up from his typewriter. "Jake is going to evict us if you keep stomping on the floor so much."

"I know, I know," said Annie, blowing the hair out of her eyes. "This is just so frustrating." She glowered at the sheet music on the black music stand with steely contempt.

"I can relate." Matt glanced down at the mountain of crumpled up pieces of typing paper around his feet. "Not a very good day for the arts, is it?"

"Well, my inadequate cello playing can't be helping your creativity very much. I don't know what I'm going to do. I have to get this piece down by rehearsal on Tuesday." A headache emerging, Annie closed her eyes and rubbed her temples. "I just can't seem to concentrate today."

A worried expression clouded Matt's face. Annie caught the change in his mood out of the corner of her eye and her blood started to boil. Every time she had a headache or had trouble concentrating, he'd act overly concerned, which was getting on her nerves. People had headaches all of the time, but suddenly because she'd had a head injury, when it happened to her, it was a major event. What worried her more than any physical symptoms, was the way she couldn't seem to control herself. A normally calm, controlled person, these days if something upset her, she'd spiral into a rage at the drop of a hat. She was constantly on edge because of it which only made matters worse.

"Why are you looking at me like that?" her voice was wary, defensive.

"Like what?" Matt tried to act innocent and clueless, which only made her angrier.

"Like you're ready to have me committed."

"No, honey, I wasn't looking at you like that."

"Well, then stop looking so worried. I'm fine. So I'm having trouble with this music. It's a very difficult piece," she snapped.

"Okay, okay. I'm sorry." He turned his attention to his typewriter and started typing furiously, punching at the keys as though they were spiders he was trying to obliterate.

Annie closed her eyes and took several deep breaths. Each time she exhaled she imagined herself expelling the ugly, angry feelings from her body, leaving only the kind, reasonable ones behind. Matt had been so patient; he deserved better than to be yelled at for just caring about her.

At moments like this she wondered if it hadn't been a mistake to get married when they did. Perhaps embarking on a marriage so soon after the miscarriage and her head injury was a bit reckless of them. After all, under the best of circumstances, marriage was a huge step. Who did they think they were, that they'd be able to surmount the difficulties that life had given them so recently?

She looked at Matt hunched over his typewriter, a pencil perched between his front teeth, his eyebrows knit together in concentration, and all of her fears disintegrated on the spot. She loved this man with every cell in her body, with every bit of her soul. There was no way she could begin to imagine her life without him. He looked up at her, the pencil hanging out of his mouth, ink smudges from the typewriter ribbon that kept needing to be straightened out, on the side of his nose. He looked positively adorable sitting there at his makeshift desk made out of an old vanity that they'd found at a thrift shop. Annie also realized for the first time how cramped for space they had become since Matt had moved in. No wonder he was having trouble writing; he had no office, no place to call his own. She was having difficulty with her music because she felt that all the starts, stops and off-key notes were disturbing his concentration. A smile slowly lit her face from within, from the light bulb that had just clicked on in her brain.

"What are you smiling at?" His face was turning a warm shade of pink, the color inching its way up from underneath his shirt collar.

"You."

"Really."

"Yes, really. I'm thinking about how much I love you. And about how lucky I am to be married to such a wonderful man."

She put down her cello and walked over to him. He swiveled a little on his desk chair, and she climbed on top of him, straddling his lap. Putting her hands on either side of his face, she leaned in and kissed him.

"Wow. What was that for?" Matt asked, a silly grin on his just kissed mouth.

"That was an 'I'm sorry for being such a bitch' kiss," explained Annie, her hands playing with the curls on the back of his head. "You don't deserve to be treated so poorly."

"I wouldn't call this treatment poor," he said, his voice was barely a whisper. "I'd call this pretty wonderful." He wrapped his arms around her and pulled her so close to him she could feel his heart beating.

"I just had an idea. A brilliant idea," Annie said as she nibbled on his neck, breathing in his clean, Ivory soap smell.

"All of your ideas are brilliant, sweetie." Matt ran his hands up and down her back and placed butterfly kisses in a line on her neck. "Does this idea involve our going into the bedroom?"

"Umm, no, I'm afraid not." Annie tried not to pay too much attention to the dejected look in her husband's eyes. "But you're going to love it!"

"Okay, then, lay it on me. What's the brilliant idea?"

"I think we should buy a house!" Annie blurted out the words with gusto, hoping to get Matt caught up in her enthusiasm.

"A house, huh?" He looked speculative. "Too much togetherness with two of us here?"

"No, I love how cozy it is. I just think that you need your own space to write and I need a place to practice that are a little further away from each other."

Matt looked around the cluttered room as if he was seeing it for the first time. He had made a small work area in which to write which consisted of the small desk, the desk chair and antique floor lamp he brought from his apartment. Annie had taken the room divider screen she had been using in the bedroom and placed it alongside his desk to create some privacy, but it didn't block the sound very well, so they had pushed it up against the wall. Her cello stand and music stand stood in the opposite corner of the small room. She dragged one of the chairs from the dining room table over to sit on when she practiced, and often left it sitting there next to the couch, because it was easier than moving it back and forth. Their bicycles leaned against the dining room wall since they had no place else to store them. There were some boxes of Matt's dishes and other items from his apartment piled in the corner of the dining room, making the apartment look as though they were just moving in or getting ready to move out.

"I guess it is kind of a disaster in here, isn't it? When you lived here by yourself it was always so perfect. It looks like a bomb went off in here since I moved in." A sheepish expression spread like syrup from his hairline down to his chin. "I've been so happy I hadn't really noticed everything piling up around us."

Annie hugged him fiercely and laughed. "Oh, honey, it's okay. It's not a disaster. Wouldn't you like to have an office though? And maybe a garage?"

His eyes lit up when he heard 'garage'. Annie laughed out loud at the sight of him nearly salivating at the idea. Her peals of laughter shook him out of his reverie.

"What?" he said, confused.

"You should have seen the look on your face when I said 'garage.' I never knew it would excite you that much!"

Blushing, Matt smiled and said, "Every guy wants a garage to call his own -- even us 'highly evolved' types."

"You don't say," said Annie. "Maybe we can put your office out in the garage then."

"Oh really." There was a devilish glint in his eyes.

"Yes, really!" she taunted him, a mischievous smile twitched at the corners of her mouth.

"I think we should talk about this some more."

"You do?" Annie was thrilled that he was interested in her idea.

"Of course I do," he said as he rose from the chair and picked her up in his arms. "But I communicate best in the bedroom, you know."

"You don't say," she murmured into his neck.

An hour later, tangled sheets became a cozy nest and they nestled in bed, her cello and his typewriter having migrated to the bottom of the priority list. Matt traced the outline of her face with his fingertips, her head upon his chest, rising and falling with each breath. The cool sunshine of early afternoon wiggled its way between the slats of the mini-blinds in the window and covered their bodies with crooked stripes. Annie's fingers followed one of the stripes from Matt's shoulder down to his hand and back up again.

"This is wonderful," she said and placed a soft kiss on his chest.

"Uh-huh."

"Do you think we'll ever get tired of this?"

"I know I won't." He kissed the top of her head and ruffled her hair.

"So, what do you think about looking for a house?"

"I think it's a good idea. Having a house and a yard to take care of means less time for afternoons like this, but we'd manage somehow."

"You are such a dork!" She punched him playfully on the arm. "House or no house, afternoons like this will always be a priority." Their priorities clearly in order, they once again disappeared under the mound of sheets and blankets.

At the first hint of sunrise, Annie slid out of bed, donned her blue chenille robe and tiptoed out into the living room. The newspaper was usually delivered early, around 6:00 a.m. and she was anxious to see if it was waiting for her on the other side of the apartment door. Keeping the security chain in place, she opened the door a crack and peered out into the empty hallway. There at the bottom edge of the door was the early edition of the Sunday paper. Smiling to herself, she closed the door, unhooked the chain and opened it again. As she stooped down to retrieve the paper, the door across the hall opened, a shaft of light seeped out into the hall, followed by the grating voice of her neighbor, Mrs. Flugle.

"Good Morning, Annie!"

"Hello, Mrs. Flugle. How are you today?"

"I'm as good as the Lord allows," said Mrs. Flugle as she bent over to pick up her own newspaper. "I had a hard time sleeping last night, with all the racket you make in there."

Annie grimaced as she watched the elderly woman straighten back up, one hand on her back, the other holding the paper. One of these days she was afraid she'd find Mrs. Flugle lying on her back in the hallway like a turtle that had been tipped on its shell and couldn't turn over, her wrinkled neck sticking out in panic, her frail arms and legs thrashing about. She always had something to complain about, whether it was her arthritis, the weather or her lazy, ungrateful son who in her eyes never did anything right. From what Annie could tell, he was a saint, who always came running when his mother called, but somehow it was never enough.

"Sorry about that," Annie muttered and slipped back inside the apartment, quietly closing the door. She wasn't sure what the "racket" was that the old woman referred to, but it didn't matter. Every time she met her in the hall or on the steps, there was some complaint to listen to, something they had done to bother her.

Back in the apartment, Annie slammed the newspaper down on the kitchen counter, a string of expletives streaming out under her breath as she set about making coffee. Every action was punctuated by an angry word or grunt, from measuring the coffee grounds to pouring the water into the Mr. Coffee's reservoir.

When the rich aroma of coffee reached Matt's nose in the bedroom, he stumbled out to the kitchen, his hair as tousled and tangled as the sheets and blankets.

"Good morning, honeybunch," he said as soon as he saw the scowl on his wife's face. "Coffee smells good." He kissed the top of her head and then went to the cupboard for a coffee mug.

"Hmmphh," Annie growled.

"Don't tell me. Mrs. Flugle?" he said, pouring the dark, steamy liquid into the mug.

"Of course." Annie took a sip from her own mug. "It was a perfectly wonderful morning until I had to see *her*."

"She is a ray a sunshine, isn't she?" Matt sat down at the table across from her.

Annie sighed, rolled her eyes at him and then began to smirk. "Positively blinding."

Matt began to chuckle and soon they were both giggling.

"I don't know why I let her bother me so much," said Annie as she settled her feet in Matt's lap. "It's just always something. No matter how hard we try, she's never happy."

"I feel sorry for her son. That guy sure has his work cut out for him."

"Well, it just confirms that we need to find a house -- a single family house. I'm tired of apartment living." Annie got up to get more coffee, offering some to Matt first.

"Unless we're on a deserted island, we'll always have neighbors, you know. Every neighborhood has a Mrs. Flugle."

"So I'm being unrealistic to want a perfect house in a perfect neighborhood? I already have the perfect husband, so anything's possible, right?"

"Okay, it's getting pretty deep in here," Matt said, laughing. "Let's see what's in the paper, shall we?"

They spent the rest of the morning searching the classified section of the paper for houses for sale and ads for open houses. More had to be done to find out exactly what they'd be able to afford and what they'd qualify for, but they had a general idea. Matt's income as a freelance writer was less predictable than Annie's salary with the orchestra, but their combined incomes would be more than enough for a modest mortgage payment. She had been fiercely saving the settlement money from the divorce and had always planned to use it for a down payment on a house someday. The substantial down payment would make the payments more tolerable. Matt also had a nest egg squirreled away; the insurance settlement from Sara's car accident. He hadn't been able to bring himself to spend a penny of it, because it felt wrong. Annie didn't want him to use it for the house; it seemed more appropriate to save it for something else. What that was, she didn't know.

"Well, we have eight we can look at today if we get going," said Matt as he snapped the cap back on the black Sharpie. "They're all in the same area, so we should be able to get to all of them, don't you think?"

"Sounds good to me!" Annie's spirits had improved with each ad they circled. She couldn't wait to go out and find their future home.

The first three houses on the list were so dilapidated and in such a bad part of the city, Annie and Matt decided not to even look at them. At first Annie had insisted they give them a chance because they were so close to Orchestra Hall, but Matt firmly overruled her. Why bother to look at something they had no intention of buying? They regrouped and started driving to the fourth house they had circled. It was further away from downtown, but still in south Minneapolis, not too far from the cemetery and Sally and Frank's house.

Annie gazed out the car window as they wound their way around the lakes and parks that were scattered about the city. As they got closer to the open house, she commented on each school, church, and park, saying how fun it would be to take their kids to each place. She chatted excitedly about how family friendly the neighborhoods looked; how it would be such a great place to raise children.

They pulled up in front of a brick tudor-style house with an "Open House" sign stuck into the lawn next to the red and white "For Sale" sign. It was too soon for any flowers to be blooming in the flower boxes that adorned the windows, but Annie could tell that it would look beautiful later in the spring.

"This looks perfect!" she crooned, craning her neck to get a better view. "Oh, look at the cute lace curtains in the windows!"

Matt turned off the ignition and sat quietly for a moment, staring straight ahead through the windshield. Annie babbled on next to him about how wonderful the house was in every way. When he didn't seem to be listening to her, she put her hand on his forearm and squeezed it enthusiastically.

"Honey, what do you think? Isn't it great?!"

He patted her hand and then gently took it in his own. "Annie, stop. Take a breath."

She withdrew her hand and gave him a wounded look. "What?"

"It's just that you've been going on and on about how great this house will be. What if it doesn't work out? We don't know anything about this place. I just don't want you to be too disappointed."

Looking down at her hands in her lap, she bit her lip to keep from crying. "Why do you have to burst my bubble so quickly, Matt? I know it might not work out; it's just fun to be excited about it." Sniffling, she looked out her window at the adorable little gingerbread house and let out a mournful sigh.

"I'm sorry, Annie. I didn't mean to do that; really, I didn't. It is a cute little place; adorable, even. I'm an idiot and a jerk to ruin the fun. Let's go in and look at it. Who knows? It might be just what we're looking for." He nudged her with his elbow. "Please?"

She slowly turned her head toward him, looking at him out of the corner of her eye first. "Are you sure?"

He nodded.

"Because I don't want you to just say that to make me happy."

"What's wrong with wanting to make you happy?" He reached over and touched her cheek with his fingertips.

"Nothing, silly, but you know what I mean."

"I do?" he joked, but then saw the look of frustration inch across her face and said, "Yes, sweetie, I really do. Let's go inside."

The house was as enchanting on the inside as it was on the outside. It was an older home, built in the late 1930s or early 1940s, but beautifully maintained and updated. There were arched doorways throughout, built-in mahogany bookcases and buffet, very similar to their apartment. All the appliances had been recently replaced, as had the roof, which was a huge plus. There wasn't much wrong with it. Try as they might, neither of them could find a cause for concern. The only fly in-the-ointment would be whether or not they could afford it. The incredibly high interest rates of the early 1980s were coming down from 16% to around 10%, which made buying a home more affordable for many people. Matt and Annie knew it would be a close call, but they prayed they'd qualify.

"So, what do you think?" Annie whispered in Matt's ear when they were in a secluded corner of the house. The faint hint of spring had coaxed many prospective home buyers out to the open houses, this one in particular. The house was crawling with people.

"I like it." Matt's voice was firm. "It's great. I say we make an offer."

Annie stared at him, her eyes as wide open as her mouth.

"Are you serious? We only decided to start looking today. Don't you think that's rushing it a bit?"

"Now who's bursting bubbles?" Matt said in hushed tones. "Houses like this don't come along every day, Annie. Look at how many people are here. If we don't make an offer, it will be gone. It's worth a shot."

Annie looked over her shoulder at another young couple that just wandered into the room. The expressions on their faces were excited and hopeful, just like hers and Matt's. Biting her lip, she turned back to Matt.

"Okay. Let's do it."

Over the course of the next 24 hours, they made an offer, signed a purchase agreement and were anxiously waiting to hear if they would be the new owners of the most perfect house they'd ever seen. Annie was grateful that she had to master the new piece of music for practice on Tuesday morning; it gave her something to do besides worry. Matt, who liked to claim he wasn't much of a worrier, took over the role while she spent the evening hunched over her cello, practicing until her fingers, arms and shoulders ached. He sat, also hunched over, at his typewriter, sometimes banging at the keys, but more often he just stared off into space, his eyebrows knit together, frown on his face.

Annie leaned back in her chair, and balancing her cello on her thigh, stretched her arms over her head, her bow still in her right hand. She closed her eyes as she bent her neck from side to side, and rotated her head in a circular motion, trying to work out the kinks. Even though her stomach had been in knots all afternoon, her practicing was going well; the piece was nearly perfect. Every time she took a break, she said a little prayer that they'd be able to buy the house. Matt had warned her to be careful what she prayed for, but she couldn't help it. She tried to phrase her prayers to say 'Please do what's best for us', but then decided to be honest and ask specifically for the house. God knew what she was thinking anyway, so hiding it beneath a benevolent request seemed like a waste of time, and just plain wrong.

The ring of the telephone was so abrupt and shrill that both Annie and Matt jumped at the sudden sound. If her heart had been beating loudly before, now it was amplified tenfold. She and Matt stared at each other, both momentarily paralyzed. Finally she said, "Will you answer it?"

Matt found his feet and leaped from his chair over to the telephone in a heart beat, although to Annie it seemed as though he was moving in slow motion. When he was almost to the small table that held the phone, his arm telescoped out from his shoulder like Inspector Gadget, his hand deftly grasping the receiver.

"Hello?" his voice sounded amazingly calm.

Annie marveled at his self-control. She tried not to hyperventilate with excitement while she waited to see if it was the realtor. As usual, Annie had worked herself into a bundle of jangling nerves as they anticipated the news about the house. If they didn't get it, she tried to tell herself that it wouldn't be the end of the world; and it wouldn't. They had both endured far greater losses than an offer on a house being rejected. Annie felt a little guilty for getting so wrapped up in it, but the possibility had given them so much happiness and hope, and it felt so good to both of them, in spite of the anxiety it produced.

"Hi Marla! How are you?" It was the realtor. Matt did his best to keep his voice steady. "We were hoping it was you!" He gave Annie a little wink as he listened to the voice on the other end. "I see. Yep. Okay. No problem. Sure. Yep. Got it. Thanks for calling." He silently placed the telephone receiver back in its cradle and turned his back to Annie.

Afraid to say anything, Annie pried the bow from her clenched fingers and set it on her music stand in front of the sheet music. She concentrated on breathing deeply, on maintaining her focus on what was really important in their lives. The sinking feeling in her stomach told her to prepare for disappointment, to be strong and brave and to be there for Matt if he needed her. It was not all about her.

"So?" she said, her voice barely audible above the traffic on the street below.

Matt turned around to face her, a huge smile on his face. "We got it, Annie, we got it!"

# The Parachute

The unmistakable twinges had started around midnight, waking her from a fitful sleep full of dreams of Dillon and Munchkin. Their precious baby faces floated in and out of her consciousness until she didn't know if she was asleep or awake. It had been a dream that awakened her and as she laid next to Matt, trying to fall back to sleep, she felt the all too familiar beginning of her period. *Damn,* she thought. *No baby again this month.*

Annie resisted the urge to cry as she had done every month since they'd lost Munchkin. In a few months it would be a year since the miscarriage. Matt had held her and comforted her every time the monthly cramps and bleeding began, assuring her that everything would be alright, that they would have a baby someday. They had both hoped that moving into their own house would take some of the focus off of thoughts of pregnancy, but it only seemed to make the yearning more intense. The apartment had only had one bedroom and so there had been no room left empty, no room put aside as the future nursery. Sometimes Matt would find Annie standing in that room, a sad look on her face, and he would gently steer her back to the present, instead of letting her aimlessly wander in the hazy world of what might never be. She never told him how grateful she was to be rescued by him at those moments, because that would have frightened him to no end. It remained her secret and hopefully always would; the feeling that while standing in that room, she would only need to take one tiny step and forever fall into a place where she would be so lost, no one would ever be able to find her let alone bring her back.

Matt stirred in his sleep and rolled toward her, arms encircling her as he did every night. She snuggled next to him, spooning in the warm cocoon of his body, and willed away the sad thoughts. Gently she reached up to hold his hands where they rested just under her chin and she kissed his fingers as they curled around hers. He gave her shoulder a gossamer kiss as he slipped into a deeper sleep.

Annie looked out of the window and searched the sky for Dillon's star. It had been difficult to find from a new window in the new house, but after a few nights, there it was, shining extra brightly, as if to say, "Hello! I'm over here!" She knew there was a good chance that the star she deemed Dillon's might not always be the same one that she'd seen the night he was born, but she didn't care. To her, any star that showed up when she needed to see it, qualified. It wasn't something she talked about with anyone but Matt, and these days she even avoided discussing it with him. She didn't want to worry him. Dillon's star was the only thing, besides Matt, that kept her grounded. She'd see it twinkling amongst lush, green summer leaves, or bare, crooked winter branches and know that it was the same world in which she'd held Dillon in her arms, if for only a short time. Seeing the star reassured her that he'd always be in her heart; that no matter what happened, that would never change.

It was a cloudy night and it didn't take Annie long to give up her search. There would be no stargazing tonight. She hadn't seen Dillon's star for days, which hadn't really bothered her because she'd been busy praying for a missed period and a pregnancy. Lying safely in Matt's arms, with no star to soothe her, another spasm of pain snaked its way through her abdomen, taunting her back to reality.

Whoever said that once you had a baby menstrual cramps were less severe, was lying, Annie decided as she closed her eyes and grimaced through the pain. Matt had moved his hands from under her chin to her belly, holding her tenderly as she tried not to squirm or writhe. When she was alone, she would give in to the waves of discomfort by moaning or groaning or curling her body into a small, hard lump of misery. If anyone else was present, however, she became stoic and the epitome of self-control, suffering in silence. It often made her wonder which was the more authentic; her stoic self or the dramatic one.

Not wanting to awaken Matt, she gingerly slid out from under his embrace, moving very slowly so that his arms wouldn't notice she was gone. He pulled her pillow close to him and kept sleeping, a contented smile on his face. She smiled down at him and silently slipped into her robe.

She reached into the bathroom cupboard with only the glow of the nightlight guiding her. Her fingers searched for a tampon but found nothing but an empty cardboard box. Damn, she thought. I was so sure I wouldn't be needing them. She padded out to the linen closet in the hall to retrieve another box and was relieved to find one there. She hadn't been that sure, which as it turned out, was a good thing. The translucent haze of the nightlight made it difficult to find the cellophane tab on the box, so Annie switched on the bathroom light. Her fingers trembled as she fumbled with the package while another spasm of cramps dug into her and held on relentlessly.

"Damn it!" she hissed and hurled the box of tampons across the room. The box landed with a small thump and bounced off the side of the bathtub.

Angry with herself for making so much noise, Annie leaned down and picked the box up off the country blue bathroom rug. Again she attempted to open the box, this time struggling to stay calm. There was a gentle knock on the bathroom door. "Sweetie?"

Chagrined, Annie reached over and opened the door with her free hand. Matt took one look at his disheveled wife, the box of tampons and the miserable expression on her face and knew the reason for the commotion. Without a word he went over to her and gathered her in his arms.

"I'm sorry if I woke you," she whispered, trying desperately not to start weeping. "I couldn't get the damn box opened."

"Can I give it a try?"

Annie nodded and handed him the box. He held the cellophane strip between his thumb and forefinger and pulled, thereby releasing the cardboard box from its clear plastic wrapper. There was another cardboard strip on the box to tear off before the top would open and free the tampons held hostage inside.

"Good Lord," he said as he set the box on the counter, "You'd think these were narcotics or something."

"Well, they are habit-forming," Annie said and then looked at him with a grim face, "unfortunately." She couldn't suppress the smirk that appeared out of nowhere.

Matt took Annie's face in his hands and kissed her. " I love you."

They looked at each other and giggled and then started to laugh harder.

"I don't know what I'm laughing about," said Annie once she could speak. "I have God-awful cramps, which means I'm not pregnant, and I needed my husband to open my stupid box of tampons."

"You forgot that it's the middle of the night," Matt said.

"That I did. Thanks for reminding me."

"And we're sitting on the bathroom floor in the middle of the night."

"Who does this?" Annie buried her face in her hands.

"Two people who are madly in love with each other, that's who." Matt put his arm around her.

"Well, you know what I've discovered?" she said, looking at him through tousled strands of hair.

"What?" He brushed the hair out of her eyes.

"That laughing relieves cramps," she said triumphantly and then doubled over as another spasm descended on her. "Sometimes."

"I'll get the Motrin," said Matt as he helped her up from the floor. "Meet you in the bedroom." He gave her shoulders a gentle squeeze.

Annie finished up in the bathroom and climbed back into bed. Matt had a glass of water and the Motrin on her nightstand and had found and plugged in the heating pad.

"I don't deserve you," she said softly as she placed the heating pad on her tummy. "Why are you so good to me?"

"You know why, Mrs. Preston." He kissed the tip of her nose. "Now let's see if we can get some sleep, okay?"

The next morning Annie hummed cheerfully as she spritzed Windex on the toaster and wiped it with a paper towel until it gleamed in the early morning sunshine. She smiled at her reflection in the stainless steel as she reached for her mug of coffee on the counter. Suddenly Matt's face popped up next to hers on the front of the toaster. He leaned forward and kissed her image shining up at them from the shiny silver surface.

"Hey - I just cleaned that!" She nudged him with her elbow.

"Oops. Sorry. I know, you want me to kiss the real you, right?" He dipped her back in his arms and gave her a proper good morning kiss. "There. Is that better?"

"Much better. Here you go." She handed him the Windex and a paper towel with a smile.

"You're in a good mood this morning," he said as he wiped his lip print off the toaster. "Not exactly what I expected."

Annie brought him steaming hot coffee in his favorite mug with the chipped handle and The Far Side cartoon on it. She had refilled her own mug as well and settled down at the table.

"I did some thinking last night," she said as she blew on her coffee to cool it down.

"Why am I not surprised?" He took a sip of coffee.

"I'm way too preoccupied with getting pregnant. You are so patient and kind to me, but I must be driving you absolutely crazy when I flip out every month when I get my period."

Matt sat quietly, waiting for her to continue.

"I'm not really living my life in the present; I'm spending all of my energy waiting for something that might never happen."

"It will happen, honey. You have gotten pregnant twice before." He placed a reassuring hand on her forearm.

"I know that, Matt, but that doesn't mean I will again. We of all people should know that there are no guarantees." She wrapped her hands around her coffee mug and looked at him earnestly. "It's not fair to either of us."

"What brought all of this on?"

"The realization that I was acting like a crazy woman last night."

"You weren't that bad." Matt said. "Everyone gets frustrated with packaging now and then..." His voice trailed off.

"You're being too kind, sweetie. I lost it and you ended up taking the brunt of it. You deserve better than that."

"Well, okay, if you say so." He smiled at her. "So, what's the next part?"

"The next part?"

"Annie, I know you well enough to know that this 'realization' isn't all that there is. You're all fired up about something this morning, and for some reason I don't think that being nicer to me is the only reason for the good mood." An astute grin worked its way across his face.

Annie straightened up in her chair and drummed her fingertips on the oak tabletop.

"Well, I thought that each month, if we're not pregnant, we should do something really outrageous; something we would never do if we were pregnant or once we have kids. That way we'll have something to look forward to. What do you think?" She squirmed in anticipation of his reaction.

"I've got to admit it's a unique way to approach it." Matt scratched his morning stubble covered chin. "Any ideas for what we'll do?"

"Actually, yes!" Her eyes lit up, making her whole face sparkle. "Skydiving!"

The grin on Matt's face transformed into a paralyzed pout, his lower lip protruding and his eyes opened wide, eyebrows arched in disbelief.

"Are you kidding me?"

"No, I'm serious! I've always wanted to do it! Don't you think it would be a blast?"

"A blast straight to your death!" His breath was rapid and shallow, his voice a panicked croak.

"Oh, don't be silly. It's very safe. Some people in the orchestra have done it. They said it was wonderful!"

"Really."

"Yes, really. You jump tandem with a professional skydiver. It's not like you just throw yourself out of an airplane and hope for the best. *That* would be crazy!" Annie got up to get more coffee. She dropped a bagel into the just cleaned toaster while she was up.

"Honey, there's something you should know about me," said Matt in a shaky voice. "I'm scared to death of heights. There's no way in hell I could go skydiving, tandem or not. Just thinking about it is making me hyperventilate." He wiped the perspiration on his forehead with the sleeve of his denim shirt. "But you go ahead if you really want to do it."

"Would you at least come with to watch?"

"Let me think about it, ok? Until this moment, I've never even thought about skydiving, let alone watching the person I love most in the world do it."

Now that she had Matt's blessing, uneasy as it was, Annie forged ahead in planning her skydiving adventure. She checked with her fellow musicians and they were more than happy to give her the names and telephone numbers of the places they had gone. It seemed that once a person has leapt from an airplane and hurled toward the earth with nothing more than a parachute, or another person with a parachute on their back, they became members of an elite club. Sort of like the "club" women join after they've had a baby, Annie thought as she wrote the information on a piece of paper and tucked it in her purse. If she couldn't belong to one club, she could belong to the other. There was nothing to stop her except a pregnancy.

The one concession Matt asked of her was to schedule the jump for the next month. It terrified him to think of her falling through the sky and the melodramatic part of him wanted her to wait, just so that he'd have her with him one more month.

"I know it's safe and all of that, but what if you're the one whose chute doesn't open?" said Matt as he chopped onions for homemade spaghetti sauce. "I just need some time to get used to the idea of being a widower again."

"Aren't you being a little dramatic?" Annie balanced a large pot under the kitchen faucet, filling it with water for the pasta. "You are not going to be a widower again. I promise."

"It's the writer in me; I can't help it."

"Okay, I'll wait until next month. Besides, Dillon's second birthday is coming up. I could jump in honor of him." She pushed the handle on the faucet down and carried the pot to the stove. "How does that sound?"

"That sounds excellent. When you put it that way, it makes more sense." He held the cutting board over the sauté pan and used the edge of the knife to slide the bits of onion into the sizzling butter.

Annie came up behind him, threaded her arms under his and hugged him, resting her head on his back. He put his hands over hers and just stood there, swaying back and forth.

"It's going to be okay, honey. Really it is," she whispered into his t-shirt. "And I'm going to have a wonderful story to tell our kids someday."

The morning of the jump, Annie was up early, listening to the weather report. The main obstacle the weather might present on the day of the parachute jump was the wind velocity. If it was too windy, it would have to be rescheduled. She had been getting psyched up for this day for weeks and if it were cancelled, she'd be disappointed for so many reasons. Annie knew that whenever she and Matt did become parents, she'd never do anything as dangerous as skydiving, so this felt like one of her last chances, at least for a long, long time. Of course, she might be looking at a long string of childless months or years; it was hard to say.

"How does the weather look?" Matt snuck up behind her as she concentrated on the morning T.V. weather report. He kissed the top of her head.

"It looks good. Sunny, no wind to speak of. It's supposed to get up to eighty degrees or so."

"Are you still excited?" He climbed over the back of the couch to sit next to her.

"I am! It's just all starting to hit me now." Her voice was tentative. "But I am excited. I just want it to be time to go!" She jiggled her leg as she spoke, the nervous excitement needed an outlet.

"I'm glad I'm coming with you."

"So am I. Yours are the arms I want to fall into after I land. It just wouldn't feel right if you weren't there."

"Don't take this the wrong way, but it's been fun to have this to look forward to, even for me."

"Well, don't you take this the wrong way, but I've been hoping to not get pregnant this month, because I was so excited for this. It's not that I don't want a baby, but --"

"But it's been good to think about something else." Matt finished the sentence for her. "I understand, honey. It's been a nice diversion for both of us. Good idea."

Annie smiled at him and curled up next to him. It had been a good month. They were still trying to conceive, but they were less intense about it. The basal temperature thermometer chart was forgotten several mornings, and some nights they opted for sleep instead of sex. Their conversations were filled with anticipation about Annie's upcoming adventure, as well as other wild and crazy things they might do the following months. They found themselves looking forward to living their lives instead of staying in the "preconception holding pattern" that they'd been in for much too long. Everything wasn't about getting pregnant and it was a welcome relief.

The drive to the skydiving center was laden with quiet anticipation. Annie was trying to stay calm, to think about anything but the fact that she'd soon be jumping out of an airplane, 15,000 feet up in the sky and free falling at a rate of 120 miles per hour. She had put two extra coats of clear nail polish on that morning so she'd be able to peel it off when she became nervous. The fingernails of her left hand we already peeled clean. Every so often she and Matt would look at each other, and they'd smile or he'd give her that adorable wink that made her melt inside. She prayed that all would go well so that she could see him wink at her for the rest of her life, and that it was a life that would last for many, many years.

They drove down a dirt road to a nondescript airplane hangar that had the word "SKYDIVING," painted on its roof in big blue letters. It looked somewhat deserted with only their car and one other in the makeshift parking lot.

"Are you sure it's today? This place looks like it's closed." Matt peered out the windshield from under the sun visor.

"I'm sure. I even called to make sure it wasn't too windy out here. Let's just go in and see."

Hand in hand they trudged up the small path to the hangar door. Annie pushed the door open a crack and looked inside. She opened the door wider and motioned to Matt to follow her. Together, they stepped over the threshold and entered what seemed like another world.

There were several people milling around the periphery of the cavernous airplane hangar. To the left was a short hallway with a rustic sign above it that said: "Restrooms." There was a vending machine on the wall between the men's and women's restrooms that sold soda pop, candy and chips. On the far right side of the hangar were what appeared to be offices, and a few chairs and table were haphazardly arranged nearby. The middle of the hangar was the part that mesmerized both Annie and Matt. Strewn on the floor were yards and yards of billowing, colorful silky fabric. Each mound of fabric had one or two people hovering at its edges, working the margins into manageable sections by folding and rolling it into small, round packs, otherwise known as parachutes.

"Wow," said Matt.

"Yeah. I wonder if one of those will be mine." Annie's voice was a whisper. She tried to swallow the brittle lump of fear that was rising in her throat and squeezed Matt's hand.

After going through a brief "training program", Annie had to read and sign a waiver, absolving the skydiving center from all liability should something go wrong. She was determined to go through with it, so she essentially skimmed the document and signed and dated it. As they told her in a very brief training, there were very few fatalities or accidents of any kind in tandem skydiving. The most common injury was broken legs, and that only happened if the person in front during the tandem jump didn't lift his feet upon landing. Annie made a mental note: Pick up feet. Broken legs would hamper her cello playing nearly as much as broken arms. They didn't say anything about arms breaking, but she figured she'd be careful with those too.

It took a few minutes to get zipped into a jumpsuit and then another fifteen minutes for Bryan, the "tandem master", the professional she'd be strapped to as she plummeted to Earth, to fasten the harness that would connect them. Another staff member photographed each connection and checked them off on a list as well. It was a safety check, Bryan had explained. Safety was a huge priority around this place. That was good to know.

The time to board the plane had arrived. Matt wrapped his arms around her and gave her a long, slow kiss.

"I love you, Annie. Have a blast!" He held up his camera to take her picture and she struck a goofy Junior Birdman pose, saluted him and hurried over to where Bryan was waiting.

"Take good care of her!" Matt called to Bryan, to which Bryan gave him a thumbs up.

"Your husband seems a little worried about this," Bryan said as they climbed into the airplane.

"He's very worried," said Annie. "He's got a huge fear of heights."

"Well, it's cool that he's okay with you jumping."

"Yes, it is." Annie sat down on the bench that ran down one side of the plane. Another bench ran down the other side and was filling up with more skydivers, all in matching blue jumpsuits. She looked out the window and saw Matt standing on the tarmac, waving to her as the plane taxied away.

Everyone straddled the benches, parachutes in neat bundles on their backs. Bryan sat behind her, explaining that when the time came, he'd hook himself to her harness, tighten it and away they'd go.

Annie took a deep breath and looked out of the small, round window. The farm fields below were looking increasingly like a patchwork quilt, dotted with Monopoly houses and tiny cars. Each minute they gained altitude was another minute closer to the big moment. Her heart hammered in her chest and she was glad that Bryan was behind her, so that he couldn't feel her fear.

Near the back of the plane, someone opened the door. The wind whipped by the opened rectangle, blowing the hair of the jumpers closest to it into instant mohawks. The thumping in Annie's chest intensified.

"Isn't that kind of dangerous?" she shouted back to Bryan.

He broke out into a belly laugh that she could feel through the straps he was attaching to her harness. "Sorry, darlin', but what isn't dangerous about this? Actually, that's normal. We've got to get out of here somehow."

Annie turned around as she felt her face turn a bright shade of red. How did she know what was "normal" in this situation? Ask a stupid question, get a stupid answer, she thought, fuming. She should be able to ask as many dumb questions as she wanted to right before she jumped out of a plane, shouldn't she?

A woman sitting across from her, who looked to be around eighty years old, reached across and patted her leg. "Don't feel bad, hon. I asked the same thing my first time."

Bright blue eyes and a contagious smile were the first things that Annie saw when she looked at the woman more closely. Gray curls stuck out from under the blue cap that was pulled snugly on her head. There was no professional jumper strapping himself to the old woman; she was jumping solo.

"How many times have you done this?" Annie asked, raising her voice above the noise of the wind and the humming engines.

"Oh, I've been doing this for years. I started with a tandem jump when I turned fifty, and I was hooked. It gives me a new lease on life every time!" She giggled like a little girl. "Of course, my kids absolutely hate that I do this! That makes it even more fun!"

Annie's heartbeat started to slow down a bit and her embarrassment faded. She realized how ridiculous her question must have sounded and decided to let Bryan off the hook for laughing at her. She felt a tap on her shoulder and turned her head. Bryan's face was right by her ear.

"Sorry I laughed at you just now," he said. "It just struck me funny."

"That's okay. This is all a little overwhelming. The altitude must be turning my brain to mush," Annie said, trying to laugh at herself.

"No, it was a legit question. We do this so much we sort of forget to explain details like that. Are we still friends?"

"Of course," said Annie. She certainly didn't want to trust her life to an enemy.

The group of jumpers in blue suits started inching their way toward the open door, scooting on their behinds up the bench. To Annie's surprise, the older woman was one of them. One by one they exited the plane and grabbed onto straps on each other's suits, preparing for their formation. Before the woman jumped, she turned toward Annie and gave her a "thumbs up", Bryan tapped Annie on the back; the signal for them to scoot up as well.

Moving down the bench with a 180 pound man strapped to her back was more difficult than she'd expected. He helped, of course, but it was odd to suddenly feel like she'd almost doubled in size and weight. Her heart was pounding with excitement now, her moment of truth was fast approaching.

They reached the end of the bench and in unison climbed over it and stood up. The open door was only a few feet away and even though she had a man with a parachute on her back, Annie backed away from it, fearing she'd tumble out into the sky. Her legs felt like jelly.

"Last chance to change your mind," Bryan shouted into her ear as they inched toward the door.

Those six words were all she needed to give her the courage she momentarily misplaced. There was no way she'd back out now. Annie Stanford Preston was not a coward, and if she had to jump out of an airplane to prove it to herself, she would.

"No way! Let's go!" Her voice was loud and clear. Bryan grinned in approval.

Just as he had instructed, she stood with her toes a couple of inches over the edge of the open door, her arms in an "X" across her chest. He held onto the sides of the doorway and they rocked back and forth as he counted, "One, two, THREE!" On "three" he flung them out into the endless expanse of blue. Annie felt the air rush past her face and before she knew which end was up, they did a swan dive and a somersault and then were free falling through the atmosphere. Her arms opened wide, she felt like an eagle soaring through the heavens. She was sure that if she looked up she'd see Dillon and Munchkin watching her, peeking out through a hole in the clouds.

# The Puzzle Pieces

"It's amazing what jumping out of an airplane can do for a person," said Sally as she peeled an enormous apple. The afternoon sun shining on the trees in the backyard made them gleam as if they were on fire.

Ever since Annie was a little girl, she had loved to watch her aunt peel apples. Sally had a way of starting at one end, and worked her way around and around, removing the peel in one long, curly strip without stopping. Annie was aways given the juicy red or green spiral as a special treat, a reward for being a good helper while they made the annual batch of applesauce and apple pies every autumn.

"What do you mean?" Annie was cutting the apples into slices for the pie filling. She had to stay on task to keep up with the lightening speed at which her aunt was peeling the bushel of apples they'd bought at the apple orchard that morning.

"Well, look at everything you've done since then," Sally said, stopping to brush a strand of hair out of her eyes with her forearm. "You and Matt went white water rafting and then did that rock climbing thing. I still can't believe you got him to go up in that hot air balloon." She shook her head as she continued peeling.

"He only did that because I did the rafting."

"And what about the burro rides down in the Grand Canyon?"

"That was crazy!" Annie laughed as she remembered the expedition. "We were both terrified of that one!"

"The two of you have had quite the summer. You definitely made the most of that vacation."

Annie nodded and smiled, remembering what had to be the best three weeks in her life. She and Matt had decided to capitalize on their decision to live life to the fullest and took a trip to the Grand Canyon, during which they did all the things that she and Sally listed. They made a lifetime of memories that would always be precious and dear.

She still dreamed about the hot air balloon ride, silently floating above the mountains, where the only sound was the whoosh of the burner as it inflated the balloon. Skydiving had been the experience of a lifetime, but in the balloon, with its peaceful motion, she felt closer to Matt than ever before. He had been terrified, but once the balloon was aloft and he had consumed a glass of wine, he managed to relax and even enjoyed himself.

The trade off had been that she had to join him white water rafting. She had tried to get out of it, saying that she didn't know how to swim, but Matt lovingly reminded her that then he could pass on the hot air balloon ride, because after all, he didn't know how to fly. Since she couldn't argue with logic like that, she complied, but was convinced that she'd fall overboard and be dashed upon the rocks. It didn't seem wise to consume alcohol beforehand, but she assured Matt that if she survived the ordeal, champagne was definitely in order. Terrifying though it was, the feeling of exhilaration and courage that riding the rapids gave her, made it worth every moment of terror.

"You'd never get me on a burro, I can tell you that!" Sally's proclamation jolted Annie out of her daydream.

"It wasn't so bad," said Annie, "now that it's over! I did get kind of attached to my burro, though. His name was Pablo. He was slow and steady; just what I wanted. Although when he wouldn't keep up with everyone else and I was lagging behind, it got a little scary." She sprinkled cinnamon and sugar over the mound of freshly sliced apples in the pie shells.

"These pies are going to be delicious!" Sally said as she finished peeling the last apple. "How about a glass of wine out on the deck once we get them in the oven? The trees are just beautiful."

"I'll pass on the wine, but you go ahead and have some." Annie's concentration was on the lattice pie crust she was constructing as she spoke.

"I have to say," said Sally as she opened a bottle of Cabernet, "marriage certainly does agree with you. You are positively glowing."

Annie smiled as she put the finishing touches on the pie in front of her and placed it in the oven. Marriage to Matt did agree with her. It was so different than marriage to Eric had been. She and Eric had never had the friendship that she had with Matt, or the passion or the devotion. So what did they have? While she didn't spend a lot of time dwelling on it, Annie had a feeling that she'd never know the answer to that question. Whatever they had, their union had produced Dillon, who had innocently changed the course of both their lives. It was the event that put everything else in motion that was making her so happy today. If she couldn't be grateful to Eric for anything else, she would be forever thankful for that. It would never cease to amaze Annie how life sometimes worked.

"Let's go outside and put our feet up. I'm bushed," said Sally. "What would you like to drink?"

"Oh, I'll just have some water. You go and sit down; I'll be there in a minute."

Sally nodded and went out on the deck, wine glass in hand. Once Annie saw that her aunt was sitting in the chaise lounge, eyes closed and basking in the afternoon sun, she hurried down the hall to the bathroom. Trips to the bathroom had become more frequent in the past couple of weeks. Her period was 10 days late and every time she went to the bathroom, she held her breath, afraid that the spell would be broken. Her breasts hurt and looked fuller than usual, she was tired all the time and was peeing like there was no tomorrow. Any normal woman would assume that she was pregnant, but Annie wasn't any woman and she definitely didn't feel normal. She wanted to have a baby more than anything, but she also knew that once a pregnancy was confirmed, she would immediately become a basket case. Suffering not one, but two pregnancy losses, she knew she'd be considered "high risk" by any ob-gyn in the world. The physiological aspects were valid and daunting, but it was the emotional roller coaster that she'd be on that intimidated her the most.

She let out a large sigh when there were no signs of her period. Looking in the mirror, she lifted up her t-shirt, unfastened her bra and poked at her breasts. They still looked bigger and were still very painful. A big grin slid across her face. There was still a chance that she could be pregnant. She quickly fastened her bra, adjusted her shirt and hurried outside to join Sally.

"I was starting to worry about you," said Sally once Annie stepped out onto the deck. "Everything okay?" She squinted at her in the afternoon sunlight.

"Everything's fine." Annie plopped down in the other lounge chair, setting her glass of ice water on the small round table next to her.

Sally peered at her over her sunglasses. "Everything might be fine, but there's something you're not telling me."

Annie tried to talk herself out of blushing, but didn't succeed. She looked down at her hands in her lap, avoiding eye contact with the one person in the world who knew her the longest and the best. Even before her mother had died, Sally had always been there, drying her tears and sharing her laughter. She knew her inside out; there was no way she could lie to her Aunt Sally.

"Well, I wasn't going to say anything until we're sure, but I think I might be pregnant." Annie's voice fluttered with suppressed excitement.

"Woo-hoo!!" Sally was on her feet, pumping her fists in the air. She bounced over to hug her niece.

"We decided not to tell anyone until we're absolutely sure, but --"

"But how could you keep news like that from me? Tell him I guessed; that I pried it out of you!" She was jubilant. "This is so wonderful, Annie! So wonderful!"

Annie wasn't even going to tell Matt what she suspected, but he knew her too well; every last inch of her. He noticed the subtle changes in her appearance nearly as soon as she did. One morning as they lingered in bed, he cupped her breast tenderly in his hand. Normally she responded to this in a positive way, but that particular morning she winced in pain.

"Sorry, sweetie." he said, his hand now repositioned on her shoulder.

"Just a little sore," Annie said in a quiet voice.

He kissed her shoulder and whispered. "And a little bigger too."

She rolled onto her back, her smile beaming up at him. He looked at her as morning sunbeams danced across her face, reflecting his love for her back to him.

Even though she was barely awake, she seemed to sparkle and glimmer, radiating something beyond description. His hands glided down her body, caressed their way from her shoulders, past her breasts and stopped at her stomach, making a protective cage. He leaned over and gently planted a kiss on her belly button.

"Why do I have the feeling that we may not be alone?" He tilted his chin up and gazed at her.

"I wasn't going to tell you until I was sure, but I think there's a chance. I'm a week late."

The line that was Matt's mouth broke into a slow motion grin and he patted her stomach gently. Then he nestled next to her, taking her in his arms, her head sheltered in the crook of his neck, his chin resting on her rumpled morning hair. They laid there in silence for a very long time, lost in their own thoughts, together.

"I didn't want to get your hopes up," Annie finally said. "It could be a false alarm."

"Sweetie, my hopes have been soaring without your saying a word." He smoothed her hair. "I'm sort of tuned in to you, you know."

"Really? You knew?"

"I might be a guy, but I'm not a Neanderthal. I've noticed little things. No tampon wrappers in the wastebasket, no new numbers counting from 1-28 on the calendar. And the changes in your body, well, .." His voice trailed off.

"So I can't keep any secrets from you, huh?" Annie reached up and stroked his cheek.

"Nope. I'm afraid not." He buried his face in her hair.

They agreed to wait until she'd had a positive pregnancy test from her doctor before they told anybody. They decided to get the test done when she was two weeks late; she didn't want to appear too anxious or be disappointed too soon.

Sitting on Sally's deck that afternoon, she had four days to go before getting tested; it may as well have been four years. It felt like forever.

"So when will you be sure?" Sally was vibrating with joy.

"I'm going to wait four more days; then I'll be two weeks late."

"What's so special about two weeks? Can't you get one of those home tests and do it sooner? How can you stand the suspense?" The questions were firing like rounds from a gun. Sally didn't even take a breath.

"I'll be really upset if I'm not, especially since there are so many positive signs. I guess I just want to make the hope last as long as I can." Tears formed in Annie's eyes as she remembered the months of disappointment that preceded this moment.

Sally saw the crack forming in Annie's strong facade and hurried over to give her a heartfelt hug. She sat on the end of the chaise lounge and took her niece's feet in her lap.

"Then wait we will," Sally said as she rubbed Annie's feet. "I'll stifle myself until then. I won't tell a soul; not even Frank. Scout's honor." She bent her fingers into the Girl Scout sign.

"Thank you, Sally. I'm sure the days will fly by." Annie did her best to convince them both of what she knew was a blatant lie.

Four days passed, each day dragging by as if it had a two ton anvil attached to it. Annie tried to be calm and ignore the fact that every little twinge carried with it the disappointing possibility that her period was starting. The orchestra was having a short break before the winter season began. There weren't any concerts to prepare for, but Annie practiced anyway, playing scales and etudes until her fingers ached. If she wasn't pregnant, at least she'd be the best cellist in her section; maybe she'd even inch closer to the coveted "first chair" position. Either way, the hours of practice would not be wasted.

On the morning of the fourth day, Annie woke with a start. She had to go to the bathroom, but she also had to take her temperature with the basal thermometer before she got up and moved around. She'd taken it every day since her period was late, and it was staying high; staying in a perfectly flat, high line on her temperature chart. As she laid with the thin, glass cylinder under her tongue, she ran through her list of things to do after she got up. First, she had to pee in the jar she'd prepared for the occasion. She'd bought a jar of Gerber Baby Food Custard Pudding, ate it and then sterilized the empty jar in the dishwasher. Having a container with a screw top seemed safer than an old margarine tub. Once that task was accomplished, she would place the jar in a brown paper lunch bag and put it in the fridge until she was ready to bring it to the clinic. After that, she and Sally were going to meet for lunch. Matt had an interview with someone for an article he was writing, which given his level of preoccupation over the pregnancy test, was a good thing. They both agreed that if he and Annie were waiting for the results together, they'd drive each other crazy.

Matt rolled over, opened his eyes and saw the thermometer protruding from his wife's mouth. "Good morning, sunshine," he said, careful not to disturb the procedure. She winked at him and gave him a little wave. Too much activity might falsely elevate the numbers, as well as their hopes. They both knew it was silly to play such games. Nothing would alter reality, but at times their reality seemed as fragile as the new life they hoped to create.

Annie slid the thermometer from her lips and peered at it in the semi-darkness.

"Yes!" She grabbed her pen and made a dot on the graph of the temperature chart. "It's still up -- even a little higher!" She raised her hand to give Matt a high-five.

He dove in for a kiss, only to get a mouthful of her pillow.

"Sorry, sweetie," she called to him on her way to the bathroom. "I've got to pee!"

Matt rolled onto his back, holding the temperature chart up to the light. He counted back to the first day her temperature had spiked, and gently noted the date. If Annie was pregnant, that would be the day their baby had been conceived; the day that a miracle occurred.

"So, what did the doctor say?" Sally tore open the pink packet of artificial sweetener and poured it into her iced tea.

"He said that they'd call later this afternoon. Probably after 4:00 p.m. or so," Annie said as she studied the menu on the table in front of her. "I'm almost too excited to eat."

"We'll have you home by then. I promise. What time will Matt be home?"

"I'm not sure; whenever his interview is over. God, the time is just dragging!"

Sally reached across the table and patted her hand. "Let's talk about something else to take our minds off of it. I know! Your first anniversary is coming up! Any big plans?"

At three-thirty that afternoon Annie pulled into the driveway, her heart beating wildly. After lunch they went shopping and Sally talked her into buying a new negligee for her and Matt's anniversary, which managed to distract her for only fleeting moments. She felt a little guilty to be more preoccupied about the results of the pregnancy test than their first anniversary. Checking the contents of her shopping bag, she smiled. Matt would love the sexy, black teddy she had gotten. Pregnant or not, their anniversary would be a very special occasion.

Once inside, she hurried into the bedroom and hid the lingerie in the box of out of season clothes that she stored under the bed. Their anniversary was about a month away and she wanted to surprise Matt. He never looked under the bed, so it was the perfect hiding place. Just when she had carefully laid the last sweater on top of the nightie, the telephone rang loudly. It startled her so much that she bumped her knee on the bedpost as she shoved the box back under the bed. Rubbing her knee, she hurried to the phone.

"Hello?" She tried not to sound out of breath.

"May I speak with Annie Preston, please?" a female voice said.

"This is Annie." A sensation in the pit of her stomach told her it was the doctor's office.

"Hi Annie. This is Sheila, from Dr. Hayes' office."

"Hi," said Annie calmly, although inside she was screaming, *Just tell me, for Pete's sake!*

"Well, we have the results of both the urine and the blood tests. Congratulations! You're pregnant!"

The words glimmered through the receiver and fell upon her, a shimmering blanket of joy. She shivered with happiness and disbelief.

"Are you sure?" she finally said. "This call wasn't meant for someone else?"

"Annie," said Sheila. "We're always very careful with these calls, but because it's you, I'm extra careful. So yes, I'm sure! Dr. Hayes wants to see you for your first appointment at around eight weeks, so would you like to schedule that now?"

Annie's mind was a whirlwind and her body was beginning to feel the same way.

She didn't know why, but suddenly she felt very dizzy and grabbed the edge of the counter for support.

"Can I call you back to schedule that? My husband might want to come with and we need to check his schedule first." She took slow, deep breaths to make the dizziness go away.

"Oh, of course. That's just fine. We'll talk to you soon. Congratulations again!"

Annie hung up the phone and sat down at the kitchen table. Pregnant. She said we're pregnant! She still didn't believe it. Pregnant! Tears filled her eyes as she let the words settle around her. Now that her wish had come true, she was elated and terrified.

What if this baby died too?

The scraping of a key in the lock diverted her attention to the back door to see Matt holding two bags of groceries, jostling his way into the room. She was out of her chair and into his arms in an instant. They would always laugh about that moment, wondering how it had all transpired; her telling him the wonderful news, as the contents of the bags spilled out onto the floor and landed around their feet without them even noticing.

The days that followed were idyllic. Annie and Matt reveled in their happy news, telling only Sally and Frank at first. They wanted to wait as long as possible to tell Matt's parents and their friends, just in case something went wrong. With Annie's history, it felt like tempting fate to do otherwise. Amid the worry, Annie was feeling good. The previous symptoms remained and were getting stronger every day. She wasn't experiencing full-blown morning sickness yet, just a little queasiness and found herself wishing for it, claiming it would be reassuring.

"Are you sure you want to go out tonight since we have the doctor appointment in the morning?" Matt said as he straightened the knot in his tie. "I know it's our anniversary, but maybe we should stay home and rest."

Annie poked her head out of the bathroom, a mascara wand in her hand. "Sweetie, this will be the last wedding anniversary for a long, long time when we don't have to have a babysitter. We'll be home early, I promise. I'm starting to feel too tired to do anything else."

"Good point." He came over and put his arms around her waist. "Can you believe that it's been a whole year since we got married?"

"Yes, and no." Annie kept applying her make-up while Matt watched, his chin perched on her shoulder. "In some ways I feel like we've always been together; in a good way. In other ways it feels like I just fell in love with you yesterday."

"Well," he said as he tightened his embrace, "that makes sense, because I fall in love with you all over again every single day." He pulled her bra strap off her shoulder and kissed the place it had been.

"Hey, mister," she said as she rotated to face him, "we'll never make our dinner reservation if you keep behaving like that." She tilted her head up to meet his and gave him a long, passionate kiss. "On second thought, who needs to go out?"

"What? I thought you wanted to go."

"I did, but I have a better idea. You go out in the other room. I have a surprise for you." Annie kissed him quickly and gave him a gentle push out the door. "I'll let you know when it's time to come back."

Matt did as he was told, a goofy grin plastered on his face alongside the confusion. Annie gently shut the door behind him and then quickly pulled the storage box out from under the bed, digging down to find the lingerie. Her heart pounding, she pulled it out and slipped out of her bra and panties to put on the unusually provocative attire. No amount of pulling, squeezing or contorting would make it slide over her hips or contain her stomach or bosom. She was working up a sweat as she tried to force her body into it, swearing a blue streak as she struggled. There was a hesitant knock on the door.

"Need any help?" Matt said in a jovial voice.

"No!" Annie snapped, her impatience overpowered any remaining sweetness. The moment she said it, she regretted it. "I'm sorry, I didn't mean to sound like that." She tried to keep the tears at bay, to keep them from spilling over into her voice.

"Honey, can I come in?"

"Okay, fine," She sounded defeated and utterly forlorn.

Matt slowly opened the door. There on the bed sat Annie, facing away from him. A black lace robe was draped over the round curve of her hunched over back, her head bent forward. He inched toward her and sat on the bed just behind her.

"This is amazing," he said as he placed a gentle hand on her back. As soon as he touched her, she stiffened.

"No it's not," she said, the tears still trying to break through.

"But you look wonderful."

"No I don't. It doesn't fit like it's supposed to!" She pulled the robe closer around her, holding it together in the front. "I bought this the day of the pregnancy test and now it's too small."

Matt rubbed her back, waiting for her to continue.

"I'm too fat!" The sobs that she'd been trying to suppress exploded from deep inside. "I'm huge!"

"Well, honey, you're pregnant," Matt said in his most understanding voice.

"I'm not *that* pregnant," she wailed. "And I shouldn't feel bad about being bigger, but I do. I'm a terrible mother!" Her emotions were spiraling out of control, a whirlpool of epic proportions. Matt had to brace himself to avoid being sucked down into the vortex with her.

"Calm down," he said. "You are not a terrible anything, sweetie. Let me see"

Sniffling, she turned toward him little bit. He craned his neck around and peeked over her shoulder. The teddy was supposed to fasten down the front, but all of the hooks wouldn't meet. Her body was straining against the delicate black lace, her blossoming breasts all but poured from the bodice, spilling over the lacy edges. She had managed to close one of the fasteners across her stomach, but the fabric was stretched to its limit, making her flesh bulge out above and below the clasp. As she sat there crying, the tears plopped onto her chest, and disappeared into her cleavage.

"Wow." Matt's eyes widened as he took in the sensual display. "You are --"

"Worse than you thought, right? If I'm this big now, what will I be in a few months? Look at me, just look at me!"

"Believe me, I am! You are beautiful, absolutely beautiful!"

"I am?" Annie finally looked up at him from her embarrassed crouch.

"Yes, you are. My only concern is that if you keep it up, you'll be so sexy and beautiful I won't be able to keep my hands off you. I have enough trouble with that as it is!" He caressed her shoulders under the lace. "You are one hot mama!"

"You're so sweet," she said, leaning into him.

"Tell you what. Even though you're turning me on big time, I think we better go out for dinner after all." Matt squeezed her shoulders affectionately.

"Why?" Annie asked, confused.

"Well, shouldn't we be careful? With the baby and all?" He patted her stomach.

"I think we need to relax. The doctor said to keep doing my regular activities. And this," she said between kisses, "is one of them. So I think we should stay right here."

"I don't know if I can wait much longer," Annie tapped her foot impatiently as she turned the pages of the waiting room magazine. She put the magazine in her lap and pushed up the sleeve of her sweater to look at her watch.

"They said it would only be a few more minutes," Matt reminded her. "Patience is a virtue." He gave her a playful wink.

"That's easy to say when you don't have a quart of water ready to burst out of your bladder," moaned Annie as her foot-tapping escalated. "I just really have to pee."

"I know, honey. I'll go and ask the receptionist how much longer it will be."

Matt walked over to the reception desk and spoke quietly to the young woman sitting there. He gestured toward Annie and then nodded, shrugged and then made his way back to his seat next to her. He leaned over and whispered in her ear.

"It should be any second now. She said the doctor had an emergency."

"We know what that's like, don't we?" said Annie, feeling like a heel for complaining at all. "I'm sorry. I'll try to be more patient."

He was just about to kiss her cheek, when they heard a nurse call her name. Annie rose and gingerly followed the nurse back to the ultrasound room with Matt trailing behind.

"This is an exciting day, isn't it?" said the nurse as she opened a drawer in the exam table and retrieved a folded paper sheet. "Everything off from the waist down," she said as she handed it to Annie. "I'll be back in a couple of minutes. You can just have a seat on the table. You can sit right here," she instructed Matt as she pointed to a stool on wheels that was next to the exam table.

The two of them locked eyes. The last time they were in an ultrasound room, they had watched as their baby's tiny heart stopped beating. Annie also couldn't help remembering her other ultrasound experience, when she found out that Dillon had died. Matt knew what she was thinking without her saying a word, and he walked to her side.

"I love you, Annie." He wrapped her in an understanding hug.

"I love you too."

"We can do this," he whispered into her hair.

"I know. We'll be fine."

Annie felt anything but fine. Ultrasound rooms held only heartbreaking memories for her. She was terrified of having another bad experience, but was determined to be strong and positive, not only for Matt and herself, but for this new precious little one inside of her.

The coolness of the ultrasound gel made her shiver as the tech squirted a blob of it on her belly. As the transducer rolled over her abdomen, she looked at the ceiling, her ears straining to hear the baby's heartbeat. The technician was stopping every so often to type information into the computer after she made various measurements. Matt's eyes were glued to the screen, his mouth hung open in wonder.

"How's everything going in here?" a familiar voice boomed through the doorway.

"Good, I guess," said Annie. "I mean, I hope."

Dr. Hayes smiled and placed a reassuring hand on her shoulder. "We're all hoping, Annie. All we can do is take this one day at a time. I know that you won't believe that everything will be fine until you're holding that new baby in your arms, and I respect that." He looked over at Matt and extended his hand. "You must be the new man in Annie's life."

"I'm sorry, Dr. Hayes. This is my husband, Matt." Annie was embarrassed to have forgotten her manners.

"Pleased to meet you, Matt." The two men exchanged a hearty handshake over her head.

"Thank you. And I'm pleased to meet you. I've heard a lot about you." Matt returned his hand to Annie's, entwining his fingers with hers, next to her side on the exam table.

Dr. Hayes smiled and then focused his attention on the black and white display on the monitor. His mouth remained in a pleasant line, but his eyes became all business as he studied the hazy images that appeared and disappeared with the wave of the technician's magic wand.

"How does everything look, Dr.Hayes?" asked Annie. She grasped Matt's hand like a lifeline.

"Well, let's see. Everything looks good. Here's the head, the spinal column, oh, and right here is the heart.

What a glorious sight! It's beating like a bass drum!" He glanced over at Matt and Annie with a huge grin on his face. "Let's see what else there is." He returned his gaze to the screen. "Hmmm. Emily, can you go back a little bit?"

The technician moved the transducer over the slippery surface of Annie's skin to where she had been moments before. Dr. Hayes motioned to her to enlarge the image, freeze it and then return it to its original state.

Annie had been watching him more than the screen, following every move and nuance. She suspected that he'd break bad news to them gently, possibly waiting to share it when she was dressed and presentable.

"What is it?" she asked abruptly. "What do you see?"

"Well, Annie, Matt. Look very closely right here. What do you see?" He pointed to the tiny pulsating black dot on the screen.

"That's the heart, right?" said Matt.

"That's right," Dr. Hayes replied. "And what do you see here?" He pointed to the screen again.

Annie and Matt squinted at the screen, the only bright spot in the darkened room. There, not far from the beating heart, was another small, black dot, it's rhythm matching the one next to it, beat for beat. They looked at each other and then at the doctor, who was grinning from ear to ear.

"Is that what I think it is?" Matt's voice was a hoarse whisper. His fingers dug into the palm of her hand as he spoke.

"Well, if what you think it is, is another heartbeat! Annie, Matt -- congratulations! You're having twins!" He clapped an enthusiastic hand on Matt's shoulder.

Annie stared at the monitor, at the two tiny dark spots, beating in sync. Twins? *Two* babies were growing inside of her? She scrutinized the image, trying to see the outline of each head, each spinal column and everything else, praying that this wasn't a figment of their imagination. The technician must have read her mind, because she quietly went to the screen and began tracing with her finger, describing each thing as she went until it was clear that there were indeed two babies. They were curved around each other like two pieces of a puzzle, fitting together like two halves of a whole.

"Oh my God," Annie finally said, holding tightly onto Matt's hand. "I can't believe it." A tear dropped from

Matt's cheek onto her forehead and she looked up at him and smiled, her own eyes filling up. "This is a miracle."

"A miracle that is long overdue," added Dr. Hayes. "Long overdue."

Even though Annie knew that Dillon and Munchkin could never be replaced, she couldn't help but wonder, as she watched the small beating images on the screen, if God was giving them two babies at once for a reason. She might never know what that reason was, but as she squeezed Matt's hand, she knew that there was more than enough love in her life for whatever it turned out to be.

# The Cradle

The arm on the scale bounced up and down several times before it balanced in the middle. Annie stood with her eyes squeezed shut, listening to the clank of metal against metal, reluctant to look at the final number.

"Do you want to know?" Sheila, Dr. Hayes' nurse was standing next to her, Annie's chart in her hand, ready to record the number.

"Not if I don't have to," Annie said, her eyes still closed. "Just tell me if I'm doing okay."

"You are doing more than okay, kiddo. You're doing great!" She slid the weights on the scale back to zeros. "Is this going to go on until you have these babies?"

"Probably," admitted Annie, stepping down off the scale. "What woman really wants to know exactly how much she weighs while carrying twins?"

"You've got a point there," said Sheila. "Most moms cringe when they see how high the scale goes. But it's healthy and normal, Annie. It's a good thing."

"I know it is," Annie said, slipping her flip-flops back on her swollen feet. "Just humor me, ok?"

"Can do. Is Matt coming today?" Sheila led Annie to the exam room as she spoke. Annie followed, waddling slowly down the hallway.

"Yes, he should be here any minute. He had to park the car."

"What a sweetheart he is to drop you off at the door," Sheila took the blood pressure cuff off it's holder on the wall. "Arm on the desk for me, please?"

The nurse deftly wrapped the blood pressure cuff around Annie's upper arm and was just starting to pump the bulb to inflate the apparatus, when there was a gentle knock on the door. "Who's there?" Sheila's eyes remained glued to the blood pressure gauge on the wall as she spoke.

The door opened slightly and Matt poked his head inside. "It's just me." His impish smile momentarily made Annie's heart beat faster. It never ceased to amaze her how excited she always was to see him, even if they had only been apart for a few minutes.

"Now, now, you two," Sheila reprimanded them. "Be careful or we'll have to start over with this blood pressure reading." She shook her head and smiled as she listened carefully to the beat of Annie's heart through the instrument's ear tips.

"Sorry," whispered Matt as he sat down next to Annie.

"No problem." Sheila smiled as she pulled free the Velcro strip and removed the cuff from Annie's arm. "Your blood pressure's good -- except for that pitter-patter moment when Mr. Wonderful came in." She winked at them and added," I can't tell you how great it is to see this woman so happy and loved." She patted Annie's belly. "Dr. Hayes should be in in a few minutes." Closing Annie's chart, she brought it with her to the door. Before leaving, she turned to them, "I am just so darned happy for you two!" And with that, she slipped out into the hallway, shutting the door behind her with a quiet click.

"So I missed the weigh-in, huh?" Matt reached for her hand.

"Yes, and that's how it should be. A girl has to have some secrets."

"But it's a secret to you too. Did you close your eyes again?"

Annie nodded defensively. "Humor me, ok, sweetie? Please?"

Just then they heard the tell-tale whistling that always preceded her doctor's entrance into a room. The door opened and Dr. Hayes entered the room. "Hello, you two!"

"Hi, Dr. Hayes," said Annie and Matt in unison, their discussion about her weight abandoned for the time being. Matt stood to shake the physician's hand.

"How's everything going?" asked the doctor as he lowered himself onto the small desk chair. "Everything's looking good; blood pressure's good, weight's getting up there, but that's what we want. You'll nurse it off anyway. Those babies are growing nicely. We're at thirty-four weeks, almost to the end of the rainbow. As I told you, thirty-seven weeks is considered full term for twins. We won't let you go past that."

"I'm just so relieved to be past the thirty-third week," said Annie, squeezing Matt's hand.

"I know, Annie. I've thought about Dillon a lot too. That was an awful thing to go through, but that doesn't mean it will happen again. I want you to try not to worry too much." He saw the incredulous look on her face. "But that's sort of like asking you not to breathe, isn't it?"

She grimaced and nodded. " It's hard not to dwell on it."

"Well, you're going to get preferential treatment, Annie. We'll do whatever it takes to make this a good experience for you. Now how about you hop up on the table and we check things out?"

Matt stood near her head as Dr. Hayes poked, prodded and measured Annie's progress. The babies' heartbeats were very loud and strong, which was music to everyone's ears. This was so unlike the appointment near the end of her pregnancy with Dillon, when the room was overcome with the chilling silence as they waited to hear Dillon's heartbeat. Annie's heart swelled with joy at the sound. Next, Dr. Hayes palpated her belly, feeling the positions of the babies.

"It feels as though Baby A is head down and Baby B is in a breech position," he said, as he deftly pushed on what was Baby B's bottom.

"What does that mean?" asked Matt, concerned.

"For a vaginal delivery we prefer to have them both head down. It's safer for the baby and the mom. Sometimes they turn at the last minute, though, so let's not worry about it now. With twins, we're always prepared for anything, so if a C-section is required, that's what we'll do. Okay?"

"Of course, that's okay," Annie didn't miss a beat. "We don't care how these babies are delivered; we just want them safe." As soon as the words were out of her mouth, she looked at Matt, hoping he felt the same way. He sat there, nodding his agreement.

"Alrighty then. Keep growing these two peas in a pod and we'll see you next week." Dr. Hayes shook hands with each of them and left the room, whistling "Brahms' Lullaby".

Annie sat on the exam table, her bare feet dangling. She looked around the room slowly, examining every square inch with guarded eyes.

"Annie?" Matt said when he realized she wasn't hopping down as she had done after every other appointment. "You okay?"

"It's just that this is the room I was in for my last appointment with Dillon." Her eyes were getting watery as she spoke.

Matt reached out and took her hand.

"I noticed it the minute they brought me in here. At first I was afraid it would be a jinx, and that we wouldn't hear the babies' heartbeats today either." She stopped and swallowed hard. Her mouth was so dry and sticky that the words were lodged at the back of her throat like frightened swimmers, frozen at the edge of a diving board. "But we did hear them. Maybe that's a sign that everything will be okay."

Matt took her face in his hands and looked into her eyes. "I know how scared you are, Annie, and you are entitled to every bit of your fear. I admire you so much for going through all of this again to have our babies. You are so brave." He kissed her forehead so tenderly it felt as though a butterfly had brushed past her, barely touching her skin. "I am forever grateful to you."

Annie put her hand on Matt's cheek and smiled at him. "And you are brave to go through this with me. I know it hasn't been easy."

"I wouldn't have wanted to miss a minute of it." He encircled her in his arms and held her close.

The door opened suddenly and Sheila popped her head inside. "Excuse me, you two lovebirds, but I need this room for another patient." She tried to act perturbed but couldn't suppress a good-natured smirk.

"Oh - sorry, Sheila!" Annie said as she turned several shades of red. "We'll be out in a minute." Matt held her hand as she slowly climbed down from the exam table.

"We'll see you next week!" Sheila chirped as she closed the door.

"Are you sure you don't want me to drop you off at the door?" Matt said as they turned into the mall's parking lot. "It looks like it could be a long walk and it's awfully hot out there."

"No, I'll be fine. Besides, I want to walk. It will be good for me." Annie's tone was insistent.

"Okay." Matt knew it was pointless to argue once his wife made up her mind.

He circled around the crowded lot twice to find an open parking space let alone one close to the entrance. It seemed as though everyone was trying to escape the heat by fleeing to the air-conditioned paradise of the mall. Cool air blasted through the vents in the car as Annie fanned herself with a paper Japanese fan that someone from the orchestra had given her. She held the hair off her neck and waved the fan back and forth in an attempt to stop the steady stream of sweat that was rolling down her neck.

"I can't believe how hot it is today," she said, trying hard not to whine. "At least the mall will be cool."

"I still say we should get central air put in," said Matt as he pulled into a parking spot. "It would be worth every penny." The car sputtered as he turned off the ignition.

"You're probably right, but it's just not in the budget." Annie folded up her fan and dropped it into her purse. "We spent our air-conditioner money last summer on our Grand Canyon trip, remember?"

"And that was worth every penny," he said, as a big grin exploded on his face. "When you put it that way, using the window fans doesn't sound so bad."

Matt scurried around to Annie's side of the car and opened the door for her. She climbed out of the vehicle as gracefully as possible for a woman over eight months into a pregnancy with twins.

"I feel like a beluga whale," Annie moaned as they walked hand in hand toward the store entrance. "I know it comes with the territory and that it's a good thing, but I still feel huge."

"Well, I think you're beautiful. It will all be worth it when you're holding little Baby A and Baby B in your arms. You'll forget all about how huge you feel now." He squeezed her hand.

"I can't wait until they're here and we can call them by real names instead of letters," Annie said as they approached the store entrance.

The baby furniture store was a wonderland of every nursery product imaginable. Cradles, bassinets, cribs, and rocking chairs were arranged in various combinations and decorated with adorable quilts, bumper pads and blankets. Annie couldn't help but think about the crib and bedding that she and Eric had picked out for Dillon. It was an oak Jenny Lind style crib, that had a teddy bear quilt and bumper pad in bright, primary colors. There had also been a matching changing table and dresser, as well as an old-fashioned rocking chair, which they had placed on order. It still made Annie feel sick to her stomach when she remembered the day she went to the store to cancel the order and to ask for their down payment to be refunded. At first the young salesman had been adamant that special order deposits could not be refunded under any circumstances. She hadn't wanted to ask for special treatment, but certainly they'd make an exception if your baby died, wouldn't they?

"I'm sorry, sir," she had started, her voice finding its way up through the muddy marsh of grief. "I know you have your policies, but my baby was stillborn last week. We could really use the money to pay for his funeral." A tear ran down her cheek and she swiped it with the back of her hand, hoping he hadn't seen.

The stubborn salesman's expression shifted a bit and the abrasive corners of his pursed lips wavered slightly as he tried to avoid making any eye contact with her. Behind his aviator-style glasses his eyes quickly swept the sales floor and then, while looking down at the cash register, he said, "I am sorry for your loss, miss. Since we have no policy for this situation, I guess we can refund your deposit." He punched some keys on the register which made the cash drawer shoot open, pulled out some bills and handed them to her. "Please accept our condolences. That should never happen to anyone."

For a brief moment he looked directly at her. She saw not a pompous, self-absorbed salesman, but a truly shaken young man who had probably never known that babies could die before they ever got to sleep in the cribs that he sold every day. Suddenly she felt guilty for having given him a glimpse of how unfair life could be. A nearly inaudible "thank you" tumbled from her lips as she tucked the money in her purse and fled from the store.

"Hey sweetie, what do you think of this one?" Matt's voice floated into her consciousness and rescued her from her memories.

He was pointing at a simple white crib. It was made up with a royal blue quilt with white polka dots and matching bumper pad and dust ruffle. Next to it was the same crib, but it had pink and white polka-dotted bedding instead of blue.

"Look, Annie!" Matt continued, "These convert to toddler beds, too! How cool is that?" He looked over at her, his face lit up like a child's on Christmas morning.

The relief she felt when she saw the white cribs and how different they were than the one she'd chosen for Dillon made her squeal with excitement. "I love them!"

"White's okay for boys, isn't it?" asked Matt as he examined the cribs in more detail. "Not that we're having boys," he added quickly. "I'm just as excited at the idea of girls, you know."

"We don't know what we're having, but I'm okay with white. I think it's perfect. Remember, we're talking babies here, not teenagers."

After talking with a grandmotherly-type salesperson, they decided to buy the white cribs, but not to purchase any bedding. Annie couldn't resist looking at the different colors and patterns as Matt went to drive the car up to entrance so that the cribs could be loaded into it. She hadn't allowed herself to plan the nursery too much, afraid to have too many dreams for these little lives inside of her. As she ran her fingers over the satin binding on a pastel blue blanket, she couldn't help but compare it to the silky smoothness of Dillon's tiny cheek and she said a silent prayer that these babies would be squirming and squalling when she was finally able to touch their faces.

It was difficult to share her fears with Matt or Sally, and so she had turned to Lora, her friend from the support group. Having buried a baby of her own, Lora knew too well the all-consuming feelings of dread that accompanied a subsequent pregnancy.

"I'm just terrified that these babies will die too," Annie said to Lora after they'd given their lunch orders to the waiter. "Did you ever feel that way?"

Lora took a sip of her ice water and gazed thoughtfully at Annie, who was busy spreading her napkin over her enormous belly. She recognized the tension and worry that had etched themselves into Annie's face, in the creases in her forehead and the apprehensive parentheses around her eyes.

"Constantly. I worried all the time, which I knew was crazy, but I did it anyway," said Lora quietly.

"Especially after having the miscarriage, I have this feeling that maybe God doesn't want me to be a mother."

"I understand what you mean," Lora said as she traced the beads of condensation rolling down her glass with her finger. "But you know what? Even if that were true, which I don't believe it is, it's too late. You're already a mother. Twice. No wait, four times. You are a wonderful mother, Annie. Nature took Dillon and Munchkin; not God."

"You really think so?" Annie's voice was thick with unspoken doubt. "I just have this feeling that if I relax too much and let myself feel happy, I'll jinx everything; that if I let my guard down, everything will go wrong."

"And it will be all your fault?"

Annie nodded in disbelief, relieved that her friend understood.

"I hate to burst your bubble, but you're not that powerful and those little darlings in your belly will remind you of that a thousand times over before they even start preschool," said Lora, chuckling. "As a parent you do have some influence over them, but not absolute power. The sooner you accept that, the more you'll enjoy the ride. You can't take all the blame or all of the credit. It's kind of liberating, when you think about it."

Annie considered what her friend said as she took a swallow of lemonade and had to admit that it made sense. If only it were that easy. Lora was more easy-going by nature and so letting go of worry was more straightforward for her. Annie had to work at it.

"You know what I finally had to do toward the end of my pregnancy with Amanda?" Lora sensed her friend's skepticism. "This might sound crazy, but to cope, I had to face my fears and imagine the worst case scenario, which was, of course, that she'd die. From there, I planned every last detail of her funeral in my head."

Annie had just dug her fork into her chef salad and upon hearing what Lora just said, stopped cold. "Then I'm not crazy. I've been doing that too."

It was a relief to know that she wasn't the only person to have spent time during a pregnancy thinking of such morbid things. Annie hadn't planned to tell anyone, not even Lora, because she thought it was so bizarre. Shortly after she'd found out they were having twins, she had been in the baby department of a store downtown, allowing herself to indulge in a little fantasy about bringing the babies home from the hospital. The newborn layettes and sleepers were so precious and tiny; her heart danced with excitement at the thought of being able to choose two of everything. That was when doubt took hold of her happiness and placing its gnarled fingers around her heart, squeezed out every last bit of hope until nothing was left but a raw, forbidding fear of what might happen. A cold, clammy sheen covered her face and she wanted to be anywhere but in a store surrounded by baby clothes. She held onto a soft blue and white striped sleeper as though it possessed the strength she needed to get through the moment and closed her eyes. That was when the idea was born; if she could face the thought of her babies dying, then she could face anything. She would not let her doubts and fears make her cower and hide, but would confront them and even embrace them, thereby stripping them of their power over her. She bought two tiny layette gowns, one in a soft yellow and one in pale green, both with little matching hats. Should the babies die, she would bury them in these. At the last minute, she bought two small terry cloth teddy bears, one in yellow and one in green, that she'd place in the casket with them. She'd also place them in a casket together, because it would be wrong to separate them. Since she hadn't had any involvement in planning Dillon's funeral, knowing what she'd want if the unthinkable were to happen again gave her a strange sort of comfort. This time, God forbid, she'd be prepared.

"The first time I thought of it," she said to Lora, "I was a little shocked at how easily all the details came to me. Then I felt guilty because it seemed sick and wrong. I mean, who does that?"

"Someone who has been through what we have and is trying to keep their sanity," Lora said in a matter-of-fact tone. "No one can judge us unless they've walked in our shoes. You do whatever gets you through the day." She took a hefty bite out of her corned beef sandwich.

"Did you tell your husband?"

"Are you kidding me?" said Lora as she chewed her food.

"I haven't told Matt either. He's worried about me enough as it is."

"Smart move," Lora said, reaching for her iced tea. "Some things are best left unsaid. I'm glad you told me about it, though. I always wanted to share it with someone, but even the support group didn't seem like the right place. It is a bit over the top."

"Well, as you said, whatever gets you though the day," said Annie as she raised her glass of lemonade in a toast.

Even though Sally had wanted to throw her a big baby shower, she had wanted to postpone it until after the babies were born. That way, she had explained, people would know if they were buying for boys or girls or one of each. Sally thought it made sense and didn't badger her about it anymore after that. In lieu of a baby shower, Sally and Lora were going to take her out for lunch and shopping the following weekend, to pick out some essentials, bedding being one of the items on the list.

The cribs were now assembled in the nursery, almost ready but definitely waiting for the babies. Annie and Matt had purchased mattress pads and some plain white fitted crib sheets, because the bare mattresses seemed too harsh and plain. Annie was nearly at thirty-five weeks and while still anxious and worried, was looking forward to completing the nursery and bringing her little ones home. She was beginning to allow herself to hope; hope with a happy ending.

# The Pea Pod

A wide beam of sunshine danced in on a fleet of dust motes, bathing Annie in a swath of soft light as she sat by the living room window. Pulling back the curtain, she looked up and down the street and then at her watch. Muttering to herself about people being late and soon being able to write in the dust on the furniture, she heaved herself out of her chair and shuffled to the closet to get the dusting cloth and furniture polish.

"You just cleaned yesterday, didn't you?" Matt was standing in the doorway to the kitchen, a mug of steaming coffee in one hand, the morning newspaper in the other.

"Yes, but look at all of this dust," Annie said as she ran a furious cloth over the sparse layer of dust on the coffee table. "Besides, I might as well make use of my time." She sprayed a generous coating of Lemon Pledge on the other half of the table and proceeded to wipe it off in a circular motion.

Matt blew on his coffee and said, "What time was Sally supposed to be here?"

"Fifteen minutes ago." Annie glanced at her watch again. "Why must she always be late?"

"That's Sally; she's never going to change." Matt got a coaster out of the end table drawer and set his mug on it. "Will I be polished if I read the paper in here?" He gave her a quick smile.

"Very funny," she said, aiming the yellow aerosol can at him, and then, "I wonder if I have time to vacuum?" She glanced at her watch again.

"Excuse me for saying so, but you seem a bit wired today. What's up?" Matt said in a nonchalant way as he settled into the overstuffed navy blue leather chair.

Annie frowned as she applied some elbow grease to a stubborn smudge on the bookshelf. "I don't know, I just feel antsy. In a way I wish I wasn't going shopping today. There's so much to do around here before the babies come."

"There's always going to be a lot to do, so you should go and have some fun. Besides, don't you need to get some baby things?"

"I suppose you're right," she said as she put the finishing touches on the mahogany shelf. "Everything Sally and Lora are getting us today will be important to have."

"There you go. Just relax and enjoy." He flashed a goofy grin at her as he turned the paper inside out to read the editorial section.

Just then there was the shrill sound of a horn honking outside. Annie turned and peered out the window. Sally's black Volvo was sitting at the curb, windows rolled down and music blaring. Annie laughed at the sight of her aunt sitting behind the wheel in her oversized sunglasses, bouncing up and down to the tunes on the radio.

"Well, I guess my chariot awaits!" Annie folded the dusting cloth into a neat square and headed toward the closet to put it away.

"I'll take care of that for you," Matt jumped up from his chair. "Who knows? Maybe I'll do more dusting while you're gone."

"You are definitely my knight in shining armor -- with a dust cloth!" She reached up and put her arms around his neck. "I love you!"

"Right back at you, sweetie," he said as he hugged her back. "Have fun today,. Take as long as you want. Now shoo!" He playfully swatted her behind as she lumbered through the front door.

Annie pulled the car door open with an already sweaty hand and leaned over to look at her aunt. Sally's curly hair was pulled back with a bright pink banana clip and large pink earrings that looked like discs adorned her earlobes. She wore a neon pink dress and matching pink canvas tennis shoes.

"Hey there, little mama!" Sally all but shrieked her welcome. "Quick, get in here and out of that heat!" She moved her purse from the passenger seat to the floor behind it. "Don't you look adorable!"

"I feel anything but," said Annie as she eased herself into the car. "Not that I'm complaining."

"Well, when it's this hot and you're that pregnant, you have every right to whine a little." Sally placed her outstretched hand on Annie's belly and patted it gently. "This never ceases to thrill me!"

Annie sat back in the seat and smiled at Sally. She placed her own hands next to her aunt's and was suddenly struck by the similarities between them; they could be her mother's hands. Even though Sally's hands bore more creases and wrinkles, the basic shape was similar to her own. Suddenly she saw her mother's hands next to her child-sized ones as they had rolled out cookie dough together, the larger hands on either side of hers like loving parentheses, fingers curled around the rolling pin handles. Visions of her mother's hands lying motionless on the hospital sheets as she lay dying crept into her mind and the motion picture of that night began to play in her head, no words, just the flickering light of uncertainty and loss, as the reel spun the sad story again. Emotion constricted her voice for a moment and just when she was going to say something, one of the babies gave Sally's hands a firm kick, which made Sally hoot with pleasure.

"Oh my God! Did you feel that?" Sally's eyes had grown huge with excitement.

Annie nodded, knowing that if she spoke, she'd start crying and wouldn't be able to stop.

"That is so incredible! It's just amazing!" Sally craned her neck and leaned down to kiss the place where the baby had just moved. "Your mom would have loved this so."

"I was just thinking about her," said Annie. "Your hands remind me of hers; they look just like mine."

Sally laid her hand next to Annie's and took a deep breath. "You're absolutely right! Would you look at that." She looked up at Annie with tears in her eyes, her lip trembling like the quiver on a bow. They sat there in silence for a moment, the only sound was breathing punctuated with sniffles.

"Okay," said Annie, summoning all of her strength. "Let's get this show on the road before we turn the car into Minnehaha Falls!"

The two women glanced at each other and burst into subdued laughter. "Yes, your mom would want us to shop our little butts off for these grandbabies of hers." Sally dug in her purse for a Kleenex and offered one to Annie once she found the travel-size pack wrapped in cellophane.

"Speak for yourself, Auntie," Annie said as she dabbed the tears from her eyes, "My butt isn't so little these days."

"Well, it had to get bigger to balance out the front of you. If it didn't, you'd fall flat on your face every time you stand up!" Sally giggled at her own remark as she turned the key in the ignition.

Lora had arrived at the mall before them, pacing back and forth in front of the entrance. She ran up to Annie and Sally when she saw the black Volvo pull up to the curb. The passenger door swung open and first one swollen foot and then another, appeared from inside, dropping down to the pavement. On each foot was an inexpensive white flip flop and all ten toenails were painted with bright pink polish.

"Don't tell me," said Lora, looking at Sally's assorted pink wardrobe items, "Sally had something to do with these pretty pink toes. Lord knows *you* can't reach them anymore!"

Annie blushed. "Actually Matt did that last night."

"He is such a keeper!" Lora shook her head, smiling.

"Yep, I know!" Annie grinned, remembering how careful he had been as he painted each toenail. He had even used a Q-tip dipped in nail polish remover to clean up the edges.

"Well, you look darling. I love your dress!" Lora helped her up from the low seat of the car. "Is it new?"

"Sally made it for me," said Annie, fluffing the skirt as she spoke. "It's really cool and comfortable."

"It reminds me of the tent dresses your mom and I wore back in the 60's," Sally said from the driver's seat. "It's hard to believe we all wore those and we weren't even pregnant! You two wait for me inside; I'm going to park the car."

Soon they were in the baby department at Dayton's, oohing and aahing over all the cute little sleepers and outfits, blankets and stuffed animals. Sally held a list in one hand, and a pen in the other.

"Have you decided on a color for the nursery yet?" Lora asked as she dug through a pile of quilts.

"Well, since we don't know if they're boys or girls or one of each, we thought we'd stay away from pink or blue. The cribs are white and that's about all we have so far."

"Oooh!' Sally's squeal reverberated off the walls. "This is adorable!"

Annie and Lora hurried over to where Sally was standing. She was holding up a bright green quilt. The design on the coordinating sheets and bumper pads was made up of pea pods splayed out in every direction, as though someone had dumped a bushel basket of the tender green vegetables onto the soft white fabric. A ruffle of the same fabric was sewn around the edge of the quilt.

"It would look great with the white cribs," said Lora as she inspected the items.

Annie stood, gazing at the quilt, trying to picture the babies snuggled into the emerald softness. "Two peas in a pod," she said in a whisper, more to herself than anyone. She cradled her belly, resting her hands on her babies, and felt them shift and turn beneath her fingers. Smiling, she decided to take it as a signal of their approval.

"I love it," she finally said in a voice loud enough for Sally and Lora to hear. "It's kind of funny, because my doctor called them that at my last appointment. Two peas in a pod."

"Will Matt like his babies being compared to vegetables?" Sally said as she examined the design on the sheets, her brow furrowed in a skeptical line.

"It's a sweet idea and he's a sweet guy, so I should think he'd be fine with it," said Annie, picturing Matt's reaction. He had been affectionately referring to the twins as "Thing One" and "Thing Two", so she doubted that it would be an issue.

"Well, the two of you are certainly like two peas in a pod, so why not carry it over to your kids?" Sally conceded.

Lora called to them from the next aisle over, elbow deep in sleepers. "Look what I found over here!"

"That woman is a shopping machine," Sally whispered to Annie as they made their way over to her.

Annie shifted uncomfortably from one foot to the other as her shopping companions sorted through racks of sleepers and rompers, choosing two of everything, one in white and one in green. Twinges of pain were beginning to reach like tentacles under her lower abdomen, settling there and squeezing until they got her attention. She frowned and rubbed her belly, thinking it would go away in a minute. Thc pain did go away and so she decided it was a Braxton-Hicks contraction and nothing to be alarmed about. Several minutes later it was back, this time reaching farther and squeezing harder, making her gasp out loud. She was relieved to see that Sally and Lora hadn't heard her, and she quietly observed the second hand on her watch make its way around the numbers as she tried to take deep, relaxed breaths. Once the hand went around once, she watched and waited, a feeling of panic rising in her chest. Stay calm, she told herself. Stay calm. She looked up to see where Sally and Lora were but she couldn't see them anywhere. Suddenly Lora's head popped up from behind a display of stuffed panda bears, and Annie waved to her to get her attention.

"I'm going to sit down for a minute," Annie said. "I'll be right over there." She pointed to a low vinyl bench that was near the escalators. Lora smiled and gave her a thumbs up.

The bench was only about thirty feet away, but it felt like thirty miles to Annie as she shuffled over to it, the pain in her abdomen starting again. She glanced at her watch; it had been about five minutes since the last one. Dr. Hayes had assured her that she would "just know" when she was in labor and that if it occurred to her to time any pains she was having, they were probably contractions. Telling herself to stay calm, she tried to appear normal, like any other pregnant woman at the shopping mall, and plastered a big smile on her face. Maybe no one would notice that she felt like hyperventilating every time she thought about being in labor, if she pretended that everything was fine. Once she reached the bench, she turned around to lower herself onto it and felt something trickle down the inside of her thigh. I'm just sweating, she assured herself. It's no big deal. Just then the tentacles gripped her again and much to her dismay, she let out an audible groan. A woman walking by stopped at the sight of her.

"Excuse me, but do you need some help?" She looked to be in her early forties and had a sullen teenage girl trailing behind her. The girl had circles of dark eyeliner around each eye and what seemed to be a permanent scowl on her lovely young face.

"I - I think I might be in labor." Her voice came out in a thin squeak. "My friends are right over there." She pointed to the baby department with a shaky finger.

"Ellie, go over and tell those women to come over here," the woman said to the girl. "Now here, let me help you sit down," she said to Annie.

The girl's mask of indifference momentarily lifted as she scurried over to where Sally stood and gesticulated excitedly toward her mother and Annie. Sally's eyes opened wide and she dropped the armful of baby things she had been holding on the counter next to the cash register and ran to Annie's side.

"Oh my God, Annie! You're in labor?!" Sally's voice was several octaves higher than usual as she put her arms around her niece. "Why didn't you say something?"

"I thought I was just having Braxton-Hicks, but then they got worse. They're about five minutes apart." She closed her eyes and winced. "I think we better call Matt."

"I'm on it!" Lora said and hurried over to the cash register to use the store's telephone. "I'll tell him to call the hospital!"

"Let's go. Matt will meet us there." Sally had recovered from her momentary hysteria and was calmer than Annie had ever seen her. "Everything will be just fine. No worries." She put out her hand to help Annie up from the bench.

The mother and daughter were still lingering there, unable to tear themselves away from the drama. The woman also assisted in helping Annie up, and once she was standing, the teenager gasped, clapping her hand over her gaping mouth. There on the back of Annie's dress was a huge wet spot. Her water had broken.

"Oh no," moaned Annie. "This is so embarrassing." She felt the back of her dress and looked over her shoulder to see how much of a mess she had made of the bench.

"There's nothing to be embarrassed about," Sally said, putting her arm around Annie's shoulders. "This is exciting!!! This means we're going to have some babies today!"

The woman and her daughter exchanged puzzled glances and then both spoke at once, "Babies?"

"Yes, my niece is having twins! Isn't that great? Thank you so much for all of your help, but we better get going!"

The two good Samaritans waved them away and amidst wishes of good luck, Sally and Lora escorted Annie out of the store was though she was made of delicate, very fragile glass. The heap of baby things were forgotten on the counter, as everyone in the store stood motionless, staring after the woman with the wet spot on the back of her dress.

Lora left her car at the shopping center and rode with Sally and Annie, just in case Annie needed anything on the way to the hospital. Having had a pregnancy loss herself, Lora knew how terrifying it was to embark on the journey of labor and delivery. She sat in the backseat with Annie, holding her hand and rubbing her back.

"Just breathe, sweetie. Nice and even. Like this, see?" Lora demonstrated several long, slow breaths.

Annie did her best to imitate her friend, fighting the overwhelming urge to tense up and scream. She closed her eyes and inhaled deeply through her nose and then exhaled slowly through her mouth. It really did help her stay focused and calm as Sally maneuvered the Volvo through the Monday afternoon rush hour traffic.

"Well, I guess I won't be needing my doctor appointment on Thursday, will I?" Annie said as the pain subsided, the adagio before another crescendo.

"Let's not worry about that now," Sally said as she changed lanes. "You just worry about staying calm."

"I'm sorry if I make a mess back here," Annie's voice tightened as the tension spread across her belly again.

"Again, no worries, missy. Just breathe!"

Sally swerved deftly into the hospital driveway, slowing to a stop under the canopy labeled "Emergency." A nurse and an orderly pushing a wheelchair met them at the door, helped Annie out of the car and wheeled her through the open emergency department doors. Matt was there, doing his best to stay out of their way, but desperately wanting to be near Annie. She caught a glimpse of him and called to him, reaching both arms out toward him.

"Oh, honey," he said, bending down to kiss her forehead.

She held onto him, breathing him in, finally feeling safe. He smelled like Ivory Soap, sweat, and Dentyne. Her armor of composure and strength crumbled the minute she felt his breath on her cheek and his hand on her shoulder.

"This is it. It's really happening." The edges of her voice were scalloped with fear, but there were also traces of peace and strength.

"I love you, Annie." Matt kissed her mouth this time and held her close.

"Hey, you two!" It was Dr. Hayes. "None of that! That's what got you into this!" he laughed and patted Annie's foot. "So, kiddo, I'll see you upstairs!"

While Matt got Annie registered, Sally and Lora helped her get settled in a birthing room. She was relieved to be placed in a room on the opposite side of the hall from where Dillon had been born. That was a place that would be forever etched in her mind and she wanted it to be for him alone. To begin this journey in that place would have been her undoing. As they wheeled her past the doorway, she could almost see the ghost of the person she used to be, along with Eric, both of them paralyzed with grief and fear, both of them so lost and alone.

Matt bounded into the room, a paper cup filled with ice chips in his hand.

"The book said you'd need these." He placed the cup on the bedside table, a white plastic spoon sticking out of it, next to a box of Kleenex. "I also brought the bag you packed." He held it up for her to see.

"Thanks, sweetie." Annie reached her hand out for him to hold. No sooner did he touch her, when her eyes grew wide and her entire body stiffened.

"Is it another contraction, Annie?" Sally was keeping watch from her spot near the window.

Annie nodded silently and began breathing in slow, deep breaths. Matt held onto her hand and started breathing right along with her. Sally kept her eyes glued to the clock on the wall, watching the second hand march around the numbers once, then twice. The thin, black hand was nearly halfway around again when Annie let out a loud "whoosh" and relaxed back onto the pillows.

"Wow!" said Lora, who had also been timing the contraction. "That was a long one! That's good! That means things are happening!"

Annie closed her eyes, her hand still in Matt's. "I kind of wish we'd gone to those childbirth classes now," she said, chagrined.

They had opted out of attending childbirth classes for a number of reasons. During her pregnancy with Dillon, she and Eric had just started going to the classes when she had to go on bed rest. If she and Matt were to go again with this pregnancy, she knew that at the first class, they would have everyone introduce themselves and say how many children they had. It would have been too painful to not mention Dillon or Munchkin, but on the other hand, she didn't want to share their experiences and cause excessive worry for the other prospective parents in the class. Instead, they read a multitude of books on the subject and just hoped that somehow they'd figure it out. So, here they were, in the throes of labor, in desperate need of some "on the job training."

"You'll be fine," Lora said in a reassuring voice. "I'll show you the breathing technique that worked like magic for me. You go 'Hee, hee, hee, hoo. Hee, hee, hee, hoo.' It worked like a charm when I had Lizzie."

"Let's try it," said Matt as he started to practice the patterned breathing. "We'll show that next contraction who's in charge around here."

Before Annie had a chance to practice, another tidal wave of pain rolled in, taking her breath away. Matt took her other hand in his, the one she had balled up in a fist, and calmly began breathing, "Hee, hee, hee, hoo." Annie kept her eyes scrunched shut and held her breath, her feet flexing stiffly. Matt didn't say a word; he just continued to breath. When the breathing sounded like a chorus, Annie slowly opened one of her eyes, and then the other. There, surrounding her bed, were Matt, Sally and Lora, all breathing in unison, "Hee, hee, hee, hoo. Hee, hee, hee, hoo." She smiled through the grinding pain at the motley crew assembled around her; Sally in her hot pink outfit, Lora's eyes shining as she earnestly breathed along, and Matt, dear sweet Matt, who looked as though he was feeling every twinge just as deeply as she was. She thanked God for these people who loved her enough to stand in a circle around her bed, all on the verge of hyperventilation.

The tension of the contraction eased, and again, she melted back into the pillows stacked beneath her head. Matt reached for the plastic spoon and balancing some ice chips on it, held it out to Annie. She opened her mouth, resembling a baby bird, and he slid the ice into it. A satisfied smile lit her face as she gazed up at him. Sally and Lora watched the exchange and traded knowing glances.

"You know what?" said Sally, as she stepped back from the bed. "You two have got this under control. Don't you agree, Lora?"

"Definitely. Under control." Lora nodded her head in enthusiastic agreement.

"So, we're going to run along and get Lora back to her car." Sally went over to the windowsill to get her purse.

"You don't have to go," said Annie, as she squeezed Matt's hand.

"No, you don't," he piped in quickly. "We'd love for you to stay."

"I'd love to," Sally assured them, "but this is your special moment; your family is being born. I want you to have it all to yourselves." She reached down and gave Annie a long, heartfelt hug.

"Yes," said Lora, "we'll come back later." She kissed Annie's forehead and then put a hand on Matt's arm. "You take good care of her, you hear?"

"I promise," he said, putting his hand over hers. "We'll call you as soon as there's news."

"You better!" The two women said in unison, laughing. "We love you!" They scurried out of the room, closing the door carefully behind them.

There was little time for reflection because another contraction came crashing in, forcing Annie and Matt to give it their undivided attention. Annie gripped Matt's hand again and they began to breathe together. They were just beginning the fifth round of the pattern, when the birthing room door swung open and Suzie, Annie's labor and delivery nurse, strode in. She reviewed Annie's chart and waited quietly until the contraction subsided.

"You two are quite a team!" she said as she studied the read-out on the fetal monitor. "From the looks of these contractions, a lot is changing in there. It's time to check and see how dilated you are. Do you want your hubby to step out?" She pulled a latex glove over her left hand and let it snap.

"No, not unless he wants to," said Annie. She dreaded this part and didn't want him to leave.

"I'm not going anywhere, if that's okay with everyone." Matt's voice was polite but firm.

"Not a problem. Okay, Annie, sorry about this, but here we go."

Matt stood by her head, smoothing her hair and kissing her forehead as the nurse poked and prodded. It seemed like an eternity until the nurse was finished and Annie let out a deep sigh.

"Well, good news! It won't be long now. Did you talk to Dr. Hayes about anesthesia?" She scribbled notes in Annie's chart as she spoke.

"I'd rather not have any if I don't have to," said Annie, "but I'll do whatever's best for the babies."

"Well, we'll talk more about it in the delivery room. Dr. Hayes delivers all twins in there, just in case we need to do a C-section. So, let's get you down there. I'll be back in a jiffy with a gurney." She swept out of the room in a flurry, a tornado in scrubs.

As it turned out, the babies were in too much of a hurry to wait for any delivery room discussions about anesthesia. Baby A, turned out to be a boy, and Baby B was a little girl. They made their entrance into the world fifteen minutes apart, weighing in at 5 lbs. 12 oz. and 5 lbs. 5 oz. respectively. They named the boy Maxwell David and the girl Mackenzie Ann; Kenzie for short,

Holding her newborn babies in her arms, Annie marveled at how wonderfully alive they felt. Warmth radiated from each of their tiny bodies as she cradled them in her arms and examined every inch of them. They had her eyes and nose but their mouths were all Matt, as well as their heads of dark curly hair. At the same moment, Max and then Kenzie opened their eyes and gazed at her with what could only be described as peaceful, thoughtful expressions. It was as though they knew who exactly who she was as they looked into her soul. She smiled down at them and whispered "I love you" to each of them and then kissed them each on the tops of their little heads. Tears of relief and joy filled her eyes and spilled down her face, getting lost in the curls on their precious little heads.

"Hey little guy," cooed Matt, cupping Max's head in his hand. "Hey little darlin'," he whispered to Kenzie, cupping her head in his other hand. As soon as the words left his lips, each baby gently startled and peered up at him.

"They recognize your voice, Matt," said Annie, her voice a reverent whisper.

"All of those lectures into your belly button really paid off!" he said, laughing softly and leaned over farther to kiss her. "You are amazing, Annie. I love you so much."

Annie closed her eyes and pressed her cheek against Matt's head as he lingered over her. The babies began to squirm in her arms, their tiny arms and legs stretching, as if to say, "Hey Mom and Dad, remember us?" They quietly shifted their attention to the two tiny miracles in Annie's arms and smiled.

Matt extended his arms and encircled Annie and the babies within them. Not only had two beautiful, healthy babies been born, but a new family had just been created as well. Annie couldn't help but think of the night Dillon was born or the day they watched Munchkin's heart slow to a stop on the ultrasound screen. The lonely, hollow places that those previous losses had carved within her expanded and let every drop of joy that she felt rush into her heart, filling it until it overflowed and spilled the delicious happiness everywhere and anywhere. No one in the delivery room was untouched by the blessed event that occurred that day; the joy was contagious and rampant. It sparkled and shimmered, and sprinkled amongst them as they went about their work, confirming their belief in the miracles they witnessed every day but that they never took for granted.

# The Pink Ribbon

The lump had been tiny, minuscule, really. Her fingers had run over it accidentally in the shower one day. Her heart stopped for a moment. That was all she remembered about that day. Her heart stopped and her world ended.

She had always done those monthly self-exams very casually, if at all. Her aunt died from breast cancer when she was forty. Her mom died from it when she was forty-five, and her grandma was diagnosed at sixty. For some reason she thought she had dodged the bullet. More than one doctor had indicated that the risk can lessen after a generation or two. Annie had managed to force the possibility to the back of her mind. She had been far too busy over the years to worry about such morbid things happening, especially to her. After all, she'd already had enough bad things happen to her.

She had her first mammogram when the twins were six months old. She was done with breastfeeding and done having babies, so she figured it was time to radiate her breasts. What could it hurt? None of her friends had had mammograms yet. She felt like a trailblazer. At thirty-three, she was younger than most of the women in the waiting area. Nervous and embarrassed, she checked in with the receptionist.

"Hi," she whispered, "I have a 10:00 appointment." Thank God she didn't have to say what it was for; they only did mammograms here.

The receptionist was an older woman, probably in her late fifties or early sixties.. At first Annie thought that she was looking at her as if she didn't belong there with these older women. That would be ridiculous. Women of all ages had mammograms, didn't they? She tried to shake off the old ratty cloak of shame and kick it in the corner, next to the rack of outdated magazines. Straightening her shoulders and standing tall, she turned to find a seat amongst the other women. She deserved to be there just as much as any of them, even if she was so young.

The other women; what a group. Not only were they much older than Annie, but they all had breasts the size of watermelons. Very large, droopy watermelons. Squirming in her chair, she sighed and glanced down at her chest. What type of fruit were they comparing her to, she wondered. Certainly not anything in the melon family. Kiwi perhaps? Apricots? The thought made her giggle a little.

"Anne Preston?" Annie's speculation about produce was interrupted by the raspy, cigarette voice of a middle-aged x-ray technician. The stocky little woman peered out over the eyeglasses that were perched on the end of her nose. She had a drill sergeant quality about her. Annie tried to swallow the lump in her throat and wondered if that would show up on her x-ray as well.

She led her to a short hallway where there were a row of dressing rooms. She gestured toward the one that still had a key in the doorknob. The key had one of those curly telephone cord key chains on it. It was blue. Annie's favorite color.

"You can get undressed in there. Everything off from the waist up. The gown opens in the front. I'll be back in a minute."

Annie almost felt like saluting. This woman made her more nervous than ever. She was afraid she'd make her drop and give her 50 if she didn't follow orders. Pulling the door shut and locking it, her fear of the unknown loomed large. The cold, drafty air made her nipples hard and pointy. When she'd worked at the grocery store during high school, the stock boys always enjoyed working in the freezer section so that they could observe this phenomenon over and over again. It was the 70s, when the braless look was "in", so not much was left to the imagination. She thought they were pigs for doing that at the time, but she wished she were back in that carefree time now, instead of preparing to have her breasts smashed in a vice, looking for cancer.

On a shelf was a container with Handi-Wipes towelettes in it with a small sign next to it: "Please remove underarm deodorant before mammograms." Next to it was a blue can of Secret aerosol deodorant spray. Annie hated the smell of Secret – body odor was preferable in her opinion. She was glad she'd remembered to throw her own anti-perspirant -- an unscented variety, in her purse that morning. The wipes were cold and clammy on her underarms and made her feel even colder and more alone.

After donning the hospital issue gown, she sat down on the bench inside the dressing room and waited for the drill sergeant to return. She double checked the ties just to make sure she wouldn't expose anything on her trip down the hall. It occurred to her that perhaps the ties on hospital gowns were really some sort of I.Q.test. They never made any sense. Just when you thought you were tied in just right, another tie would materialize out of nowhere and you'd have to start over. Of course it really made no difference, because they'd be untied in a matter of minutes and her breasts would be exposed to the world anyway – or at least to Brun Hilda, the drill sergeant.

There was a sharp rap on the door. "Ready?"

Annie reached over to open the door as she stood up. "Yep," she squeaked. "I'm all set."

No words were further from the truth. She was not all set. She was terrified. Her mom had been around fifty when she had her mastectomy, but Annie vaguely remembered a scare, a biopsy, when she was a little girl. Her mom had to stay in the hospital overnight and to Annie it seemed like an eternity. She could still remember how desperately she had missed her. No matter how hard he tried, her dad just couldn't fill her shoes. She felt sick to her stomach – a feeling no doubt caused by her intense feelings -- and whenever she was sick, nobody but her mom could make it better. As an adult, she felt bad that she'd put her dad through "parenting hell" during that time, but she hadn't known any better. She was acting on her feelings – something she learned not to do so much after that.

She found her legs and followed "Sarge" down the hall to the torture chamber. She'd heard about mammograms and it didn't sound pretty. The room was small, making the x-ray equipment look even larger than it was. It took on the persona of a breast squishing monster awaiting its next victim. Sarge busied herself in the corner, pushing buttons and turning dials.

"Okay, honey," she barked without looking up, "put your left breast on the plate." She continued getting the monster ready for action.

Annie cautiously eyed the contraption. She looked at the plate that Sarge had referred to. It was at chest level, a smooth, cold square of steel. The metal plate seemed a little high – it didn't seem physically possible for her to put her breast on it without standing on a step stool. She started to panic again.

"I'm sorry," she started, "but how exactly do it do that?" Her shame made her blush as she said it.

The x-ray tech came over next to her. While she needed the help, she was afraid of what might come next. The husky little woman took her left breast in cold, rough hands and placed it on the plate as though she was a butcher, weighing a piece of meat. It was humiliating.

"You flat chested gals always have a little trouble. When you're bigger it's really easy to just lob it up there."

She then proceeded to compress her breast, which meant she had to adjust and tighten another plate on top of it. It was squished like a pancake. Annie had no idea that her precious little kiwis could spread out and cover that much area. If it hadn't been so horrifically painful, it might have been amazing. She couldn't believe how much it hurt.

After Sarge tightened the screws, she lollygagged her way back to her command center. Hurry up, Annie thought, her eyes watering, take the damn picture!

"Okay now," she barked, once behind the window, "don't breathe." She pushed a button and the machine started to knock and clang. It startled her so much she gasped. That startled her even more because she'd been ordered not to do that. Oh no, she thought, her heart beating wildly, I'm in trouble now! Luckily Sarge hadn't seemed to notice her disobedience. She was busy turning dials and resetting the machine.

"Okay – good." She came out of her lead-lined cubicle and came over to Annie. Finally, she released the death grip on her poor little breast. Annie looked down at it to make sure it was still normal, or if it actually looked like the piece of tissue paper she felt it had been squished into. Relief washed over her when she saw that it was okay – a little red, but it had bounced back admirably. She wondered how larger breasts fared and couldn't believe she was giving this much thought to the subject – she almost felt like a man. It was briefly disturbing, being so obsessed.

Sarge was busy repositioning the plates. "Okay, now, honey," she said, "here we go again." Annie shuddered and followed orders.

That had been her first mammogram – the first of many. It had turned out to be just fine – as had the rest of them, until the last one. When she heard those results, the previous ones didn't matter at all. Who cares if they were fine? What did that get her now? If anything, they'd given her a sense of false hope. She had begun to feel as though they were a waste of time. Why keep going through that year after year if it always turned out normal? And then wham! Right between the eyes – or the breasts, so to speak.

Fear began to creep through her veins, icy and cruel. It slowly moved at first, starting in her heart and spreading outward. Or had it started in her head, gravity making it trickle down, invading the rest of her like a silent, slimy enemy? She wondered how there could be room inside of her for both the cancer and the fear, but then she realized that they went hand in hand, like peanut butter and jelly; co-existing quite nicely. After a while she couldn't remember where the fear had begun and it didn't really matter. It was there, mocking her, threatening her. How would she tell Matt? How would she tell Max and Kenzie? Is was so unfair, but wasn't that the way cancer was? It was never fair.

Dr. Hayes had called on a Tuesday, asking her to come into the clinic to discuss the results of the needle biopsy she'd had the previous Friday. He told her not to worry, but that she might want to bring Matt to the appointment. Looking back, that was when the fear dug in its bitter claws and began to settle in. She had managed to ignore it or keep it at bay in the days since finding the lump, but then no one had wanted a special meeting; everyone was telling her everything would be okay. Matt and the twins were out of town on a series of college visits. Her schedule with the orchestra had prevented her from joining them, but this was the first run through; when they narrowed down the list, she'd go on the follow-up visits. So, as much as she would have wanted Matt there, she didn't want to wait to talk to the doctor. She scheduled the appointment for the next day.

It was a picture perfect popsicles-in-the-park kind of day, the first really hot day of the summer. Driving by Lake Calhoun, Annie could see that the beach was already filling up with sun-bathers staking their claim for the best place to soak up the sunshine. Warnings about skin cancer obviously ignored, given the numbers of bodies stretched out on beach towels, some golden brown, others as white as the underside of a carp. Adding extra pops of color were the bright red ones, already burned to a crisp by the powerful late morning rays. Annie shook her head, knowing that if they weren't traveling with Matt, her kids would probably be at the beach with the rest of them, snubbing their noses at fate and the endless health warnings that were constantly hurled in their direction.

The clinic's parking lot was steaming, the heat rising in hazy waves from the generous expanse of asphalt that stretched out before her. She parked as far from the building as she could, deciding that she could use the exercise. It reminded her of the last doctor appointment before the twins were born, when it had been so hot and steamy. Matt had dropped her off at the door that day, ever the gentleman. She felt a sharp twinge in her heart at the thought of him and how the news she was about to hear would devastate him. He had been so wonderful to her and had made her so happy; she hated the fact that she'd have to cause him any worry or pain. Life could be so cruel.

Annie sat in the patient consult room, her foot tapping nervously against the wooden chair leg. The telltale whistling outside the closed office door announced Dr. Hayes' arrival. It was comforting to know that some things never changed.

"Hi, Annie." Dr. Hayes entered the room. "It's good to see you." He put a gentle hand on her shoulder and then sat down across from her.

"Hi, Dr. Hayes." She put on her best fake smile for him. "Matt is with the twins on a college visit so he couldn't be here today. So, it's just me." Her voice sounded strange to her, as though she was speaking in a rain barrel.

"It's hard to believe those kids are nearly out of high school. It seems like only yesterday that they were born." He shook his head and chuckled. "It makes me feel old."

As Annie kept the polite phony smile pasted on her face, the speed of her foot tapping accelerated slightly. She knew that his bedside manner dictated that he make friendly small talk at the beginning of an appointment, but she wished he'd just get down to business. After all, this small talk wasn't that different from the small talk that preceded the biopsy procedure last week. Perhaps he was dreading this as much as she was.

"Okay, Annie. Here's the deal. The biopsy tells us that the tumor is malignant." He looked down at his hands and cleared his throat. "Stage III."

The words reverberated in her head. Tumor. Malignant. Stage III. It felt as if all of the oxygen was being sucked out of the room as she tried to assimilate the information. Dr. Hayes seemed very far away, his voice tinny and distant.

Annie closed her eyes and tried to inhale deeply, but found she couldn't breathe. Behind her eyelids a movie depicting her life was playing in Technicolor, but it had no sound. In an instant, she saw Matt, Kenzie, and Max, the three anchors of her existence; her reasons for living. Matt as the handsome young writer she met when she was suffocating in a sea of grief, flawlessly turned into the distinguished middle-aged man that she kissed good-bye that very morning, the gray in his hair glistening in the early morning sunshine. Max and Kenzie were transformed from fresh little babies into chubby toddlers along the way to the young adults that had folded themselves into their father's blue Volvo, travel coffee mugs in hand, as they left to visit their aspirations and dreams.

Why hadn't she gone with them? She had stayed behind because of the orchestra's concert schedule, but now that seemed like such a trivial reason. She had looked forward to several days with the house all to herself, eating popcorn for dinner if she felt like it, or watching a marathon of "Little House on the Prairie" episodes. Of course at the time, she hadn't known that today her doctor would be telling her she had cancer. Cancer. The word itself conjured up images of suffering and death. She knew it didn't always end that way, but it was hard not to fear that it might. Her mother died from breast cancer, and Annie still remembered every step of the journey with amazing clarity.

Since her father had died years before, Annie found herself thrown into the role of caretaker at the tender age of sixteen. When her friends were flexing their newfound driver's license freedom by cruising around the lakes on spring afternoons, when the promise of summer was so ripe you could taste it, Annie was driving her mom to radiation treatments, reading outdated magazines with tattered pages while she marked time with all of the other cancer chauffeurs in the dingy, well-worn waiting room.

She recalled one day in particular, when she had to miss the youth symphony try-outs because her mom had an appointment. Frank and Sally were out of town and there was no one else to bring her, so Annie let go of a dream she'd had since she was a little girl. Instead, she drove her mom to an appointment that was supposed to save her life. At her mother's request she played a cello solo at her funeral. Little did she know that the youth symphony conductor was at the funeral. As she pulled the bow across the strings of her cello, he saw in her the emotional and technical qualities he was seeking in a first chair musician. The next day she was given the position without ever having completed the audition.

It had been a bittersweet victory. Her mother's dream had been to see her little girl perform onstage at Orchestra Hall. The next spring, at the end of her junior year in high school, Annie sat first chair in the state youth symphony concert. She found it hard to see her music through the tears that filled her eyes as she played. Each note was for her mother, and she knew that she was smiling down on her, for she felt her loving presence in every measure.

Annie was glad that neither one of her children played a musical instrument. As much as she loved music, she never wanted to drape them with expectations that would lead them to music through parental guilt. It was important to her that her children find passions that were unique to each of them. Annie and Matt were equally as adamant about the twins developing their own tastes and interests and did not expect them to mirror the other sibling in any way. Since they were different genders there were natural disparities, but in many ways they were also very similar; similar in ways that their parents didn't begin to realize. They had their own language, their own "secret code" and could communicate volumes to each other by only exchanging glances. A magical telepathy also seemed to exist between them, for sometimes they'd emerge from separate rooms simultaneously, spurred on by the same thought or intention.

Annie imagined them now, having one of the best days of their lives, visiting the two schools at the top of their respective lists. Max's favorite touted an exceptional college of biological sciences, while Kenzie's professed to be top notch in psychology and law. Max hoped to become a physician one day while his twin sister aspired to become a lawyer, much like her "Aunt Gwen." Matt and Annie were extremely proud of their children's dreams, but would often marvel to each other how neither one of their offspring gravitated toward the arts. In many ways it was easier this way; no one had to fill the shoes of a parent. They were free to forge their own trails, to be in charge of their individual destinies.

She then imagined how they would react to the news that she had cancer. Would it affect their plans for college? Neither school was very far from the other, but they were enough of a distance to require up to an eight hour drive from home. For a moment, Annie was thankful that her children might be far away while she was in the throes of chemotherapy, but in the next moment, she couldn't imagine being separated from them at such a difficult time.

"Annie, are you with me?" Dr. Hayes's voice was gentle, treading lightly into the minefield of her thoughts. The sound of it snapped her back to reality.

"Yes, I"m sorry. I was just thinking about Matt and the kids." Her voice caught in her throat, finding it difficult to make its way past the stalagmites of emotion that had suddenly sprouted there.

"Of course you were," he put an understanding hand on her arm. "When will they be home?"

"Not until the day after tomorrow. They're visiting Northwestern and the Illinois Institute of Technology." The words were ragged and strained, and floated in the air between Annie and her doctor.

"Do you want me to call Matt? I'll deliver the news if it's of any help."

Annie glanced over at the man who had seen her through another one of the worst moments of her life. He appeared to be agitated, clearly needing to so something, anything to help her through this one. His face bore the agony of having to shatter someone's world in one word. She felt nearly as bad for him as she did for herself.

"No, I couldn't ask you to do that. I need to tell him but I'll wait until they get back. I can't have him driving all that way with that on his mind. Besides, the kids have tours scheduled and I don't want to ruin that for them."

Dr. Hayes just sat there silently, his brow furrowed, a frown tugging down on the corners of his mouth. Annie glanced over at him and realized that he needed her reassurance. It was role reversal at its finest.

"There's nothing that has to be done for the next few days, is there?" She searched his face for any trace of relaxation or softness, but there was none. When his reply wasn't forthcoming, her foot started to jiggle again and her heart resumed its erratic rhythm. "There's no rush, is there Dr. Hayes?"

"The sooner we act the better. Time is of the essence, although one or two days shouldn't make a significant difference. I can tell you this, though. If Matt and the twins were here, I'd be admitting you to the hospital this afternoon." His face remained clouded in concern. "When do they get back?"

"Thursday sometime."

"Promise me you'll schedule the surgery for the day after they get home."

"I promise." The words squeaked out of her mouth.

"I'll get Margo in here to help you schedule it. And Annie -- also promise that you'll call if you need anything."

"I will." She found it hard to look at him, to see how visibly upset he was for her.

"Okay. Well, good. I'll be in touch." He patted her hand and then made himself stand up and leave the room.

It wasn't two minutes before Margo, another one of the nurses she'd known for years, came into the room. Margo was blonde and hovered somewhere around fifty years of age. Somedays she looked closer to fifty-five while other days, anyone would swear she was in her mid-forties. Today was one of the "older" days. She sat down in the chair that Dr. Hayes had just vacated and looked at Annie with forlorn puppy dog eyes.

"I am so sorry, Annie."

"Thanks, Margo. It's going to be okay, right?"

"Of course it is, kiddo!" She patted Annie's knee. "You know, Dr. Hayes is the best we have for this. A few years ago he transitioned from obstetrics to this. You're in good hands with him."

It bothered Annie that Margo, a health care professional for many years, couldn't bring herself to say "cancer" or "oncology." Instead she called Annie's condition "this." Obviously Margo had never had "this"; otherwise Annie was sure she'd be able to say the word.

"He said to schedule surgery on Friday. He still has a 9:00 a.m. open. How does that work?" Margo looked at her expectantly, her pen poised over the scheduling form.

"That will be fine, I guess," Annie said as she tried to visualize the family calendar and what was scribbled in the square for that day. "It doesn't sound like I have much of a choice." She tried to laugh a little, but the sound that escaped her lips was flat and dull.

The world seemed to be infused with fog and moving in slow motion. Annie walked out to her car from the clinic feeling like a different person; a sick person, a cancer patient. How could one word have the power to change life so quickly?

The moment she felt the twinge in her heart, she realized that she knew the answer to her question. Twenty years before the word had been stillborn instead of cancer, but her whole world stopped and changed in an instant. At the time when Dr. Hayes had uttered that devastating word, she had no idea that she'd be losing more than her baby; she'd lose her marriage as well. Perspiration formed on her upper lip as she prayed that the same thing didn't happen this time.

Reaching her car, she leaned against it, relieved to have found it in her current state of mind. She looked around the parking lot at the different people coming and going. From their outward appearance she couldn't tell if they'd been to the clinic to receive bad news like hers or if they'd just gone in for a routine checkup. Some of them would be going home, stopping to pick up milk and eggs on the way, this day like any other. Others, like her, would drive home, struggling to come to terms with words that shot around their brains like small steel balls against flippers in a pinball machine. Malignant. Stage III. Tumor. Surgery. Keeping their cars on the road would be an enormous feat let alone attempting to run any errands.

Finally behind the wheel, Annie said another prayer for Matt, Max, and Kenzie, that they'd have the strength they'd need to get through this next chapter in their lives. That done, she pulled out of her parking space and headed for home.

## The Dog

The snuffling and whining was so pitiful; it was almost more than she could bear. Rolling over onto her right side, Annie drew in a large breath and hoisted herself up on her elbow. The motion irritated her incisions more than she'd expected and a small moan escaped from her lips. The whining increased in intensity. She stretched her neck over the edge of the bed and locked eyes with two large, brown, very sad eyes.

"Oh, Howard. What's wrong?"

They had rescued him from the Humane Society the year the twins started first grade. Annie and Matt missed them so much, they ran out to fill the void that had been created in their lives during the school day. He was a black and grey terrier mix with long, coarse hair. Once Annie saw that he only had three legs, the back right one having been amputated just above the knee, he was the only dog for her.

"No one else will take him," she told Matt as they observed the little dog run up and down the concrete kennel. "Look how sweet he is. He's like a little Toto dog."

Life wasn't easy with Howard at first. He was a runner. When he first came to live at the Preston home, he'd try to escape every chance he got. After a particularly close call between him and a UPS truck, Matt and Annie decided that they had to fence the backyard. Annie had pleaded for a white picket fence, but Matt convinced her that it wouldn't be "Howard-proof" and a chain link fence was installed. Eventually Howard settled in and settled down, content with his new home. He became best friends with Max and Kenzie, following them around as they moved through the various stages of childhood and adolescence. Matt always had a buddy as he sat at his typewriter and then his computer, a trusted critic of his latest writing project.

The person to whom Howard was most devoted was Annie. He seemed to sense that it was she who saved his life. In return, he was always there for her, particularly if she seemed unhappy or in need of comfort. He'd nudge her hand and lick it, giving her his own brand of doggie kisses. Howard was her constant companion when she had one of the many migraines that had plagued her since her head injury in Paris. He'd curl up next to her and stay there until the pain passed and she could face the world again. He was a lifesaver in a fur coat.

Howard looked at her with pleading eyes, much the way he had the day they found him. He circled around and around, wagged his tail and barked again, looking both endearing and desperate.

"You have to go o-u-t, don't you?" Annie slumped onto her back and sighed.

It was such an ordeal to get out of bed. At thirteen, Howard was developing some problem with incontinence. Accidents had become a common occurrence, especially if his requests to go outside were ignored. Where were Matt and the kids, anyway? She knew that she'd been asking for a lot of help lately, but it was only when she was really desperate, wasn't it? Her eyes shifted over to the nightstand next to the bed. It was cluttered with prescription bottles, two Kleenex boxes, a small bottle of lotion, a tube of lip balm and a plastic water mug with an accordion straw sticking out of the top like a floppy Jack-in-the-box. The white tulips that Matt had given her when she came home from the hospital were just beginning to droop, several big, curved petals were hanging on desperately, as if they couldn't bear to leave the others.

Reaching with her fingertips, she nudged the closest box of Kleenex over a bit, exposing the small bell which had been hiding amongst the collection of personal care items. She leaned over further in an attempt to reach the bell, but knocked it onto the floor instead. It landed with a soft thud onto the Oriental rug, startling Howard, who gave out a small yip of surprise.

"Damn."

Howard whined again, the sounds sounding more urgent than before.

"Okay, okay," Annie said, as she pulled herself up to a sitting position. "Ooh. Ouch."

Pausing a moment to catch her breath, she looked out the window to see Matt, Max, and Kenzie playing Frisbee in the backyard. No wonder they couldn't hear Howard whining to go outside; they were already out there. Anger flared inside her, competing for space with the pain and pity. It had only been a day since she came home from the hospital, three days since her surgery. How could they just ignore her like this? Howard yipped again, imploring her to get moving. He stood by the bedroom door and wagged his tail. His nails tapped out an SOS on the oak floor as he paced back and forth, whining continuously.

"I'm coming!" Her voice was harsh, and Howard looked at her with confusion as he did his "I wanna go out" dance.

Wincing, she slipped her old chenille robe on over her t-shirt and sweat pants and shuffled to the door. Passing the mirror she caught a quick glimpse of herself, but refused to linger. She wasn't ready to see how awful she looked; she'd wait a while for that, thank you very much.

"Come on, Howard," she said, patting her leg as she started down the hall.

Howard scampered happily down the hall after her, slipping and sliding on the highly polished hardwood floor. Feeling a little lightheaded, she reached out and touched the wall with her hand, stopping for a moment to regain her momentum. She hadn't been up and around much since the surgery and this little adventure was proving more challenging than she'd expected. Ever the loyal companion, Howard stopped and looked up at her, tilting his head from side to side, as if to ask, "Are you okay?" After a second she started walking again, taking smaller and slower steps, and he slowed his pace to match hers.

As she approached the kitchen, she could hear the teasing voices of Matt and the kids drifting in through the open windows. The happy sounds hovered over the pile of dirty dishes on the counter, slid down the front of the cupboard, and landed in a puddle on the white tile floor. Anger boiled within her again as she surveyed the mess. They knew how much dirty dishes bothered her. How could they just leave them and go outside to play Frisbee of all things?

Howard emitted a woeful whine as Annie stood there, debating whether or not she should start doing the dishes. He nudged the back door with his nose, as if trying to open it himself and then looked back at her.

"I'm sorry, buddy. Here you go."

She pushed the screen door open and Howard dashed out into the yard, racing to his favorite spot under the tree by the fence. When Matt saw him zoom by, he looked up to see Annie framed in the doorway, her mouth set in a grim line. He raised his hand to wave at her, but she had already turned around and was going back into the kitchen. He made a "time out" sign with his hands to Max and Kenzie and hurried toward the house.

"Hey, sweetie, what are you doing up?" Matt said in a cautious voice once he was inside. "Why are you doing the dishes?"

Annie was standing in a cloud of steam rising up from the hot water filling up the sink, her hands resting on the edge of the counter, her posture tense and foreboding.

"Obviously I'm doing what the rest of you didn't have time for; the dishes and letting Howard out." She kept her back to him and plunged some cereal bowls into the hot, soapy water.

"I'm sorry, honey," said Matt, walking over to her. "We were going to do it --"

"When?" Annie interrupted him. "You know how much this bothers me! And poor Howard. All of you just leave him in here. How was he supposed to get outside?" She took a greasy frying pan and dropped it into the sink, causing soapy suds and water to splash up into her face and all over the front of her robe. "God damn it!" Stepping back, she lifted her arm to wipe the suds from her face. The movement stretched her incision and she gasped in pain.

"Honey, please calm down. This isn't going to help anyone." Matt was trying to be the voice of reason, but it did little good, as the storm was already brewing.

"Don't tell me to calm down! How do you suppose I feel looking outside and seeing the three of you having such a good time without me?"

"We thought you were sleeping, Annie. Howard was sleeping on the floor by the bed, so we went out to get a little fresh air. Is there a law against that?" Anger and frustration skirted the edges of Matt's voice. "The twins are seniors in high school, but they're still kids. They needed to burn off some energy. I know this is harder for you than anyone else, but give us a break. We're doing the best we can."

He folded his arms over his chest and stood there, looking out the window at Max and Kenzie. They had stopped tossing the Frisbee and were sitting under the willow tree, gently petting Howard, deep in conversation. Annie followed his gaze and took in the sight as well. They were such good kids; they had put their lives on hold to be there for her the past week. Coming back from their college visit trip with Matt, they had been bubbling with excitement with their plans for the future. It had broken her heart to have to tell them about the cancer. She had wanted to wait a week or two, but Dr. Hayes was adamant; there was no time to waste. And so began the rest of their summer, taking care of their sick mother. She didn't even try to hold back the tears.

"I'm sorry, Matt. You're right." The sobs spiraled up from deep within her. "It's just that for a minute I could see what it will be like without me." She wiped her nose with the back of her hand, but the tears kept coursing down her cheeks.

Matt came up behind her hand put his hands on her shoulders. "Well, it would never look like that, because we wouldn't be happy. Besides, we're not going to be without you."

Annie leaned back into him and he gingerly wrapped his arms around her, being careful of her incisions. The tension began to melt away as they stood there, her head on his chest, his face buried in her neck. When Annie felt his tears on her skin, she wiped her hand on her robe and then lifted it to his face.

"Oh sweetie," she said, patting his cheek. " Please don't cry."

"I can't help it. I can't even think about life without you. That is not an option." His words were drenched in viscous emotion. "We're going to beat this."

"I know, I know." Annie's eyes never moved from Max and Kenzie. "But I can't not think about it. Sometimes. Just a little."

He turned her around to face him and took her face in his hands. They looked into each other's eyes, just as they had that first night in the parking ramp, so many years ago. As always, Annie felt as though he was looking directly into her soul. She briefly lowered her eyes, afraid to let him see the fear that was lurking inside. After she blinked away the tears, she raised her chin and smiled up at him.

"Kiss me?"

"I thought you'd never ask."

The screen door slammed and Kenzie swept into the kitchen, her curls shooting out in all directions. Her eyes were wide with panic and alarm.

"Something's wrong with Howard!"

Matt and Annie, still locked in their embrace, turned their heads in unison at her announcement. "What?"

"He's shaking and acting weird. It's like he's having a seizure or something!"

Without saying another word, the three of them hurried out to where Max was kneeling next to Howard. The little dog was on his back, his paws in the air, shaking violently and crying. Max was trying to comfort the dog with a litany of soothing words as he scrunched down next to him, but Howard's writhing continued.

"What's wrong with him, Mommy?" Kenzie was crying now, her face contorted and red, just as it always had since she was a baby.

"I don't know, honey." Annie ran her hands over her daughter's wild mane as she tried to calm Kenzie's fears as well as her own.

Matt had his cell phone out and was dialing the vet clinic's emergency number. He left a brief voice mail and then kept his phone ready as they waited for the vet to return the call.

"Was he acting normal before he starting having the seizure?" Matt started gathering the information that he knew the vet would need.

"It seemed like it," said Max, glancing over at them. "Didn't it, Kenz?"

"Yeah, he was just like he always is. Then he just got really still and then starting shaking. Is he going to be okay?"

Annie took her hand away from Kenzie's head and knelt on the ground next to Howard. The poor little dog was suffering so, jerking and drooling as his eyes rolled back in his head. He had never had a seizure before which made Annie suspect that there was something seriously wrong. What it was, she didn't know. What she did know, was that it would be especially unfair for them to lose Howard right now when they all needed him so much. She couldn't help but think that faced with her own mortality, a dog's life would be put in perspective, but it wasn't. Suddenly it seemed more important than ever.

The vibration and accompanying ringtone of Matt's cell phone jarred them all. He glanced at the Caller ID display. It was the veterinarian. He stood up and walked over to the other side of the yard, away from the others. They could see him nodding his head, gesturing with his free hand, and pacing back and forth as he listened to the voice on the other end of the phone. Annie knew it was bad; it was a feeling that washed over her as she watched her husband's body language. It was a language she had seen too many times before, the language of immediate despair. Across the lawn dappled with sunshine and leaf shadows he finally flipped his phone shut and strode back to the vigil they were keeping under the tree.

"Dr. Phelps said that she'll meet us at the clinic. We're supposed to wrap Howard tightly in a towel or a blanket so that he feels safe. She said that now that the seizure's over, he'll be tired and lethargic."

"What did she say is wrong with him, Daddy?" Kenzie's plaintive voice reminded Annie of how she sounded when she was three years old, asking why the sky was blue and the grass green.

"She won't know until she sees him. She would've come here, but she might need to take an x-ray." His voice was matter of fact but Annie could see the panic behind his eyes, "Let's get going."

Max came running from the house with a large orange, red and yellow beach towel and Howard's "blankie", a tattered and torn old baby blanket that had once belonged to him. He laid the towel on the ground next to Howard and then tucking the blanket next to the quivering dog, wrapped the towel securely around him. Annie's heart skipped a few beats as she marveled at how calm and deliberate her son was during this crisis. Calm and steady, just like his father. It gave her hope and strength for the journey ahead, not only for Howard but for all of them.

"I just need a minute to get dressed," said Annie as she remembered what she was wearing, and she started toward the house.

"Oh. Um, Annie, are you sure you should go?" Matt said, putting a hand on her arm. "You just got out of the hospital."

"I know that, but I'm not staying home. I'm not." The look of determination in her eyes dared Matt to stop her.

"Okay," he said, knowing that look all too well. "Let me help you then." He grabbed her hand and they walked as quickly as she could to the house.

The trip to the vet clinic reminded Annie of the trip to the hospital the day that she'd learned that Dillon had died, the day they lost Munchkin, the day she learned she had breast cancer. She was beginning to recognize it now, an aura the color of navy blue storm clouds that hovered and swirled around them as Matt maneuvered the car on its route to the clinic. The sense of impending doom weighed heavy on Annie's shoulders and she tried not to see the hope and expectation for miracles in her children's eyes.

The examination was short but thorough, the diagnosis delivered much too quickly. Dr. Phelps ran a nervous hand through her short gray hair and looked at them with compassion. "It's a brain tumor, just as I feared. I'm so sorry."

The family's shoulders dropped collectively, as if they'd all been holding their breath and had just had the wind knocked out of them. No one spoke at first, but one by one they reached for each other's hands as they stood around Howard, who was lying passively on the exam table.

"Is there any treatment?" Annie was the first to speak.

"Well, it's not in a good location for us to surgically remove it, and I'm afraid that chemo and radiation usually don't work."

"One of my friend's dogs had cancer and they gave him chemo," said Kenzie, determined to fight for Howard.

"It is an option in some cases, but not this time. I'm afraid the treatment would be a waste of time and money and it would be very hard on Howard."

"So what do we do?" Matt asked the question that nobody could.

"Euthanasia is the most humane option."

The words fell on them so heavily that they all visibly slumped some more. To Annie, Max and Kenzie became little children again. She wanted to gather them in her arms and never let them go, but she stood where she was, holding onto each of their hands instead. Locking eyes with Matt, she tried to ask him silently for his thoughts. In the past they would have retreated to another room to discuss it privately, but this felt like a group decision. Max and Kenzie had already been initiated into the world of sickness and health with her cancer diagnosis. It made little sense to exclude them from the discussion about their beloved pet.

"Wow," said Matt. "We weren't expecting that."

"It's a difficult situation," said the vet. "I understand how hard it is. Often times an animal has been sick or suffering prior to a decision like this. While that doesn't make it any easier, at least it's not so sudden."

"Is Howard suffering now?" Max asked, petting Howard's back as he spoke. Howard took a deep, heavy breath, barely opening his eyes to look at him.

"It's hard to know," said Dr. Phelps. "The seizure took a lot out of him."

"Do we have to do it right now?" asked Kenzie, tears welling up in her eyes. "Can't we take him home?"

"I'll give all of you some time alone to talk it over," said the vet, stepping out of the room. "I'll be back in a few minutes."

The four of them stood in a circle around the little dog who seemed oblivious to everything but Max's hand on his back. The tail that always wagged back and forth like a furry metronome was still, his pink tongue hanging out of his mouth as he panted and struggled to breathe normally.

"Honey, I understand why you want to take him home; so do I. But do we want that for Howard or for us?" Annie smoothed Kenzie's hair away from her face.

Kenzie raised her blue eyes, blurred with tears, and looked at her mother. Her bottom lip trembled violently, and she wiped at her tears with the back of her hand.

"I think we all know the answer to that," Matt said and put an arm around Kenzie's shoulders.

Dr. Phelps came back in and they told her their decision. She told them they were doing what was best for Howard and brought him into the adjacent room to insert the catheter into his leg. Wrapped in his blankie, she carried him back into the room and gently placed him on the table. They each took a turn to say "good-bye" to him before the medication was injected into the flexible narrow tubing. It only took a minute before his breathing slowed and then stopped. It seemed to take forever, but for Annie, it was over much too soon.

# The Scarf

It had been a rough night for both of them. The latest round of chemotherapy had run roughshod over Annie both physically and emotionally. The nausea started sooner than it had before and was violent and relentless in its intensity. Even though she initially tried to spare Matt the unpleasant task of taking care of her as she draped herself over the toilet, the reality of the situation was that after a bout of vomiting, she was rendered too weak to wipe off her mouth, let alone drag herself up off the floor.

As she laid in bed snoring softly, Matt laid next to her, his arm placed protectively around her thin shoulders. His own breath harmonized with hers in an odd, sweet melody as they inhaled and exhaled together, matching breath for breath, heartbeat for heartbeat.

Opening her eyes, Annie could see by the outline of light around the room-darkening shades, that morning had arrived. She turned slightly to see the time on the alarm clock next to the bed, moving only her head so as not to disturb Matt. The bright red numbers on the alarm clock glared at her. It was 9:45 a.m., much too late to still be in bed. In spite of her illness, Annie made a point of getting up and dressed every day, no matter how she felt. Today was different though; she couldn't summon the strength. Instead, she laid there, her eyes trained on the light filtering in from outside, too weak to even turn her head. Matt stirred, rolling over on his side so that he was facing her.

"Hey sleepyhead," he said. He was going to tousle her hair playfully as he always did, but as he opened his eyes, he stopped, his hand frozen in midair.

There on her pillow, was a mass of hair, a soft downy nest around her head. Even in the dim light of the room, he could see several bare spots on her scalp where the hair used to be. He swallowed the brittle lump of fear that filled his throat and went ahead and placed a gentle hand on her head anyway. Until now, she hadn't lost any hair, much to her relief. It was the one thing she dreaded more than anything; she had always been so preoccupied with her hair. The doctors warned her that it would happen eventually, but since everyone was different, it was difficult to predict when. She reached over and put her hand on his chest.

"Good morning, sweetie," she said, her voice raspy from the night's events. "I'm sorry about last night."

"Stop that. There's no need to apologize. I thought we'd established that after the hundredth 'I'm sorry' last night." He traced his fingers down the curve of her face.

"I know, but I feel bad. Just because I'm up doesn't mean you should be. This is going to wear you out."

"Annie. However tired I get is nothing compared to how you feel. Stop apologizing, okay?" His patient tone was getting stern.

"Okay, okay." She removed her hand from his chest and stretched both of her arms out in front of her, a motion she always made just before getting out of bed. Matt cleared his throat.

"Um, honey?"

"Yeah?"

The look on his face and the stillness of his hand on her head stirred whispers of apprehension within her and ever so slowly she reached up to her head, her fingers almost magically resting on one of the bald spots.

Her eyes widened during the dreadful moment of understanding, immediately filling with tears.

"Shit." Her voice was nearly inaudible. She closed her eyes. The tears spilled down the sides of her face, making wet spots on the pillowcase where they dripped along her ears. Before Matt could react, she reached up with her other hand, both hands investigating the cruel surprise that had happened while they both slept. He looked at her and waited for yet another part of her world to crumble.

"Well," she said as she opened her eyes again, "now I can stop worrying about when that's going to happen." Her voice was surprisingly calm. She raised herself up on her elbows and bent her neck around to look at her pillow. "Impressive," she said in a matter-of-fact tone as she surveyed the mound of hair.

"You're taking this very well," Matt observed, his words measured with caution and concern.

"I've been thinking about it a lot. You know, what would I do, how would I handle it. Of course I was praying that I'd be one of the few who is spared the hair loss, but deep down I knew this day was coming." She gathered the loose hair in her fist, examining it with a newfound clarity and resolve.

"Is there anything I can do?" Matt said as he rubbed her shoulder.

"Yes, as a matter of fact there is. I want you to shave my head."

Surprised, he took his hand away from her and sat straight up, the covers falling in a puddle around his waist. "What?"

"I want you to shave my head. Now. Today. There's nothing worse than having it fall out in clumps and patches. It would be like reliving this moment over and over again. And besides, it looks terrible; much worse than a bald head."

"Wow. Well, okay. I can do that." He paused, scratching his own head for a second. "You're sure."

She gave her head an emphatic nod so sharp that a few more strands of hair drifted down onto her lap. "I'm sure."

A gentle knock on the bedroom door interrupted their conversation.

"Mom? Dad?" Max's voice was tentative.

"Come on in, Max," said Matt.

"I was just getting worried; you're usually up by now." Max being the first-born of the twins tended to be the caretaker, while his sister was the freer more elusive spirit. Never one to be left out, however, her face appeared over her brother's shoulder.

"We were both getting worried," she piped in, her eyes adjusting to the darkness. "Those new shades you got really work. It's like pitch dark in here." She emerged from behind Max and bounced over to the window. Grabbing the cloth ring on the end of one of the cords, she pulled down slightly and then held on while the shade went up, rolling around itself. Morning light spilled into the room, washing Annie and Matt in sunshiny brightness. Matt felt for Annie's leg under the sheet and gave her a gentle squeeze as they waited for the bomb to drop. She looked at him and smiled.

"Mom!" Kenzie said when her eyes took in Annie holding handfuls of hair. "Oh my God! Mommy!" She let go of the shade which sent it spinning around and around, the cord flipping wildly until it was completely wrapped around the roller. The window shade forgotten, she was at her mother's side before the shade stopped spinning.

Max, always more cautious, stood dumbfounded in the doorway, his mouth agape at the scene. His gaze went from face to face until it settled on his mother. For the first time since Annie had started her journey with cancer, Max was letting them see him cry. Big round tears fell from his eyes and ran down his cheeks. Without fail, ever since he was little, he'd been embarrassed to cry in front of people, trying to be the tough guy. This had always confused Annie and Matt, especially because Matt was so open about his feelings and readily shed tears if a situation moved him to do so. There was never any doubt how Kenzie was feeling, her sleeves perpetually full of hearts, but Max was more guarded, more reserved. Now however, every ounce of pain and fear he'd kept inside the past few months could be seen in each tear, exposed and magnified. Annie's reserve crumpled when she saw him struggling and she had to fight back tears of her own.

"Oh, Maxie, sweetie, come sit by me," Annie said, patting a spot on the bed next to her. "It's okay, really."

Max looked over at his dad. Matt gave him an understanding smile and nod.

His eyes averted, Max made his way over to Annie's side of the bed and sat down on it so gently, it felt like a butterfly landing there instead of a teenager on the brink of adulthood.

"Does it hurt?" His voice was tentative and somber.

"My head?" Annie touched the top of her head with her hand. "No, not really. That's a good question, though. You'd think it would, wouldn't you? No, it's just kind of breezy."

"It's just that you're so obsessed with your hair most of the time. Aren't you upset?" Seeing his mother so calm was clearly a bit unnerving for him.

"Well, Maxie, there's nothing I can do about it, so I've decided not to get all bent out of shape. It's just hair; it will grow back."

"In fact," added Matt, "your mom wants me to shave her head today, so she doesn't have to go around with this molting look."

Max's mouth dropped open at the news, as did Kenzie's. Annie felt her face flush and the knot in her stomach twist. She didn't want them to be ashamed or embarrassed by her, but she didn't know what else to do. Shaving her head or not didn't make a difference; her hair was falling out regardless.

"Seriously?" Kenzie was incredulous. "That is so cool!"

"Yeah!" Max said, grinning through his tears.

"Wait a minute," said Annie. "You guys think it would be cool?"

"Of course it's cool, Mom," said Kenzie, her tone bordered on patronizing. "Your head is a great shape. You'll look awesome!"

"What I think is cool," said Matt, "is that your mom is showing cancer who's in charge here. She's being tough and she's kicking butt."

Annie cringed at the comment, although she knew he meant well. She wanted to be strong and tough and positive, but it wasn't at all how she felt. It took everything she had to pretend that she was a kick-ass woman who wasn't letting a little thing like losing her hair get the best of her. The truth was, she often felt as thought the disease had already gotten the best of her; that she was becoming a hollowed-out shell with nothing left inside of her but the toxic streams of chemicals that were coursing through her veins. Losing her hair made her feel that since there was nothing left on the inside, the monster was starting to destroy her on the outside. Wasn't losing her breasts enough? What would be next? Would her nose fall off, or would she begin to lose fingers and toes, one by one?

Annie knew that she had to keep such irrational thoughts to herself. Her family would seriously question her sanity if they had any idea she entertained such gruesome notions. No, those things were best kept hidden deep within her heart. Looking at the light shining from within both of her children she knew she had to keep the charade up as long as she could; forever, if possible. She just didn't know how long forever would last. If she couldn't be strong for herself she'd be strong for them. For them and for dear, sweet Matt.

"So," she said, swallowing her sadness and fear like a mouthful of day old coffee, "let's do this!"

The clippers hummed and buzzed as Matt carefully ran it over Annie's scalp. Shards of sun-streaked hair fell around her shoulders and onto the bathroom floor. Matt had suggested they cut it first and then shave it, but Kenzie had insisted that it would be much more dramatic if they left it long and shaved it that way. Annie didn't really care; she just wanted it done.

"There," said Matt, cupping his hands over her bare head. "You are beautiful, honey." He leaned over and kissed the newly exposed skin.

"Yeah, Mom," agreed Kenzie. "Your eyes really stand out. They're huge!"

Max was sitting on the edge of the bathtub, observing the rest of them. He hadn't said a word yet.

"Max, what do you think?" Annie turned around to look at him.

"I think I'm next," he said, standing up. "Dad? Will you do the honors?"

"Are you crazy?" Kenzie laughed so hard she snorted. "You're going to shave your head too?"

"Why should Mom be the only cool one in the family?"

Matt looked down at Annie, gauging her reaction. "Well," he said, "not that it isn't your hair, Max, but I think it depends on how your mom feels about it." He squeezed her shoulder and winked. "Maybe she wants to be the only cool one."

Annie regarded her reflection in the mirror, at the same time seeing her mop-top curly-haired son over her shoulder. Suddenly she saw him as he was when he was a chubby toddler, full of curiosity and energy, his silky curls bouncing with every exuberant step. His curls had always been his trademark, just like the dimples that appeared on either side of his mouth when he smiled, and here he was, ready to shave them off, for her. The twinkle in his eyes preceded the dimples every time, and she could see his eyes twinkling now, for the first time in a long time.

"I think it's a wonderful idea," Annie said, her voice catching, her eyes filling with tears, "if it's really what Max wants."

The dimples deepened as Max's smile grew. He gave Matt two thumbs up and gave his head a determined nod. "Go for it, Dad!"

Matt turned on the clippers and started in on Max's hair. Curls dropped to the floor like leaves falling from a tree in autumn.

"Now that I've practiced on your mom, I can really cruise," said Matt as he dragged the trimmer carefully over Max's left ear. "Maybe I missed my calling; I should have been a barber."

"I can see it now," Annie said, "Preston's Tonsorial Parlour. Shave and a haircut, 10 cents." She sang the last part, cracking herself up, and laughed until she cried.

"Okay, Mom," Kenzie said, rolling her eyes, "whatever you say. I swear, this whole family is going bonkers right before my eyes!"

"Oh well," said Matt as he finished up his son's new look, "there are worse things." He used a small whisk brush to sweep the hair from Max's shoulders. "Not bad if I do say so myself!"

Max rubbed his sleek, shiny new head with both of his hands and turned to Annie, grinning. "This is so cool! It feels so smooth. Wow. The guys are going to freak!"

"Should we make it four for four?" Matt turned toward Kenzie, the clippers still in hand. "We could be like 'The Coneheads' only without the cones."

Kenzie's eyes grew to twice their size and her hands flew up to her headful of long, mahogany curls. A look of fear paralyzed her face for a moment and then she relaxed a bit, the distress dissipating. "You're kidding, right?" She looked from Matt to Annie to Max and back to Matt again.

Matt only raised his eyebrows and revved the clippers as he rubbed his own head. Annie stood up and took the clippers out of his outstretched hand.

"Of course he's kidding," she said, giving Matt a reproachful look. "Unless you want to, of course."

Kenzie twisted a tendril of hair around her finger, and chewed on her lower lip. If Max's curls had been his trademark, hers were her crowning glory. Annie had told her time and time again that Kenzie had the best hair in the world, much better than hers had ever been. Some of Kenzie's favorite memories were of playing "Beauty Shop" with Annie, when they would create elaborate hairstyles and then take pictures of them, just like in the fashion magazines. Reading her daughter's mind, Annie unplugged the clippers from the wall with a sharp snap which startled them all.

"Actually, I think this should just be a mother-son experience," Annie said as she put her arm around Kenzie's shoulders. "Not that I don't appreciate the attempt at camaraderie; it's very sweet of you and your Dad to be willing to make such a sacrifice, but a totally bald family would be a little creepy, don't you think?"

Kenzie let out a loud sigh of relief and she hugged her mom. "Thanks, Mom," she whispered in her ear. "I owe you about ten million."

"No worries, sweetie." Annie whispered back and kissed her cheek. She patted her daughter's hair as Kenzie left the room, following her brother down the hall. He was hurrying off to call his buddies to tell them about his new hairstyle, or lack of it.

"So, you don't want me to shave my head?" Matt stuck out his lower lip, pouting. "I was starting to look forward to it."

Annie reached her arms around his neck and tipped her newly shaved head back and gazed up into his eyes. He wrapped his arms around her and pulled her close to him, covering her head with kisses.

"I love you so much, Annie. I just want you to know that I'd do anything for you. Anything."

"I know you would, sweetie. I love you so much for that and everything else." She buried her head in his shoulder, nuzzling in like a puppy. "The best thing you can do for me is stay just the way you are. I always want to remember you just like this."

Just then Kenzie came bounding back into the room, a wad of colorful cloth in her hand.

"Sorry to interrupt, but this is for you, Mom." She thrust the fabric out toward Annie. "I made it for you in art class."

As Annie took the glossy blob from Kenzie's hand, it unraveled, revealing itself as a large, rectangular piece of silk, covered with streaks and squiggles of pink, teal, blue and purple.

"This is beautiful, Kenzie." Annie held the scarf by the top two corners, letting it hang down between her and Matt. "I didn't know you'd made anything like this. You made this in school?"

"Remember that final project that I 'lost'?" Kenzie shot her dad a conspiratorial look. He winked back at her over Annie's head.

"This is it?" She looked from the scarf to her daughter's impish grin.

Kenzie could only nod, because when she saw the tears in her mother's eyes, her eyes filled as well.

"We were in cahoots with the art teacher," explained Matt. "Sorry, honey."

Annie's mind traveled back to the student-teacher earlier in the year, when the young female art teacher with the pierced nose and jet black hair had reported with dismay that Kenzie's final project in her Art and Textiles class hadn't been completed; the only black mark on an otherwise stellar academic record. It was at the beginning of Annie's journey with cancer and while it had disappointed her, she decided not to make an issue of it. Things had shifted around on her priority list and the twins' grades were not as close to the top as they had once been. Now that they were preparing to go off to college, the ever important G.P.A. was competing with chemo for her attention.

"We were working on the designs when you first started chemo. I decided right then and there that I'd make a scarf for you to wear, when, you know, it was time." Kenzie twisted a curl around the index finger of her right hand, and dabbed at her eyes with a Kleenex with the left one.

"It was my idea to surprise you with it," said Matt. "The teacher was all for it; she thought it was a great idea."

"So I'm the only one who thought your grades were slipping?"

"Pretty much." Kenzie said, looking down at the floor and then up at Annie again. "You're not mad, are you?"

"No, I'm not mad." Annie encircled her daughter in a warm hug. "I love it. And I love that you had a fun surprise to look forward to! Will you help me put it on?" She handed the scarf to Kenzie and settled herself in front of the mirror.

Matt left the room as Kenzie began to wind the bright fabric around Annie's newly shorn head. Her fingers were deft and loving as she worked to cover her mother's baldness; the new statement of her condition to the world. The scarf wasn't hiding the fact, but rather it celebrated the beauty of the battle that all of them were fighting together.

Annie looked at her reflection in the mirror and wondered when her cheeks became so sunken, her eyes so haunted. The absence of the mane of thick, wavy hair accentuated all of her other features, possibly to a fault.

She forced herself to look beyond the obvious and to concentrate on her daughter, the beautiful, lively creature who stood behind her, wrapping her head in silk. When did she become so breathtaking? Everyone said that

Kenzie looked so much like her, and Annie blushed at the thought, feeling conceited and flattered. Kenzie caught her mother's eye in the mirror and gave her a smile and a wink. Closing her eyes, Annie offered up a prayer, that she would live to be old and gray, to see the woman her daughter was becoming.

# The Diploma

People were milling about in the bleachers, looking for sections of rows that were long enough to hold grandmas and grandpas, aunts, uncles and cousins. The slant of the early evening sun was shining across the football field at such an angle that everyone was holding their hands up over their eyes, in a squinty salute, as they searched for a place to claim as their own. Fragmented notes of "Pomp and Circumstance" escaped from under the white and red striped tent as the band, minus the seniors, practiced its selections for the evening. Annie winced as she surveyed the expanse of aluminum.

"Are you okay?" Matt had seen the frown that so often accompanied a sudden bout of pain.

"I'm fine. It's the band; the flutes are flat." She took a moment to squeeze his hand. "I appreciate the concern though, sweetie."

"So, where should we sit? I don't want to make you climb too far."

"Over there is okay." Annie pointed to a spot a few rows up. "It looks like there's room for Frank, Sally, and Gwen behind us"

"Okay. I'll hurry up there and save it. You'll be okay?" Matt hesitated before leaving her side.

"I'm fine, Matt. It's a few rows of bleachers, not Mt. Everest," she said, laughing.

"Just take your time," he said and then leapt up the steps to lay their jackets and commencement programs on the two rows of bleachers.

Annie grasped the railing that ran up the middle of the steps and began to climb. She had insisted she was fine, but each step felt as though it was straight up the side of a mountain. The past few months of treatments had sapped her strength so much that most days it was an effort to even get out of bed. Matt had wanted her to use a wheelchair to go to Max and Kenzie's graduation ceremony, but she had refused with a vengeance.

"No! I am not going to be wheeled into that stadium like an invalid or an old woman. I am young; I can walk and I will walk!"

Matt stood rooted to the floor, his mouth agape at the display of fury he just witnessed from his wife. She had been so weak the past few days; he didn't know if she'd even be able to attend the event, let alone climb into the stands. Sally had suggested the wheelchair as a last resort. Annie had been too proud to be wheeled to her chemo appointments, but perhaps graduation would be an occasion worthy of the embarrassment. Now, seeing Annie rise up in her bed before him, like a phoenix from the ashes, a small smile found its way onto his face.

"Okay, okay. No wheelchair." He walked over and put his hands on her feet. "Although I have to admit, if mentioning the wheelchair makes a little bit of you come back, I just might have to suggest it every day."

Faced with the vertical climb in front of her, Annie wondered if she'd made a mistake. Had she used the wheelchair, she could have been down on the field, closer to the graduates, but she didn't want to use her illness as an excuse for special treatment.

She wanted to be like all the other moms, to blend into the crowd of proud parents, not be ostracized to the sidelines. Taking a deep breath, she raised her foot up to place it on the step in front of her. Her fingers tightened on the railing as she used all of her strength to push herself up, bringing her other foot with her. Sweat trickled down her back as a shaft of sunlight danced across her shoulders. Exhaustion shook her arm as she struggled to complete her task and she prayed no one was watching. Relief enveloped her like a cocoon when out of nowhere, Matt swooped silently to her side, offering a hidden boost to her elbow.

"Hello, m'lady," he said quietly into her ear.

"Always my knight." Her voice was barely audible as the band continued to practice. "Isn't that suit of armor a bit warm for today?"

"Nope. I added extra ventilation." He squeezed her arm. "Do you want to see where?" An evil grin played across his lips and he wiggled his eyebrows up and down.

"I'd elbow you, but I'm conserving my energy for clapping," Annie said. "But look out later on. Consider yourself warned."

"Okay, sweetheart. I can't wait."

They'd reached the saved seats. Matt straightened the red and black plaid stadium blanket on the narrow bench and gently helped Annie ease herself onto it. She had lost so much weight that sitting on the cold, hard aluminum would have been extremely uncomfortable. So as not to draw attention to her, Matt plopped down next to her on the leftover section of blanket. He found her hand and took it in his, lacing their fingers together as they had every day since they'd met. Exhausted from the climb up the steps, closing her eyes, Annie rested her head on his shoulder, trying to regain her strength.

"Aren't you two cute?" a voice chirped from behind them. "Just a couple of lovebirds!"

Annie's eyes fluttered open and she turned her head in unison with Matt, to see the silhouette of a tall, shapely woman towering behind them. A tiny place in the pit of her stomach twisted and broke open as she realized who it was; Marla Emerson, in all of her surgically enhanced glory. Insecurities she thought were buried and gone forever began cavorting around in her gut, bringing back memories of past betrayals and sadness. She wrestled them down the best she could, silently reminding them that they belonged to her days with Eric; that Matt would never do anything to hurt her or to make her question his devotion.

As odd as it sounded, Matt's love for her seemed to grow right along with the cancer. Whenever she felt as though she had nothing left and wondered how much more he could stand, he never failed to give her whatever she needed. It had occurred to her more than once, how different the scenario would have been had she gotten sick when she was with Eric. It would have been difficult for him to hide how inconvenient it all was for him; the trips to the hospital for chemo, the night sweats that drenched the sheets and the wretched sounds of her heaving into the toilet at all hours of the day and night. Where Matt was there for her every step of the way, Eric would have had to go out of town for business, or would have to entertain clients. For every time Matt kissed her and told her she was still beautiful, Eric would have looked at her bald head and scarred chest under hooded eyes, not quite managing to hide his revulsion. Part of her knew that she would have died by now if she had been with Eric, because there would have been nothing to live for. She thanked God every blessed day for her three reasons for living: Matt, Kenzie, and Max. The three of them kept her fighting even when it would have been so much easier to curl into a ball and fall asleep forever.

That was why it was so alarming to feel the insecurities coming back to life; they had been dormant for so long. Annie had been under the impression that they had died, along with her feelings for Eric, but here they were, worming their way back into her soul, as though they'd never been gone. Was it the way Marla was resting her hand on Matt's shoulder or was it the low-cut dress that accentuated her spectacular breasts?

As if on cue, the places where her own breasts used to be, began to ache.

"Annie dear, I must say, I don't know how you do it," Marla said, her sympathetic hand still on Matt's shoulder, "but then you have this absolute gem of a husband, don't you? I swear, every woman in this school is so jealous of you!"

Annie smiled up at her, craning her neck to see around Marla's breasts. She was speechless. Telling a woman who has lost both of her breasts and all of her hair that every other woman is jealous of her because she has such a wonderful husband, did not exactly create warm, fuzzy feelings. What it did, was fuel every insecurity that Annie ever had, giving them enough power and intensity to light up the entire football stadium. Annie's stomach churned and her head began to pound. Matt tightened his grip on her hand.

"Well, Marla, you have it all wrong," Matt said as he straightened his shoulders to deflect her hand. "You should all be jealous of me, because I get to spend my life with this beautiful woman." He raised Annie's hand to his lips and kissed it.

"Yes, well, of course." Marla was now the one who was at a loss for words. "Oh look! There's Paul. I better get going! See you later!"

"Who in blazes was that?" Sally and Gwen appeared on the steps next to them.

"That was Michelle Emerson," Annie said, trying to sound pleasant. "She's the president of the PTA, among other things."

"Hmmph," snorted Sally. "Looks like trouble to me. I saw her touching Matt's shoulder the whole time. Who does she think she is?"

"Yes, Sally, but I could have sworn I saw Matt's middle finger standing a little straighter than the rest when he kissed Annie's hand," said Gwen as she winked at Matt and Annie. "Nice one, Matt."

Matt lowered his head and blushed. "I try."

"I wondered why she took off so quickly," Annie said, giving Matt a fist bump.

"Is Frank here?" Matt said as he looked in the stands.

"He's parking the car," said Sally, settling down next to Annie. "He'll be here in a minute. Now tell me about this Marla person."

Annie proceeded to tell her aunt, in hushed tones, about Marla Emerson, the self-appointed, self-anointed "Super Mom" of Lakeside High School. Marla was the consummate overachiever when it came to her children, her house, her appearance. Her husband was an overachiever as well, and as a result was never at any school functions because he was always working. In what Annie perceived as a desperate plea for attention, Marla had gotten breast implants the year before, shortly before Annie's breast cancer diagnosis. One area in which Marla did not achieve anything, was that of sensitivity. At school conferences that year, shortly after Annie's surgery, Marla commented on the irony of their situations: Annie had her breasts removed and Marla had hers enhanced. Annie had been at school alone that evening, since Matt was on a writing assignment, and so she'd had to endure Marla's cruelty on her own.

At the time, she was too preoccupied with recuperating to fully experience the true meaning of the insult. Later, when she told the story to Matt, he had been livid.

"That bitch!" Sally was livid as well. "Where'd she go? I want to go and slap her silly!"

"I'm just glad that once graduation is over, she'll be out of our lives forever," Annie said, fanning herself with the commencement program.

"Unfortunately there's people like that everywhere," said Gwen. "But it looks like you two can handle whoever comes your way."

The drum major signaled for everyone to stand, and the band started playing "Pomp and Circumstance" again, marching along the track, leading the graduating seniors into the stadium. The students walked in two lines, their black caps and gowns blowing in the evening breeze. Annie leaned on Matt as she stood on her tip toes to see the kids she'd known since that first day of kindergarten. She couldn't believe that they were graduating from high school and heading out into the world, just like Kenzie and Max. Two by two they made their way along the track, smiling and waving to their families and friends in the bleachers. Some of them wore sunglasses, some of them wore the braids indicating academic achievement. Some wore flip flops and some wore high heels. It was a conglomeration of the class clowns and teacher's pets, disappointments, and dreams and Annie couldn't imagine how she could have missed it.

Her eyes were trained on the lines of students marching in front of them, watching for Max and Kenzie. In their robes and mortar boards, they all began to look alike, and she was suddenly frantic that she'd miss them.

"Do you see them yet?" she asked Matt, tugging gently on his arm.

He shaded his eyes as he peered out onto the field. "There," he said, pointing, "is that them?"

Rounding the corner came Max and then Kenzie, both grinning from ear to ear, waving to various people in the stands. Annie's breath caught in her throat at her first glimpse of them, much the same as it had the first time she'd held them in her arms. They were so grown-up and confident as they strode along with their classmates, ready to lasso the future. Her heart ached a little as she watched Kenzie brush the curls out her eyes and then wave directly at her. Kenzie then nudged her brother and pointed to them. Max waved and gave them a thumbs-up, his dimples visible from hundreds of feet away.

Suddenly they were back in kindergarten, bravely walking into their separate classrooms, and leaving her behind. She had been terrified for them, being without her or each other for the first times in their lives. They proved her fears wrong and flourished and blossomed in kindergarten and every grade that followed. Now she realized that she had been terrified for herself, at the thought of losing her babies forever. The tears that filled her eyes blurred her view, and she had to blink them away so as not to miss a single moment. She was so proud of them.

The sun sank lower and lower in the sky as the assistant principal read the names of the graduates, and one by one they marched across the stage, clutching their diplomas, to shake the outstretched hands of the superintendent and the principal. Annie's heart beat faster and faster as they got further along in the alphabet; L, M, N, O, and finally P. She fidgeted and squirmed, already having peeled every bit of clear polish from her fingernails. It was then she heard it: "Mackenzie Ann Preston." She clutched Matt's hand as their little girl glided across the stage, beautiful and strong. As she flipped the tassel from one side of her cap to the other, Annie clapped her hands together gleefully, tears streaming down her face. Then came "Maxwell David Preston" and there was their little boy, who seemed to become a man as he strode across the stage and firmly shook the superintendent's hand. He looked out into the crowd as he flipped his tassel and smiled a smile that could have broken the heart of every female in sight. Annie looked at Matt while he watched his son and daughter go through this rite of passage and her heart doubled in size, it was filled with so much joy.

The night was bittersweet as Matt and Annie made their way through the maze of graduates and families out on the football field after the ceremony. She was hugged by more people than she could count, was told she looked great, and that she was in everyone's thoughts and prayers. As she watched Kenzie pose for pictures with her girlfriends she got a lump in her throat as she thought about how the group would scatter in the fall, each going to a different school, each following a different path.

They had been best friends since kindergarten and now, as she heard them promise that they'd always be "best friends forever", she felt a sharp stinging in her heart as she wondered how long their forevers would be. Max was hamming it up with his buddies, mugging for the paparazzi of parents, slugging each other and acting like the little boys that part of them would always be, no matter how old they became. Annie loved how Max was so much like his father and she imagined what Matt had been like at that age. Her only regret was that she hadn't met Matt sooner, so that they would have had more time together at the beginning, when they were younger. Now, surrounded by so much excitement and talk of the future, Annie was overcome with the fear that had been gnawing at her body and soul for months, the fear that there would be a future that did not have a place for her in it.

Wiping away the tears she smiled as Matt put an arm around the shoulders of his children who stood on either side of him. Annie waited for them to lean in toward each other and smile at her. She was just about to take the picture when Frank came up behind her, tapping her gently on the shoulder.

"There's someone missing in that picture," he said, putting out his hand for the camera. "You get over there where you belong, missy."

"I'll be in the next one," she said and repositioned her family in the viewfinder.

They smiled at her as she snapped the picture, not knowing that as she did, she was etching them upon her heart, seeing them as they would be forever without her.

# The Kitten

A lone scarlet leaf broke free of its branch and floated aimlessly past the window. It was joined by a bright gold leaf from another tree and they performed an impromptu pas de deux, swirling and twisting their way to the ground. Drifts of leaves were piling up against the trees, and along the fence, like red, yellow, and orange confetti decorating the yard.

Annie readjusted the pillow that kept slipping out from behind her back and settled in to admire the tranquil autumn scene. She was sitting on the three season porch, in the tan leather recliner that Matt had gotten for her. There was a lift mechanism in the chair that she could use if she didn't have anyone to help her get up. It made her feel like an invalid, but she was somewhat relieved to have it. The chemotherapy regimen over the summer had been brutal, making her weaker than ever. Her oncologist was pulling out all the stops, doing everything possible to stop the cancer in its tracks. It had metastasized to her lungs and was resisting the powerful arsenal of drugs that had been prescribed.

Everything was more difficult now that she was so weakened by lungs that could no longer function well. Her days were punctuated by frequent naps, naps that would creep up and surprise her mid-sentence, carrying her off to a restless, unwanted slumber. Matt always felt guilty for leaving her alone, whether she was in bed or up and around. Annie, on the other hand, often welcomed the time alone because then she didn't have to try so hard; she could just be. Sometimes she was lonely, but it was hard to see the look of helplessness in Matt's eyes. It broke her heart and she didn't know how to make him feel better. The cavalcade of fall leaves dancing outside her window took her mind off her worries and lulled her into another fitful nap.

Suddenly she felt an unusual weight on her feet, as though someone had set a small pillow on top of the afghan that was keeping her warm. Keeping her eyes closed, she decided she was imagining things and tried to climb back into her interrupted dream.

"Hey hon," said Matt in a hushed voice next to her ear.

"Hey." She opened one eye and squinted at him. "I must have dozed off again. Sorry."

"No need to apologize. You need your rest." He tousled the ends of her silk scarf, much like he used to do with her hair.

She gave him a small smile. "What's up?"

"Well, I brought you a present."

"A present? But I don't need anything."

Just then a small squeaky cry came from the pillow on her feet.

Looking down, she could see that it wasn't a pillow at all, but a tiny calico kitten, curled up in a puffy little ball. She could see two blues eyes peering up at her as its little mouth opened to make its plaintive sound.

"Oh my God, Matt! Oh, it's so cute!"

"And it needs a home. How about that?" He reached down and gently picked up the precious ball of fur. "Here, little kitty, meet Annie."

She lifted her hands to accept the kitten and holding it close to her chest, tenderly patted its body with her free hand. The little calico purred and reached up to lick her hand.

"She's adorable! But why? You don't really like cats."

"Well, they're not that bad, especially if you get to know them as kittens," Matt said, smiling at her reaction. "Besides, this house needs a pet. I know you've missed Howard a lot. So have I."

"I *have* missed him," Annie said as she gazed at the kitten. "He was such good company. Not that you aren't, of course."

Matt gave her a playful punch on her shoulder. "Of course."

"And a cat is less work," she continued. "Does she have a name?"

"Nope. That's your job."

"Hmm. I'll have to give that some thought. Oh - I know! How about Clara?"

"Clara the Calico Kitty. I like it!" Matt reached down to pet the newest member of the family.

"Hello little Clara!" Annie tried the name out and the tiny fuzz ball meowed and licked her hand. "Oh! I think she likes it, too!"

"Clara it is, then!"

"Do we need to get kitty things? A litter box, food dishes?" Annie's maternal instincts were kicking into high gear. "Do you need some little kitty toys too?" She held the kitten up to her face and talked to it in a high, singsong baby voice. Matt grinned at how goofy she was being and grabbed the camera to take a picture of the happy moment. The camera was always nearby these days, so that anyone who was there could use it to record special memories and moments. Seeing the camera in Matt's hands, she struck a silly pose with Clara so that he would take another picture.

"The Humane Society had some supplies there, so I think we're set for awhile," said Matt as he reviewed the pictures on the camera. "I just love these digital cameras. It's so cool to see the pictures right away."

He turned the camera so that Annie could see the pictures of her and Clara. Annie smiled and cooed at how sweet Clara looked, but she could never get used to seeing herself without hair. She was wearing one of the scarves that Kenzie had made for her, but it was still very obvious that she was hiding her baldness, which was in essence, broadcasting her illness to the world. Not only was she bald, but she had become so thin and gaunt. Mirrors were something she avoided as much as possible these days, and really, why not? She had no hair to blow-dry or style, no make-up to apply. Seeing her reflection reminded her of a reality that she'd rather forget. She looked up at Matt and put on her happiest face.

"Thank you so much, sweetie. She's perfect."

He placed his hand on her cheek and she turned her face to kiss it. She missed the intimacy that was such a big part of their relationship. These days his hand on her shoulder, a kiss on her cheek were about as intimate as her condition would allow. It hurt her so to not be able to lie with him the way she used to, feeling his skin, the beating of his heart next to hers. They had always looked forward to when the kids would go to college, when they could make love whenever and wherever they wanted. Now the warmth and weight of a small kitten had become a substitute for the warmth and weight of her husband's body entwined with hers. She had to find the good in everything, to appreciate the little things, even when she felt like screaming.

"I know it's not the same as having Max and Kenzie around, but maybe she'll help. At least I hope she will." He placed his hand on her shoulder.

"At least she won't leave her shoes or dirty dishes all over the place."

They sat and watched Clara explore her new surroundings, stalking the edges of the tablecloth and pouncing on the fringe on a pillow as though she were out in the jungle. Matt rolled a small plastic ball with a bell inside of it past the kitten and she ran to catch it, doing a clumsy somersault and sliding on the hardwood floor, the ball nowhere to be found.

"Cats really are good entertainment," said Matt as he retrieved the ball from under the skirt of the sofa and rolled it again. "She could do this all day."

"Or not," Annie said, laughing, as the kitten instantly lost interest in the game and started licking her paws, displaying typical "I can't be bothered" feline behavior.

"Boy, I sure didn't see that coming," said Matt, feigning disappointment. "They grow up so fast."

"Well, honey, that's why they say 'dogs have owners and cats have staff'." Annie jiggled the edge of the afghan in an attempt to cajole Clara out of her attitude.

Matt grinned and watched Annie coax Clara back into being a kitten again. He sat back on the sofa and patted the space on the cushion next to him. Clara immediately climbed up the side of the sofa and then up onto his leg.

"Hey, kitty, who invited you? I was inviting your mother to join me." He smiled at Annie. "You feel up to a little snuggling?"

Matt looked so handsome, sitting there with an expectant, hopeful grin on his face. He had aged well; he still took her breath away. The wrinkles that appeared around his eyes when he smiled made him even more attractive to her, each one earned with many smiles and equally as many tears. His hair had gotten more gray during the past year or so and he now had a thin spot on top, which she dubbed his "sympathy bald spot" although they both suspected it would have appeared whether she had cancer or not. She knew that the forlorn, tired look in his eyes was due to her illness and for that she'd be forever sad. The eyes that once twinkled with mirth and love were now laced with apprehension and fear. Why did life have to be so difficult? Why did God have to rob this wonderful man of both of the women he loved so deeply and so well? He was the best thing that had ever happened to her; there was no doubt in her mind.

For the first time she pushed the button on her lift chair and allowed it to raise her gently up to a standing position. Matt was going to get up to help her, but she held up her hand as a signal for him to stop. Respecting her wishes, he stayed seated and kept petting Clara, who had cuddled up on his lap. The motion of the chair was smooth but swift, and left her feeling slightly lightheaded when she got to her feet. Taking a minute to adjust, she closed her eyes and prayed for the strength she needed to get across the small room, which she accomplished with less difficulty than she'd expected.

"It's so nice to sit here together," said Matt as she settled in next to him. He put his arm around her and gave her a delicate squeeze.

Clara stretched out her paws and turned her head to look at Annie. Without so much as glancing in Matt's direction, she repositioned herself onto Annie's lap and went back to sleep, her purring a soft vibration in the background.

"You really think it's nice to sit here with your bald, sick wife?" Annie said, her voice prickly.

"Yes, as a matter of fact, I do."

"You're sure about that."

"Annie, if you're trying to pick a fight, I'm not in the mood." Matt's calm demeanor prevailed. "What's the deal?"

Annie looked down at the kitten on her lap and sighed. Why was she trying to pick a fight anyway? She had just gone from feeling so full of love for Matt that she didn't know if she could contain it, to being defensive and insecure. What was wrong with her? Besides cancer, that is. She had been determined not to let her illness define her life, and here she was, letting it control her every thought and mood. There had been so many people that she'd known over the years, who once they had cancer, it was all they could talk about. Suddenly it became the excuse for everything, their ironic reason for living. It had occurred to her that some people missed their disease once they went into remission, because they were no longer special, no longer eliciting preferential treatment from the world.

The days when she was just another mom at school conferences, the grocery store or the shopping mall had become a distant, precious memory. She had never liked being the center of attention and now, the looks of pity that were cast her way were enough to make her want to run and hide. Gwen had encouraged her to create a blog where she could keep everyone informed of each step of her journey; every treatment, every change in the prognosis. Then, Gwen had explained, people would know the details and every conversation wouldn't end up being about her illness.

"But Gwen," Annie had said, trying to keep her voice pleasant, "I don't want everyone to know every detail. It's private. There are better things to talk about."

"Don't you see, Annie? People are concerned about you." Gwen had insisted, her french manicured nails drumming on the arm of the sofa.

"People are nosy. Case closed." The finality of the statement had been enough for Gwen. She never brought it up again.

Annie had stayed true to her philosophy and had managed to avoid making a big deal about her situation. The only help she accepted was if it made life easier for Matt or the kids, and then it was met with appreciation and a side order of guilt. She wanted to be "Super Mom" and have her family's memories be of how she was always there for them, no matter what; not of a parade of friends and neighbors carrying tuna casseroles and Rice Krispie bars through their living room.

Now that Max and Kenzie were off at college, there was less of everything to be done and life had taken on a more relaxed feeling. Even though they had been quite helpful and self-sufficient during the past year, the sense of urgency and responsibility had diminished a bit since they were no longer living under the same roof. Annie missed them terribly, but having them gone made her downward descent less precipitous, at least in her eyes.

What she didn't know was that Max and Kenzie were each keeping in close contact with Frank and Sally, as well as Matt. They called and emailed Annie frequently, but the conversation was kept light, at her insistence. She wanted to know all about their classes, their new friends, and surroundings. When they'd steer the conversation toward her, she'd veer off on a tangent and bring it back to them again.

"It will be good to be able to talk about Clara when the kids call now," Annie said, ignoring Matt's question. "They always ask how things are here and I never have much to say. Lord knows they don't want to hear about my T-cell count or last doctor appointment."

"Well, actually, they do, Annie. They feel very isolated from all of this since they went to school."

"And that's a good thing, Matt. I don't want them to dwell on "this" as you call it. They're young and should be having the time of their lives." Annie could feel the redness creeping up from her neck to her face.

"But you're their mother and they love you. It's only natural for them to be concerned." Matt's words were coated in caution.

"You know how I feel about this. Why do you always insist on bringing it up?" The fight she had been trying to start a few minutes ago now threatened to be well underway.

"Because it's important. Look, Annie, I know that you don't want a repeat of what you went through when your mom was sick, but it's not right to go to the other extreme either." Matt had taken his arm out from around Annie's shoulders and was resting his elbows on his knees. He studied the palms of his hands as he waited for the bomb to drop.

Instead of a bomb dropping, however, Clara did her job and diverted their attention from the discussion by being her cute, cuddly, kitten self. She stood up to stretch and in the process, did an accidental back flip off of Annie's lap, onto the shag area rug the color of cinnamon. Looking up at them, she blinked as if to say, "What happened?"

"Oh no!" Annie said, and laughed, unable to stay mad any longer.

Matt reached down and scooped up the calico comedian, planting a kiss on her tiny pink nose. Annie reached over to scratch behind her ears and the bomb was detonated for another day.

# The Camera

The phone rang, startling both Annie and Clara out of their respective catnaps. Annie had just entered the lovely final phase of REM sleep and was confused and disoriented as the telephone continued to ring several more times.

"So you're not going to get that?" she said to Clara who responded by licking Annie's chin. "Okay, okay. Just a minute." She grabbed the phone, "Hello?"

"Mom? Did I wake you up?" It was Kenzie.

"Hi sweetie! How are you?" She did her best to crawl out of the sleepy cavern she had been curled up in.

"I'm good. I just had my Psych mid-term."

"How'd it go?"

"Pretty good, I think. I hate multiple choice tests, though. I always over analyze everything."

"You and me both," laughed Annie. "They were always my downfall. So what's up?" She could tell by her daughter's tone that this was about more than her mid-term.

"I was just wondering why you guys haven't sent any pictures lately," said Kenzie. "Max and I thought that getting the digital cameras would be a great way to keep in touch, but we're sending all of the pictures."

Annie squirmed in the recliner. Clara decided to hop down and find a patch of sunlight on the floor to snuggle up on and went back to sleep. *Sure, desert me in my time of need,* Annie thought as she tried to compose a good excuse.

"Our pictures are all boring compared to yours," she finally said. Even she thought it sounded lame.

"Mom, you know that's not true. What about that little kitty Dad got for you? I don't want to wait until I come home at Christmas to see her. She'll be so much bigger by then."

"That's true," Annie said, stalling, "but she'll still be cute."

"Mom, what's going on?" Kenzie sounded suspicious.

She could never keep anything from Kenzie. As a small child, Kenzie had a knack for sensing every mood change Annie had, sometimes even before she realized it herself. Once after she and Matt had had a silly argument, two year old Kenzie had climbed next to her on the bed and offered her beloved blanket to her. "Here Mommy," she had said, "make it all better." Annie had been successfully fighting back the tears until that precious act of kindness melted her resolve and she began to sob, holding both the blanket and Kenzie to her heart.

"Nothing is going on," she said, hoping her lies couldn't be detected over the telephone.

"Then will you please send some pictures? Of Clara and of you and Dad? Please?"

Annie wasn't used to being scolded by her daughter. She agreed to email some pictures to both Kenzie and Max, wondering if she could photoshop some health back into her images before hitting "Send". It was the end of October, and there had been some changes in Annie's appearance since the kids left for college in late August. She hadn't realized it herself until she had seen the picture Matt had taken of her and the kitten, but there was no denying it. Max and Kenzie would see how much thinner she was and the sickly pallor of her skin and want to come home. At the very least they'd become distracted and their studies would suffer. That wasn't an option as far as Annie was concerned, as they were both on scholarships and needed to keep their grades up.

Matt was gone for the day, working on a writing assignment, and she'd have to wait until he got home to take more pictures. Kenzie hadn't given her a deadline, thank goodness, so she had some time. An hour later, interrupting yet another nap, the telephone rang again.

"Hello!" Her aunt's voice was bright and sunny.

"Hi Sally - how are you?"

"Fine. Care for some company?"

"Sure."

"Good. I'll be right in. I'm out in your driveway!" The line went silent, followed by a knock on the door and a "Yoo-hoo!" as she let herself in with her own key.

Sally always entered a room with a commotion, never gliding in quietly or unnoticed. She bustled in carrying a large bag of groceries in one hand and a casserole in a thermal carrier in the other. Placing her wares on the dining room table, she then sailed onto the porch and gathered Annie into a gentle hug.

"How's my favorite niece?" She gave Annie's cheek a big kiss.

"Good."

"I brought you some food. The lasagna is ready to eat now. Do you want some?" Her eyes surveyed the room for something, anything that might need to be done, as she spoke.

"Thanks, but I'm not too hungry right now. Maybe later."

"Definitely later. Isn't that husband of yours feeding you?" Sally looked her up and down, her disapproving frown growing with every inch.

"Yes, he's feeding me. I'm just having trouble eating these days. No big deal." Annie sank a little farther under the afghan.

They heard some plastic rustling in the dining room and turned to see that Clara had discovered Sally's bags of goodies. The kitten had scampered up onto the table and was poking at the bag with her nose.

"Oh for heaven's sake," Sally said, laughing, and went over to the table. "Listen, little miss furball, you stay off the table!" She nuzzled the kitten, bringing her back to Annie on the porch. "She's a stinker, isn't she?"

Annie nodded and then said ,"Okay, fess up, Sally. Why the sudden visit?"

Sally looked at her, surprise stretching over her face. "What do you mean?"

"You always call before you're in my driveway. In fact, you're usually running late. So what gives?" Annie peered at her as Clara attacked the fringe on the afghan.

Sally's cheeks flushed with color, an obvious sign that she'd been found out. Annie knew it well. She also knew that she'd have to give her aunt both the time and the space to tell her story. Sally was not one to be rushed, hence her tendency to be tardy. The older woman settled herself on the end of the sofa closest to Annie's recliner and ran a hand through her somewhat disheveled, gray-streaked hair.

"The twins are worried about you, honey. Kenzie called me today and said that you sounded different on the phone."

"She woke me up! Of course I sounded different." Annie couldn't believe her ears.

"She also said that you and Matt haven't sent them one picture from that new fangled camera you have," Sally added.

"So?"

"So why haven't you?" Clara was now pouncing at Sally's feet, which bobbed in continuous motion as she spoke. "And don't lie to me. You're not very good at it. Never have been."

Annie shifted her gaze to the tree branches swaying in the October wind. Nearly all of the leaves had fallen, but there were still a few stubborn stragglers hanging on. She could relate to their tenaciousness but also envied the ones who had accepted their fate and had floated with graceful dignity to the ground below. If anyone understood her, it was Sally. It was time to trust her with the truth.

"The thing is, since the kids have gone to school, things have gotten worse. I didn't realize how bad I look until I saw a picture that Matt took of me with Clara. I don't want them to see me this way, Sally. I don't want them to know --" The rest of her words were swallowed up by the huge sobs that percolated up from the bottom of her heart.

Sally stayed on the sofa, and leaned forward, taking Annie's hands in hers. She didn't say a word, but waited patiently while her niece cried the tears she had been storing deep inside. Even Clara was trying to be patient, curling up near Annie's hip alongside the arm of the chair, purring contentedly as she licked her paws.

"I don't want them to know that I'm dying," she finally said quietly.

Sally drew in a breath, but didn't speak right away. Annie's words hung in the air between them, like the dry, faded leaves, defying the wind to knock them to their unavoidable destiny.

The doctor's prognosis had been guarded and grim the last time Annie had gone to see him. There were fewer treatments available to her; they just had to hope and pray that the cancer would either stop growing or at the very least, slow down. She and Matt had decided to keep the news to themselves for a while, until they had come to grips with it themselves. After several weeks had passed it became clear to both of them that they may never come to grips with it. Each of them had been dealing with the sadness in their own way, and while they did their best to be there for each other, there were times when the burden was crippling in its enormity. The number of people who really understood was very small, so Annie had gotten very good at hiding her feelings. It was just easier that way. When her Aunt Sally was around, however, her guards fell away. Sally had walked in similar shoes when her sister, Annie's mother, was dying.

"Your mom felt the same way," said Sally, still holding Annie's hands. "She wanted to protect you from everything she could."

"That always drove me crazy," Annie said. "Now I know why she did that," her voice trailed off to a whisper.

"Yet you want to keep it from your kids." Sally's voice was gentle.

Annie looked at Sally as she formed her thought, wanting desperately to make sense at a time when nothing made sense at all.

"It drove me crazy when Mom kept things from me, but it also drove me crazy to have my life revolve around her cancer. I sound like such a brat to say that, but it's true. While other kids were getting excited for prom and graduation and college, I was excited if Mom's chemo had gone well and if her T-cells were improving. I always promised myself that I'd never do the same thing to my own kids."

"How can you expect to keep a promise like that? You can't predict or control the future. We take what comes and make the best of it. Your kids have an excellent dad to help them handle things; they aren't doing it alone like you did." Sally was indignant, her face turning a bright shade of scarlet.

"I wasn't alone," Annie said, afraid that she'd hurt Sally's feelings. "You and Frank were there the entire time."

"Oh, sweetie, I know that, but it's not the same. You had already lost your dad, and then were faced with losing your mom. That had to be horrible. I just don't want you to make the mistake of shutting your kids out."

Annie's head popped up in surprise. "Have Max and Kenzie told you that?"

Sally took a minute to choose her words carefully. "They've kept in touch. It's not easy for them to be away from home right now. I'm sure you know that."

"Yes, I do, but it's also important for them to live their own lives. They'll never get these years back." Now it was Annie's turn to be indignant.

"My point exactly," said Sally. "Let's say you are dying. You may not want to burden them, but do you want to deprive them of something else they'll never get back?"

"What's that?"

"Time with you, my dear." Sally's gaze was direct and firm. "Hence, the camera. They don't want to miss a moment, And do you really want them to?"

Annie looked away, tears springing to her eyes. Was there never an end to the tears? She'd thought long and hard about her children going through their lives without her and it never got any easier. She knew what it was like firsthand, a fact that she couldn't ignore. While Sally had been an excellent substitute, how many times had something happened when Annie had wanted her mother there? Weddings, funerals ,and everything in between, her mother's absence had been keenly felt, never a minor twinge, but a sharp, penetrating pain that reached to her very soul. She missed her father as well, but there was something more visceral about her mother. Perhaps it was born from the fact that she had come from within her; perhaps mothers and children did have an irrefutable bond because of biology, but then what about the mothers who neglected or abused their children? Wouldn't they be neglecting and abusing themselves if the bond was that remarkable?

The rarely used camera sat on the end table, a haunting reminder of the urgency of capturing moments in time. When the twins had been small, the old Canon A-1 was always within reach, always charged and ready to catch something cute, hilarious or precious. In the days before digital photography, the trips to the one-hour film processing store were essential and expensive, but worth every penny. Now images could be viewed instantaneously and either saved or deleted. Annie wished that the film that recorded her gaunt, tired appearance could be sent away and never return. She felt ugly and diseased, afraid that the twins would be repulsed by her, but she knew that the truth could not be hidden from them; that would be equally as cruel. If someone had denied her access to her mother during those final weeks and months, she would have been angry and devastated. As painful as it was, she knew that she had to cooperate with what her children wanted, and do the best she could to captivate that which had become the essence of Annie, even though she already felt like a ghost of the person she had been.

Reaching over to pick up the camera, she handed it to Sally and struck a pose, holding Clara up next to her cheek. "Say 'Cheese', Clara!" and Sally snapped the picture.

# The Book

Matt sat hunched before the computer, the light from the screen casting a shadow on the off-white office wall behind him. A cup of cold coffee sat on the desk and next to it a half-eaten plain bagel, on a wrinkled white paper napkin. His fingers were nimbly dancing across the keyboard one minute and angrily jabbing the "delete" key the next, erasing everything he had just written. Then came the heavy sigh, the litany of expletives emitted on an exhale and the dance began again.

Annie peeked in from the hallway and instead of saying anything, stood there in silence, hidden in the darkness. She had always loved to watch Matt write. He was like a creative cyclone, rotating wildly as ideas and words spewed out and attached themselves to the empty page in front of him. The typewriter he'd sat hunched over in the earlier days had been replaced by a computer, which made the words easier to change, but Annie missed the clickity-clack of the typewriter keys. Before she had known when he was in the midst of a creative explosion just by listening. Now she had to tiptoe down the his office to look, the new creative process being so much quieter. He never minded if she interrupted him, but she tried to do so as little as possible. She had never liked it when her cello playing was interrupted, finding it difficult to get back into the same mindset, and she knew that it was the same way for Matt, although he'd never admit it.

He'd been especially understanding during the past few months, never complaining if she needed help, but lately he'd been working on some big project, one that he'd told her very little about. It had been Matt's habit over the years to bounce ideas off her and to share his work with her, but this time it was different. He was being very private and elusive. Annie wasn't sure if he was just being thoughtful, assuming she didn't feel up to it, or if he had lost interest in discussing ideas with her. She couldn't blame him; she wasn't what one could call "vibrant" the past several weeks. Her naps were getting longer and more frequent and much of the time she felt rather foggy and sluggish. She often found that by the time Matt had finished telling her about something, she'd either forgotten the beginning or had dozed off in the middle. It was hard for her to see the sadness in his eyes, the look of feeling utterly useless. It was harder still to not see it, to be left out of the process altogether.

"Knock, knock," she said in a quiet voice so as not to startle him. "Can I come in?"

In spite of her efforts, he jumped a little and swiveled in his chair toward the doorway. Right before he turned, he closed the screen on his computer.

"Of course you can. You don't have to ask, you know." He patted his lap, his longtime signal for her to sit on it.

Annie crossed the small room, trying to take normal steps, standing tall, instead allowing the pain to make her bend into a knot. She lowered herself onto Matt's lap, and he wrapped his arms around her, a safe port in the storm.

"Your butt has sure gotten boney," he said, teasing. "We need to get some more meat on those bones."

She leaned her head against his and closed her eyes. "You know that's not going to happen."

"Always so worried about your weight." He shook his head and smiled sadly. "Maybe now you believe me. If you'd gained about a hundred extra pounds when I told you to, you'd have just enough padding now, when you need it."

"Yes, sweetie, I should've chowed down back then. If only I had known I'd have a built-in weight loss program like this in my future." She punched him playfully on his shoulder, but didn't have the energy to laugh.

Matt grimaced at the comment, but only because she couldn't see his face. "Would you have really wanted to know?" his voice came out in a raspy whisper.

Annie waited a moment before she answered him. It was the age-old question she'd been contemplating ever since Dillon died. Would she want to have a crystal ball? Would knowing what the future held be a blessing or a curse? While she was pregnant with Munchkin and the twins, she had longed for a glimpse into the future, just enough to know that they'd be born healthy. She used to bargain with God, asking Him for just a tiny peek, and then she'd never ask for anything again.

Of course, God was wise to that request, hearing it continually from everyone everywhere. People would promise to never ask for anything and then as soon as a prayer was answered, they'd be back asking for something else. When Munchkin's heart slowed to a stop during the ultrasound, Annie shot angry thoughts toward the heavens, mocking the very thought that she'd believed her prayers would be answered, that this baby would be alright. Eventually she learned to accept that everything happened for a reason, or at least she thought she did, until her cancer diagnosis. Now she didn't know what to believe, her faith in answered prayers shaken yet again.

"No, I guess I wouldn't. Unless I could change the bad things, that is."

"Always trying to shake things up, aren't you?" He tousled the ends of her scarf and kissed the back of her head.

"Can I ask you something?"

"Sure."

"What are you working on? You've been working like a crazy person in here."

"Oh, it's nothing. Just an idea I had for something." Matt's words were stilted and self-conscious. He ran a hand through his thinning, curly hair.

"Oh. Okay." Annie tried to hide her disappointment by putting a big smile on her face. "Well, carry on. I think I'll go and lie down."

Matt helped her to her feet and started to help her walk to the bedroom. She shrugged his hand away as if to say, "I can do it myself" and shuffled out of the room. Once in their bedroom she closed the door and let the tears she'd been suppressing spring from her eyes. Matt really hadn't wanted to tell her about the project he was working on; she'd become useless to him in so many ways.

Standing in front of the large mirror on the double dresser, Annie contemplated her reflection. Mirrors were something she'd avoided ever since she lost her hair, especially if she was alone. In front of Matt or the kids, especially Kenzie, she'd put on a brave act, pretending it didn't bother her, that she had embraced her new look. To be honest, however, she thought she looked hideous without hair and she didn't know if she'd ever learn to accept it before she died. Her sunken cheeks and the dark circles under her eyes didn't help matters any. She looked like a concentration camp prisoner from World War II; there was no denying it. Not that she looked worse than any other cancer patient; it wasn't a contest she aspired to win.

To complicate things, Matt had been stalking her with that damn camera for weeks. He didn't seem to understand how ugly she felt; he didn't respect the limits she had unsuccessfully attempted to establish. Every time she turned around, she'd see the flash of the camera or hear the click of the shutter. Matt would just grin and act innocent, as though he just couldn't control himself. He had always been generous with compliments for her and if anything, her cancer had caused an increase in his attentiveness. Annie never doubted his sincerity, but she detested the fact that there was an illness at all. She would have preferred complaining about his lack of attention, like so many of her friends did about their husbands. Instead she was blessed with a treasure of a man who not only gave her attention, but anticipated her every need, except the need to be done with this battle. He didn't seem to be able to see her as she was; he saw her as she used to be, and she didn't know how to handle it.

That was why his secrecy about his latest project baffled her so. If he saw her as she used to be, he'd be talking her ear off about it, instead of deftly closing his laptop when she entered the room, thinking she hadn't noticed. Maybe it wasn't a project at all; perhaps he was on some internet dating site or dabbling in porn. She scolded herself for even thinking such a thing, but she could hardly blame him. Sex was a distant memory for them, one of the most painful casualties the cancer had left in its wake. Until she had gotten sick, their love life had been full and active. The daily challenges of raising twins and getting older had never put a damper on the joy they found in each other. Their desire never faded; it had only grown stronger with each passing year. Annie knew that Matt's frustrations must be more intense than hers, since she was preoccupied with the ravages the cancer was having on her body and mind. For all the advances made in modern medicine and cancer treatment, there was little if any help for the emotional toll it took on spouses and families. There were support groups, but there never seemed to be the time or energy to attend the meetings. It didn't feel right to sit and whine to strangers about their personal struggles, when all they wanted to do was to spend every possible moment with each other. If Annie's cancer was going to take years to play out, perhaps a support group would have worked for them. The sad truth was, time was running out. In many ways Annie wished she could stop the clock, but in many ways she had looked forward to being done with the chemo, the lab tests, the relentless medical machine. It had taken over their lives at a time when there so little of their lives left for them to share. It seemed a shame to waste a moment.

"Knock, knock."

Annie looked up from her perch in front of the mirror and saw Matt peeking his head through a crack in the door. She quickly raised her hands to her face to wipe the tears away and said,"Who's there?"

"Just your stupid, lonely husband. Can I come in?"

"Of course. It's your room too."

He slid into the room and sat down next to her on the edge of the bed. They sat side by side, their thighs and shoulders touching. Matt reached for Annie's hand.

"I'm sorry, Annie. I'm not trying to keep secrets from you, but that's what I've been doing, isn't it?"

"It feels that way, but it's okay. You need to do what you need to do. I know I'm not as "with-it" as I used to be. Your work shouldn't suffer because of me, but I know it has. So, I'm the one who should be sorry."

"Are you serious or are you just trying to make me feel worse?" He nudged her with his elbow.

"I'm serious. Even though you keep telling me to stop apologizing, I am sorry that this is happening to us." She looked down at their intertwined fingers and sniffled. "Until this happened, I always felt like I was enough for you, and now I don't."

"What makes you think that? Because I haven't told you about the project I'm working on?"

Annie kept looking down, but nodded.

"Anna Banana, what am I going to do with you?" Matt shook his head as he spoke. "I was going to wait to show you this, but come with me." He stood and gently pulled her up. Hand in hand they walked to his office.

He gestured for her to sit in the desk chair. Leaning over her, he booted up the computer and clicked on an icon on the desktop. Up popped the dedication page of a book, a book dedicated to her. She turned to look at him, but could only see the silhouette of his face in the twilight shadows of the room.

It was a book comprised of pictures of Annie, Matt, Max, and Kenzie, accompanied by text Matt had written. There were pictures of the early days, when Annie and Matt had first met, pictures of Annie's apartment, pictures of the orchestra, of Paris, and wonderful random pictures from their wedding. Then came the pictures of Max and Kenzie, from the first bulge in Annie's stomach, to the ultrasound pictures, to the first photos of them in their isolettes shortly after they entered the world. The years scrolled by with each click of the mouse and Annie marveled at the masterpiece before her. It wasn't long before they arrived at the recent years, the twins at their various high school awards banquets as well as goofy pictures taken when no one was looking. It made Annie smile to see Howard on so many of the pages and that was as it should have been, for he was as much a part of their family as any of them. Finally, the images on the screen were of their current life, of little Clara, of Annie in her lift chair, taking an unexpected nap, the scarf on her head askew, showing the baby fine, downy fuzz coming in at her hairline. It struck Annie as she examined the picture, how young and at peace she looked as she slept. She couldn't help but wonder if that was what she'd look like in death. Her heart hurt to see what Matt had to see every day and she wondered how he was enduring it.

"This is amazing. But why?" She couldn't take her eyes from the screen as she waited for the answer.

"It was Kenzie's idea. She thought it would be good to have a pictorial story of our lives. It was my idea to add some writing. It's not going to published or anything like that. It's just for us." He kissed the top of her head.

"When were you going to show me?" She could hardly speak, the words getting caught on the spiderweb of emotion in her throat.

"I wanted to wait until I had it printed. I'm almost finished, so it won't be long. Do you like it?"

His question hung between them like the translucent veil that had covered her face on their wedding day, attempting to hide the excitement and anticipation that permeated the room. Annie couldn't take her eyes from the screen, mesmerized by the beautiful prose that Matt had written. His account of their first meeting brought back so many treasured memories and for a brief moment she felt as though it was twenty years ago, waiting for the elevator, going to the support group meeting for the first time.

"This is beautiful, Matt. I love it." She reached out to the computer screen, her fingers touching it carefully, as though it were a precious, hand-woven tapestry. "Thank you."

Matt smiled down at her, contentment softening his expression, the sharp angles of anxiety and fatigue momentarily erased.

"I'm sorry if my working on it made me seem distant or preoccupied. There was no other way to do it."

"I understand, sweetie. It's worth every minute I wondered about what you were doing in here." She squeezed his hand as she spoke. "This will be so wonderful for Max and Kenzie to have after. You too."

"What are you talking about, after?"

"You know what I'm talking about," she said gently.

Matt lowered his eyes to an invisible spot on the floor, a frown appearing on his face. He often behaved this way when Annie talked about dying. It was a fact he did not want to face, even though he knew it was true. He'd been by her side during the entire ordeal, every doctor appointment, every chemo treatment; certainly he knew what was going to happen. Annie knew too well that there was a difference between knowing something and accepting it. She couldn't blame Matt for turning away from the truth; she had done that for months herself. There had been a time early on in her illness when Matt had been more realistic about what needed to be done than she. Now they had flip-flopped their positions, with her looking reality straight in the eyes and Matt, shielding his gaze. The creation of this book, however, told Annie that he did realize what was ahead of them and it made her heart ache.

"You know what this book reminds me of?" she said, guiding the conversation down a slightly different path. "It reminds me of my charm bracelets. It's like each page is about one or two of the charms."

The two bracelets, which she always wore on her right wrist, had become significantly looser due to the weight she had lost, and slid freely up and down her arm whenever she moved. There were seventeen charms on each one, depicting the many phases and adventures of her life. Sally had given her the first bracelet with one charm on it after Dillon had died. The charm was a bright blue star. From that point on, friends and family knew what to get Annie for her birthday, Christmas, or to commemorate a special event. Annie bought many of them for herself, for the private moments that nobody else would understand or care about. The bracelets were two of her most prized possessions and she rarely let them out of her sight. Matt lifted her hand towards his face to look at the charms more closely.

"You know, you're right. I hadn't thought of that. These bracelets really do represent your life, don't they? I guess I've gotten so used to seeing them, that I don't really *see* them anymore." He slowly turned the bracelets around her wrist.

"They represent our life. There wouldn't be nearly as many charms if it weren't for you. You've given me so much over the years; so many things to celebrate and remember."

"Well, something tells me that you would have had a very full life without me," Matt said.

"I can't imagine my life any other way. You have made it perfect, Matthew Preston." She brought his hand to her lips and kissed it tenderly.

The sigh that came from Matt was long and slow, full of disbelief and desperation. It seemed to rise up from the bottom of his soul, and brought with it shards of disappointment, lost dreams, and bittersweet memories. In it, Annie could feel the grief and pain he was living with every day, trying to save her and knowing that he was losing ground.

"This is far from perfect," he finally said, hanging his head.

"That all depends on how you define 'perfect'," she said, her hand on his back. "We've had so many good years; we've been so happy. To me, that is perfect."

"I know, but I'm selfish. I don't want it to end." His voice sounded thick and wounded.

"Oh sweetie, neither do I. Neither do I."

## The Dragonfly

It happened on a Friday, when the beginnings of spring were trying to break through the last remnants of crusty ice lining the sidewalks and driveways. Tender shoots of green made a polka dot design on the lawns, still barely covered with a thin sheet of snowy whiteness. The sun had barely shone that day, mimicking the mood that pervaded the house and those inside it.

Matt had called Max and Kenzie earlier in the week, when it became clear that the end was near. The timing was impeccable; they had each just finished their mid-term exams.

*Leave it to Mom to do what's convenient for us,* Kenzie thought as she stuffed her suitcase with whatever she could lay her hands on. Later, when she unpacked it, she'd find a hodgepodge of items, much like the random assortment of things she used to cram into her "Hello Kitty" backpack as a little girl before she went to daycare each morning. Once Annie and Matt had gotten into a huge argument over the whereabouts of several window cranks, each accusing the other of misplacing them. Kenzie, being the helpful three year old that she was, ran to get her backpack, unzipped it and showed her parents the cranks that were lying at the bottom. They looked at each other, bewildered, and then burst into uncontrollable laughter. From that point on, if anything was missing, Kenzie's backpack was the first place they looked.

Digging through her suitcase, Kenzie reached down and pulled out one of her roommate's flip flops instead of the cell phone charger for which she was searching. She sat down on the bed, the flip flop in her hand, and burst into tears. Her long curls fell over her face, creating a veil of privacy, a safe place to hide for the moment.

She couldn't believe this was happening. It was so unfair. There were so many things she had wanted to tell her mom and now it was too late. Why hadn't she made it a priority to call home more than once a week? At first she had called more frequently, but as the months passed and she became more acclimated to college, the need hadn't seemed as great. By the time she and her brother came home for Christmas break, she had been shocked at how Annie's condition had deteriorated; she had gotten so thin and frail. If Kenzie were honest with herself, she'd have to admit that seeing her mom like that had frightened her. It made her avoid calling home.

Max had preferred sending emails to Annie over making telephone calls. Being the less talkative twin, he'd write long, heartwarming messages to his mom. She began to anticipate their arrival daily, Max writing them during his late night study sessions. Annie cherished these notes and saved every one in her computer. She had told him in a reply email, that she was getting to know a whole new side to him, a side that she knew was always there, but that he had not yet discovered. He often wondered if her illness was bringing them closer, or if he would have written the same notes to her just because he was away from home and missed her.

"Kenz, can I come in?" Max stood in her doorway. His hair had grown back nicely and he had a two day beard going, making his face look dark and somber.

"Oh. Sure." She glanced up at him, shoving her hair out of her eyes with both hands. "This really sucks, doesn't it?"

"Yeah, it does." Max ambled over and plopped down on the floor next to her bed. He picked up one of the throw pillows that she'd tossed on the floor and started absentmindedly flipping it in the air. "You okay?"

"No, I'm not okay. Our mom just died. How can I be okay?" Kenzie said through the tears that started coursing down her face.

Max's expression froze, his mouth a straight line, his eyes round and anchored on the taffeta covered pillow in his hands. He and Kenzie had always been close, their "twin's telepathy" often reading the other's mind. Being away from each other for the first time in their lives hadn't weakened their bond, but the situation was making their communication a bit fuzzy.

"Sorry," he said in an emotional whisper. "I should have known that."

"Oh Maxie -- what are we going to do?" As usual, she looked to her "minutes older" brother for guidance.

"I don't know, Kenz. How do you think Dad's doing?"

She looked at him and merely shrugged.

They arrived home in a whirlwind only hours before. Frank met them at the airport; neither Matt or Sally wanted to leave Annie's side. Their flights arrived within minutes of each other and they frantically ran through the airport to the car to get home to their mom. Matt had told them that there wasn't much time left, that Annie was waiting for them to get home. It placed an even greater sense of urgency and tragedy on them than they already felt. It occurred to Kenzie that if her mom was waiting for them, then maybe they shouldn't hurry so much; maybe she wouldn't die after all, if they took their time. Even if they weren't with her yet, knowing their mom was still in this world, would keep them safe just a little while longer.

"I wish I had called her more," Max said, his voice barely audible. "It's weird to think that I'll never hear her voice again." He punched the pillow still in his hands.

"Me too," said Kenzie, blowing her nose loudly. "Can I tell you something?"

"Sure. What?"

"I was sort of afraid to call her. I didn't know what to say, you know, once she started getting worse. Telling her about my trivial day-to-day stuff seemed pointless. There she was, dying, and I was talking about stupid problems with my roommate. It just felt so wrong." Kenzie peered at her brother through her mane of hair that had fallen over her face again.

"Yeah. I know what you mean. I don't think it was wrong to tell her that stuff though. She liked hearing about normal stuff. It made her feel more normal."

"I guess. Well, it's too late now." Kenzie stared at the floor, her face a mask of dejection and grief.

They sat there in silence. The punches that Max inflicted on the pillow became gentler and Kenzie had wrestled her wild hair into a haphazard bun, finally getting it out of her face. What do you do when you're eighteen years old and your mother dies? There was so much life ahead of them that they had hoped to share with her; she was supposed to be a part of it.

"Even though I knew that Mom wasn't going to get better, I always imagined my life with her in it," said Kenzie, breaking the troubled stillness. "I pictured her at my graduation from college, at my wedding. All of those big days."

"I can't picture our birthdays or Christmas without her," Max said. "It's hard to think of this house without her. Or Dad." His voice broke as he said the last words.

Max was worried about his dad. At Christmastime he had seen Matt crying, all alone, his bent figure outlined by the lights twinkling on the Christmas tree. He had seen his dad cry many times before, but this time had been different because it was about Annie. It was one thing to cry at the loss of a pet, but the loss of a spouse had to be so much worse. The vision of his dad crying that day had etched itself in his mind because it captured the essence of a grief and loneliness that was too great for words.

"I know," said Kenzie. "They were always together, especially since she's been sick. So many of my friends' parents are either divorced or wish they were. I always felt lucky because our parents actually *liked* each other. Now we only have one parent. How lucky is that?"

"We're still lucky, Kenz. We've had two parents who loved us very much and still do. Even though Mom died, I don't feel like she's really gone."

As Max said the words, he could still see the image of the coroner wheeling the body bag out the front door, taking his mom away. They had all given her one last hug, one last kiss and then left the room so the coroner and funeral director could do their jobs. They stood holding onto each other, Matt, Max, Kenzie, Sally, and Frank, as the hearse drove away into the night. Max had kept watching until the red tail lights faded off into the distance. He never wanted to forget that moment; he wanted to make it stop before the lights disappeared forever. Frank and Sally left shortly after, as though they wanted to follow Annie, not letting her out of their sight.

The door opened a crack. "Knock, knock," said Matt.

"Hi Dad." Kenzie got up and went over to Matt, reaching up to give him a hug. Max got up and joined them.

"I've always loved our group hugs," Matt said, rumpling the hair on both of their heads at the same time. It went unsaid for the moment that one member of the group was missing, although they all felt the absence.

"What's up, Dad?" Max said, his hand still on his dad's shoulder.

"I just wanted to talk to the two of you about the funeral." Matt sat down on the floor, leaning his back against Kenzie's bed. "Mom had some pretty definite ideas."

"I know," said Max. "She told me about some of them in one of her emails."

"She tried to tell me about it in one of our phone calls, but I changed the subject," Kenzie said. "It was too sad."

"Well, one of the things she wants is for each of you to be given one of her charm bracelets at a certain point in the service. She said she'd be flexible about just about everything else but that." He looked from his son to his daughter and back again.

Kenzie unsuccessfully tried to stifle a giggle. "That sounds just like Mom, doesn't it? Saying she'll be flexible about something she has no control over?"

"Who's to say she doesn't?" said Matt, chuckling a little. "Your mom is one influential woman."

They all sat there, smiles on their faces, as they remembered Annie's persuasive, stubborn streak. She did have a way of getting things done and getting them done her way, even though she could convince everyone that it had been their idea.

"Okay, so what else does she want?" Max was anxious to hear the rest. He also wanted to give his mom whatever she asked, this one last time.

"She wants live cello music. Jen has already agreed to do that. They picked out some songs together. She also wants everyone to wear bright colors; no black. And she wants wine and hors d'oeuvres at the wake, so people have more to do than stand there and feel uncomfortable."

"It sounds like she wants a party," said Kenzie. "I don't think anyone is going to be in a party mood, do you?"

"No, but your mom wants us to try. She really believed in all of that "Celebration of Life" stuff. That's why she wants you to be given her bracelets; she felt like they represented her life and she wants to celebrate that. It's hard for me to accept too, but I promised her."

"Well, then we don't have much choice, do we?" Max said as brightly as he could.

"I just can't believe this is happening," Kenzie sobbed. "Why did Mommy have to die?"

Matt put his arms around his little girl as she wept; Max stayed where he was, looking down at the floor, trying not to cry. It wasn't that he didn't think he should, he just didn't want his dad to feel torn between which one of them to comfort. Annie and Matt had always been good at giving the twins plenty of attention and it had suddenly occurred to Max that those days were over. They only had one parent now, and since he was the oldest, Max decided at that moment, that he'd let Kenzie receive the comfort. He'd do his best to grow up and be there for his dad and his sister. After all, they'd need him more than ever now.

"What else does she want at the funeral?" Max tried to keep the conversation going.

"She wants 'The Dragonfly Story' read; and the one about the star from The Little Prince."

"Is that the one that was read at Dillon's funeral?" Max said, a faraway look in his eyes.

"Yes, it is, Maxie. How did you know that?" Matt was surprised to hear his son mention Annie's first child.

"Mom wrote about it in one of her emails. She said that she was never afraid of dying because she always knew that whenever that time came, she'd be with Dillon again. Then she told me about that story, and I found it and read it. I always wondered why she was so obsessed with stars."

"Wasn't there another baby, Dad?" Kenzie said.

"Yes, we lost a baby in a miscarriage before we had you two. We called her Munchkin." The twins looked puzzled, and he added, "It's a long story." He then proceeded to tell them about Paris and all that happened there.

"Wow," said Kenzie when he was finished. "That is so romantic. Who knew our parents were so cool, Max?"

"Well, just remember that we were a lot older than you guys are; we were both out of college, established in our careers; we'd both been married before," Matt said, putting special emphasis on older and out of college.

Matt hoped that Annie wasn't going to put a hex on him on her way to heaven. She had always been very private regarding the story of Paris and Munchkin, especially when it came to the twins. She preferred they learn the details when they were older and past the dangerous years of adolescence and early adulthood. They had known about her short marriage to Eric and about Dillon, but that was all. Matt had told them about his marriage to Sara as well, and about her tragic car accident. As parents, they decided that those stories gave the twins enough background information for quite a while and it had made sense. Now that Annie was gone, it felt right to Matt to tell them the rest.

"Don't worry, Dad. I'm not going to run out and get pregnant," Kenzie said a little too flippantly. "It's just cool to hear what you and Mom were like before you had us. You know, when you were actually people."

Matt laughed out loud for the first time in days. "Oh, so what have we been all these years if not people?"

"Well, parents, of course. Totally different. Although as parents go, you're pretty amazing," said Max, clarifying what his sister meant.

"Oh, well that's good to know," Matt said. "Your mom would have loved this conversation." He felt the lump in his throat expand and he couldn't stop the fresh batch of tears. "Sorry, guys. I'm going to have to do this for a while."

"No worries, Daddy," said Kenzie, wiping away more tears of her own. "We're right there with you."

"What's 'The Dragonfly Story' about, Dad?" Again, Max tried to rein them in from getting lost in their grief. There would be plenty of time for that later.

"That was one your mom came across when our neighbor's ten year old daughter died from leukemia. They read it at her funeral, as a way of helping all of her classmates understand the concept of death. Mom always loved how it talked about how life doesn't really end, that it just changes form and makes us free."

"I sort of remember that happening. We were just little, weren't we?" Kenzie's voice wavered a little, thinking of what that girl's family had experienced at the time.

Matt nodded. "Yep. You were in first grade. It was the first time that anyone you knew died."

"Yeah, I remember how she used to ride our bus and then all of a sudden she was gone," said Max. "I hadn't thought about that for a long time."

"It's funny how death can bring people closer," Kenzie said. "Now I understand why those people have been so nice to us since Mom got sick."

"Well, they know what it's like. It makes people more compassionate, or at least you'd hope so." Matt grabbed a Kleenex and blew his nose. Then he leaned his head back on the edge of the bed and thought about how much he missed Annie already.

It was decided that at the funeral Max would read the story from The Little Prince and Kenzie would read "The Dragonfly Story". Matt would give the eulogy. None of them knew how they'd find the strength to stand in front of everyone and produce coherent thoughts and words, but knowing it was what Annie wanted would help them through it. Once he was standing in front of the church full of people, Max understood why the bracelets had been given to him and Kenzie only moments before the readings. As he looked at the bracelet he had slipped onto his wrist, he felt the warmth of his mother encircle him and his pounding heart calmed to a more relaxed pace. She was here with him at that moment and would always be.

Right before Kenzie made her way to the pulpit, she noticed that a new charm had been added to her bracelet; a dragonfly. She rubbed it gently with her thumb and thanked Annie for thinking of this one last detail. Looking at the charm made her heart soar, knowing that her mom wasn't really gone, but had just moved on to a place where she didn't need the bracelets anymore.

The End

## Acknowledgments

Many thanks to: my husband, Chuck, for believing in me from the beginning; to Sara S. for reading and re-reading my manuscript and countless words of encouragement; to Geri B. and Robin M. for taking the risk of reading a friend's first novel; to my writer's group, Kris, Joan, Lynne, Theresa, Becky and Laurel, for giving me a reason to write even when I didn't feel like it; to Sarah O., for a glimpse into the life of a professional cellist; and finally to my daughters, Lindsey and Amy for adding to the charms on my bracelets and the charms of my life.

Nancy Manther

CPSIA information can be obtained at www.ICGtesting.com
Printed in the USA
BVOW041710140512

290104BV00001BA/9/P

9 781456 608668